Europe, Mother of Revolutions

Europe,
Mother of Revolutions

Friedrich Heer

Translated from the German by
Charles Kessler and Jennetta Adcock

PRAEGER PUBLISHERS
New York · Washington

BOOKS THAT MATTER

Published in the United States of America in 1972
by Praeger Publishers, Inc., 111 Fourth Avenue,
New York, N.Y. 10003

© 1964 by Friedrich Heer
English translation © 1972 in London, England,
by Weidenfeld and Nicolson Ltd.

Library of Congress Catalog Card Number: 72–180867

Printed in Great Britain

Contents

I

Prelude

THE NINETEENTH CENTURY

The nineteenth century was one of the most unusual and significant of centuries in the history of Europe. It was a century of reaction and revolution, innovation and rigid adherence to established values, a century of juxtaposition: on the one hand rococo grace, the beauty, the regulation, of the Old Order and on the other the ugliness of industrialisation, the rebellious, revolutionary attitudes of a youth inspired by 1789 and the French Revolution. It was a century of great hopes, great disappointments, and of fear.

In every field of life, in political, intellectual, social and religious affairs, it is possible to see manifestations of this fear: in the state police, in political, racial and religious censorship, persecution, and in the resultant increase in voluntary exile of both individuals and whole groups. It was this fear, felt both by men of the Old Order, reactionaries, and by those subjugated to the demands of reaction, which, in part, made the nineteenth century an age of suffering, poverty and unease, influences which even now, in the mid-twentieth century, are making themselves felt. And yet these are not our only heritage. The nineteenth century was also the beginning of a new era in the history of man, and to that too we are heirs. In two great periods, 1790 to 1810, and 1890 to 1910, the creative spirit of man produced a tremendous flowering – in science, technology, literature and art, in the desire for discovery, experiments and reform. It was a time of great aims and great achievements, which prepared the way for man's conquest of space. And in studying the events, the changes, of those years, we are forced to recognise, beyond all else, one fact: man's desire to improve, to excel, was making itself irresistibly felt, the wish to rise above those former tendencies which would ultimately have plunged Europe into total self-destruction.

For their boldest projects, in politics, philosophy and literature, the men of the nineteenth century drew on the example of their immediate ancestors, on ideas and precedents dating from the eleventh to the eighteenth centuries. Descendants of these men, in the twentieth century, have gone even further, searching consistently and logically right back to the origins of man in both

East and West. For when one is faced with the total transformation of man, the whole of his history must be examined in the closest detail.

Nineteenth-century Europe begins in 1789 and lasts until 1914, or even perhaps 1945, when the first atom bomb was dropped. Yet if one studies the faces of the men and women of different countries living around 1900, one cannot fail to notice one very striking fact: by origin and background, by generation and stage of intellectual maturity, these so-called contemporaries belong to totally different historical periods. In 1903, for example, Giuseppe Sarto, then sixty-eight, was elected pope. He was six years older than Clémenceau and King Edward VII, five years younger than the Emperor Franz Joseph. Yet this was also the time when the Russian Social Democratic Labour Party split into Bolsheviks and Mensheviks; Lenin was thirty-three. Rutherford, who during those same twelve months came to the conclusion that radioactivity results from the disintegration of atomic nuclei, was thirty-two. Einstein, Otto Hahn and Paul Klee were twenty-four, Robert Musil twenty-three, Ezra Pound eighteen. Stravinsky was twenty, Picasso twenty-two, and Chagall sixteen. Churchill was twenty-nine.

The antitheses between these 'contemporaries' were epochal. They lived, thought and acted as if belonging to different eras. The same wealth of antitheses existed around 1800, and it was this that determined the material affluence, the penury, the greatness, the poverty, and above all the creative power, of the nineteenth century. Yet when twentieth-century thinkers and historians use of the nineteenth century such epithets as 'ambiguous', 'inconsistent', 'dubious', they are merely underlining our own inability to gauge, much less understand, the many antitheses and phenomena arising from this coexistence of non-coevals.

Heidegger called the nineteenth century 'the darkest of all the centuries of modern times'. Goethe spoke of its spirit as 'beyond conception'. If one studies the events of one single year, 1889, with all its then current and future implications, one gains some idea of the century as a whole.

In 1889, the year of Hitler's birth, the Celtic movement achieved its breakthrough in Britain with W. B. Yeats' *The Wanderings of Oisin*. Gerard Manley Hopkins, the Jesuit pioneer of modern versification, died unrecognised. Bernard Shaw published *Fabian Essays in Socialism*. *The Nether World* of George Gissing described the misery to be found in London's proletarian underworld. Jules Verne, in *Robur the Conqueror*, depicted a machine-age dictator-superman. Germany was scandalised by Gerhart Hauptmann's first play, *Before Dawn*. It was also the year of Hertzka's and T. R. Stockton's visions into the future, *Freiland* and *The Great War Syndicate*, respectively. Prince Peter Kropotkin published his *Memoirs of a Revolutionary*. In 1889 Nietzsche's mind gave way.

It was in 1889 that Houston Stewart Chamberlain began his twenty-year residence in Vienna, a British Germanophil, anti-semite and Wagnerian, an important figure whose character combines barbarity and culture to the point where he becomes virtually the symbol of his century. His aphorisms, opinions and demands, later adopted by Hitler, are counterbalanced by the humane outlook of *Man and God*.

The first of Hermann Schell's six volumes of Roman Catholic dogma appeared in this year. His aim had been to try and reconcile Catholicism with the modern age, and he is representative of the many intellectuals who were drawn into the religious maelstrom of the late nineteenth century.

On 18 May Bismarck made his last speech in the Reichstag. Earlier in the year Crown Prince Rudolph had shot himself; it was the assassination in 1914 of his successor as heir apparent, Archduke Francis Ferdinand, that was to set loose the eruptive forces which in two world wars destroyed old Europe. Youth everywhere was beginning to feel and express a deep restlessness; Hermann Conradi's *William II and the Young Generation* and Michael Georg Conrad's *German Clarion Calls* were published. The industrial and technical age saw its achievements reflected in the World Exhibition in Paris. Gauguin portrayed himself with a halo, and painted Christ on the Mount of Olives with his own features: works which were greeted as blasphemy by the *bourgeois* and, by many artists and writers, as a manifesto.

It was in Paris too that the Second International was founded. Sidney Webb published *Socialism in England*. Victor Petrovic Klushnikov's novel, *Egyptian Darkness*, portrayed the savage anti-semitism which was infesting Europe, and many Jews fled Russia to seek refuge in Austro-Hungary or further afield.

This record of a single year is a pointer to the greatness and wretchedness of the nineteenth century. It is a jumble of incompatibles: the far-reaching effects of many of the events are hard to assess. But it reveals that characteristic split between reactionaries and progressives.

That was one fact of the nineteenth century. Another may be found symbolised in a recently recovered portrait of Heinrich von Kleist, on the front of which was written *Subjet suspect – Henry de Kleyst – Poète Prussien,* and on the pack *511p. – Surveillance militaire – Personnage suspect.* Kleist had been arrested on German soil by French military authorities on suspicion of espionage. He was given a number and would remain 'suspect' for the rest of his life. He is a symbol of that rule of authority by which any person, once marked out on whatever grounds ('demagogue', 'liberal', 'radical', and many others), from then on remained under constant surveillance, a number in a case history, not an individual.

One cannot separate the greatness of the nineteenth century from its extreme wretchedness and poverty, for these were suffered even by its best minds and most creative spirits. The 'sufferings of the masters' in Thomas Mann's phrase, should be accorded due respect by heirs to the nineteenth century, who should also remember those countless others who could neither make themselves heard, nor attain their ends.

Every encounter with the nineteenth century is an encounter with ourselves and the elements at work within us. We of the twentieth century will rise above its problems only to the degree in which we face up to them. Not one of the nineteenth century's major enigmas has yet found a sound and satisfactory answer.

IN THE WAKE OF THE GREAT REVOLUTION

Talleyrand, a man of charm, wit and intelligence, whose power survived not only the revolution but the many changes of government which followed it, once said: 'He who did not know life before 1789 has no idea of its charms.' He himself had recognised and enjoyed the beauty of the *ancien régime*, with its style, culture, women, civilisation. With Metternich, he laid the foundations of the Europe of the Restoration. Yet in 1789, while still a bishop, he played a crucial part in the first act of the revolution. He destroyed the power of the Church in France by instigating the confiscation of its lands, and was the first bishop to swear allegiance to the new constitution. When the power of the Holy Roman Empire was destroyed, a power which had lasted one thousand years, he sold bishoprics and abbeys to whichever prince bid most.

Balzac has portrayed with vivid, vicious skill, the avarice and greed of the French bourgeoisie, and Talleyrand, as foreign minister to the Directory, the Consulate, the Emperor Napoleon, the restored Bourbons and the July Monarchy, acquiring with time the most enormous fortune, did nothing to belie the accusation. His gratuities alone amounted to more than sixty million livres. He is, in fact, the symbol of those men, profiteers, politicians, financiers and men of letters, who understand the art of survival through every change of power.

Talleyrand's career is not only a model of successful opportunism. It indicates the continuity, often ignored, which exists between the eighteenth and nineteenth centuries. Despite the political turmoil, a fairly wide section of society, related by interest if not by class, managed, even in France, to maintain their way of life, their social status, their economic leadership. This is one reason why the Revolution and the Restoration, the Enlightenment and Romanticism, have so much in common. Great and small men fall, but not those in finance, industry and administration. Men of Talleyrand's calibre successfully outlived all changes: having no illusions, they knew when to give way.

How different was Saint-Just, proud twenty-six-year-old who shared Robespierre's fate of the 10 Thermidor. Supreme example of the link between Romanticism and the Revolution, he represents that young generation who in 1789 kindled their own funeral pyre. These men, Danton, Robespierre, Desmoulins, were all in their twenties, as were most revolutionaries – Luther's followers, Napoleon's generals, the early Romantics, and the founders of twentieth-century science. And with these early revolutionaries a chain reaction of youthful rebellion seems to start that was to last throughout the century.

Saint-Just, with his longing for heroism, his belief in the future, his fatalism,

4

once said: 'Great men do not die in their beds.' 'He who starts revolutions, who desires to do good, will rest only in the grave.' Epitomising the link between Romanticism and the Revolution, he also wrote 'I wish to go my way without arms, without defence, followed by love, not fear.'

He called for the death of the king in 1792, of the Girondists in 1793, of all nobility and suspects in February 1794, of the Hébertists in early March and Danton at its end. Yet this was not a fanatic's frenzied thirst for blood, but his tragedy. The men of the Revolution saw themselves surrounded by plots and counterplots, by men who, thanks to money and influence, attacked them from the centres of power. The rulers of Europe were antagonistic, the civil servants of France unreliable. A minority with passionate beliefs, the revolutionaries, lived in constant fear, and it was this fear which, as throughout the century, instigated the Terror – as in the 'red terror' and 'white terror' in twentieth-century Europe.

But if fear lay at the roots of the Terror which evolved in France during the Revolution, in Robespierre it was linked with a somewhat different emotion. From his early years when he had attended the opening of the States General at Versailles as deputy for Arras, he had been disgusted by the hypocrisy, the corruption and debauchery of all men in power, whether in society, religion or politics. He was filled with a passionate desire to purify France. Condorcet called him a *chef de secte*. Jacobins complained of his sermonising. Religious and political fanatics saw him as the future Messiah of a New Age. Cathérine Téhot, his sister-in-law, made it her mission to help him in his vocation, his desire to separate 'good from bad'.

'Separation of good from bad' was a major preoccupation of revolutionaries at that time, and led in turn to the development of counterplots and to the rise of Bonald and de Maistre, two political ideologists whose writings were to be accepted as dogma by right-wing thinkers throughout the nineteenth century.

Robespierre, himself an active Catholic until 1789 and a defender of the minor clergy to the end, maintained that atheism was aristocratic. The people, he believed, were basically good, though easily seduced into sin. It was his vocation to purify them, to reconcile them with the Supreme Being, to reclaim on their behalf liberty, equality and fraternity. He played the part of a new Moses who set fire to the statue of Atheism in a liturgical feast arranged by his friend the artist David for Whit Sunday 1794.

David, Jacobin and later court painter to Napoleon, had exhibited his *Brutus* in 1789, and at this point a new atmosphere entered the arts. The painting was seen by people of all classes for, with the Revolution, art had become an act of political faith. David himself proclaimed: 'each one of us is accountable to the nation for the talent conferred on him by nature'. His theses indicate the increasing tendency of the time to combine art with politics. In 1791 the *salon*, formerly reserved for members of the Academy, was opened to the whole art world. The Louvre was created in 1792, the

Revolutionary Arts Club in 1793. Drawing lessons became part of the curriculum at the *écoles centrales*. The people were encouraged to deploy their creative talent in all spheres of art.

Revolution and the arts have always been closely connected, and in particular, revolution and literature. Burke and Tocqueville even accused writers of being responsible for the Revolution. Voltaire and Rousseau in particular were blamed, although in Voltaire's case this is quite wrong, and even in Rousseau's inaccurate. Voltaire, a man of the *ancien régime*, abhorred sentimentality and the idea of rule by the masses. Rousseau, on the other hand, was foremost in a literary movement which extended throughout Europe, the significance of which lay far beyond the limits of the Revolution and Romanticism in their narrow sense. Naturally the young revolutionaries had read Voltaire and Rousseau, but the significance of this lies in what they read into the works and took from them.

Voltaire, ultimately buried in triumph at the Panthéon, attended by the ill-fated monarchy and worshipped by all France, once estimated the true connoisseurs of French literature at two to three thousand. Up to the time of the Revolution, literature, like 'art', had been for the enjoyment of a very few. It was now open to a new public and, as a result, became politicised, sentimentalised, popularised and generally radicalised, a development which may be seen today in Asia, Africa and the Americas. The popular press took over this process and in the second half of the nineteenth century made enormous profits, but both literature and people paid a high price for their democratisation.

Camille Desmoulins (1760–94) provides an excellent example of the close link between politics and the arts which evolved in the nineteenth century and continues today. His polemical writings, of a natural literary brilliance, bear the stamp of Desmoulins' personal happiness and his political fervour; he was later to pay the very highest price for his genius. The speech he made before the Palais Royale reveals his mastery of language, of its emotive forces: 'What differentiates the Republic from the Monarchy? One thing only – freedom of speech. What is the best weapon of a free people against despotism? Freedom of the press. And the second best? Freedom of the press. And the third best? Freedom of the press.' Nor was his denunciation of the Terror any less courageous or apt.

Desmoulin's greatness was the greatness of all politically engaged writers, and in his brilliance and fearlessness he was the forerunner of many: of Zola and his *J'Accuse* in the near civil war conditions of the Dreyfus affair, of Camus, active in the Resistance and in his denunciations of the machinery of terror in Algeria.

Four days before his execution in 1794, Desmoulins wrote to his wife: 'I dreamed of a republic which would win over everyone. Never would I have believed that men could be so cruel and unjust.' All over Europe young men and women felt this terrible disillusionment and disappointment at its disastrous outcome, and in many former supporters of the Revolution may be found the counter-revolutionaries of 1795, 1821, 1830, 1832, 1848, 1870, and 1919.

The self-destruction of a revolution and the obliteration of hope in its adherents is but one phenomenon in the great complex of tumultuous events which spread throughout Europe after 1789. Another is the fact that, despite the Terror and ultimate failure of the Revolution, there were men, Kant among them, who, undeterred, remained true and active in pursuit of their aims. A third significant aspect of the Revolution is that its effects were felt throughout the nineteenth and twentieth centuries not only by virtue of its ideals, but also because of the gory pictures and tales of horror recounted of it. French émigrés, carrying the story of the Revolution into the drawing rooms of polite society all over Europe, portrayed it as the work of the devil. As an inevitable result pamphlets and articles were published which provided food not only for the Revolution's adherents but also for its enemies. Of these the most important are Burke's *Reflections*, published in 1790, Bonald's *Theory of Power*, de Maistre's *Reflections on France* and Chateaubriand's *Historic and Moral Essay on Revolution*.

A GREAT COUNTER-REVOLUTIONARY: JOSEPH DE MAISTRE

Joseph de Maistre (1753–1821) – a follower of Bonald, that man of strength and conviction who confined himself throughout his life to one great aim – was one of the most important and active counter-revolutionaries of the age. Like so many great patriots down through the centuries, de Maistre, the intellectual leader of right-wing thinkers and of all anti-revolutionaries, was not a 'true' Frenchman. Like Joan of Arc, who was born on the borders of Burgundy and France, like the borderland Romans in Spain and Africa at the decline of the Western Roman Empire, like the expatriot Germans of the twentieth century, he upheld the traditions, the patriotism, of the 'mother country' with greater dedication than those brought up within its boundaries.

De Maistre was born on 1 April 1753, at Chambéry, Savoy, received his education from the Jesuits and in 1772 joined the legal profession at Turin. As a young man he frequented the company of Freemasons, enthusiasts and occultists, men from whose circles came the inspirations and plans of the Romantic Movement, the Revolution and the Counter-Revolution. He read the current political treatises, associated with followers of Martinez de Pasqually, was much influenced by Saint-Martin, formulator of that quasi-religious, political axiom of 'new thought' and the Revolution, 'Liberty, Equality and Fraternity'.

In September 1792, following the entry of French troops into Chambéry, de Maistre fled to Geneva. There in the confused atmosphere of anxiety, anticipation and hope reigning in French-speaking Switzerland, with refugees arriving every day, the full significance of the revolution was forced upon him and sealed his future political career. Between 1794 and 1796 he completed at Lausanne his *Study of Sovereignty*.

While at Lausanne he had been employed as 'correspondent' to the king of Sardinia. Four years later, in 1797, he was summoned to Turin, in the service of the new king. On 17 May 1803 he arrived at St Petersburg as Sardinian envoy, and stayed there until July 1817. St Petersburg and the estates of the Russian nobility were at that time the meeting place of the 'other Europe', especially of French and German opponents of the Revolution and Napoleon. Here, too, could be found adherents of the Enlightenment and the Neo-Classical age, Voltaireans, Rousseauists of all political colours of Pasqually, Saint-Martin and Jakob Bohme. It was indeed a mixed society, the backwash of the European eighteenth century, avidly received by the intellectually and spiritually starved Russian mind.

This was the Russia in which de Maistre lived, thought and worked, and which he hated; his mind constantly preoccupied with Europe. At this period he wrote his *Evenings in St Petersburg* and *On the Pope*, works whose concepts were fundamental to counter-revolutionary Europe and the Curial absolutism of the nineteenth century. At this period he was also closely connected with Madame Swetschin and those Russians whose great hope was to witness the religious and political rebirth of Europe under Tsarist rule, a hope in which lay the seeds of the Holy Alliance.

In the last letter de Maistre wrote before he died, he said: 'the French Revolution is of a satanic character which distinguishes it from everything seen so far and perhaps ever to be seen.' He felt sure that this view was shared by many of his contemporaries throughout Europe. Indeed, although in 1861 the Catholic *Neue Zürcher Nachrichten* stated in a leading article that the French episcopate warned citizens against the *Cité Catholique*, this movement, based on the conviction that the Revolution and all its subsequent effects were the work of the devil, was supported by many leading Europeans of the day.

De Maistre deliberately fell back on epithets taken from Dante's and Milton's descriptions of hell in his comments on the Convention. Yet he was, in fact, one of the Revolution's most avid students, regarding it and its effect with the hypersensitive eye of hatred. 'The creators of the French Revolution and its new constitution are felons, fools and lunatics'; the Revolution was a 'cancerous growth', the republic 'criminal and impotent through and through'.

Implacable in his condemnation of the Revolution and all its fruits, de Maistre was convinced that destruction was the only method by which the world might be rid of this work of the devil. He himself advocated the use of terror, which, when wielded by the revolutionaries, he had attacked. Like so many before him, he maintained that 'War is divine'. An upholder of the vengeful God of the Old Testament and of Islam's, he believed, as did Pierre Teilhard de Chardin, in 'La messe sur la monde'. All men, all events in history, were but a sacrifice on God's altar, a preparation for after life. 'God is always on the stronger side', therefore, maintains de Maistre, it is up to man to create the stronger side to fight for God's cause, to the greater glory of God.

For only he whose cause is just had the right to kill. Killing motivated by the devil's agents is necessarily murder.

In illustration of his argument de Maistre quoted the massacre of St Bartholomew's Eve, for Protestantism was to him 'the foe of mankind', a secular heresy, a perpetual insurrection. This view of Protestantism inspired papal pronouncements like *Mirari Vos* throughout the nineteenth century. The pastoral letters of Italian and South American bishops still reveal its influence, as do many of the Roman Catholic histories and sermons. The idea that Protestants are communists is little different from de Maistre's conviction that they are the equivalent of Jacobins.

As forefather of the *Action Française* and French chauvinism in the nine-teenth and twentieth centuries (the tradition he founded can be traced right down to contemporary ultraists), he saw Protestantism as the 'mortal foe of all national good sense'. 'Let us assume that this law (abrogation of the Edict of Nantes) lost France 400,000 individuals. That corresponds to just about one thousand people less in Paris. Nobody would notice.' He was unaware how close this cynical calculation of manpower brought him to nineteenth- and twentieth-century revolutionary leaders. Napoleon had said much the same to Metternich at the peak of his career. It is not surprising, therefore, to find de Maistre, in his *Letter to a Russian Nobleman*, extolling the Spanish Inquisition as a model of justice and mercy. The ancient Greek methods of justice and democracy, so much praised by Voltaire, were an anathema to him. He hated the Greeks and the Greek spirit. Likewise he hated (and admired) Voltaire and the whole trend of the eighteenth century in France. Both hatreds are significant.

In the eighteenth century the Greek genius, that spirit of Hellas which represents life, love, enlightenment and tolerance, was revived, and had a considerable influence on German and English Romantics, German idealism, philosophy and religious thought. Consequently, the nineteenth century was stirred by a wealth of ideas inspired by the Greek spirit, though, in fact, the movement had little or nothing to do with classicist or political Philhellenism. To the youth of Europe, Russia and Poland, Byron represented the link between and key to all the ideas and ideals of the Greek renaissance.

De Maistre's hatred of this influence was inflexible: 'I do not know Asia or Greece, but I know the world; I have not the slightest desire to see how things are there.' The Eastern Church, like all other churches not subject to Rome was, he considered, insignificant. He was not alone in this illusion. The papal 'wooing' of Russia in the nineteenth century was based on the same idea. The attempt failed because Rome demanded of Russia a submission that Russia could never give. For behind Russia stood the Greek spirit, something of which de Maistre became conscious, during his years there as Sardinian envoy.

He identified the French eighteenth century with Greece and all its vices: licentiousness, anarchy, despotism, and the power of writers. It was the philosophers, those intellectuals with their fatal belief in the goodness of man, who had paved the way to the revolution. De Maistre, convinced of the basic evil in man, believed in ruthless subjugation and control, whereas the Greek spirit believes in man's capacity to mature, to progress. Greek theologians coined formulae that bring to mind Lessing and Teilhard de Chardin. De Maistre upheld a pessimistic view of man which has become the basis of all totalitarian ideologies, ecclesiastical or political, in the nineteenth and twentieth centuries.

De Maistre held only one weapon to be valid against the free-thinking, luxurious eighteenth century: the guillotine. *Salut par le sang.* The world had to be purged of its dissenters by the power of blood. (How similar to Robespierre's attitude!) He expressed this idea even in the first of his St Petersburg discourses, where, in his 'portrait of the executioner' he maintains that 'the scaffold is an altar. ... The executioner ... an exceptional being. ... His creation like that of a world.' 'All greatness, all power, all subordination depends on the executioner. He is the terror and the unifying bond of human society. Remove this mysterious agent from the world and ... order will yield to chaos, thrones fall, ... society disappear.' This acknowledgement of the need for an executioner, expressed in the same cold, passionate language as that used by Robespierre and Saint-Just, is an open admission of a major secret of the *ancien régime*: that its order was based on absolute power over life and death.

It is not strange that de Maistre, holding such views, should stand against the tide of progress. Science, that is the natural sciences, all knowledge of the universe and philosophy, should be controlled by the rulers of the church and realm who would provide the people with the truths they needed to know. The people themselves had no right to any knowledge whatever, except *pour s'amuser.*

In 1794 the Revolution founded the *École Polytechnique.* The *Naturforschende Geselschaft* had come into existence the previous year at Jena. The Revolution was welcomed by a new European *élite* of inventors and scientists as the beginning of a new epoch. In England these were the men associated with Erasmus Darwin (grandfather of Charles) and his Moon Society. The younger Watt, Walter, Jackson and Dalton belonged to the Parisian Jacobin Club in 1792. In 1796 Laplace published his *Explanation of the Astronomical System* and in 1800 Cuvier's *Anatomic Comparison of Petrified and Living Animals* appeared. Herschel discovered infra-red rays in the same year. Alexander von Humboldt's first exploratory voyage took place between 1799 and 1803. In 1801 Oliver Evans produced his steam automobile and Trevithick and Vivian put the first steam engine on iron rails in 1804. In 1807 Fulton designed the first technically feasible steamship. Dalton's atomic theory was published in 1808, and Lamarck's theory of the origin of species in 1809. In 1811 the Krupp steel works were founded at Essen.

De Maistre was not alone in his hatred of this progress. Fear of history, of evolution, was to bear strange fruit in the nineteenth and twentieth centuries. Men of the Old Order felt instinctively that the natural sciences and new historical scholarship were opening gates to a universe so gigantic that it would inevitably overwhelm the static notion of God and the stability of power and religion, just as today Egypt's temples have been drowned in the Nile waters of the Aswan Dam.

De Maistre had great admiration for Egypt, its pyramids, its temples and canals. 'There everything has order, has its proper place. All the great edifices of power, St Peter's at Rome, the Alhambra, the Louvre and Versailles, the arsenals at Brest and Turin . . .', all these architectonic achievements represented one sole idea: they were the achievements, the symbol, of totalitarian states. In de Maistre's admiration is revealed the Janus head of reaction: in order to defeat the political structures of the Revolution it looked both into the past and into the future. De Maistre's visions of ancient despotism foreshadowed the dictatorial structures of the twentieth-century European Right.

He considered the 'civil and religious despotism of the Caliphs' to be the best form of government, for despotism strengthened the nation, created a national heroism. The Arabs were the elect of God, destined to harass and reclaim degenerate Christians. Religion became, to de Maistre ever more a political factor, the 'mortar of the political stronghold'. Without the restoration of the Old Order, religion was finished. Theocracy, papal rule, monarchy and the establishment of ancient authorities were all closely linked. Failure to wipe out democracy, the French Republic, the effects of the Revolution spelled the downfall of Christianity.

De Maistre showed only too clearly how close was the link between European reaction and Counter-Revolution and what they attacked. Rousseau had proposed a *religion civile*, a religious-political loyalty to the state, and Abbé Coyer had also advocated the politicisation of religion in 1775, saying that a priest's first allegiance was to his country, that boys were born to serve and die for the state, that patriotism should be encouraged by the solemnisation of religious festivals. The Revolution had incorporated this fervent nationalism into its creed, giving religion an even stronger political flavour, a process then continued by reaction in its turn. The concepts of the 'good Catholic' in the nineteenth century, and more especially in France, of throne and altar, the defence of the Papacy and its temporal dominions, the fight against Revolution, republicanism and 'modern' satanic science, art and literature, were finely interwoven.

There are two ways to read de Maistre. One is to take him literally. In that light he was the arsenal for the nineteenth-century's civil wars and a broad path leads from him to the *Action Française*, fascism and other twentieth-century dictatorships of the Right. But if we read him carefully a different view of de Maistre emerges, and with it the full extent of his personal drama and tragedy. Through his hatred resounds admiration. De Maistre was fundamentally a child of the eighteenth century he abhorred. He employed the weapons of the Revolution against the Revolution. His style owed its bite, its rhetoric, its diction to the same school as Desmoulins, Saint-Just and

Robespierre. Secretly, he admired those scribblers and puny philosophers who had succeeded in shattering the old France, convulsing the world and setting a question mark for ever over an order which had held for more than a thousand years.

2

England – Mother Country of Romanticism

Es sind viele anti-revoluzionäre Bucher für die Revoluzion geschrieben worden.
Burke aber hat ein revoluzionäres Buch gegen die Revoluzion geschrieben

NOVALIS from the *Athenaeum*.+

Many anti-revolutionary books have been written *for* the Revolution;
Burke, however, has written a revolutionary book against the
Revolution

England might be said to have led the way into the nineteenth century. The Romantic Movement and the Industrial Revolution first emerged there. It was the hope of some, deluded by the great disparity between rich and poor – Disraeli's 'two nations' – and by Britain's benevolent attitude to revolutions abroad and their refugees, that world revolution would start there. Political Romanticism, a movement to evolve all over Europe in the years 1800–48, was to find its hero in Byron. And that nineteenth-century lament, 'God is dead' was first formulated by English poets.

But the developments in political and revolutionary thought were not to find their outlet only in the Romantic Movement. Conservatism was just as inevitable, and in England, as nowhere else, the legal and political institutions, heritage of the Middle Ages, were jealously preserved. Burke's writings and Malthus' *Essay on the Principle of Population* were to provide both the basis and prop of the principles of the ruling classes – those men in politics, the church and industry, to whom the growth of the masses represented a terrifying and very real threat. Inwardly convinced of their right to power, possession and property, they were determined on the ultimate destruction of any revolt or uprising. Wellington and his government are an example of such thoughts. The massacre of French 'upstarts' at Waterloo found its counterpart at home, at Peterloo: 60,000 were brutally dispersed from St Peter's Fields, Manchester, in August 1819, inspiring Shelley, then living in exile in Italy, to write his poem *Mask of Anarchy*:

> I met Murder on the way
> He had a mask like Castlereagh

13

Very smooth he looked, yet grim;
Seven bloodhounds followed him:
All were fat; and well they might
Be in admirable plight.
For one by one, and two by two,
He tossed them human hearts to chew
Which from his wide cloak he drew.

Examples such as Peterloo of the real fear that possessed the classes and of their ruthless methods of repression, stimulated intellectuals to even deeper criticism. Like Shelley they began to question the existing state. Members of the Established Church, to mention just one of the prosperous institutions of the time, were naturally to hold that their active opponents, those children of puritanism and forerunners of the Jacobins, were the anarchists. There was a dread that the horrors of the French Revolution should find a repetition in England. Revolts took place with increasing frequency, even in public schools. The Birmingham home of the dissenting minister and pioneer of modern chemistry, Joseph Priestley, was burnt down by a mob in the name of 'King and Church'.

Change was inevitable. The questions posed by Shelley's poem were to be repeated not only in art, but in religion, philosophy and science. The piety of the church, the rigid structure of society and politics, seemed but a mask, concealing chaos, hypocrisy and self-interest, and its rulers, at whose whim the people suffered, the true anarchists.

England, the first country on the threshold of the Industrial Revolution and faced with the resulting problems – paralleled today in the new states of Africa, Asia and South America – was totally unprepared for the speed of change brought about by the rapid expansion of towns to keep pace with industry, and the resultant misery, ugliness and squalor. The whole structure of society was thrown into relief. The upper classes appeared cynical, self-interested, the lower classes deadened, uncouth. No wonder that sensitive men should counter such a grim aspect with dreams of beauty. The growth of Romanticism in England was closely linked with the Industrial Revolution. In 1749 Horace Walpole, author of the 'gothick' novel *The Castle of Otranto*, began rebuilding his house at Strawberry Hill as a Gothic castle. In 1757 Thomas Gray deserted his research at Cambridge to write the lay of a Celtic bard. 'Back to nature' became the cry, implying only too clearly not merely a longing for beauty, but a retreat into the past. The poets who answered it were much influenced by those repressed and despised peoples, the Irish, Welsh and Scots, with their romantic traditions and settings.

There was a revival of the Scots ballad in the years 1727–30. New ballads were written, such as James Thomson's 'The naked, melancholy isles of farthest Thule', 1730. James Macpherson (1736–96) was a product of the new Celtic movement. A child of poor Highland peasants, his early years were spartan in the extreme. Like so many of the young men of the *Sturm und*

Drang period, dreamers and revolutionaries in England, France, Germany and Russia, he became a teacher, at the local charity school in Ruthven, near Kingussie, Inverness, and later private tutor in a family.

Macpherson published a small volume called *Fragments of Ancient Poetry: translated from the Gaelic or Erse Language*, by the bard Ossian, which held a unique position in the literature and thought of the time. Although it has now been proved that these poems were a forgery, their immediate effect was very significant. European youth heralded Ossian as the symbol of a world which no longer existed, a world of nature and love. Pantheism became a recurrent theme. Ossian was the signal for hope in repressed peoples, for a search into the past, for a 'rediscovery' of national epics. The uproar these poems caused was amazing. The new hopes, nationalist fervour and creative activity they inspired were counter-balanced by quibbles as to the authenticity and origins of the epics. Dr Johnson himself held that the Scots were a 'nation that could not write and could therefore have no ancient literature'.

Thomas Percy, however, student of Chinese literature and later author of *Runic Poetry* and *Reliques of Ancient English Poetry*, was impressed by Macpherson and himself greatly influenced the early German Romantics centred round Herder. It was a time for research and discovery among the emergent peoples, and had valuable and far-reaching effects in the fields of lyric poetry, folk song, philology and history.

Fifty years later, in 1819, Keats noted that 'Chatterton was the purest writer in the English language', a significant tribute to a boy who committed suicide at the age of seventeen, by one of the greatest poets of that frustrated generation which included Shelley and Byron, Hölderlin and Kleist, Pushkin and Lermontov.

Chatterton grew to adolescence in the neighbourhood of St Mary Redcliffe, Bristol. Since the seventeenth century his ancestors had made their living as masons and caretakers of this church. The beauty of its Perpendicular Gothic style made a deep impression on the young boy. Left fatherless, he was sent to the local charity school and, at fifteen, was articled as junior clerk to a solicitor. His life there was humiliating: he shared a bed with the servant, took his meals in the kitchen. No wonder that he sought refuge in dreams, populated an imaginary mediaeval Bristol with heroes of his own making, and finally came to invent, and see himself reincarnated in, Thomas Rowley, poet and monk, whose works he then set out to produce. A doctor and a pewterer became his first and only patrons. When he told them the truth about the poems and revealed himself as Rowley, they refused to believe him.

Chatterton fled to London, filled with ambition, a great longing for action and also a premonition of death. The last writings of this very gifted young poet reveal the hate and despair he flung in the faces of the rich and powerful. As late as July 1770 he wrote to his sister, 'I must be one of the great. The affairs of state suit me better than commerce.' Like Hölderlin and Nietzsche, like the poets of Russia, Poland, Hungary and Italy with their songs of freedom, Chatterton was fully conscious of the political significance of a poet's work. Racked by the discrepancy between his feelings and external conditions, he is symbolic of aspiring European youth of that period. Deep within he knew himself to be great and capable of achieving genius, yet outside was London, alien and indifferent. He tore up his manuscripts and took poison. His suicide set a pattern for the nineteenth century during which so many poets, painters and other artists were to follow his example or seek self-destruction in drink, passion or drugs.

In Chatterton glowed the embers of anger and rebellion that fired the generation of Byron, Keats and Shelley, and which found its own reflection in him. Between these two generations came Blake (1757–1827). Born above a shop in a plain house like all the rest in Broadwick Street, Soho, he suffered as a child from visions of the prophet Ezekiel and of God, a face looking at him from the fire. The visions continued throughout his life. He felt the great men of the past dining with him as his guests and once asked Isaiah and Ezekiel how they dared to maintain that God had spoken to them: were they not afraid of being misunderstood? He heard Isaiah answer: 'I saw no God, nor heard any, in an actual way, yet my senses discovered the infinite in everything. Then I was persuaded, and remained confirmed, that the voice of honest indignation is the voice of God. I cared not for consequences, but wrote.'

In the fullness of his years Blake was a healthy, pugnacious little man, a sort of 'Christian bulldog'. At sixty, when English Romanticism was nearly spent, he was poor and lonely, an engraver who belonged to an outmoded school. He spent his last years in almost total obscurity.

Very little is known about Blake's youth, but his father had joined a small sect of early Swedenborgians and in 1789 Blake and his wife became members of the Great Eastcheap Swedenborgian Society. The Swedenborgians in France constituted an important leaven both for the Revolution in the years around 1790, and for the Counter-Revolution around 1800. Their influence in England was similar in many respects. The founder of these societies, Emanuel Swedenborg, was the son of a bishop. He had studied mathematics, physics and astronomy and was a fervent reader of Newton. He arrived in England for the first time in 1710.

A remarkable man, both visionary and scientist, his approach to work was cool and exacting. He considered that the stars played a large part in men's lives, but true to the scientific methods, used himself and others as the subject of his experiments. Swedenborg's *Arcana Coelstia* (in eight volumes, 1749–56) was devoted to the study of the celestial spheres, of the supernatural. Yet he did not ignore the events taking place in the world. He loved London, where he lived till his death in 1772; and he loved the English people, the mentally, spiritually and politically homeless sectors of the lower middle classes who showed such a burning interest in the relationship between the natural and the supernatural, in the changes in political and ecclesiastical affairs. Inspired by the restlessness and curiosity of these Londoners, he evolved his politico-religious prophecy which assured them that the downfall of the establishment was near. State and church would fall, like idols long since decayed. In 1757 the Last Judgement would take place and from this would arise a new church which would create a new realm for man, the individual.

'England awake, awake, awake!' How often this cry is to be heard in Blake's work, as in his magnificent *Jerusalem*. Whereas the cry, 'Germany awake!' was inspired by certain circles of German Pietism, 'England awake!' was drawn from the sermons of John Wesley. Together with Swedenborg, this man had exercised great influence on Blake. Crowds, twenty-, even thirty-thousand strong, of miners and artisans, the ordinary people of England, would await Wesley on his missionary journeys. In the course of his life he gave more than forty-thousand sermons and travelled two hundred and twenty thousand miles. Utterly indefatigable right up to his eighty-fifth year, he was inspired by the desire to rescue the English people, condemned to misery by poverty, drink and exploitation, from the clutches of the devil. His capacity to inspire faith produced a revivalist movement which formed followers not merely in other sects, both in Britain and abroad, but eventually in the Church of England itself. There is some justification for the view that Wesley saved Britain from a repetition of the French Revolution.

John Wesley was a genuine prophet. But what was Blake? The words 'prophet' and 'poet' were synonymous to him. 'I know of no other Christianity, no other God than the freedom of both body and mind to exercise the divine arts of the imagination.' God exists only in man. 'Man is the power of imagination. God is man and exists in us and we in him . . . Imagination is the eternal in man. Imagination is the Divine Body in man . . . .' God is the creative process in man. Blake, the painter, designer, engraver and poet, read and visualised the Bible as a gigantic experiment in imagination, an almost inexhaustible reservoir of visions. The heaven and hell of the Old Testament prophets are an allegory, for Blake, of the conflicting forces in the human mind and spirit, where alone they exist.

Only in the exercise of the imagination does man live, feel, see God, practise God's powers, reveal them to the world. Art and religion become inextricably entwined. Only the imaginative man, the true artist, is religious. The unimaginative, non-erotic, impercipient, uncultured man is a barbarian, a murderer, with no right to his claim to Christianity. Blake's subconscious attack on the churches and the Christianity of the time began at this point, but it was the religious intellects and artists of the nineteenth century who were to attack the Church most vehemently. The English Romantics, led by Blake and followed by Byron and Shelley, were but a prelude to Novalis, Hölderlin, Kierkegaard and Nietzsche. 'We are all coexistent with God, Members of His Divine Body.' And Blake, conscious all the time of this belief, once wrote: 'I am in God's presence night and day. And he never turns his face away.' His wife, to whom his last words were spoken, said of Blake in the long years of old age, poverty, loneliness and exhaustion, 'He is always in Paradise'. And this paradise was the imagination. 'One power alone makes a Poet: Imagination, the Divine Vision.' To Blake the worlds of vision and thought were one and the same thing.

Blake took his illustrative work very seriously, studying at length all art forms, and finally coming to the conclusion that the art of the ancient peoples, the Babylonians, Egyptians, Indians, Greeks and Romans, had been in imitation of the art of the Hebrew patriarchs: the fount of all art, based directly on the revelation of God. This original art had been lost but in his own visions and work Blake began to rediscover it. The Romantic notions of primal art, universal art, the origins of the history of man in pictures and forms are, like Goethe's universal literature, inseparably bound up with the religious pan-humanism of Blake and his kind. Blake saw man, despite his innate religious beliefs, as threatened by enemies on all sides, by the 'God of the Jews', by the puritanical Christians, their churches and priests, by the materialism of post-Newtonian science, by industrialisation. Jehovah is the 'false', the 'evil' God, a murderer with the church as his agent. The true God is spirit, love, eternal life. True Christianity is infinite remission. That is what Blake tried to express in his *Jerusalem*, a poem which took him sixteen years to write and illustrate.

Blake was deeply disturbed by the rape and ruination of man in contemporary society, by the destruction and violation of mankind by court, church, state and university. He saw Europeans corrupted by materialism, Englishmen made callous by the spirit of Newton and by industrialisation. He himself never visited an industrial centre, but shrank from those 'dark satanic mills' of his prefatory poem to *Milton*. He longed for the return of England's 'green and pleasant land' where men lived in harmony:

> O Earth, O Earth, return!
> Arise from out the dewy grass
> Night is worn
> And the morn
> Rises from the slumberous mass.

In 1800 Blake left London to seek the rural surroundings of Hayley. This flight from depression and melancholy into the peace of nature was to become characteristic of a later stage of Romanticism, epitomised by Wordsworth, Coleridge and Southey. But it should not be forgotten that this reaction followed a more powerful emotion: enthusiasm for world revolution.

In the circle of his English Jacobin friends of 1790 Blake was convinced that the 'Revolution of the world' should be total – a complete transformation of all ecclesiastical, political and social institutions, a liberation of the sexes, of women, of love. He was one of a group of supporters of the French Revolution who used to gather at 72, St Paul's Churchyard in the rooms of the printer and publisher, Joseph Johnson. Others to be found there were William Godwin, Thomas Paine, Fuseli and Mary Wollstonecraft. Their main belief was that the new age would depose Jehovah, symbol of kings and priests of the Old Order. Godwin, one of the dissenting ministers of the time, wanted abolition of the Church, the army and the prisons. He fought for the rights of women and married the early feminist and assistant of Johnson, Mary Wollstonecraft. At the same time Olympe de Gouges was fighting for the rights of women in France; vainly, however, since the Revolution had been made and ruined by men, and had left to women only the scaffold, street and *salon*.

The outstanding personality in this circle of artists, writers, printers and young women was Thomas Paine, born in 1737, the son of a Quaker stay-maker. His pamphlet, *Common Sense*, published 1776 in Philadelphia, two years after his arrival in America, paved the way for the Declaration of Independence. In 1787 he returned to England. Paine was an important link between the American 'Revolution' (i.e. the independence movement, for its leaders were never prepared to admit its revolutionary character), the French Revolution, and the apparently imminent British Revolution. His *Rights of Man* (1792), a classic definition of the principles behind the American and French Revolutions, was a counter-thrust to Burke's *Reflections*. On Blake's advice he fled to Paris immediately after publication, escaping the law by a mere twenty minutes.

Blake's hymnic poem, *The French Revolution*, was written in 1789, set up in type in 1791 at Johnson's house, but never published in his lifetime. In 1793 he composed his *America*. At this period of his life he was much influenced by Mary Wollstonecraft, at that time the friend of Fuseli, who revealed to him the wretched status of women, the long connection between social distress, prostitution and spiritual bondage. Twelve years later, at Chichester, Blake had to answer a charge of assault against a 'disgraced sergeant', John Scholfield. The indictment was for 'sedition', the official word used against any man suspected of harbouring revolutionary tendencies. It was only the first of a long series of humiliations for Blake. But the crowning blow which destiny had in store for him came in 1831 when a very close friend destroyed all the manuscripts which remained unpublished at the time of his death. This destruction of anti-puritan, revolutionary writings by over-zealous relatives and executors was a fate which only too often befell nineteenth-century writers, artists and thinkers.

Between 1789 – the date of Blake's *Songs of Innocence and of Experience* – and 1821–2, when Keats and Shelley died, English Romanticism reached its peak in Blake, Coleridge, Wordsworth, Shelley and Keats. Byron stood on a lone promontory. To the day of his death, the ideals of the 1789 Revolution retained their powerful impact upon him and his enthusiasm for them never died, despite the strain placed on it by despair, chagrin and boredom.

> The sun is warm, the sky is clear
> The waves are dancing fast and bright
> Blue isles and snowy mountains wear
> The purple noon's transparent light.

These are the first lines of the *Stanzas Written In Dejection Near Naples*, and, despite the title, the words show clearly how happy were the days which Percy Bysshe Shelley (1792–1822) spent in Italy. During this period he translated certain scenes from Goethe's *Faust* – a significant occupation, for in Shelley himself may be found something of Faust and Prometheus, those bringers of light, the friends of mankind and opponents of entrenched oppression. Shelley wrote *Prometheus Unbound* in Rome during one of the happiest periods of his life and finished it in the late summer of 1819. It was the symbol of man's best and most creative qualities. In his preface, Shelley calls Prometheus the personification of the highest perfection in moral and intellectual nature, impelled by the purest motives to the best and noblest ends. Prometheus calls men to fight against the evil, hunger, illness and misery which prevails under Jupiter's rule. He is an incarnation of the 'principle of hope' in Ernst Bloch's sense. He gives man the power of speech and thought: 'And speech created thought,

> Which is the measure of the universe;
> And science struck the thrones of earth and heaven'
>
> (Act II, scene 4).

Prometheus is the pioneer of man's way to cosmic rule. Between 1860 and 1914 Russian poets and thinkers were to proclaim this cosmic future for mankind. Their technically-minded heirs are seeking to put the prophecy into practice.

With Prometheus as symbol of the best in man, love became the creative principle. Love generates good and demands no reward just as a moral life is complete in itself without need of an after-life. Prometheus challenges Jupiter as representative of all the father figures of the old world, the kings, priests and gods who, as Shelley and his fellow thinkers were convinced, had no further future. Jupiter is the embodiment of tyranny, cruelty, superstition and lack of culture. In the first act Prometheus sees a vision of Christ and all the evil that Christianity had caused. He sees how Christ, through Christians, has become a term of abuse, a fact noted again by Friedrich Engels in his study of the working classes in England. Shelley himself had rejected Christianity by the time he was eighteen. His classical, and more especially Greek, outlook made him resist vehemently the ties of any dogma. His *Necessity of Atheism*, 1811, maintains that atheism is essential for the release of man's creative and religious powers. He himself was proud of being an atheist, was determined to avoid the constraints of established religion in order to be able to create with total freedom. Through the influence of Shelley one sees again in the nineteenth century something of the Greek spirit of rebellion against Rome, which, again and again since the days of Pelagius, has enriched the English mind and creative ability. He revived some of the oldest Greek themes of spiritual optimism, and his visions of the future possess those Utopian qualities found in the early French socialists, in Victor Hugo, and in America and Russia in the nineteenth and early twentieth centuries. The world would no longer be a place of misery. Health, love and freedom would rule the earth, with woman standing equally beside liberated man. Mankind was to be bound to God only as a free being. In his *Essay on Christianity* Shelley writes of the indivisible tie between God and man. The perfect human and divine character is identical. Man, by becoming like God, fulfils most exactly the bent of his nature; God comprises everything that constitutes human perfection. Therefore he is a model according to which the excellence and greatness of man can be assessed, while the abstract perfection of human character is the essence of God's actual perfection. His *Hymn of Intellectual Beauty* (1816) and *Adonais* (1821) sing the praises of this new conception of the relation of God and man.

Influenced by the ideas of Byron, currently working in Ravenna on *Cain*, Shelley began to evolve a new titanic Christology. Christ, the sacrifice to a cruel deity, combines with Satan and the legions of Titans, and Shelley comparing his own Prometheus with Satan, believes that Christ will be freed from the cruelty of dogma by the new Titans.

'Prometheus', 'Satan', 'Titan', 'Orpheus', 'Dionysus', ancient names resurrected from myths and former faiths, were invoked not only by Shelley, but by many of the young revolutionary generation around 1800, 1810, 1820, as a manifestation of their belief in the coming of a greater man, a greater god. Shelley believed that it was the poet's mission to release into the universe these primal creative forces (*Defence of Poetry*, 1821). The great poets of mankind, Moses, David, Solomon, Isaiah, Christ and the Apostles, had guarded and kindled the divine fire, burning in it all evil, sin and death.

The poet is a seer, prophet, immortal herald. The poet is a pariah, an eternal fugitive and outcast on earth. John Keats (1795–1821) became only too aware of this twofold truth, this double image of the poetic being that haunted poets in the nineteenth century when, mortally ill at the age of twenty-four, he entered on the most creative period of his life, the period of *Ode to Psyche, Ode to a Nightingale, La Belle Dame sans Merci.*

> Beauty is truth, truth beauty – that is all
> Ye know on earth and all Ye need to know

The famous closing lines of the *Ode to a Grecian Urn* epitomised not only his belief in the identity of truth and beauty, but furthermore that truth is the name for that ultimate reality which imagination alone, and not argument, will reveal.

The powerful upsurge of the irrational in the last decade of the eighteenth century and the conviction of the poet that man's path lies midway between horror and beauty is reflected in three magnificent poems, *The Ancient Mariner, Kubla Khan* and the first part of *Christabel*, written in 1797–8 by the twenty-five-year-old Coleridge. They are an expression of the extreme mixture of feelings provoked in the hearts of English Romantics by the French Revolution. Wordsworth was another to whom the utter failure of the French Revolution caused bitter disappointment, yet during the years 1797–1807 he recovered much of his equanimity and as early as 1802 was able to begin his *Ode* to *Intimations of Immortality*. In later years he was accused of being cold and hard, but he had in fact, merely retreated into himself. His first enthusiasms took on a quieter form, and like Coleridge and Keats, though unlike Blake, he grew to reject that paragon of European Romanticism, Byron, whom Goethe and Mazzini, Germans, Poles, Russians, Italians, Spaniards and Portuguese, hailed as leader of the younger generation.

The figure of Byron presents even today something of an enigma to students of literature and thought. In England he was certainly not popular, and even on the Continent the attitude towards him was ambiguous. He has been called the first modern poet of whom it has been impossible to decide whether, he was the genius *par excellence* or a complete charlatan.

Byron's own quizzical survey of the situation is to be found in his *Detached, Thoughts* for 15 October 1821:

'To begin then – I have seen myself compared personally or poetically in English, French, German (as interpreted to me), Italian and Portuguese within these nine years, to Rousseau – Goethe – Young – Aretino – Timon of Athens – 'An Alabaster Vase lighted up within' – Satan – Shakespeare – Buonaparte – Tiberius – Aeschylos – Sophocles – Euripides – Harlequin – The Clown – Sternhold and Hopkins – to the Phantasmagoria – to Henry VIII – to Chenies – to Mirabeau – to young R. Dallas (the Schoolboy) – to Michael Angelo – to Raphael – to a *petit maître* – to Diogenes – to Childe Harold – to Lara – to the Count in Beppo – to Milton – to Pope – to Dryden – to Burns – to Savage – to Chatterton – to 'oft have I heard of thee my Lord Biron' – in Shakespeare – to Churchill the poet – to Kean the actor – to Alfieri, etc., etc., etc. The likeness to Alfieri was asserted very seriously by an Italian, who had known him in his younger days: it of course related merely to our apparent personal dispositions. He did not assert it to me (for we were not then good friends), but in society.

'The Object of so many contradictory comparisons must probably be like something different from them all; but what *that* is, is more than I know, or anybody else.

'My Mother, before I was twenty, would have it that I was like Rousseau, and Madame de Stael used to say so too in 1813 ... I can't see any point of resemblance ... Altogether I think myself justified in thinking the comparison not well founded. I don't say this out of pique, for Rousseau was a great man, and the thing if true were flattering enough; but I have no idea of being pleased with a chimera.'

The whole passage is unmistakably Byronic, but it is the last phrase which is of particular significance. Byron had no illusions about the age he lived in. He saw the situation clearly and with insight, and what he saw embittered him. It is this bitterness and despair that lies at the root of his melancholia. His most cheerful moods were usually nothing but a cover concealing the deepest depression, as his wife Annabella once said: 'at heart you are the most melancholy of mankind, often apparently when gayest'.

Byron knew himself to be basically a realist and he felt nothing but contempt for the moody Romanticism of Continental poets, for the Romantics' conception of 'imagination'. To him the poet was not a higher being, a god. He considered nature, love and emotion as adequate inspiration for art.

His devotion to nature, however, was genuinely religious:

> My altars are the mountains of the Ocean,
> Earth – air – stars – all that springs from the great Whole,
> Who hath produced and will receive the Soul.

Nature is the stage on which man fights perpetually for his freedom. His attitude to London, on the other hand, was uncompromisingly realistic:

> A mighty mass of brick, and smoke, and shipping,
> Dirty and dusky, but as wide as eye
> Could reach . . .

It was the capital of a country corrupted by the cant of the church and state, ruled by men who masked their merciless control with a flow of fine words. On the 13 January 1821 Byron noted: 'Dined – news come – the Powers mean to war with the peoples. The intelligence seems positive – let it be so – they will be beaten in the end. The King-times are fast finishing. There will be blood shed like water and tears like mist, but the peoples will conquer in the end. I shall not live to see it, but I foresee it.'

Italian, Polish, Russian, French, Greek, and Hungarian poets, Romantics and national revolutionaries, felt this strain of promise and revolution in Byron's 'romantic' writings. Not that he bothered to conceal his thoughts:

> For I will teach, if possible, the stones
> To rise against Earth's tyrants. Never let it
> Be Said that we still truckle unto thrones; –
> But ye – our children's children! think how we
> Showed *what things were* before the world was free!

He was a resistance writer, in word and deed, and stands between Saint-Just (whom he mentions in his diary for 1813) and the long series of writers-cum-revolutionaries that leads via Mazzini and Petofi to T.E.Lawrence and Malraux. He attacked in plain words both the government of George IV with its leader Wellington ('the best of cut-throats'), and the Holy Alliance, those rulers of Europe and the world who wish to enslave mankind:

> Shut up the bald-coot bully Alexander!
> Ship off the Holy Three to Senegal;
> Teach them that 'sauce for goose is sauce for gander'
> And ask them how *they* like to be thrall.

He accused England of betraying the people's hopes, of promising them

23

freedom and then conniving at, even aiding, their captivity. All his poetic heroes, Cain, Don Juan, Manfred are portrayed in combat with tyranny, whether in heaven or on earth.

Despite the effect of his works on writers and thinkers of the time, Byron himself, like many other aristocrat and political activist, did not think much of literature. In a letter from Venice to Thomas Moore, 28 February 1817, he said frankly that he did not view it as his true vocation, 'But you will see that I shall do something'. Ten days earlier he had written, 'It is no great matter, supposing that Italy could be liberated, who or what is sacrificed. It is a grand object – the very *poetry* of politics. Only think – a free Italy!'

To alter the prevailing state of affairs, whether through wars of liberation or revolution 'is . . . the very *poetry* of politics'. That was to prove the point of departure for the ideas of the right-wing Romantics – Karl Marx was a direct product of Romanticism. The explanation of the enthusiasm and inspiration which Byron's writings instilled into the youth of Europe lies in their fusion of the poetic and political. In him both elements were pure, vital. He believed in the dictum that a poet's vocation is to help man towards a worthier existence. He believed in man's release from bondage, whether self-incurred or not. He spared neither his health nor his fortune in the cause of Greece, although he quickly perceived that the true tragedy of the Greeks was that they were preparing, by savage cabals and civil war, to throw themselves into viler conditions than any they suffered 'under the Turkish yoke'. He sees this but involves himself nevertheless because he knows that the Greek episode is but a prologue to the passage of man, through tragedy, to a happier future.

A happier future? The way to that was barred by the French Revolution, political man's fall from innocence. It had been the 'upshot of a plot', a conspiracy of murderers, criminals and cheats. It would need a crusade to overthrow it. And because this 'armed doctrine' had its own great strength, the war would be a long one. Such, in short, was the content of Burke's writings.

Edmund Burke (1729–97) was one of the most influential thinkers of the Western world. In the nineteenth and twentieth centuries his disciples have included moderates, 'liberals', 'conservatives', radical nationalists and fascists. His ideas have become a kind of dogma, almost a religion to them, according to which the French Revolution continues and will seem to continue until such a time as its seeds have been destroyed for ever. He represents that principle of intervention which was used by the Holy Alliance 1815–48, and by the Western powers in Russia 1918–22, namely that every state has the right to intervene in its neighbours' affairs should anarchy, tyranny or inhumanity take a hold there. In the opinion of some of Burke's American disciples, this should be the purpose of the United Nations.

Burke's *Reflections Concerning the Revolution in France*, a violent polemic written in the first years of the Revolution, appealed to deep-seated instincts, the desire to remain in power, in possession, in position, at any price. Among his French and German admirers the work released retrogressive, archaic tendencies which, in the major irrationalist movements, are always only too ready to come to light. History and religion would be used to support their theories. Burke's rationalism, his political and religious conceptions were more typical of the eighteenth than the nineteenth century. He held religion to be a political weapon, a means of maintaining order, of supporting the state, an opinion held also by Hobbes, Justus Moser, Edward Gibbon, and later by such atheistic Catholics as Charles Maurras. It was a view of religion which enabled sceptics, cynics, free-thinkers, and rationalists with a Voltairean bias, to come together as a 'national front'. In France the coalition of the liberal upper-middle class, atheists and free-thinkers with ultra-conservatives and clericals in the fight against the revolutions of 1830, 1848 and 1870 had momentous consequences.

Burke's hatred of 'Marianne', of '*la* révolution' – which Delacroix had depicted as a woman storming the barricades – was exacerbated by the not infrequent difficulty and unhappiness of Irishmen's relations with women, with sex, some taking refuge in drunkenness and brawling, others in orgiastic excesses – long before James Joyce – to release the explosive tensions. The 'neurotic' nature of nineteenth-century politics was right in looking instinctively to his dour, emphatically masculine Irishman for support, and in this connection it is important to look once again at the characteristics of Talleyrand's *dolce vita* prior to 1789.

Laxity of morals was one of the fundamentals on which the gaiety, wit and lack of inhibition of the *ancien régime*'s aristocratic and upper-class society rested. Neurotic anxiety and unease appear to have played no part in circles where vice and virtue were paraded with equal candour. With the advent of puritanism and terrorism in political, religious and social life an element of rigidity, hypocrisy and mendacity seems to emerge in the relationship between the sexes. The increasing neuroticism of political conditions in Germany in the years between 1870 and 1941 was paralleled in the private sphere with an hysterical fear of 'obscenity' and the belief that sex was a satanic vice.

In nineteenth-century Europe the disturbance of the political, mental and spiritual balance of affairs has intimately connected with the aggravation of sources of sexual conflict. In order to appreciate how this complex situation developed from the intemperate mode of life of the *ancien régime*, it is necessary to turn to the writings of William Beckford and Marquis de Sade, men whose works have, significantly enough, remained practically unstudied until the middle of this century.

William Beckford, of Fonthill Abbey, son of a rich Lord Mayor of London, was born in 1760. At the age of ten his education was put in the hands of Alexander Cozens, a naturalised Russian who claimed to be an illegitimate son of Peter the Great. This man was highly esteemed as a painter of water-colour. He was also a lover of occult arts and may have been responsible for introducing Beckford, who was greatly influenced by him, to black magic. Certainly he incited his pupil to learn Persian and Arabic. Both in England (possibly since the days of Roger Bacon) and in France, occult aspirations had often gone hand in hand with the knowledge of Oriental languages and culture. At any rate in 1781 the circle of Beckford's friends included an old Arab. He also frequented the society of Count Philipp de Loutherbourg, a painter, stage designer and (Beckford's own description) 'mystagogue', a pupil of Mesmer and Cagliostro.

For Christmas of that year Beckford arranged a select party, a party never to be forgotten because of its combination of eroticism, epicureanism, enthusiasm, Romanticism and leanings to mortal terror. Those invited included his cousin Louisa Beckford, to whom he was passionately attached, and William Courtenay, a beautiful young boy of thirteen who several years later accused Beckford of being responsible for having lead him into homosexuality. What actually happened at this party of spoilt, highly-strung, perhaps perverted young people and their dubious friends remains unknown. Did they among other things, celebrate black masses? Louisa's letters to William, before and after, contain horrific insinuations:

William, my lovely infernal! how gloriously you write of iniquities. Not all the saints in paradise could withstand your persuasive eloquence, and like another Lucifer you would tempt Angels to foresake their coelestial abode, and sink with you into the black infernal gulph. Converts to your faith would crowd from every starry world, and the wide expanse of Heaven be left desolate and forlorn . . .

How much of this was overwrought imagination, how much a hint of dark and evil play? Impossible to tell. What is apparent is the spiritual affinity between Beckford – a highly talented writer who by the age of seventeen had a tale of damnation redolent of delight in destruction, crime and wickedness to his name – and the works of the Marquis de Sade.

Fame came to Beckford with the publication of *Vathek*, a 'Transcription of Arabic Stories', which he maintained had been written, in a state of trance, over a period of two days and one night. In fact he had worked at it for several months. Its strangely powerful style is a cross between irony and lament and leaves the reader both fascinated and horrified. It was written in French, which he held to be the sacred language of Orientalism, and if we remember Guillaume Postel and the tradition of French Orientalists from the sixteenth to the eighteenth centuries, he had some justification.

The impact of this book was far-reaching and lasted late into the nineteenth century. Its Caliph Vathek is depicted as a superman with the mark of Lucifer on his brow who undertakes a series of journeys to hell. Satan is a handsome youth of twenty with aristocratic features, a gentle voice and an elusive air of melancholy (a self-portrait in some respects of the author). The main focus of the story, however, is the journey through hell of a pair of unhappy lovers. Torn between ecstasy and despair, they remain dissatisfied while surrounded by idle stimulations, splendours and excesses: here were Louisa and William Beckford, dissolute descendants of old families, tasting the fruits of evil and destruction. It is not unlikely that they practised all the perverted horrors of black magic and sacrificial rites.

The principle theme of *Vathek* was that greatness exists only in evil, a decadent theme artistically deployed with the help of an overcharged sensibility, titillation and romance and framed in a style which anticipates Nietzsche and the *poètes maudits* from Baudelaire onward. Such an expert in decadence and the search for hells in the human heart was Donatien Aldonse François de Sade.

THE MARQUIS DE SADE AND THE DEATH DANCE OF EUROPE'S RULERS

Sadism: the word is emblematic of the general decline, the 'dance of death', of the ruling classes in Europe at the end of the eighteenth century, and de Sade's life, spent in the description and practice of sexual cruelty, become a symbol of that age.

As far back as Ugo de Sanza (Hughes de Sade) in the twelfth century, his family shows a record of indulgence in extravagance and high living. The men held important ecclesiastical and social positions which enabled them to fulfil their desires without hindrance. The women, in particular Laura de Noves, Petrarch's Laura, who married Hugo II in 1325 and became the model for much lyric poetry, were the lovers of high-standing officials, and anticipate de Sade's 'heroines'. His own father, Jean Baptiste Joseph François de Sade, was a colonel in the Papal Cavalry of Venaissin (1730), envoy at the Russian court, later Elector of Cologne and, in 1760, Field Marshal. His mother, Marie-Eléonore, came from a subsidiary branch of the Bourbon family and was related to Richelieu. His uncle, Abbé Jaques François Paul Aldonse de Sade, whose influence on the Marquis was considerable, was a man of culture and wide experience with women.

De Sade was born at the Hôtel Condé in Paris on 2 June 1740. At ten he was sent to the Collège Louis-le-Grand; at fourteen he entered the army; at sixteen saw active service, and at twenty-three married the rich Renée Pelagie de Monteuil. In the same year, 1763, he was arrested for the first time for licentiousness combined with cruelty. Two affairs, at Arceuil in 1768 and Marseille in 1772, revealed to a wider public the close connection in his psychoneurotic constitution between masochism and sadism. He fled the country but was arrested in Chambéry on the orders of the king of Sardinia and thrown into Miolans, a prison built in the twelfth century, the Bastille of the Dukes of Savoy. His twenty-eight years of incarceration with its few brief respites had begun. He managed to escape, lived in hiding for a time and then on his own estates. In 1777 he was imprisoned at Vincennes, where his initial sentence of sixteen months was later extended to five and a half years. One night, while at Vincennes, he fell asleep over a copy of the *Life of*

Petrarch and had a vision of his ancestress, Laura, speaking 'lofty, mysterious words' to him. During his periods in prison he spent much time expanding his knowledge of painting, sculpture, the theatre and literature. He considered himself to be a literary man, an *homme de lettres*.

It is in a letter to his wife, who retained a deep affection for him and tried constantly to obtain his release, that we find one of the best portraits of the man. With typical candour and self-honesty he writes: 'Domineering, irascible, passionate, extravagant in every way. Where morals are concerned, possessed by a grossness of imagination that does not have its like. That, in a word, is how I am. And another thing: take me as I am or kill me, for I shall not change.'

De Sade was a prisoner at the Bastille from 1784–9. On 1 October 1788, he made a *catalogue raisonné* of his writings. In this are listed fifteen octavo volumes, two of tragedies and comedies, four of stories; he wrote seventeen plays in all. There is also an extensive collection of letters, mostly written to his wife, 'truly Shakespearian monologues' in which de Sade's ruthlessly blunt ego confronts itself with the abyss of his own personality and with the world.

He was moved from the Bastille on 4 July 1789, but the Revolution did not release 'this monster' until 2 April 1790. In 1793 he was once again imprisoned and this time sentenced to death. Robespierre's fall saved him, but he spent 312 days in four of the Revolution's prisons. On 6 March 1801, he was arrested once again and in 1803 was transferred, thanks to the efforts of his family, to the lunatic asylum in Charenton-Saint-Maurice. Here he was allowed to take charge of the asylum theatre, which had been established for therapeutic purposes. He died there on 2 December 1814. His will, dated 30 June 1806, instructed that he should be buried in a wooden coffin 'without any ceremony' in a forest on his Malmaison estate.

De Sade introduced one of his works with an aphormism from Seneca: 'True freedom is to fear neither men nor gods.' This could well be taken as the motto of his own life. He was dedicated to a religion of evil, according to which God created and perpetuates the world through evil, humanity exsist in evil and the world will ultimately return to evil when its term is spent. In his *Dialogue between a Priest and a Dying Man* (Vincennes 1782, published 1926) he maintains that nature is cruel and destructive, that there is no God. His writings are full of reflections of this kind.

Against the God-idol of Christianity, the 'throne-and-altar' faith and belief in virtue as these were preached from the pulpit and mouthed by hypocrites, de Sade set the notion of man's total rebellion, taking it to its logical conclusion of total destruction, total outlawry and total dictatorship. If man is forced to be entirely dependent on himself in a state of nature apparently without logical cause and effect, should he not do anything and everything of which he is capable? Man's highest potentiality and power lies in crime, in murder, in the subjugation of others and their appropriation as raw material for any and every passion known to the individual. Juliette, at the end of her horrifying report on her crimes and life, says 'I admit that I love iniquity passionately, that it alone stimulates my senses and that I shall adhere to its principles with my last breath.'

Juliette is the 'heroine' of *La Nouvelle Justine, suivi de L'Histoire de Juliette, sa soeur* (1797). Her friend, a main character in the book, is the criminal Lady Clairwil. It is of crucial significance that de Sade put his doctrine into the mouths, and illustrated it through the behaviour, of those who belonged to Europe's ruling class before 1789, aristocrats, ecclesiastics, men of finance. Here, even though in distorted and extravagant fashion, a member of the aristocracy described something of the reality that lay behind the power and rule of the time, something of the monstrous brutality and contempt for humanity that was accepted in practice by its victims and perpetrators as 'the will of God'. Whereas the nineteenth and twentieth centuries have preferred to veil the total right of the stronger party in Christian ideology, de Sade frankly declared Christianity to be a fiction. Juliette analyses, dissects Christ with cold, scientific precision and asks, 'Imbecile Christians, what do you propose to do with your dead God?' Elsewhere she says, 'man must dare to do anything, without fear.' Nature knows only one law, that of the stronger. If the weaker resists, he is at fault. Remorse is contrary to reason and pity to sin.

La Nouvelle Justine was the culmination of de Sade's invective against the old world. Through perverted humour, and surrealist settings, his tale becomes a dance of lust and death, a caricature of the fear among the ruling classes of the rise of the masses. The descendant of a family which for six centuries had served the papacy in many different capacities, he goes on to discharge with unparalleled ferocity his wrath and contempt on the contemporary Pontificate. Juliette is received by Pius VI. He not only celebrates black masses in St Peter's in order to win her favours, but enters a spirited plea for murder and the extermination of all enemies and creatures of lesser breed. At the court of Naples Juliette is told that the ruins of Pompeii and Herculaneum are favourite scenes for royal excesses. At his palace King Ferdinand possesses a unique theatre: its stage is fitted for the performance of seven different forms of execution and fifty ravishingly beautiful boys and girls, whose pictures are displayed in the auditorium, can be killed there at will. The master of ceremonies to these orgies is Vespoli, the Royal Confessor. This travesty was de Sade's depiction of the Baroque order which revelled in the terror of death. His revolutionary theme was that the men of power in Europe before 1789 were no better than cannibals.

In 1815 and again in 1825 the publication of *Aline et Valcour, ou le Roman Philosophique* (1795) was forbidden. The novel portrays an ideal state logically socialised down to the last detail, and compares it with the depraved, cannibalistic state of Butua. In October 1785, while still in the Bastille, de Sade began the fair copy of *Les 120 Journées de Sodome ou l'École du Libertinage*. It is the story of four psychopaths aged between forty-five and sixty, who come together at a lonely castle in the Black Forest. De Sade portrays them as important officials of state, church, government and finance. During their stay at the castle, they make use of forty-two victims and the text consists of their descriptions of six hundred types of perversion. The book is only partially completed and drafts read rather like a clinical treatise. As in so many of his works, de Sade shows himself here to be a forerunner of Freud, the psychology of the subconscious, and, in particular, the sexual pathology of the late nineteenth and early twentieth centuries. Apart from its scientific aspect, however, the direction of his political and philosophical attack also deserves attention. At one level the members of his most select society are simply portraits of textbook 'sadists'. At another, through their contribution to our knowledge of nature and humanity, they serve the important purpose of undermining the premises of Christianity.

In *Justine* we read the following passage:

When anatomy has been brought to perfection, there will be no difficulty in demonstrating the relationship between man's constitution and his appetites. What will you do then, you *pedants, hangmen, warders, law-makers and tonsured riff-raff*, when we have got that far? What will become of your laws, your morality, your religion, your power, your paradise, your gods and your hell, once it has been shown that this or that current of fluid, or a certain grain, or a degree of acidity in the blood or the juices will suffice to subjugate man to your torments of vengeance?

This was more than a premonition of hormone research and pathological analysis. De Sade understands that murderous instincts and passions arise with such devastating force in man's 'nature' precisely because that nature is concealed, violated and suppressed by the 'pedants, hangmen, gaolers, legislators and tonsured rabble'. In fact, the Marquis disclosed that urge to destruction which caused Sigmund Freud, between the two world wars, to realign and extend his principles of psychoanalysis.

In the nineteenth century neuroses and psychoses, severe mental and psychosomatic diseases, were initially encountered in small minorities and communities, only later affecting larger groups. De Sade exposed the close connection between impotence, perversion and political incapacity. The characters of his *Journées de Sodome* were not only caricatures of the epitaph of pre-1789 *dolce vita*, but prophetic silhouettes of the figures of Europe's *danse macabre* which led to 1914. Such men, rulers by class, could not control the dangerous upsurge of the masses. To outsiders the connection between sexual and political incapacity may not be very apparent, but it was crudely and often visibly manifest in the courts of Constantinople, St Petersburg and Peking, all of which waned at the same period.

In his novels and tracts de Sade described three recipes for happiness: life on a socialist isle, the terror of the Baroque order and the unbridled craving of the ego prepared to pay any price, including self-destruction, for its satisfaction. He explored the weird possibilities open to man in his pursuit of happiness. The attention now devoted to his works, some of which were published for the first time in France, America and Britain after the Second World War, reflects the fascination exercised on contemporary minds by this seer of 1790 and 1800.

3

German Society in the Age of the French Revolution

In 1770 Germany, seen through the eyes of a traveller, a man of culture, was a haven of peace: small towns, the residences and courts of noblemen and prelates, markets, castles, monasteries and convents, the upper classes maintaining their comfortable standard of living, the aristocracy bent on pleasure, the states and princedoms managed by officials. To outward appearances it was still the Age of Enlightenment of Frederick the Great's last years of rule, with princely courts imitating Louis XIV, the Regency and French Rococo. As Count Manteuffel wrote to Christian Wolff, the philosopher: 'Germany swarms with potentates, three quarters of whom scarcely have common sense and who are the bane of mankind ... Tiny as their territories are, they imagine humanity to have been created on their behalf.' Nevertheless, those were peaceful days. There was no industry, no war, no religious stir, no major intellectual unrest to attract the stranger's attention. The manor houses, with their libraries, their beautiful antiques, their parks and lakes, were to remain undisturbed until the devastation and annihilation of 1945.

German, meaning at that time Protestant, culture spread its influence throughout Europe. German poetry, German antiquities, the German past, held the interest of the upper and middle classes of that rich, self-assured, satiated eighteenth century. At Konigsberg, in Prussia, Immanuel Kant in 1781 defined 'the land of pure reason as an island ... that lies in the ocean of illusions, dreams of power, adventures; the sea is both the whirlpool of loss and destruction and the ocean of freedom and infinity for which the soul craves, however much reason clings to the island's boundaries, to the finite.'

Kant, until his death in 1804, lived in fear of a relapse into barbarism. Should one of the great ethical forces, mutual love and respect, lose its hold, 'then the chaos (of immorality) will swallow up the whole realm of (moral) being like a drop of water'. He knew only too well that the enlightenment in Germany was confined to isolated circles and was conscious of the possibility that the tumult erupting from hard-pressed German hearts and minds might well come to compare with England's Promethean visions and France's explosive revolutionary force.

By the middle of the eighteenth century an intellectual storm had begun to rise over those placid, sleepy lands among men who had lived too long in pietistic, enlightened, rationalistic circles and communities. Following a mere spring shower, spread over two to three generations, the first clap of thunder hit Germany in 1800. By 1815 the worst seemed over, the main fires it had started, quenched by political reaction. Yet many small sparks continued to glow. With Marx, Kierkegaard and Nietzsche they burst into flame, and in France and Russia kindled important conflagrations. This German movement questioned radically every aspect of life as known to the Old European Order, in matters of state, church, religion, thought and sentiment.

It was during the course of Germany's quiet eighteenth century that the works were composed which cleared the path for nineteenth-century intellectual exploration and at the same time raised the dams which were to stem the ensuing flood of ideas. The men who started the movement were all essentially products of the eighteenth century: Kant (1724–1804), Klopstock (1724–1803), Hamann (1730–88) and Herder (1744–1803). Schiller, apotheosis of German middle-class enlightenment, was of the eighteenth century (1759–1805). Novalis, polar star of the young Romantic movement and greatest pointer to the twentieth century, was born in 1772 and died in 1802.

In 1755 European equanimity was shattered by the Lisbon earthquake, which revealed the very real crisis afflicting Christianity. While on the one hand a stream of pamphlets defended such an apparently inexplicable occurrence as God's just wrath against a sinful humanity, on the other side indignation against this 'God' and theology for the first time united all Europe's best intellects, from Voltaire to Kant. Goethe, six years old at the time, subsequently stated that the Lisbon earthquake was responsible for his loss of Christian faith.

In 1755 Kant's inaugural dissertation appeared, and in 1756 his tract on the earthquake, condemning the 'criminal presumption' of those who ventured 'to claim insight into the intentions of divine counsel'. In 1763 he described the system of metaphysics prevailing up to that time as an 'abyss' and a 'dark ocean without land or light'.

In 1774 Goethe's *Werther* was published, a slim volume which was to be interpreted by the youth of Europe as a revolutionary manifesto. Napoleon carried it in his military pack. Students enthused over it. To others, especially in Germany, it was a sweet poison, leading to suicide.

Kant's *Critique of Pure Reason* appeared in 1781, and was regarded by himself and several of his later followers as the last major attempt to defend the old concepts of divinity, immortality and human dignity.

In 1788, a year before the beginning of the French Revolution, Prussia fired the first salvo against the Enlightenment with its issue of the Woellnerian Edict on religious affairs. This statute was to prove a very fruitful source of inspiration for censorship provisions and all the paraphernalia of cultural policy from 1815 to 1848.

In 1789 the Prussian corporal's cane was for the first time publically stigmatised by liberal thinkers as the symbol of military and political reaction. On 8 August of the same year Jean Paul set down his vision of Christ defunct and the cry which European writers during the first half of the nineteenth century would continually recall, 'God is dead'.

In 1790 *Faust, a Fragment,* was published.

In 1791, Herder's *Ideas on the Philosophy of Mankind's History* appeared. In his youth Herder had sung the praises of Peter the Great and dreamed of becoming Empress Catherine's counsellor. During his sea journey to Nantes, bringing in its course his transformation into a truly revolutionary philosopher, he still favoured the notion of himself as a future Zwingli, Calvin or Luther in Livonia. Instead he was to become the laureate of the 'awakening peoples', whose songs advocated the destruction of the old, decayed, ruling classes. Herder wished for a Germanic note to replace the Jewish in Christianity and in *Adreasta* postulated a Jewish migration to Palestine. And this in precisely those years when a mentally alert German *élite* were beginning to frequent Jewish drawing-rooms in Berlin and had initiated that meeting of German and Jewish minds which until 1933 was to be of such significance to German intellectual life.

The first version of Schiller's hymnic *The Gods of Greece,* printed in the year of the Woellnerian Edict, began to reveal his own opposition, and that of other intellectuals, to the 'establishment' predominating in all Christian denominations. Seven years later saw the publication of Goethe's *Wilhelm Meister's Years of Apprenticeship* (1795). This book, resented by many members of the upper classes, was acclaimed by the younger generation, along with Fichte's ideas and the French Revolution. The first performance of Schiller's *Wallenstein* took place in April 1799. For German youth Wallenstein became the symbol of a man of action, reshaping history with the Germans as his chosen instrument. In the same year Hölderlin turned against all forms of orthodoxy and in his *Germania* (1801) gave the Germans a sense of being a people whose significance could change world history. The magazine *Athenaeum,* issued from 1798 to 1800 by the two Schlegel brothers, intimated aphoristically the 'inexorable' revolutions and future prospects of the nineteenth and twentieth centuries. Another weekly, *Der Neue Mensch,* republican in sentiment and distinctly radical on social questions, was published at Flensburg in 1796–7.

Despite the fact that Germany in the eighteenth century had not yet felt the effects of the Industrial Revolution as such, unrest and social discontent was beginning to make itself apparent in many groups and classes. The position of the peasants was wretched, and from 1790 onwards disturbance and unease were reported in the rural areas of Saxony, Prussia and Silesia. Beggars were common. A third of Cologne's total population of 40,000 is said to have consisted of paupers, a state of affairs reminiscent of mediaeval Paris and Florence. The number of Berlin's inhabitants grew from 50,000 in 1712 to 140,000 in 1799 (excluding a military establishment of 45,000). Its suburbs contained a working population of 70–80,000, whose domestic conditions were appalling.

The penury of private tutors, impoverished lawyers, doctors without fee-paying patients, authors without fee-paying publishers or without readers (German language writers rose from 3,000 in 1773 to 6,000 in 1787) was the hallmark of the 'lettered proletariat'. Sheer necessity brought these men to revolt. Hunger was common in the houses of men like Jean Paul and fear for the bare necessities of life, pursuit of an appointment, the strain of nocturnal toil on their literary work, consumed the poets of the *Sturm und Drang* and early Romantic period. Even Schiller, despite the highest patronage, never succeeded in shaking off crushing pecuniary distress. And an intellectual who lost his office, benefice or chair, was doomed, for not everybody possessed Jean Paul's and Mörike's capacity for flight from everyday penury into the realm of creative imagination.

'Germany's most important revolutionary publicist prior to 1848' was the title justly conferred on Andreas Georg Friedrich Rebmann (1768–1824). Most of his radical writings were concentrated in the years 1790–4, time when the Austrian and Hungarian 'Jacobins', as well as Wekhrlin, Hülsen and Fichte, were deploying ideas representative of a fundamental change which alone renders subsequent developments such as 'Romanticism', 'Classicism, and 'Idealism' intelligible.

Rebmann described in his *Letters Concerning Erlangen* (two volumes, Frankfurt and Leipzig 1792) the distress caused among the early industrial proletariat by the reduction in the number of stocking-looms:

> Friends, I have witnessed scenes here which make a humane man's flesh creep. Five or six naked children, covered with sores and scabs and wrapped in rags, writhing in the bleak cold of a damp attic. Boiled potatoes are the poor sufferers' only food, while the youngest of them hangs parched from its mother's breast, which can yield no milk because the mother herself is starving.

In 1796 he wrote: 'And yet this race of crowned devils did not die out with Louis XI. In Germany in 1796, four years before the close of the eighteenth century, there are princes who sacrifice not merely a few infants, but a good part of all their vassals to their folly and iniquity . . .'

Wieland, in his essays on the French revolution of 1789–92, goes even further. He maintains that European man had 'come of age. The old authorities have been indisputably overthrown'. For even in Germany, according to Wieland, the people were considering how to 'strip off the old fetters' and '*beginning to surmise a possibility that self-help may prove the way*, should hope of help be disappointed by those who are still credited with enough goodwill to help gladly if they could . . .'

The words of Wieland italicised here draw attention to the incalculable significance of the French and American Revolutions for the nineteenth and twentieth centuries. These revolutions (as Hannah Arendt has shown so clearly) were the progenitors of a period in which the feasibility of altering the human condition by political action was discovered. After centuries of contemplation, of metaphysics, which seemed to be 'above' man's social situation, but was in fact often not equal to it, a mode of thought was evolving which would take this situation in hand and make it possible for all aspects of it to be discussed frankly and publically.

During the period following the Revolution, however, this state of affairs did not mature in Germany. The Terror into which the Revolution had degenerated coupled with French occupation of much of the territory of the Holy Roman Empire, gave rise to reactionary sentiments even at a time when republican and revolutionary hopes were animating German youth. The attitudes of Schiller, Goethe, Novalis, Hölderlin, the two Schlegels and the men around Fichte and Hülsen are incomprehensible unless seen against this broad background of 'patriotic', 'national', 'true blue' and Christian reaction to the French Revolution.

Counter-revolutionary propaganda had been appearing in Germany for some time before the Revolution. The dispossessed Jesuits had established a centre at Augsburg and had, since 1784, been issuing 'disclosures' to prove that freemasons, disciples of the Enlightenment were seeking the 'overthrow of established states and religion as well as the repeal of all order'. The Bavarian Privy Councillor, Karl von Eckartshausen, published a pamphlet in 1791 entitled: *What Contributes Most to Contemporary Revolution? And What is the Surest Means to Forestall Them in the Future? A Text for Princes and Peoples to Ponder.* Two years later he published a book *On The Danger that Threatens Thrones, States and Christianity with Total Ruin*, explaining that the Enlightenment and the Revolution were a conspiracy on the part of philosophers and that the sole remedy lay in an alliance between altar and throne.

Count Friedrich Leopold Stolberg had predicted the Revolution in an early poem, in 1755. He was an enthusiastic partisan of the events of 1789, but the years of the Terror shook his faith to such an extent that he became one of the most fervid adherents of the anti-Weimar group of counter-revolutionaries. Stolberg is a text-book example of blind adherence to a cause turning into blind hate, and a symbol of the reaction felt by so many Germans who had originally welcomed the Revolution. It is possible to quote dissenting opinions from almost any member of the intelligentsia of that period, but such quotes would be deceptive. There was a continuous if unavowed interaction between the Revolution and almost all German thinkers of importance. They knew that the effects of the Revolution would continue, but hoped to direct it according to their own ends.

In 1794 leading German intellectuals were invited by conservative factions to join the newly-formed league of sovereigns in a propaganda offensive to save the country from the 'menace of anarchy'. Goethe, however, whom they had hoped to enlist as star-supporter, declined on the grounds that it was impossible to combine princes and writers in this fashion.

The correspondence between Goethe and Schiller must be seen in its political context. For them the vital question was how to do away gradually with the remnants of feudalism in Germany, how to gain certain social benefits from 1789 without revolution.

WEIMAR AND SCHILLER

On 26 August 1792 the National Assembly in Paris passed a resolution conferring on *sieur Gille, Publiciste allemand*, the title of *Citoyen français*.

The leaders of the French Revolution were well aware that poetry and politics, writing and freedom went hand in hand. The poets of all nations with their songs of freedom form, whether they know it or not, a Holy Alliance, a vanguard in the cause of humanity. There were men in 1792 who knew that Schiller (although the official recorders could not even spell his name) was in the first rank of such poets. The outcome, however, was farcical. Schiller deposited the deed of honour bestowed upon him by the French revolutionary leaders at the sleepy, easy-going town of Weimar, in the library of a Duke who – not ungifted, but eccentric, cunning, and in his own way a bohemian – knew only too well how to govern 'his' officials, who included Goethe, Schiller himself, Herder, Fichte, and all the rest. This act of submission was symbolic of the fate of so many German poets who lived their lives dependent on the favour of their patrons.

Even in Schiller one finds the element of a great man who has not fulfilled his destiny, and the life of this tragedian must be seen in itself as a tragedy. When he died, an autopsy showed that his intestines had shrunk to the size of a fist. It was incomprehensible to the doctors how he could have lived so long. For fifteen years he struggled with illness and death, tormented by pain and sleeplessness. He never escaped penury. While he was writing *Don Carlos* he could hardly afford paper and ink. That he did not become the preceptor of German thought, a role to which he knew himself destined, was not entirely the fault of the Germans. It was due in part to a profound sense of personal failure. He believed, after the disintegration of the French Revolution, that change could only be effected within the individual personality.

In May 1781, at the age of twenty-one, he published at his own expense but anonymously and under a false imprint, eight hundred copies of a 'drama'. The revolutionary preface and some of the text was toned down during the course of typesetting. The action was also transposed, at the wish of the Mannheim impressario, Dalberg, from contemporary life to the close of the Middle Ages. It was first performed on 13 January 1782:

> *Die Räuber* cost me my family and my country ... Now I have dissolved all personal ties. Henceforth the public means everything to me – it is my study, my sovereign, my friend. I belong to it alone. I shall submit myself to this and no other tribunal. It alone I fear and respect. There is something of greatness in the feeling that I have no fetter but that of the verdict of the world, need appeal to no throne other than the soul.

Thus ran Schiller's announcement of the periodical *Rheinische Thalia* in 1784. It was something of a revolutionary manifesto. Five years before the French Revolution he thereby proclaimed himself a 'citizen of the world who accepts everyone into his family and extends brotherly affection to the cause of all . . . ' Here in German was *liberté, égalité, fraternité*.

What were the 'soul' and the 'public' whom he had appointed as his only judges? The soul was the storm-tossed mind granted no peace from radical-pietistic and irrational promptings, as well as the haunt of a chiliastic political ecstacy which Schiller bore within him and which Walter Muschg has correctly interpreted as of great importance in *Die Räuber*. As for the public: 'Nothing is more coarse than German public taste at the moment and it is my earnest intention in life to work for a change in this calamitous state of affairs, not to mould myself on it.' But that was eleven years later. By then Schiller had recoiled both from the idea of the French Revolution and the 'coarseness' of the German public. He was certain that the German middle class would start no revolutions. Such a trend would be confined – the proof of it was furnished by the revolutionary unrest of 1789 in the south-west of the country – to elements secretly in touch with the proletariat, fostering popular revolutionary movements which had been pulsating since mediaeval days. The proletariat, together with German 'Jacobins' and the turbulent, unemployed, intellectuals would cause revolutionary unrest. He feared the alliance of that plebian agitation with religiously inspired political fervour and a brazen, undisciplined intelligentsia.

Schiller himself had the makings of all this in him, in the inheritance of his Swabian ancestors, both actual and spiritual, whose search for the 'Kingdom of God' was by no means confined to heavenly spheres. He quailed before the progress of the Revolution and its Terror because he was himself familiar with that temptation to resort to terrorism which comes so easily to both proletarian movements and individual anarchists. Many of his followers in Russia, Poland and the Balkans have sensed instinctively this potential in him.

Schiller's partiality for the rebel, the political assassin and even the criminal has, in fact, frequently been noted. High politics, violent action and criminality were to him a fascinating kaleidoscope. 'And perhaps the great miscreant's way to the great and righteous Judge is shorter than the lesser's . . . '

In 1793 he confessed: 'I am so far from believing in the start of a regeneration in political life that current events rob me of all hopes thereof for centuries ahead.' This was the tragedian Schiller's most tragic error, derived from the depths of his pessimistic nature. Again and again German 'idealists', their hopes of change in the state of things disappointed, would give up too easily and retreat into this sort of scepticism.

Yet in 1793 Schiller also wrote: ' . . . for art is the daughter of freedom'. In art, in the realm of art as he understood it, Schiller sought and found freedom, 'the free ascent into the regions of the ideal'. And here begins the tragic misunderstanding of Schiller. Members of the middle class and the

38

academic world found a justification for retreat into their 'inner realm' of culture in Schiller's 'idealism', whereas he himself saw art as a preliminary education for man: as a preparation for political liberty. Frustrated (both by his nature and by the circumstances of his life) as a politician, a man and leader of the people, he undertook the gigantic labour or *introversive political activity*. For Schiller this meant the education and refinement of popular taste through his periodicals, his criticism and his support for and censure of certain individuals (among them the two Schlegels and Fichte). With his plays, his lyric and hymnic verse, his philosophical essays Schiller fought against an illiterate and increasingly illiberal age for a cosmopolitan future and a Germany that would lead mankind. In *German Greatness* (1801, an unfinished poem), he says: 'Our language will dominate the World', and, of the German future: 'Just as this nation stands at the centre of all European nations, so is it the pith of humanity, where others are the blossom and the leaf.'

The expression of such sentiments put Schiller at the heart of the 'German Movement' with its Messianic flavour. But in contrast to Fichte, who allowed himself to be carried away by the rising tide of Nationalist fervour, Schiller tried to see beyond the movement's limitations. In his capacity as political preacher in the realm of inner freedom, he remained equally aloof from and critical of any awakening of the common conscience, like the renewed interest in Christianity, which seemed to him irretrievably linked with the proletarian capacity for unrealistic enthusiasm, superstition and terrorism.

To the same degree he rejected the French Revolution in its Jacobin manifestation and its cult of antiquity. For him there could be no rebirth of ancient political virtue and greatness. They had been totally destroyed by Christianity. A product of German eighteenth-century enlightenment, he fought against the political Romanticism of the last quarter of that century and in his resistance to every form of metaphysics, knew that he was supported by Goethe: 'As you yourself say,' he wrote to Goethe on 9 July 1796, 'healthy and beautiful by virtue of its very essence, Nature has no need of morality, of natural law, of *political metaphysics*. You could well have added that it has no need of divinity or immortality for its support or durability. Those three points around which all speculation ultimately revolves, may provide a mature and perceptive temperament with material for poetic play, but they can never become the subject of serious concern and necessity.'

Schiller did not believe that Christianity had any positive contribution to make towards man's progress to inner (and later, presumably, outer) freedom. What this negation can have meant to him in the way of mental suffering and disappointment can only be surmised. As a child he was destined for the ministry, but as a youth, at his sovereign's request, he studied medicine instead of theology. Later, as a grown man, 'he was haunted by longing for an undefiled pulpit'. Thus Schiller, convinced that Christianity was not fit for the task of reshaping man, had to find some other medium. The answer he found was art. Art must take its stand against revolution, which it can subdue. In the Prologue to *Wallenstein*, Schiller accepted the challenge thrown down by the French Revolution:

> And now, at the century's solemn end,
> When even truth itself is turned to fiction . . .
> . . . may art upon its shadow stage
> Attempt yet higher flights; indeed, it must,
> Or else be put to shame by life's own stage.

HÜLSEN AND THE SOCIETY OF FREE MEN

'The dominion of the Church cannot last much longer,' wrote August Ludwig Hülsen to August Wilhelm Schlegel and Sophie Bernhardi on 8 July 1799, 'and when its downfall finally occurs a new Heaven will open above us and symbols will no longer obscure the view of its gods. *Life* is with them, and they alone are life; but men seek death and each one strangles the next, from Aristotle to Fichte.'

Men seek death by fencing themselves off inside a metaphysical system, a closed society or church. The Society of Free Men set out to destroy this self-occlusion, first at university (Fichte's students at Jena, 1794-99) and later by leading active lives.

Hülsen was born at Premnitz near Potsdam in 1765. Destined for the Church, he became tutor to a young man called Fouqué who was later to become one of those Romantic poets who had nothing in common with the great contemporary movement except the epithet 'Romantic'. It may be that Hülsen, so upright and sincere, recognised this trait in his friend and pupil. But, his own enthusiasm roused by the French Revolution, he was deeply hurt when Fouqué, instead of accompanying him to university, took a military commission. He left Prussia and adopted a false name. Throughout the nineteenth and early twentieth centuries many students, revolutionaries and members of underground organisations, were to do the same thing, adopting pseudonyms which they deemed appropriate to their role of pioneers in a new society.

Hülsen was thirty when he enrolled at Jena under Fichte, and his personality made a profound impression on fellow students, such as Schelling and Hölderlin. Fichte, who was as much a personal friend as his teacher, wanted to secure a professorship for him. But Hülsen was never considered successful by his contemporaries, either as a citizen or a literary man. Like his friends in the Society of Free Men, he remained, until his death, opposed to all forms of nationalism, condemning the 'abstract Germanomania' of the times. These men made great efforts to achieve a deepening and civilising of student life, and together with Fichte fought for the abolition of duelling, war and capital punishment. Their lives and outlook reflect in many ways the difficulties, successes and failures encountered by that young German generation.

Erich von Berger, a German from Denmark, exercised the greatest influence in the group. In essays written in 1794–5 he dealt with 'France's political rebirth and the great gospel of reason emanating from Germany'. Like many of the Romantics, he visualised a new age of man in which fear would play no part. 'No work-houses and charity institutions and man-traps and standing armies!' 'Prison keeps shall fall!' 'Immense turns of fate are pending. He indeed will be able to regard himself as fortunate of whom it shall not be said at the end of the race that he fled his destiny.'

The life and work of another member of the group Johann Schmidt, illustrates the sound basis of outlook of the Society of Free Men. Originally a theologian, during his student days Schmidt was a passionate participant in the Society's debates on the State and established religion, war and capital punishment. In 1810 he was elected to the Senate of Bremen. As its representative at the Congress of Vienna he was instrumental in obtaining autonomy for the Hanseatic towns. At a later date Treitschke affirmed that his intellect had been among the finest of those who attended the Frankfurt Parliament. As the liberal-republican mayor of his city, he was the founder of Bremerhaven and the driving force behind Bremen's rise to prominence during the nineteenth century.

Berger, Schmidt and Hülsen had all felt the 'electrifying impression' made by Fichte (risen from the lowest strata of society) and believed in his annunciation of a 'new man'. Hülsen described the feeling which bound them together as the belief in the equality of all men. Fichte maintained that a new epoch had arrived, that of the individual. With the turn of the century he foresaw that certain men and influences presented a threat to this progress. He wrote to Wilhelm Schlegel that, having studied Christianity at great depth, he felt more and more clearly how incompatible it was with the freedom of man. He greatly feared a strong reactionary trend and criticised the incipient fashion, led by the Schlegel brothers, for admiratory mediaeval chivalry. The knights in his opinion, had been tyrants. He adds: 'I would far rather that the great mass which we call the people should knock us all, academics and knights, over the head, for *our* enjoyment of position and privilege is only possible by virtue of *their* misery. Work-houses, penitentiaries, arsenals and orphanages are huddled around the temples where we want to venerate the Godhead.' 'If you still wish to see any greatness in knights and gentlemen, you must first forget man.'

FICHTE

There is practically no philosophical, political or religious label of any importance which has not at some time, been applied to Johann Gottlieb Fichte (1762–1814), and it is certainly a fact that much that has happened in the nineteenth and in a good part of the twentieth centuries can be traced back to his thoughts, aims and plans. Whenever a major intellectual or social crisis has occurred in the last one hundred and sixty years the spell which this 'unarmed prophet' exercised on German and European youth has become apparent. For he was the first great plebeian to gain a hearing in the German intellectual world at the dawn of this new era, taking hold of words and using them as no one had done since Luther, Münzer and Lessing.

At twenty-six, on the 24 July 1788, one year before the French Revolution, Fichte wrote his *Random Thoughts during a Sleepless Night*. For him the root of the corruption he saw about him, the 'night' which shrouded contemporary Germany was first and foremost the disparity between the sexes; the 'disdain and corruption of the female sex'. Women were corrupted through the fault of men. 'The main reason for our moral depravity – contempt for married life.' Fichte maintained that it was impossible to wed in such a state of affairs. The status of marriage reflected the utter confusion surrounding all social, political and ecclesiastical matters. Diagnosing a general condition of moral decay, he tried, in his capacity as educational reformer and preceptor, to regenerate politics through improvement of individual moral standards.

In his youthful political writings he saw the French Revolution as the 'consequence of long-standing intellectual bondage'. He launched a pungent attack on the conservative publicist, August Wilhelm Rehberg, who in 1793 had great success in Germany with his *Inquiries into the French Revolution* based on Burke: 'no pedlar in the service of a state openly hostile to the French Revolution should be heard in such an inquiry'.

But even as a young man Fichte was more interested in education than politics. His motto was: 'Yield everything, but never freedom of thought.' He charged governments with paralysing that freedom through religious edicts (like Woellner's and the Prussian censorship ordinances of 1788), transforming man 'into the machine that you want and thereby moulding him to whatever purpose you please'.

As a young plebeian he shared to the full the anti-Semitism of his class. Temporarily suppressed by authority and hushed up in Berlin drawing-rooms, anti-semitism increased rapidly at the outset of the nineteenth century, spreading via the lower-middle classes to the mass of university students. In Fichte's eyes the Jews had the power to exploit unpunished the ordinary citizen. 'I see no way of conferring civic rights on them other than by chopping off all their heads in a single night and screwing fresh ones on them, void of even a single Hebraic notion. I see no other way of safeguarding ourselves against them other than by conquering their promised land for them and shipping the lot off there.' Did these views serve as models for the *Kristallnacht* pogrom of 1938, Himmler's ideas of transporting Jews to Palestine, and worse things still? On the other hand, he wrote to his wife about Dorothea Veit, daughter of Moses Mendelssohn and the mistress, and later wife, of Friedrich Schlegel: 'Praise of a Jewess may sound odd coming from me but she has sapped my belief that no good can come out of this nation.' And as first rector of Berlin University he was to take a strong stand against anti-Semitic student excesses.

Such was Fichte, a man of passionate emotions who had a basic feeling of goodwill towards every class and nation, but whose own exuberance of style betrayed him into demagogic phraseology, later to be used by a class of intellectually, morally and politically uncontrolled youths: a plebeian whose tongue and pen ran away with him.

By 1793 he had become known as a 'democrat', an epithet as significant and dangerous then as the terms 'liberal', 'socialist' and 'communist' have since become. It is proof of the liberalism of Weimar at that time that in 1794 such a highly controversial figure as Fichte was nominated a colleague of Schiller at Jena.

At this period Fichte was beginning to believe firmly in mankind's right to equality. His *Natural Law* of 1796 attempts to establish scientifically the equality of all men before the law. The true property qualification was, according to him, work, and he felt that the state was responsible for seeing that each man was able to live on the increment of his labour. He favoured a form of unemployment benefit. He also argued that the final source, basis, and reality of all political sanction lay with the people, and consequently that they could never be said to be 'in rebellion', since they were themselves the highest tribunal and, as such, responsible to God alone. 'To render it possible to maintain that a people has rebelled against its sovereign neces- sitates the assumption that this sovereign is a god, a point likely to be difficult to prove.' This was, however, precisely what, in the aftermath of the Revolution sovereigns did try to prove – that they had been set up *over* their peoples by divine right.

Sixteen years later Fichte, in his *Jurisprudence*, gave up his earlier dream of a system of ephors to act as agents of 'pure reason' between the people and its executive. During the intervening decade and a half of spiritual and political upheaval when the audiences at his lectures numbered as many as five hundred at a time and his listeners held him to be the spokesman of hope for Germany, he had realised that the majority of students would resist any reform of their way of life and thought.

On 12 October 1789 he wrote to Hölderlin's friend, Franz Wilhelm Jung, privy councillor at Mayence and head of the educational commission set up in the territories on the left bank of the Rhine that had been ceded to France: 'I should like to remain active as long as possible through the written and spoken word: that is the object of my life.' He suggested the foundation of an institute of learning on trans-Rhenian soil which should be devoted to the benefit of 'all mankind' and the 'union of the French and German intellect', an idea which found great sympathy among German 'Jacobins' and left- wing thinkers. It was the right-wing Germans and French who advocated war instead of alliance and friendship.

Fichte viewed the dawn of the nineteenth century with feelings of appre- hension. It was a time when intellectuals had to sell themselves to the highest courtly bidder in order to live, and Fichte himself had no illusions about this state of affairs. He said he would have gone to Russia if he had been offered membership of the St Petersburg Academy of Sciences. Indeed, it is tempting to see Fichte in the company of de Maistre, Mme Krudener and the French and German *émigrés*, as educator and reformer of Russia, successor there to Leibniz, secular heir to the two centuries' old pietistic German efforts on behalf of Russian culture, schooling and religious devotion. He remained, however, in Germany, bound to the 'deluded Germans', in particular by the effect the 'Atheism Dispute' had on him as well as on German public opinion.

The 'Atheism Dispute' started in 1798, when political and religious reactionary circles as an integral part of their 'international plot' theories, were fond of denouncing as Jacobins any intellectually independent personalities. Fichte accepted a contribution to his *Philosophical Journal* by Forberg, with the title 'Evolution of the Concept of Religion'. It was a time when European intellectuals were suffering harsh criticism from the Vatican for any support they gave to evolutionary theory. But Forberg was not a cautious man, and Fichte, who annotated the dangerous article, while dissociating himself from its author, still paid tribute to his merits. Both Forberg and Fichte abhorred dogma, and Fichte was convinced that 'in the Forberg essay a genuinely Kantian, sceptical atheism shines through'.

Forberg himself was a convinced atheist: 'I have never had need of faith in my life and I expect to persist in my resolute disbelief to the end, which for me is total.' As for Fichte: 'What they call God is simply an idol', whose favour has to be sought by means of ceremony and incantation. He maintained that the 'real atheists' were the worshippers of this idol, and that worship of the idol was the destruction of all morality, as it left man dependent on the caprice of his *own* goodwill.

In his attack on the image of deity as presented by Protestant orthodoxy, Fichte was also attacking the absolutism of German princes and churchmen. His criticism had its roots in that of the Protestant non-conformists of the sixteenth to eighteenth centuries, and paved the way for reaction against all forms of orthodoxy in the nineteenth. As a result of this publication, he was dismissed by the Weimar authorities, for he refused to recant.

The personal consequences of this episode were of even greater significance than the material ones. He was profoundly upset by Jacobi's *Autograph Letter to Fichte*, 1799, accusing him of atheism and nihilism. Such criticism had far more effect on his way of thought than the attacks of political and religious obscurantists, for Jacobi demonstrated that for Fichte the principal rule was: 'I shall have no other gods than myself and my own individuality', a charge which led Fichte to revise completely his own scheme of ideas. The re-examination of his religious concepts and, in turn, of his political and 'national' way of thought was, however, important both to himself and to succeeding generations of Germans. It is possible to observe, sentence by sentence, *the birth of reaction* from out of his acute inner perplexity. There is still much to be learnt from this formative process. Assailed as an atheist, he developed, with the same pietistic sincerity which had inspired his previous way of thought, a form of mysticism which combined the qualities of the fourteenth-century Meister Eckhart and Johannine evangelism.

'All our life is His life. We are in His hand and remain there; no one can tear us away. We are eternal because He is.' In the *Instruction in a Blessed Life*, 1806, the last in the series of great lectures preceding the *Addresses to the German Nation*, the theme was complete submission to God. 'Man cannot create his own god. But he can quell his self as the real negation and shall thereupon be absorbed into God.'

In April 1813 Fichte made an official approach to become a lay military chaplain at the Prussian headquarters, 'where the volunteer guards are recruited mainly from students', his aim being to 'fill military leaders with a sense of God', as he noted in his *Self-Critical Journal Entries*. He saw himself in a role previously played by the quasi-political military pastors of the Reformation and Counter-Reformation, and later by the National Socialist *Führungsoffiziere* and army chaplains. Death forestalled his plan.

His secular 'sermons' were a straightforward continuation of his religious ones. He wrote his *Addresses to the German Nation* as a form of religious instruction, as an appeal to the Germans to allow themselves to be educated in the widest sense. He saw the language of the 'primal German people' as the most sacred religious and political unifactory principle, and from this later readers could, if they wanted, deduce a gospel of rabid nationalism.

Fichte writes: 'A total change in the methods so far practised is ... the only means of maintaining the existence of the German nation', and in order to achieve this aim he stipulated that there should be a 'national education' which, penetrating to the very heart of the individual, would effect the necessary changes. Children should be separated from their parents and reared in state institutions, functioning like small, self-supporting communities and situated in rural areas. All would depend on the stimulation of 'spontaneity', pleasure taken in activity as such. Fichte quoted Pestalozzi as his authority. Liberal school reformers, founders of private and boarding schools, and others of similar calibre, were able in the nineteenth and twentieth centuries to quote Fichte as their authority. So have communists and national socialists.

According to Fichte the institutions should be operated by an overall plan and complete authority be delegated to the teachers. Pupils were to be as wax in their hands: 'You must so mould him ... that he shall be quite incapable of wanting anything but that which you wish him to want.' And consistent with this same conception of education, Fichte demanded the creation of a state which would take in hand, firmly and rigidly, the training of its citizens from the cradle to the grave. What Rousseau had suggested to the Poles as their sole means of national rehabilitation, he now proposed to his compatriots. The outlines of the *Closed Commercial State*, his national socialist and national communist Utopia of 1800, were already discernible in his *Natural Law*.

'The most important maxim of any well-organised police force is essentially the following: it must be possible to identify any citizen at any time, wherever he is ... ' 'Everyone should carry a pass issued by his nearest authority.'

'Members of the community should not be able to hold a meeting in a house without the police being informed ... and the police must require an account of the purpose of the meeting and supervise that the stated purpose is actually fulfilled, domestic rights on such occasion falling into abeyance. ...' 'No one may leave a locality without specifying where he proposed to go...'; ' ... the source of all evil is simply and solely disorder. In a state established along these lines, the police will know at nearly every hour of the day where any member of the community is and what he is up to. ...'

The comment has been made recently, with some justification, that Fichte's concept of the 'ordination' of youth is reminiscent of 'the pernicious initiation rites of the Far East'.

The *Closed Commercial State* provides a model of a socialist-communist state, with special stress laid on the creation of a good work ethic, based on the conviction that religion is the best stimulus to action. He felt that all 'communication with foreigners should be forbidden ... ' and 'above all the state must refuse to have anything to do with foreign trade'. In this self-sufficient state citizens should gradually be weaned from such desires as did not really contribute to their welfare.

One man, two years Fichte's junior, protested against this closed society. He was a native of Breslau whom Kant had enlisted to read the proofs of his *Critique of Judgment* and who had himself in 1800 composed a tract *On Perpetual Peace* which was Kantian in principle while gently correcting the master on a few points. This objector was Friedrich Gentz, the future assistant to Metternich and leading publicist of the reactionary forces.

Fichte himself considered his 'self-sufficient commercial state' but one stage in man's lengthy future evolution. According to him the progress of mankind would take 'myriads' of years, and he divided the time into five stages, of which three had already run their course. The fourth was approaching, and the fifth would be a *state of complete vindication and sanctification*, guided by a man who should represent the highest genius of the nation a man whose role would be much the same as that of the prophets, and only through a man of learning could mankind fulfil its destiny.

The dissertation *Patriotism and its Reverse* argues that learning is the truly great achievement of man, and Fichte points out that German patriotism was not love of Germany, but love of the ideas which were being put into effect in Germany. Certainly Europe in the nineteenth century and America in the twentieth, did look on German knowledge, German scholars and scientists rather as oracles, the true heirs of the French Revolution, a faith which was only slightly shaken by subsequent events.

For Fichte, as he proclaimed in his capacity as first Rector of the newly-founded Berlin University, the German man of learning was at once both the seer of the nation and the overseer of its education, with the university as his instrument. This university was to be, Fichte hoped, the mother-church of all universities in Germany in the nineteenth and twentieth centuries. Certainly the small community founded in November 1810 with twenty-five professors and two hundred and fifty-six students was to grow into something rich and powerful. Great figures in German intellectual life and learning stood godfather to it and determined its future, world-wide recognition: Wilhelm von Humboldt, Schleiermacher, Hegel, Savigny, Ranke, Mommsen, Koch, Harnack, Max Planck . . .

Revolutionaries of the Left and Right, and reactionaries masquerading as protagonists of revolution on the Left and Right, can cite Fichte in their cause. So can all idealistic, religious and humanist reformers who are concerned with the 'fusion of the eternal with the temporal' (a principal theme of the *Addresses to the German Nation*).

'Remember, so that you may become noble and strong at the thought, that of yourself you are nothing, but *through God everything; yet act as though there were no God to help you and you must do everything by yourself* as indeed He does not want to help you other than the way in which He has already helped you, by giving you unto yourself.'

This may serve as a maxim for theistic and atheistic humanists, as well as for men of learning who, as scholars and scientists, are atheists and, as members of their church, are theists.

REVOLUTIONARY ROMANTICISM, A PROGRAMME FOR 'WORLD REVOLUTION'

One of the most fundamental themes of the lives and works of men such as the Schlegel brothers, Novalis, Hölderlin, young men on the brink of a new century has been expressed by the words of Friedrich Schlegel: 'Religion for us . . . is no subject for idle discussion, but for the most serious pre-occupation: it is time to lay the foundations of a new one. That is the objective, the focal point of all our efforts.'

Certainly in the nineteenth century there were endless attempts by artists, philosophers, scientists, sociologists, to frame new religious concepts. The scope was infinite. The revivalist movements of theism, pantheism and Christianity paraded as new religions, and with them the developing atheistic creeds.

Golo Mann has said: 'European politics in the nineteenth century lived on the French Revolution.' This aphormism was equally true for the century's intellectual history and for the 'German movement' of around 1800. Novalis too, made a similar connection in his essay, *Christianity or Europe* (1799): 'It is historically noteworthy how that grand iron mask with the name, Robespierre, tried to find in religion the hub and driving force of the Republic.'

Turning to Europe as a whole, he continues:

For countries other than Germany it is only possible to say that with the coming of a peace a fresh and better religious life will swallow up other temporal interests. Of Germany, on the other hand, it may be confidently said that signs of a new world are manifest and that it makes slow but sure strides in advance of the rest of the continent. Whereas the latter is absorbed in war, speculation and party politics, the Germans are applying themselves with immense diligence to becoming partners in a new and better epoch of civilisation, which in time will give them a substantial ascendancy over the others. There is a tremendous ferment in the sciences and arts. A boundless intellectual impetus is under way.

Novalis believed in the brotherhood, the unity, of all parties: 'The brother you have in common is the heartbreak of the new age.' A fraternal revolution to inspire Europe's awakening . . . the ideas of young men around 1800 were but an early intimation of the ideals of the 'young Europe' movement of the years between 1832 and 1848. Novalis's Christianity took the form of a third Christian power, a successor to Roman Catholicism and Protestantism, which would act as mediator between the old and the new worlds and lead mankind towards freedom. This great dream of a Johannine Christianity was propagated again, with individual adaptations, in 1830, 1848, 1945, by Lamennais, his friends and his intellectual heirs. Similar waves of hope swept the world at John XXIII's announcement of the Second Ecumenical Council in 1960.

The Schlegel brothers did not share their friends' hopes, for their eyes were trained on a vision of world revolution which went well beyond the bounds of any fresh version of Christianity. Their hopes, revealed in the pages of the *Athenaeum*, embraced the entire condition of man and his total conception of himself, nature, society and history in relation to the arts, science, and all inventive processes.

The Schlegels' background was literary. Their father and two uncles had been dramatists, essay writers and translators of English works. Hanover, where the current ways of thought were coloured by Leibniz, and English ideas, was their first home.

The *Athenaeum* was founded in 1797, and the Schlegel brothers regarded it as a means of calling an awakening German community to come together in a brotherhood and to adopt a shared philosophy. Six issues, in three volumes, were published in 1789, 1799 and 1800. The first edition numbered 1,250 copies, a very high figure for an undertaking with such lofty pretensions. There have been furthermore, three reprints in the last periodical's sanguinary hopes and the revolutionary programme of its young editors.

Analysis of the *Athenaeum*'s content show three main trends: criticism, a cultural programme and a 'promulgation of the mysteries of art and science'. It sounds innocuous enough; let a few extracts speak for themselves.

Specification by way of stresses and dashes is an admirable piece of *abstraction*. To me four letters signify *Gott* and half a dozen dashes a million different things. How simple *the management of the universe* becomes, how attractive it renders the concentricity of the mental realm. Grammar provides it with its dynamic. Armies are set in motion by a single word of command, nations by another – freedom.

Novalis thought of these notes of his as 'pollen'. Rather they were sparks flying upward into the twentieth century – keen apprehension of 'abstraction', sensitivity to the importance of symbols, concise expression, 'formulae' in art, literature, technology and politics, and a reaching out into the cosmos which has since become a reality by means of computerised formulae.

We dream of travel through the empyrean. But is not the empyrean within us? the profundities of our spirit are unknown to us. . . . Eternity, with its two worlds, past and future, is within ourselves or nowhere. The outer world is the shadow world, casting its shadow into the realm of light. . . .

This is Plato, turned on his head. It was at this point that German Romanticism took its decisive, ill-fated turn: world revolution could subsequently take place only in the spirit. Only the inner realm of man would be illuminated by its flare.

'If you have a weakness for pursuing the absolute which you cannot resist, the sole escape open to you is constantly to contradict yourself and link opposing poles of argument.' This is dialectics applied to the inner life, a law governing the creative element of the personality which lives, displays and deploys itself in contradictions.

'We have a mission – to civilise the world.' Milton, Saint-Just, Robespierre had all sounded this revolutionary fanfare. Men of the nineteenth and twentieth centuries, their minds beginning to awaken, were to take it up in counterpoint.

Various titles for the Schlegels' periodical had been under consideration before *Athenaeum* was finally selected. *Freya*, recalling the efforts of Klopstock and his Teutonic bards to establish a truly German, national mythology was among the rejects.

The arch-enemy of these early Romantics was not the French or any other nation, but the philistine, the *petit bourgeois* with no pretensions to or understanding of sensitivity and culture. Novalis anticipated the censure of Marx, Kierkegaard and Nietzsche on the individual estranged from his true self, living a lie and animated by an alienated consciousness.

'Workaday life is everything to the philistine. . . . The peak of his poetic existence is attained on the occasion of a journey, wedding, baptism or church service. These satisfy and frequently exceed his boldest aspirations. *His so-called religion has no more effect on him than an opiate.*'

As the French before them, the Schlegels and their friends became aware that politics and literature, society and written word, are closely connected and have a considerable influence on each other. Literary criticism is political criticism as well as criticism of social and contemporary conditions in general. Thus it was at this period that the novel, regarded for hundreds of years as an inferior poetic *genre*, came into its own again as the form most suited to the aims of this rising generation. 'Novels are the point at which literature comes into most immediate contact with social life.' This explains Friedrich Schlegel's well-known passage in the *Athenaeum*:

> The most outstanding trends of our age are represented by the French Revolution. Fichte's teaching and Goethe's *Wilhelm Meister*. Anyone objecting to their juxtaposition because he regards no revolution as important unless it manifests itself loudly, lacks the ability to view history from a broad and detached perspective. Even in our own cultural studies, meagre as they are and usually looking like a collection of annotated alternative readings to some lost classical text, some small book here and there makes more mark than all the bustle of the crowd which at the time took so little notice of it.

Revolution and romantic poetry are closely interconnected. Indeed Schlegel, in his *Fragments*, interpreted this new form of verse as the essential element in the movement. It outstrips the French Revolution and advances the progress of mankind because, being both poetry and philosophy, it is the 'permanent revolution' (which Jefferson and Robespierre each in their own way, had envisaged so differently).

'Perhaps an altogether unprecedented epoch would dawn in the arts and the sciences if the coalescence of philosophy and poetry were so general and so intimated that it became quite common for a number of complementary personalities to compose such works jointly.'

A coalescence of poetry and philosophy – this seems like an invocation of Hölderlin's 'communism of spirits' which would bring about the true transformation of man and his surroundings via revolution, the strongest influence of the incipient age, and religion, the strongest of the past.

Schlegel maintained that the 'revolutionary wish to realise the kingdom of God is the driving force behind progressive development and the start of modern history. What is irrelevant to the Kingdom of God is purely incidental.' And it was precisely his recognition of the paramount significance of the 'kingdom of God' for man's 'progressive development' that provided Schlegel with the text for his criticisms of established religion.

> The claim that there shall be but one Intercessor is highly biased and presumptuous. Surely, for the perfect Christian . . . everything should be a means to mediation . . . The life of a truly canonical (i.e. exemplary individual must have symbolic character throughout. On that assumption would not every death be one of propitiation? To a greater or lesser degree, that is. And would not that admit of a number of extremely striking conclusions?'

With Novalis, and, to some extent, Hölderlin, there began a consecration of death, new form of death for the new type of man. Poets, political martyrs, empiricists, would sacrifice their lives to their calling. They went into nothingness, fully accepting that it meant obliteration of their personal identity, but confident that through their death they would aid the continuation of their aims and beliefs. Such deaths were to become frequent. The circumstances might vary, but within a broad context there would be a similarity of purpose much like that anticipated by Schlegel in the preceding passage.

The ideas of the Schlegel brothers and their friends as expounded in *Athenaeum* had a Fichtean flavour. To this category belonged the thesis that man's ego contains God and actively creates a new world. The periodical was the appropriate forum for Hülsen's essay *On Natural Equality Between Men*.

> What is quite certain is that only by looking into the future do we come back to the past and both of them, past and future, originate and have their entire purpose solely in the present.

> Our belief in the future ought therefore to acquire reality and assurance through our current performance. The concept of future equality between men is therefore either practically geared to our active working life or of no consequence whatever and lacking justification even in that vacuum.

> Time is relatively no more than a facet of the moment in which we do something. If we do nothing, we are nothing, and time, as far as we are concerned, does not exist.

> *Mankind is our God*. Through him we are and we continue. Not one of us can die without the pleasure of life being destroyed in us all. So whoever you may be, poor sorrowing soul, none shall attain a higher Heaven without you . . . the eternity we evoke *rests within ourselves*. Hence everything really amounts to a single world comprised of untrammeled, continual action on our part.

The humanism of a Camus or Sartre in 1944 conformed to this spiritual outlook of Hülsen in 1797.

Three years later Friedrich Schlegel began to develop his *Ideas* basing it on a new ideology appropriate to the new epoch mankind was entering. 'It is time to tear aside the veil of Isis and to reveal her secret. Let him who cannot bear the sight of the Goddess flee or perish.'

'Eternal life and the invisible world is to be sought only in God . . . Release religion and a new mankind will arise.' An enigmatic, ambiguous aphorism. From what, from whom, from which powers is religion to be released? From Church, dogma, state, Bible or traditional Christianity? It is, however, certain that Schlegel and a handful of his contemporaries conceived their own, the 'Romantic', revolution as in no mean degree a religious one.

The *Athenaeum* issue for 1800 reveals two things: on the one hand the efforts made by the whole German Movement to supersede the French Revolution and its effects and to go one step further into the future; on the other, the change in Romanticism that would lead to 'reaction', the seeds of an alliance with its political counterpart, the traditional establishment of princes. It is of greatest significance that the Schlegel brothers' programmatic and revolutionary periodical combined both ingredients – 'permanent revolution' intellectually, and sweeping reaction.

'Try to recognise the constituent elements in culture and mankind; then worship them, especially fire.'

The 'fire-worshippers' who followed Heraclitus and the adherents of this German Movement were Feuerbach, Marx, Heine, Nietzsche and Lasalle. They stand in contrast to the 'stone-worshippers' who relied on the lithic qualities of the Church and God (Luther's 'rock of ages') to ban death and overcome revolution.

'Morality without a sense of paradox is vulgar.'

The great novels and dramas of the nineteenth and twentieth centuries are stamped with awareness of this axiom: Dostoevsky, and Stendhal, Balzac and Flaubert before him; Strindberg, Ibsen, Shaw; Proust, Joyce, Musil.

Reading Schlegel's propositions now, they seem like rockets reconnoitering the night sky of the nineteenth century to seek out its potential.

'The few revolutionaries thrown up by the revolution were mystics as only contemporary Frenchman can be. They shaped their characters and their actions by an act of religion. In ages to come it will appear as the Revolution's highest purpose and distinction to have been the most vehement goad to the then static religion.'

There are two points here. First, the mystic trait in Saint-Just and Robespierre. Secondly, the significance of the Revolution in releasing a new religious consciousness in mankind which was seen for the first time as a unity.

The last number of *Athenaeum* included a poem by Schlegel: *To the Germans*. He adjures them to recall their former greatness:

> ... Europe's spirit expired; in Germany rises
> The spring of the new age; everywhere breaks forth
> A host of heroes, fans the lively spark
> Of Latin nature, and Rome awakens,
> And Hellas, whose gods had vanished away ...
> Like true knights, to fight the spirit's Holy War.

Germany Awake! an invocation to the German peoples to inspire Europe. From this Germano-European patriotism was to arise, with a mere shift of mood and key, a shriller, narrower nationalism.

The last of Schlegel's *Ideas* was devoted to Novalis. 'His thoughts are nuclei', wrote Schlegel. Destructive of other concepts, they are also fissiparous. Coldly calculating technical intellects and articalists and others of similar sympathies, were all able to cite him in their favour.

NOVALIS

Novalis (1722–1801), born Georg Friedrich Philipp von Hardenberg, son of

Heinrich von Hardenberg, known to us as a patron of Fichte, was the first to use the term, 'Romanticism', by analogy with 'Classicism'. Yet he himself was not a Romantic. He studied law, administration and then the physical sciences. At Freiberg he obtained a grounding in chemistry, physics, geology, metallurgy and, in particular, medicine, which interested him the more not only because he had an immediate object for study in the symptoms of his own fatal illness, but because he saw his brother and Sophie von Kuhn die of tuberculosis before him. This child, twelve when he met her, who died in 1797, was the outstanding event of his life, and the label, 'romantic', has often been attached to his feeling for her.

Although Novalis was not a Romantic as such, he was at pains to put to the test what the Romantics preached. He felt it important to synthesise all the sciences, past and present, in order that man should have the means at hand to perform a major task – the transformation of himself and his circumstances. He believed in an encyclopedism which, going beyond that of the French, would combine all knowledge available to man. His 'scientific bible', as he called it, was to bring together all the schismatic sciences. 'The syncretic policy of intellectuals', he wrote to Friedrich Schlegel on 7 November 1798, 'should pave the way for the genuine practice and true process of reunion.' Discussions which take place between scientists and artists of all types today are but reflections of his initial hopes.

But who would be capable of conceiving and bringing into effect the all-embracing synthesis envisaged by Novalis? Only a man who felt in his ego the strength of God and was able to realise this potential. Novalis himself once proposed a mathematical formula for the conception of God: 'God is sometimes 1.00, sometimes 1/00, sometimes 0.' His precedent for this lies in the twelfth-century Platonists of Chartres, and many others, who tried to formulate the conception of God in speculative, mathematical or geometric formulae.

Novalis has often been reproached with leading a double life – as a diligent, conscientious official on the one hand, and poet and dreamer on the other. Such an accusation is unfair. His was no split personality. But he was certainly a much weakened man, and this, like his death, was due not to his 'Godhead formulations' but to tuberculosis. It was the physical exhaustion of a mortally sick man that led him to give up his 'haphazard cerebrations', as he once described his intellectual excursions.

To realise his boldest ideas would have required the cooperation of palaeontology, biology, chemistry, mathematics, depth-psychology and, not least, all the facilities provided today by cybernetics. All this would, he thought, have made it possible for him to calculate retrospectively the processes of the universe's history and to conceive and work out the future of mankind in a cosmos made more comprehensible by this knowledge.

He wrote once: 'Where are we going? Always home.' There was in Novalis something of that archaic and basic faith which may be found in the very old and very young. He really did believe that he was going home – into the

53

all-powerful lap of creation. His brother Karl was playing to him on the clavichord when, in March 1801, he passed quietly away in his sleep.

HOMELESS GERMAN YOUTH

German Romanticism was, in its origins, the artificial product of the youth of a totally disorientated age, homeless and without root, living in a capital and country as artificial as the Romanticism it produced.

The sons of parsons, small officials, estate owners and artisans from remote rural areas, these youngsters, fugitives from their physical and spiritual fathers alike, came together in Berlin during the year 1790–1800. Dissatisfied with life as it stood, hungry for experience, haunted by fears and hopes for the future, they wanted to attain success, standing and money as quickly as they could. They mocked their family faith cynically and sceptically, dreaming dreams which rose far beyond the world of their pietistic and patriotic parents into the realms of fantasy.

Alert and hypersensitive, these young men, blasé, angry and enthusiastic, lived in a time when the society of the Prussian capital, senior civil servants and pontiffs of the literary enlightenment, was devoting itself wholeheartedly to a riotous life of amusement, gaming and every sort of occult activity, and the lower classes were involved with every variety of sectarianism.

Prussia, the home of many of the intense artistic products of German Romanticism had itself become a work of art. Its direct origins in a highly disciplined religious order of chivalry, the state had become a political structure which inspired admiration, dread and emulation. Yet at this stage, following the death of Frederick the Great, Prussia had entered a period of disorientation which was to persist right up to its defeat at Jena.

Frederick William I, that most unromantic of Prussian rulers, had been possessed of the desire to 'make new people', to 'make Christians'. It is precisely this 'making', this art of contrivance, political in his case, that characterised Prussian Romanticism. It sprang from a belief that man can and should fashion himself anew through the power of his imagination, a process visualised as one of mechanical skill. Jean Paul and E. T. A. Hoffmann presented pictures of man working as a craftsman on the mechanism of his own self in order to effect a magical, artistic transformation. Such employment of technical skill had, however, been anticipated by Frederick the Great, son of Frederick William I.

The synthetic state of Prussia created by a sovereign equally synthetic, was described by Ernst Moritz Arndt, just before its collapse in the following terms: 'Sagacity, justice, vivacious versatility on all sides. Yet all clockwork. Because pace seemed paramount, the soldier, perfect example of puppetry, enjoyed the highest position and esteem.'

Frederick the Great planned his state as a creation, an exercise in intellect and rationality. The depth of his failure corresponded to the height of his aims. He has been praised for his religious tolerance. This most probably sprang from an unconscious recognition of the fact that his state and its official church were totally incapable of fulfilling the deep and basic spiritual needs of its people. Where religion should have been there was a terrible abyss, equally obvious to Kant and to the sectarian movements which sought to turn it to their advantage.

In this troubled time, Germany's restless youth came together in their capital, Berlin, in Jewish drawing rooms, where they met men of the officer classes, French *émigrés*, guests from other German states, Englishmen, Russians and Poles. Their wealthy, witty hostesses slandered in pamphlets hawked outside their own doors, had risen overnight from the ghettos. But they made one tragic error: they believed that that present scintillation – the delight derived from unconstrained, intelligent, broad-minded, humane company – would last. In these *salons* Romanticism of the Berlin variety found its home. This was the scene set for the entry of Ludwig Tieck.

TIECK

Ludwig Tieck (1773–1853) was the son of a Berlin master ropemaker. Troubled as a child by nightmares which would have shattered the mental equilibrium of most men, Tieck, being exceptionally gifted, put these experiences to good use, and became the perfect man of letters. There was little in this field to which he could not turn his hand. He started with Rambach, a 'factory' which produced trashy horror novels to satisfy an insatiable European demand. Tieck worked on the production line, inventing episodes, verse inserts, telling climaxes. He set up on his own, writing such different works as *The Life and Death of Saint Genevieve*, *Prince Zerbino* and *Puss in Boots*, a mixture of fairy-tale and satire on the Berlin of the time, with its pedants, philistines and monarch of 'chameleon-like character'.

Could one say the same of Tieck himself? It is doubtful whether even the notion of 'character' could be applied to him if one wishes to imply by it an ineradicable stamp of personality. Tieck was interested in flux, perpetual modification, transmutation. 'Only in change are we aware of time.' He felt that any man could become anything: a criminal, saint, bird, man, woman, witch, or, at the very least, a good or bad actor. Man is a puppet of infinite scope whose wires, in Tieck's opinion, can and should be pulled by writers. There is no emotion which the puppet cannot be called upon to depict. Tieck stands half-way between the propaganda of terror and ecstasy so successfully communicated by the heavenly visions and hell-fire preachings of High Baroque and the bitter-sweet horror and Kitsch of modern propaganda as practised both by totalitarian states and the entertainment and consumer industries. He was a magician who knew how to strike every note in the emotional scale. He applied his skills to freeing his sentimental, brutally hard-headed, prying contemporaries from their new vices: boredom, frustration, lack of love, and the bitter knowledge of their own inner emptiness.

Tieck was an 'engineer of the soul', not altogether in the manner that

Stalin wanted authors to be, but with the requisite technical and artistic expertise. Art is the opium of the people, although Marx said that it was religion. Everyone, but particularly those members of the lower classes whose life is mere drudgery, need art for their entertainment, to fill their daydreams. In the nineteenth century art became the successful rival of religion as an opium for the people and, as producer of Kitsch, emotional rubbish and sentimentality, its associate. There was a fundamental link between Kitsch, the 'sensitive' long short story and the deluge of 'devotional' trinkets and cheap religious literature that flooded the popular market in the nineteenth century.

Tieck, the perfect professional, the juggler of words, experimented arbitrarily with his public and material. He was curious to see what would happen if time – which, Tieck believed, we are only made aware of through change – should lose its logical sequence, going backwards as well as forwards, if the hero should turn out to be a murderer, the wife a sister. His writing was a constant experiment, carried out on himself and on mankind. Ever since 'Romantic' literature in all its various manifestations in the nineteenth and twentieth centuries, has remained an experiment on and with humanity, research into the depths of man, a test of possible human behaviour patterns. The test was also a temptation, and led into those depths where for centuries accumulated layers of material had been stored by old and experienced sorcerers, alchemists, occultists, theosophists, and Rosicrucians.

Tieck 'discovered' Jacob Bohme. Together with the young, eager, inquisitive, impious intelligentsia of Berlin in his day, he released the sluices of dams that were long since worn out and from its very outset, the nineteenth century was flooded with the flotsam and jetsam of archaic and primal cultures. Their magical relics were ardently salvaged and dragged into the daylight by puny Fausts, starved of soul and craving substance. It was the 'modern' literary man who fused the first *entente cordiale* between an ultra-alert, all-challenging intelligentsia and pristine occultism and magic.

But what becomes of magic and its practice when it runs wild? What happens to the sorcerer's apprentice when he cannot exorcise the spirits he has invoked? What becomes of the charms he has used? Goethe's poem on the subject was as prophetic of the frightful possibilities inherent in black (or political) magic as was the Prologue in *Faust*, while *Faust* itself was a prelude to the tragedies of the nineteenth and twentieth centuries.

Tieck, as the 'sorcerer's apprentice', uncovered in his writings, and revealed to a wide public, an awareness of things which Freud, Jung and more recent psychologists have laid bare with great caution and would in part prefer to cover up again. Evil powers effect man suddenly and incomprehensibly, as Luther discovered, and as Tieck and his followers realised. The same fear, the awareness of hostile forces gripped outstanding and influential authors. The uncanny riddles and satanic influences surrounding man filled their works and infected their public. Shortly after the First World War German film-makers, heirs to this type of Romanticism, tried once more in a peculiarly equivocal way to conjure up this irrational fear of an incomprehensible and alien world. Here was a parallel to the situation that existed in the years around 1800, the result of a crisis of confidence, of the inability to trust anything or anyone, either sovereigns or revolutionaries, love or nature, reason or feeling, man or God. Was not everything simply illusion – the product of the illusionist's art?

THUS SPAKE ZARATHUSTRA – WEIMAR, 1805

In 1914 at Weimar, whose kaleidoscope fate has played such an important role in nineteenth- and twentieth-century German history, a piece was published called *The Monologue of a Demented Creator*. It had been written by Friedrich Gottlob Wenzel in 1805.

It is a wondrous thing I hold here in my hand. As I watch it through the magnifying glass, the confusion on this globule increases from second to second – or century as they call it down there. . . . That speck of dust crawling around down there calls itself man. When I created it I thought it was perhaps worth it, just for curiosity's sake – a somewhat hasty judgement, I admit. But I happened to be in a good mood at the time, and anything new is welcome in this everlasting eternity where there is nothing to do to kill time.

Let us pause briefly to note that boredom was the inspiration which led that Romantic artist God, to create man.

He continues with the admission that he still finds pleasure in 'the colourful world of flowers',

but this minute speck to which I gave the breath of life and which I called man, does fret me now and again. The tiny spark of divinity which I gave it rather over-hastily, has sent it quite crazy. Of course, I ought to have realised that such a tiny portion could only cause harm. The poor creature doesn't know where to turn and its inner sense of God just leads it into ever greater muddles, without its ever getting to the bottom of things.

'This speck, with its divine deficiency, builds little houses whose ruins it regards two seconds later with amazement and imagines to have been the dwelling of gods.' Finally – and this is the worst – the speck has begun to think of itself as God and to construct systems of self-esteem. The devil, I should have kept my fingers from making it! – But what am I to do with it? – Let it hop about up here? That would be intolerable. It gets bored enough down there and tries to kill time even in the brief second of its existence. How incomparably more bored it would get in this eternity which even alarms me! Yet I should be sorry to destroy it utterly; it dreams so often of immortality, and simply because it dreams of it, believes it will attain it. What am I to do? Really, even I am at My wits end! Supposing I let the creature die, over and over again and each time obliterate its tiny spark of self-recollection, so that it is resurrected and wanders around once more? That will pall in the long run too ... The best thing is to postpone any decision until it occurs to me to appoint a Judgement day and I get a better idea.

Thus spake Zarathustra, in 1805. Man, a crazy speck, afflicted with boredom; a puppet imagining itself through its own system of thought to be God.

This *Monologue* is deeply revealing of the current state of affairs. Fichte and Schelling were busy constructing their arrogant 'systems' to comprehend God, reality, the world. Hegel was about to start on his version of the game. And at that very moment this fantasy revealed the futility of it all. What was to become of man, when even Nietzsche's consolation had, in 1805, been rejected as farce? What was to become of man when even God was a bored bungler?

The devout atheism of the nineteenth and twentieth centuries set out to destroy a Christian doctrine that could think of nothing better than a forthcoming Judgement Day, perpetual hell, and 'a tedious Heaven'.

JEAN PAUL

Over the vaulting lay the dial of eternity. It bore no figures and was its own hour and minute hand. But a black finger pointed towards it and the dead wanted to see the time it showed.

A tall and noble form, His lineaments creased with unending pain, sank on the altar from above, and all the dead cried, 'Christ, is there no God?'

He answered, 'There is none.'

The Shadow of each departed quivered and the trembling passed from one to another.

'I searched the planets, I ascended to the suns, I flew along the Milky Ways through the deserts of heaven', Christ went on, 'but there is no God. I descended as far as being throws a shade, I peered into the abyss, and I cried, Father, where art Thou? Only the sound of the unruled eternal tempest met my ears while, though there was no sun, drops from the gleaming rainbow of intrinsic essence fell into the chasm. And when I gazed towards the divine eye in the limitless world above, it stared at me from an empty, bottomless socket. – Shriek forth, dissonances, rend the shadows with your shrieks, for He is not!'

The ashen shadows scattered like frost's white gossamer melting in warm haze. Emptiness. Then there came into the temple a sight hurtful to the heart, children woken from their graves who threw themselves down before the tall form at the altar, crying, 'Jesus! Have we no Father?' He, with streaming tears, replied, 'We are orphans, you and I, we are without a Father.'

Thereupon the dissonances screeched yet louder, the tottering temple walls shivered apart, the temple and the children were plunged forward, the sun and the whole earth followed them, the entire structure of the world and its infinity sagged past us, and above, at the peak of limitless nature, stood Christ gazing down at the world structure pierced by a thousand suns, which now resembled the pit burrowed into eternal night where the stars of day shine like miners' lamps and the Milky Ways like veins of silver.

And Christ, when He saw the grinding throng of the world, the torch-dance of the heavenly will-o'-the-wisps, the coral banks of breaking hearts, and how one world globe after another split its smouldering souls across the sea of death, raised His eyes to the nothingness and the empty infinity, saying, 'Inflexible, mute nothingness! Bleak, eternal inevitability! Blind chance! Are these things known among you? Why are the structure and I struck down? Chance, do you discern it when you stride with hurricanes through the starry snow-drifts of death, blow one sun about another, and obliterate the constellations' glittering dew with your passing? How alone is each of us in the universe's catacomb! *I am but beside me – O Father! O Father!* Where is Thy eternal breast that I may rest upon it? Alas, if each is his own father and creator, why may he not be his own angel of destruction too!'

This is an excerpt from what French, Spanish, Italian, Polish and Russian poets and philosophers have regarded as one of the most revealing documents of the nineteenth century. The initial version was written in 1789, the first year of the Revolution. Its author was Johann Paul Friedrich Richter who called himself Jean Paul in honour of Jean-Jacques Rousseau. In 1790 it was published as *Dead Shakespeare's Lament among the Dead in Church that there is no God*, but six years later as *Dead Christ's Harangue from the Building of the World that there is no God*.

Other men had had such visions. Hegel's last works covered up the nothingness he perceived in his youth. Jean Paul does not wait that long. Even as he sees the vision, the poet wakes to find it was only a dream, that he is reconciled with his God. Not that Jean Paul did ever really forget this early nightmare – in none of his later work did he mention the father he so stirringly evoked as spokesman for the dead Christ. For a long time he was preoccupied with the idea of evoking a dream of hell vivid enough to portray his dread of nothingness and the total destruction of man. He finally created it in the image of a battlefield, perhaps because he had a presentiment that the global civil war beginning in the nineteenth century would create hell on earth.

Jean Paul (1763–1825) was a favourite with women, and a controversial figure among his contemporaries. Some held him to be greater than Goethe, others treated him with contempt. Yet although he was almost forgotten in the nineteenth century, in the twentieth he achieved tremendous acclaim as a 'German Dostoevsky'. He and his contemporaries were suffering from the realisation that they were living in a post-Copernican world, Jean Paul's achievement was to have exorcised the despair he induced by his own cosmic visions.

Jean Paul first started to query man's attitude to religion when a student at Leipzig in 1781–90. He knew himself to be living in a post-Christian age, an age without God. If there was to be new faith in God and man it was essential, in the light of the great revolution and those still to come, to be clear first of all about Christ, and it was thanks to Herder that He was presented to Jean Paul's contemporaries as a man, 'divine disguise'.

Jean Paul's works were composed against the sombre background of his time, a time when it seemed as if nothing would withstand the disintegrating effect of the French Revolution and when world revolution, the complete overthrow of all existing forms of order could apparently take place, like a sudden storm out of a blue sky. He saw 'mankind proceeding towards its Promised land through a red sea of blood. ... Can you be certain (he wrote in a letter of condolence to a young couple who had just lost their daughter) that the tender creature would not have been too severely battered by the bloody waves of the future, which are already welling up? We are in the evening of our life and dusk is all around.'

From 1790 onwards after years of personal and professional disaster, he was beset by a frenzied urge to create and used every means available – coffee, alcohol, music – to stimulate his imagination. With the help of 'magic power' he skimmed over the desolate present, living only in yesterday and tomorrow. The imagination makes use of the 'moment' to release the ego into the infinite – into a future which, as a hope never to be fulfilled, merges with the Beyond.

In 1820 he published his *Dream of the Universe*, the account of a journey on which he was guided by an angel-like figure: 'We flew so swiftly through the throng of innumerable suns that they were barely able for a moment to diffuse into moons before dissolving behind us into particles of mist. ... Now I took fright at the boundless Cimmerian prison of creation. Its walls began here in front of the dead sea of nothingness in whose fathomless gloom the jewel of the luminous universe perpetually went down.' Rebuked by the angel for his fears he goes on: 'My eyes were opened and I beheld a great ocean of light. ... The eye could take in what was nearest and what was farthest away, at one and the same glance. I saw the colossal expanses we had flown over and the small firmaments that they contained. In the ethers of light the suns shone merely as ashen blossoms and the planets as black buds.'

Jean Paul's masterpiece was *Titan* (1800–03), which earned him the title of the 'German Dostoevsky'. It showed how despite imagination and intellect, a gifted man might destroy himself and his fellow men. This work was originally a reaction against Weimar and Goethe, stimulated by *Wilhelm Meister*, which had insisted on the Theatre's civilising force. For Jean Paul the theatre was synonymous with depravity. On this point he was at one with Herder who, as superintendent of the Weimar stage, fought a long pamphlet war with Goethe and the Grand Duke on their alleged corruption of youth, women and Christians generally by the public representation of their libidinous 'affairs'.

Jean Paul's memories of Weimar society combined pleasure at the company of some of its female members such as Charlotte von Kolb, and humiliation as a *petit bourgeois* at the hands of the men. His refuge was Herder's house, the centre of resistance against Weimar within the Weimar stronghold.

'What they complain of is disguised egotism and undisguised superstition. That is why they sun themselves in the company of someone who suffers from neither.' Jean Paul was well aware that he was such a person. But six months later, looking back on his experiences, he said: 'Weimar is for me an isle in the Atlantic, sunk beneath the waves. I can hardly believe that I once disembarked on those Tahitian shores.' His rejection of this distant world of luxury and forbidden pleasures made him a part of the powerful reaction which raged on all sides throughout Germany against the Weimar of Goethe and Schiller.

WEIMAR PHOBIA

The reaction against Weimar, a feeling shared by such far-flying groups as the enlightened intelligentsia of Berlin, the north German Protestants and converts, the central German middle classes, the Bavarian conservatives and both the enlightened and Catholics of Vienna, is significant as a symptom of the inner and outer complexity besetting Germany, land of 'poets and philosophers', at that time. And the nature of this reaction may be seen most clearly in Germany's attitudes to Schiller and Goethe, men despised during their lives only to be set on pedestals and idolised, after their death.

In 1810 Count Leopold Friedrich Stolberg asked Goethe to cooperate in his 'Patriotic Museum' scheme to bring together in literary form the opposition to Napoleon. He can hardly have been surprised to receive a refusal, for, as he wrote in a letter to Princess Galitzine: 'We live in strange times. Seldom can the kingdom of God have been in such obvious struggle with the kingdom of Darkness. In human perspective it could well seem that Darkness shall envelope the earth. All the more splendid then shall be the victory of Light.' The seat of Darkness to which he referred was Weimar, a den of atheism, the 'home' of Schiller and Goethe.

Count Stolberg was not only the critic. Schlegel ridiculed Goethe's book on Winckelmann in which, as he wrote, 'he frankly avows his paganism. Never before has he so completely abandoned himself to his inner profligacy.' Stolberg burnt with great solemnity his copy of *Wilhelm Meister* and, at Schiller's death, condemned his admiration for the Greek Spirit, as Bonald and de Maistre had done before him; 'So Schiller is dead. God rest his soul.

For philosophy, religion and the standards of truth and beauty his death is a gain. His gifts sufficed for glittering falsehood, not veracity.'

Weimar was an island, a seductive island ruled by the powers of darkness, as an anonymous writer observed in 1800 in the periodical, *Der Genius der Zeit*, that reservoir of professed humanism and resentment against Weimar.

No one tries to sing in chorus. Each is a soloist, seated alone in the shade of a tree, turning his back on the rest and ignoring their existence. In other words, closely akin though they are by reason of their identical aspirations and love of the muses, these intellectuals nevertheless live thoroughly divorced from one another, each an island unto himself.... Like elephants, these great men (Wieland, Goethe, Herder) seem by their mutual proximity to impede and inhibit one another in their movements.

There was some justification for this view. Herder died a lonely and embittered man at Weimar in 1803. Jean Paul, with the affection of a true friend, fully grasped the nature of the situation: 'His feelings were hurt. The cancer gnawing at him was his political and literary discontent.'

Was Goethe any less lonely? Probably not. He never held illusions about his status in Germany.

GOETHE

'*Er ist ein Vulcan, aussen überschneit, innen voll geschmolzener Materie*'
(He is a volcano, snow on the outside and full of molten matter inside)
JEAN PAUL

Goethe, the dormant volcano: this is perhaps one of the most perceptive comments on Goethe and his life. He himself was only too aware of his volcanic qualities, and his life becomes a series of more or less successful attempts to quell the fire, regardless of whether its nature was divine or satanic, to plant flowers on the lava screes, to avoid the destruction, not only of others, but of himself.

All through his life he felt the need to take refuge from the miseries of the age, from the lack of character in Germans, from the upsurge of his own innermost feelings, and he sought this refuge in general ill health. A few years before his death, recovering from a serious illness, he said: 'The weight of three thousand years' illness plagues me.' It was a serious statement. He saw Europe, its Christianity, and its spiritual and intellectual condition as a source of disease, infecting and poisoning its peoples and individuals. Like the young Herder, he had wanted as a young man to leave the confines of an ailing Europe and return to the 'spring of life', the healing waters of the Orient. From 1814 on his thoughts turned more and more towards India and Iran in whose traditions he believed he could trace a divinity of infinite life and infinite regeneration.

Eckermann reports Goethe as saying: 'Let mankind last as long as it will, there will be no lack of obstacles to inspire its creativity or troubles of every sort to help develop its faculties. Men will become more intelligent and discerning, but neither better nor happier, nor more effectual; or if they do, simply for limited periods.' Goethe believed that at some stage God would get bored with humanity as it was and (a reference to the Lisbon earthquake) destroy everything in favour of a fresh creation. 'But', he adds, 'a good time will probably elapse before this happens and for thousands of years yet we shall be able to find pleasure of every kind on this dear old earth.'

He felt a deep concern for human life and for every other living being on earth and in the universe. But he was afraid that the gigantic accumulation of disease, madness, wickedness, the heritage of the world's history, was bound to destroy man. In his final years he sensed, with consternation, the approach of destruction on a grand scale. Was not the span of mankind, particularly of cultured man, coming to an end? Even in his early years he was conscious of what Nietzsche was to formulate as his epitaph: 'In German history Goethe is an episode without sequel.' Ortega y Gasset in 1932 and Karl Jaspers in 1949 both restated the aphorism in their own way. This German virtuoso of life has been buried under a mountain of sculpture, anthologies of quotations, classic editions, celebration speeches, school essays and (by no means least) nineteenth-century philological and interpretive studies of his works. The volcano, so eager to dispense life, was effectively extinguished. Nietzsche viewed Goethe 'as the most fascinating chaos, not before but since creation, that there has ever been'. It was a chaos that Goethe both feared and venerated, for he knew very well both how constructive and destructive his creative capacity could be. Even at the age of twenty-three he had been horrified by the senselessly destructive quality of nature, and looking back as an old man saw his work as a lifelong effort to master the terrible effect that the French Revolution had had on Europe.

Essentially he was a lonely man. Even the women who kindled his passion were unable to assuage his sensuality for more than a fleeting moment. It was not until he met Charlotte von Stein that he experienced the primal, healing power of woman, and he celebrated this in his work, producing verse of an almost sacramental nature. The intensity of his feelings threatened to overcome him, and he fled to Italy. Time after time he was to flee from Charlotte's influence and from the grand duke's ramshackle state which he had tried in vain to reform. He went no less than seventeen times to the Bohemian spas, where he met not only the Empress Maria Ludovica and Marianne von Eybenberg but also the seventeen-year-old Ulrike von Levetzow. Yet behind the Olympian mask of the small, graceful, finely-built old man lay unease and fear.

Goethe, the son of well-to-do Frankfurt parents, loved the beauty of life of the Rococo age. His many love affairs and adventures scandalised his contemporaries. Yet he himself was conscious, even in the second half of the eighteenth century of something that was to impinge on the spirit of some of the greatest as well as lonelist artists of the nineteenth century: the deadly power and influence of the erotic urge.

For many Goethe is chiefly known as the author of *The Sorrows of Werther*, a work personifying rebellion, the revolt of youth against the constraints of a false morality, of the 'new man' against a philistine society, with its egoistic, stagnant tendencies. There is so much of Goethe in this work, the insanity, the near suicidal state of mind, that for years he could hardly bear to speak of it. Half a century later he prepared a new preface, the opening poem of the *Trilogy of Passion*.

'Neither God's love, nor that of nature is tender.' Goethe was convinced that creative existence ruthlessly subjugates other and weaker forms of existence, using them to its own ends, consuming them. This was a supreme law, recognisable in its fruits, and he was well aware of the danger inherent in his concept and of the threat he represented to himself and others.

But Goethe was essentially an optimist and he wanted men to be educated with a practical, sober, warm-hearted appreciation of reality. He put his own ideas into the mouth of the priest in *Wilhelm Meister*:

> Mankind is simply the sum of all men, the world no more than the sum total of its forces. These are often at odds with each other and, inasmuch as they seek their mutual destruction, nature keeps them going and resuscitates them. . . . *Every* predisposition is of importance and must be developed. . . . The teacher's task does not lie in preventing error, but in giving guidance to his erring charge and indeed allowing him to drain his error to the full. Therein lies the teacher's sagacity.

These concepts brought on him the criticism of many German educationalists, who were far from sharing Goethe's opinion that the German 'lack of character' was the result of too servile a system of education.

He knew that eternal revolution was out of the question in Germany, and looked with compassion on the misery of the poor and illiterate. He felt that the people had been betrayed by the conscious and unconscious frauds of state, church and patriotism. With a mixture of compassion and horror he watched fascinated as mankind progressed through a series of individual tragedies: 'Man has to be crushed yet again. Every individual of any exceptional quality has but one purpose on earth. His mission fulfilled, his continued presence is no longer necessary.' He knew, as an old man, that it would not be the dreams of poetic bards and revolutionary protagonists which liberated Germany, but the building of good roads and the extension of the railways. Yet at the same time he sensed that capitalism, both a creative and a destructive force, would change the world to a point where poetic fancy, the appreciation of beauty, would no longer have a part to play, where vulgarity would achieve victory over everything noble and transcendental. He felt that a plebeian force was growing, ready for every sort of enthusiasm and act of madness. Right up to his death he retained this fear that the prosaic tendencies of the age would finally overcome all possibility of divine inspiration.

Goethe had grown up in a world of 'ghosts'. The intellectual riches of Old Europe, rotten now, were vanishing from the minds of those living in what was left of the Holy Roman Empire. Watching the last Imperial Coronation at Frankfurt, he felt he was seeing a procession of spectres. History, it seemed to him, was an unbroken dance of phantoms, full of horrors and void of good sense. The Baroque, to which he himself owed so much, he now regarded as mendacious and vilely calculating in its appeal to the instincts of the lower classes. He was no less sceptical of the Reformation, remarking: 'The sole point of interest in the whole affair is the character of Luther, and that too is the only thing that really impresses the masses.'

It was his own distinctive form of religion that brought him into conflict with the Christianity of his age, although for a time Herder's and Schelling's Johannine evangelism impressed him. His language is steeped in biblical expressions, especially from the Old Testament. As a mature man, however, he had no hesitation in pressing beyond the boundaries of Christianity, that is to say, beyond the spiritual and intellectual maladies of Europe, back beyond Moses to the pure sources of older, holier, more comprehensive piety and wisdom. In so doing, he reforged a link with his youth and his early Strasbourg discussions with Herder. After 1814, having firmly decided in favour of Oriental mysticism and the views of the Persian non-conformist, Hafis, he introduced the whole of ancient Iranian and modern Persian symbolism into *Faust; Part II*, aiming thereby to supersede Christianity with a religion belonging to man's greater, older past, and greater, richer future. Goethe was in search of a God who would be above the wrangling and partisanship of Christianity.

He looked beyond the confines of a miserable, faction-ridden, reactionary and narrow-minded Europe, partly benumbed, and partly ready to explode to real contact between an East and West world, abounding in healthy antitheses and intellectual pluralistic as well as religious diversities. He knew this broader world to exist within himself. He spent his life in conversation, spoken or written, with friends of all nationalities, and it was only within the circle of these friends that he found Europe. Outside this world, his enemies could condemn him at will.

As a medium for cosmic currents and radiations, his points of reference lay thousands of years back (and continued perhaps into the future). All his life he felt himself to be in touch with nature and constantly affected by its ceaseless promptings. He sought its signs in leaf and stone, skull and feather, colour and wind, soil and cloud formation. The circle of the seasons and the orbit of the universe held him under their spell. To him the sun was divinity, the intellectual and spiritual gold of cosmic alchemy and the artist of eternal transmutation, breathing fresh life into his mind and body.

Goethe knew that the Golden Age of kings, gods, priests and prophets was past, that mundanity and loneliness awaited the individual, together with a great fear, a fear of the universe, of death: 'The individual gets lost, the memory of him disappears, and yet he and others care that it should be retained.' It was with these words that he drew up his plan for *Dichtung und Wahrheit*: the will to survive, by word and work of creation.

The loneliness man feels when he undergoes some profound evolution of his personality was one of the nineteenth-century's most oppressive experiences. This was a cup which Goethe had tasted to the dregs.

HÖLDERLIN

> My love belongs to the human race. Not the depraved, menial, lazy specimens we encounter only too often, however limited our experience, although even in them I love their inherently fine and great proclivities. *My love is for the human race as it will be in centuries to come.* My dearest hope, the belief that keeps me strong, is that our grandchildren will be better than we are, that one day freedom will prevail and that goodness will thrive better in freedom's hallowed tropics, than in the icy zones of despotism.

With these words, written in 1790–91 – the year which, according to Pierre Bertaux, 'must be called one of man's decisive moments' – Hölderlin placed himself alongside Schelling and Hegel, their minds alight with Heraclitus' concept of fire and the blaze of the French Revolution. What was it he hoped to find there? A manifestation of the godhead, a reincarnation of God and thus a revival of true faith in Christianity, in the whole of history and nature, a vision of a new Europe arising from the fires of an ancient Greece whose roots lay buried deep in Asia.

In January 1797, writing to Johann Gottfried Ebel, he described his time in terms which struck those who rediscovered him on the eve of the First World War and between the two wars, as particularly apposite to their own feelings:

> ... my one consolation is that all the tumult and disorder must necessarily lead to annihilation or a new order. But there is no such thing as annihilation, *so the world's youth must revert out of our decay.* Surely we can say that the world has never yet presented such a manifold appearance as it does today. It is a gigantic miscellany of contrasts and contradictions. Old and new! Culture and crudity! Malice and passion! Egotism in sheep's clothing and egotism in wolf's skin! Superstition and scepticism! Servitude and despotism! Senseless cleverness, idiotic good sense!

Two years later, in a letter to his brother, he outlined in broad terms his view of mankind ending with a dedication to its service: '... and should the Kingdom of Darkness seek to break in by force, then let us throw away the pen and, in God's name, go where the need is greatest and where we are most needed!' So Byron thought and did when he went to participate in Greece's struggle for freedom.

With his *Hyperion* (1797) Hölderlin threw himself into the struggle for the liberation of all mankind. He considered that it was the philistine, the contemporary German, the new barbarian who stood in the way of man's evolution, and the words he put into Alabanda's mouth were unsparing: 'The question is not whether you are willing. You never are, you serfs and savages! It would be vain to try and improve you. But care must be taken that you do not bar mankind's path to victory.' In *Hyperion* he describes with a realism tinged with bitterness the effect that the Germans as a nation must produce on anyone striving for a new human order: 'Barbarians by origin they become even more barbarious through effort, knowledge and even religion, utterly incapable of any divine sentiment whatever, rotten to the core. . . . One is faced with craftsmen but not fellow creatures, priests but not fellow creatures, masters and menials, youngsters and elders, but not fellow creatures.' He ascribed this condition to the effect of their religion. He was afraid of the 'German God', as tenth-century Slavs, as the youthful Herder had been, a withered, harsh, hard-hearted god ruling over state of nature that meant nothing to him, a god judging and damning a human race for which he had no sympathy, a god whose representatives on earth, the priests, were scoundrels and corrupters well versed in all forms of deceit who were leading a poor, deluded nation astray. Against this dead God of professional religiosity Hölderlin preached a revolt springing from the naturally good human heart.

It would constitute a total misinterpretation of his verse, work and historical importance to overlook the intimate connection between Hölderlin's life, his sober political thought, and the prophetic quality of his poetry. His genuine modernity is to be sought precisely in the inseparability of these contrasting elements.

Against the old, dead god of his German barbarians, the contemporary Christians, Hölderlin appealed to the 'god of youth' who had formerly manifested himself in Hellas in many shapes. Dionysus-Bacchus and Heracles were among those he favoured. As demi-gods become entirely human, long-suffering and victimised, expending their strength in heavy labour, they displayed the pure face of divinity in mankind. He was convinced that 'great pain and great longing are man's best educators', and that 'he whom the gods love sustains great joy and great suffering'.

Hölderlin invoked Greece not as a dream of ideal harmony but as possessing the essential of thought and life, since the Greek spirit alone, by virtue of its trinitarian spiritual structure, had allowed for and created the blossoming of man.

De Maistre, Bonald and the nineteenth-century Roman Curia feared and hated the Greek spirit, which threatened to subvert all church segregation. Greece to them was the mother of chaos, heresy and revolution. Hölderlin, Shelley, Byron, Nietzsche, and all the other nineteenth- and twentieth-century adherents to the Greek Spirit were convinced, on the other hand, that this spirit was the essence of life, the incarnation of divinity here on earth. Hölderlin's Greece was the home of all the positive revolutions of mankind. He spent three years in France, in the Bordeaux area, where resistance, in the political and military sense of the word, as familiarised by the two wars, had existed since the twelfth century, and during this period felt he had gained even deeper insight into the nature of those southern peoples who shared his philosophy.

Camus said of René Char, a fellow resistance-fighter: 'In his work poetry became a healing fire. It blazed up like those large bonfires in his native region which scent the air and feed the earth. We were at last able to breathe again. Nature's secret, the living waters and the light broke into the room where poetry had so far found its pleasure in shadows and echoes. This can be acclaimed as poetic revolution.'

The same can justly be said of Hölderlin and his self-imposed duty to resume 'after a long eclipse an arduous and scarce tradition'.

It is surely not mere chance that the fair copy of his *Celebration of Peace* should have come to light only in our own day and in the intellectual and spiritual situation prevailing after the Second World War at once became the occasion for a global 'dispute about peace'. This work was a trumpet-call of spiritual revolution comparable to Marx's *Communist Manifesto*, Nietzsche's *Thus Spake Zarathustra*, and Victor Hugo's greatest hymns.

Hölderlin was fully conscious of the unprecedented character of his subject matter – the reconciliation of the 'gods' with Christ, an 'alliance' between God and man, the return to the fold of all life, all nature and all history on the occasion of a great communion. The *leit-motiv* of this poem is the tragedy that would secure the universal peace of the future. He interwove his themes, his personalities and his symbolic warnings in phraseology of the utmost delicacy, perfectly aware that this was the only convincing way to evoke the 'communion of the spirits'.

Hölderlin believed that the great reconciliation could be brought about through a maturation of joy and pain; and that peace would come only when all religions and philosophies were reconciled. But even he was not sure whether the very suggestion of such a reconciliation was not presumptuous.

The Christ of Hölderlin's conception was not the Christ of German Christians, but the Johannine Christ, the cosmic Christ, Christ the unifier, the bringer of peace, who on the eve brings together the good, the pure and the pious of all ages, of the world's history to await the dawn of a New Kingdom when the earth will be transformed into a paradise.

In his great hymns Hölderlin had first sought earthly paradise of Hellas. Later he found it in everything – the Swabian landscape, the banks of a river, in bread or wine. At the outset of the nineteenth century which was destined to create so many hells, the overwhelming power of Hölderlin's poetic vision found its expression in resounding verses that describe a transfigured earth – an entire epiphany, a shining manifesto of the Godhead, the threshold of peace.

On completion of *Celebration of Peace*, Hölderlin broke down, exhausted and burnt out. Inspiration had come to him in a brilliant illumination of the senses. Who exactly he had in mind, as the 'Prince of the Feast' no one knows, for Hölderlin knew that names are the snares through which gods and men decay. He left all open: the universe, mankind, God, purpose, being, birth and fire.

HEGEL

Georg Wilhelm Friedrich Hegel (1770–1831) held the view that history had, strictly speaking, already come to an end; 'History moves from East to West, Europe is simply its end, Asia its beginning.' (Introduction to *Philosophy of History*). As far as he was concerned there was only one task left to man: to comprehend history. Hegel saw himself as a mediator between man and revealed religion. 'Only the perception that what has happened and continues to happen every day comes neither alone from God nor yet without God, but is essentially His work, can reconcile the spirit with history and reality.'

He regarded himself as the saviour of Christianity through its purification in his philosophy: as arbiter of the Godhead and his thoughts, deeds and suffering in the world. At heart he was all theologian, at first revolutionary, later belonging to the post-Napoleonic Restoration. He was a typical member of the German middle class, a professor and a philistine, convinced he would be a success. His life was conducted at two different levels, but without the slightest tendency to schizophrenia.

The first of these two levels was that of the 'higher reality', philosophy. This, in his mind, was not for the 'common man'. In fact, it was a luxury, and fell into two distinct sections: the exoteric, which provided a more or less intelligible explanation of the world along lines suited to state, church and the middle-class outlook, and the esoteric, which was far too dangerous to be revealed to the masses and which clearly revealed what had long been evident – the death of God, the decay of religion and Christianity in particular, and on all sides decay of the Old European Order.

The second level at which Hegel lived was that of the true son of a Stuttgart official with Austrian Protestant ancestors. As such Hegel accommodated himself to the political trends of the day. At first he was in sympathy with the French Revolution. Later, however, in post-Napoleonic times, he had no objection to siding with the re-established order. There is nothing surprising in this. As a political publicist once commented, nearly one hundred years after Hegel's death: 'The inconsistency of his writings, with their politico-philosophical flavour, is such as to provide a colourful quarry for liberal, socialist, conservative, religious, atheistic, national and international ideas. Hegel's theory of history is at the same time a system of historical determinism and a mystically disguised form of belief in progress.' Hegel himself might well have laughed at this comment.

To the end of his life the grace-and-favour professor (at his Berlin inaugural lecture on 22 October 1818 he introduced himself as 'appointed by grace of His Majesty the King') each year cracked a bottle of wine to celebrate the anniversary of the fall of the Bastille. He knew that the French Revolution had been the greatest event since the foundation of Christianity.

His letters were as commonplace as his philosophy was exclusive. He had no intention of writing for everyone's benefit, considering the dangerous times in which he lived. He was by nature a Lutheran theologian and knew it. He gazed into the loneliness of a gigantic cosmos where the rubble of millennia, an enormous mass of apparently purposeless material 'manpower' as it was later to be called had been accumulated, and saw instead the raw material for the Godhead and the process of history. His task as he saw it, was to make sense of the seemingly senseless and to give congruence to the incongruities which are present in all epochs. He wanted to be a bringer of salvation and conciliator. And he did not hesitate, at certain crucial moments in the definition of his own philosophy, to state in plain language the enormous price that mankind has to pay at each stage for progress towards freedom.

As a young man, he was an avid reader of Lessing and Rousseau. Under the influence of Herder he examined the serviceability of Christian concepts for a new popular religion. It was inevitable that Herder's occasionally violent anti-Semitism should effect him. The tragedy of the Jewish people 'can only arouse loathing', while its faith is 'a religion derived from and appropriate to calamity'. Christianity was equally impossible as a state institution. 'Everything depends on subjective religion.' He pleaded for the 'invisible Church' and on behalf of all heresies against the establishment. He did not believe in the 'so-called Resurrection'. His criticism of ecclesiastical Christianity led him to evolve the concept of alienation – a state to which the individual is reduced by the 'positive religion' of the Church, which imposes external discipline but fails to effect any internal awakening.

His reading, when he was a private tutor at Berne and Frankfurt as well as in subsequent years, included Montesquieu, Gibbon, the Church historian Mosheim, English periodicals and political and economic tracts. Early liberalism of the Swabian variety, tinged with French Revolutionary ideas, are merged in him with Western European enlightenment. But German nationalist enthusiasm never appealed to him. Instead, he pledged himself to the political humanism it implied. Man, to become an apt and willing member of society, should learn to think properly. He should train himself and train his fellow citizens. The five addresses he gave during his rectorship of the Nüremberg Aegydien Gymnasium from 1809 to 1815 were fully consistent in their educational aspects with the tenor of his earlier studies.

From Berne he wrote to Schelling, 'Religion and politics have conspired with one another. The former has taught what the latter has wanted: contempt for the human race and its incapacity to become anything worthwhile on its own.' The miserable state of religion in Germany, he felt, was indivisible from that of politics. That he made plain in his *Verdict on the Printed Report of the Deliberations in the Assembly of the Provincial Estates of the Kingdom of Württemberg in the Years 1815 and 1816.* Important passages from this work anticipate the criticism which was to be directed at the Frankfurt Parliament of 1848–9.

In his view sentimentality and fanaticism in religious, intellectual and political matters gnawed at the Germans like a cancer. His inaugural Berlin address of 1818 was devoted to attacking their ailments, which he analysed as lack of faith in common sense, lack of confidence in science, and lack of faith and confidence in themselves. They were without 'belief in the power of the spirit'. In the preface to his *Philosophy of Right* he launched the comprehensive rebuke that 'in the sloppiness of their hearts' they had destroyed the millennial structural balance of polity, society, and sound reason.

He stoutly opposed the irrationalism which he saw springing up at every turn in German hearts and minds. Germans, he told them, are a species which likes to babble most about mind when it is being most mindless, and most about life when it is being most sterile. They 'mouth the word "people" most often just when they are showing how utterly selfish idle arrogance can be'. What is more, thanks to a piece of 'colossal presumption', they arrogate to their egotistic 'erudition' and 'feeling' judgement over existence over the whole of reality. Hegel threw in their faces his conviction that 'authority is the root of knowledge. This, the authority of God, applies even to sentient knowledge. It is, like itself, direct.'

The business of the German professor and the German university, according to Fichte, was to act as mentor and to facilitate initiation into prime and ultimate reality. He and Marx, the professor *manqué* and lifelong pupil of Hegel regarded their work primarily as guides to the future. Hegel, on the other hand, was also sure of his role as guide to the past. Contemporary, cognisant existence meant, in his eyes, elucidation of history and appreciation of the bygone which was fulfilling itself so gloriously in the present. What the morrow held was totally indeterminate.

The purpose of history is the glory and honour of God. History manifests both the radiant and the terrible nature of the Godhead. Hegel, following the grand tradition of thought introduced into Germany by Anselm of Havelberg and Rupert of Deutz in the twelfth century and transmitted to eighteenth-century *Swabia* via Nicholas of Cusa, asserted that man does honour to God by recognising Him in history. 'The honour of God is also that of the individual, though not his especial honour. The latter lies in knowing that his conduct to the honour of God is the Absolute. In this he is with the truth and has contact with the Absolute. He is therefore with himself.'

Naturally enough history contains, besides significant to the progress of man, an infinite amount of superfluous detail. Individuals are only important as the medium through which history achieves its ends: 'It may be that the individual will suffer injustice. That is not history's concern. Individuals are the means to its process – comment all too dangerous in its possible connotations. Hegel dared to say a thing like this because to him, in the final analysis, history meant infinite suffering on the part of God. According to him the divine essence is only too aware that it is 'participating in the fate of the finite. God dies in order to be resurrected, and in history death is both fraught with purpose and a process of rebirth. Recognition of this fact does not temper its severity but increases it.'

How did Hegel come to know all this, the meaning of being and history? How did he arrive at his 'identification of God with the dialectical method' (Karl Barth)? Gnosticism, German mysticism (familiar to him originally through Mosheim's *History of the Church*) and Lutheran piety merged into the primal form of his dialectic for the first time in the fragment written at Frankfurt, a speculation on Good Friday. The divine must die; God resurrected encompasses all the contradictions of being; grief and sunderance are as pertinent to His essence as the noblest harmony.

'The tremendous pain of the negative' must be carried over into God. He is occurrence, movement, action, a process of reason and love. Logic is the delineation of this process. *The Trinity and logic are identical.* The Spirit is nothing but the revelation, life and manifestation of God.

'With Hegel the logical process has a threefold significance; theological, scientific, and cosmic.' 'Logic is . . . the prime and true self-revelation of God in the element of pure thought' (I. Iljin).

Hegel's logic arises tectonically from the fusion of two laws: the logical law of contradiction ('schism', 'emnity') and the Christian law of love ('concrescence', 'contact'). That is, the reappearance of magic in Christian garb because 'concrescence' contains the old magical desire for transmutation and amalgamation inherent in the search for the philosopher's stone.

Hegel, a creative genius, subconsciously jumbled together the currents of major historical outlooks and beliefs, just as he consciously summoned and dismissed peoples and epochs, bestowing meaning on them, or depriving them of it, according to the logic of his ideas. He was aware of the mystic character of his speculations: 'Speculation is mysticism' because 'the nature of speculation is . . . uniformity of opposites, coincidence.'

'God is not simply an idea, but the Idea itself.' The Idea is a triad, or trinity, the magic formula of transmutation. 'The Idea, the Absolute Idea, is occurrence.' The occurrence, in the shape of God's life in the world, takes place in the well-known triadic ritual of the Idea's discharge and absorption of its antithesis, absorption being understood as both subjection and preservation. Enhanced and satiated by life and the experience of death (like the passive metal in alchemical operations), the antitheses is reabsorbed into oneness.

In history the inner, effluent and refluent drama of the Godhead is accomplished at enormous cost. God dies a thousand times and in a thousand ways in order that man shall learn from His example the art of dying. 'God Himself is dead.' Hegel repeatedly quoted from the second verse of a Protestant hymn by Johann Rist (1607–67) where the *leit motiv* of his thinking was foreshadowed. 'God, through death, has reconciled the world and reconciles Himself eternally with Himself.' 'It is the true God Who sacrifices Himself.'

The Universal Spirit can have no consideration for its victims. Right is on the side of those who act in accord with it and have power. The Romans were in the right against the Greeks, the Spaniards against the Incas, the Europeans against the Asiatics. The Germans are in the right against all foregoing peoples. Hegel was a prophet who, his face turned to the past, forecast Germanisation of the world as the climax of history – his own application of the ancient sacral doctrines of the Three and the Four Kingdoms. The Kingdom of the Father lasted from Late Antiquity until Charlemagne; the Kingdom of the Son until the days of the Emperor Charles v; the Kingdom of the Holy Ghost was that of the modern Protestant world in which there had been a reconciliation of state and church, the inner and outer realms, the individual and the community, faith and science, heaven and earth. The Germanic Kingdom, reaching its culmination in contemporary times and the Prussian state, was the last of the Four Kingdoms.

Hegel regarded himself as living in the 'old age of the Spirit'. In the course of a vast process the Spirit – God, history – has spent itself. The future? Unfathomable and unintelligible; no good was to be anticipated from it and it was no concern of the Spirit. 'No other interpreter of history has cared less for the future than Hegel' (Golo Mann).

Yet he could not entirely avoid a glance at the future, for it was always possible that the Universal Spirit would abandon Europe.

Then America is the land of the future where in ages to come . . . the significance of history will be revealed. It is a land for which all those yearn who are wearied by the historic arsenal of old Europe. Napoleon is supposed to have said, 'cette vieille Europe m'ennuie'. But what has so far happened over there is simply an echo of the Old World, an expression of alien animation, and, as a land of the future, it concerns us here not at all. He was equally unconcerned about the Slav world. It had not, in his opinion, made any impression as an autonomous factor in the sequence of reason's configurations, the realisation of the Universal Spirit in the world's history. 'Whether this may still happen is not our business here.'

Nevertheless a totally different note was struck in a letter to a Baltic Germano-Russian pupil. Hegel wrote that Europe had already become a kind of cage in which only two sorts of people seemed able to move at their ease, those who possessed keys and those who had found themselves a place where the bars did not worry them. Anyone unable to rally sincerely to one another's party would do better to devote himself to an enjoyable epicurean existence and to retain his privacy, a status no higher than that of a spectator but all the same of great efficacy. He went on to contrast this European cage with Russia's future. Other modern states had apparently attained the target of their evolution, passed their zenith, and were now in a condition of deceleration. Russia, on the other hand, had in it an 'immense potential for the development of its vigorous nature'.

It has been justifiably said that 'Hegel is on the side of ideas with official blessing.' Certainly no princely Jack-in-office or panegyrist of a ruling system could have been more conformist than Hegel when acting as official speaker, and his speech at the tercentenary of the proclamation of the Augsburg Confession is an example. He abased his illustrious principle of reconciliation by solemnly declaring that princely power and the Church had been reconciled in Protestantism and that 'unity, based on freedom, between the secular order and the Faith, that is, Lutheranism' had become a reality. At Berlin University he thoroughly enjoyed his life and the power it brought with it, and he maintained a prudent attitude of mind to those above, below and against him. One cannot, however, totally explain his political ideas as being dependent on his status as a Prussian court philosopher, for they were formulated long before he had any hope of the Berlin appointment. He believed quite firmly in the idea of an eternal pattern, a cosmic justice ruling the universe. All order, for him was rooted in right and 'the basis of right is the indwelling spirit and its point of departure is the will, which is free, so that freedom constitutes its substance and purpose. . . .'

To Hegel the state was the kingdom of God on earth, ruled by order, and thus it had the sacred right to subjugate its members as mere 'limbs'. There was, however, one point which disquieted him in this state, or middle-class society: the fact that it was revealing itself as an umbrella organisation for the interests of the individual, a state where work, the masses, poverty were simply structural concomitants. He saw very clearly the misery of a capitalist society, with its resultant isolation of the individual, herd-instinct and poverty. He saw that 'middle-class society is going to be driven . . . over its own boundaries . . . in order to look for consumers, and therewith essential raw materials, among peoples behind it in the means of which it has superabundance. . . .' In fact, he stood on the brink of modern capitalism, colonialism and European economic imperialism.

It is possible that Hegel did not care to pursue the train of his thoughts. He certainly became tired and infinitely resigned. There were no illusions left to him. He saw Old Europe as a heap of ashes, Christianity spent, and modern literary forms as worth nothing.

Despite the fact that Hegel himself died disillusioned, and that he became, after his death, a subject of ridicule, nevertheless he lit dialectic fires which have survived until today in Marx and Friedrich Engels, in Lenin and Mao Tse-tung, helping these men to an awareness, a wisdom and knowledge of life, of the preservation and resolution, in history and in life, of the antitheses and contradictions which Hegel had sought to salvage and shelter.

4

European Romanticism

During the nineteenth century German thought, German philosophic and literary currents, occupied a very significant place in European culture. Most of the European intelligentsia of the period were agreed that 'truth survived in Germany alone'. For this fact one woman was very much responsible – Madame de Staël – whose own passionate nature, together with the position she held in society, the men she had loved and those she had entertained as guests at Coppet, gave her an unusual depth of understanding of all strata of society and, even more important, of the conscious and sub-conscious levels of emotion. For, with her work *De l'Allemagne* (1810), she first gave France and the whole of Europe an awareness of its situation at that time.

Madame de Staël's work was both the fruit of her own travels in Germany in 1804 and 1807, and the practical application of her study, *De La Littérature considérée dans ses rapports avec les institutions sociales* of 1800. On the first of her trips she was looking for a tutor for her son, and finally employed August Wilhelm Schlegel, of whose assistance she then availed herself in writing her book. Its publication created a sensation and it was regarded in Europe as the manifesto *par excellence* of anti-Bonapartism. Napoleon himself was extremely angry, ordered the destruction of all copies and banished Madame de Staël to Coppet for having dared to invoke the spirit of Germany in preference to that of Gallic classicism. Living in constant fear of his revenge, she fled to Moscow, and finally to London. Here the first English edition of her book was published, with an important preface by Crabb Robinson, an old friend from Germany. Later, after the first fall of Napoleon in 1814, she returned to France to correct the proofs of the French edition. She finally died in Paris, an exhausted woman, but having ensured the penetration of the German spirit into France and being acclaimed, albeit posthumously, the 'divine inspiration' of the young French Romantic movement.

It is a pity that Romanticism, a misleading term, should be the only name for the movement which between 1789 and 1848 engulfed the youth of Europe like a bush fire. The outcome of an impassioned enthusiasm, it began in England between 1790 and 1800, spread through France in the early nineteenth century, to Italy and Spain in the years 1820–30, and then, via

Portugal, Holland and Sweden, to Poland, Russia and Hungary. The programme of the movement may perhaps be summed up in the words of the Spaniard Jose Larra: 'Freedom, for literature as for the arts, for industry, for commerce, and for conscience; that is our motto and that of our epoch!' And by 'freedom' was meant liberation from impediments to the imagination, the expression of feeling, and love, from the trammels of classicist forms and academic dictatorships, from spiritual curbs, and from the fetters imposed from within and without.

A high percentage of French, Polish, Hungarian and Italian Romantic achievement was the work of spiritual *émigrés* subjected to a society which, with harsh and autocratic disregard for the individual, categorically demanded adjustment and subjugation to its standards. Today French, American, and Russian youth, as well as a larger group of intellectuals who felt constricted by mass society, are strongly attracted to this European Romanticism of 1800–48 because of its affinity to their own social situation.

Out of the frustrations suffered by German and French Romantics grew European socialism, Marx and Engels, and the radical criticism of Christianity – widespread and complex phenomena, the effects of which have lasted well beyond the nineteenth century. For that reason it will be useful first to turn to a secondary theatre of operations, Italy, where the great battle of spirit, mind, and intellect took place, sometimes in apparently anomalous forms.

Around 1800 Italian thought was characterised by a deep resignation. Vincenzo Russo reflected the outlook of the majority of his compatriots when, in 1799, he wrote: 'In Europe the Swiss alone qualify for freedom.' Nevertheless the Spanish revolt against Napoleon, documented in the songs of Gabriel Garcia y Tessara and Juan de Arriaza y Superviela, inspired the politically Romantic lyrics of Mameli and Mercantini and between 1821 and 1848 every Italian city of any importance had its native poets chanting nationalist verses against the Austrians. Florence had Niccolini, Genoa had Mameli, Naples was the home of Poerio, Venice of Carrer, Brescia was represented by Scalvini, Modena by Giannone, and Parma by Sanvitale.

The circumstances of these Italian poets were for the most part precarious. Many lived in exile. Others withdrew into a world of their own. Only very few, like d'Azeglio and Gioberti, managed to attain any real social standing. Chateaubriand, Lamartine and Victor Hugo in France, or Saavedra and Martinez in Spain, enjoyed positions of notable influence both socially and as diplomats, and were the forerunners of Claudel, Saint-John Perse and others.

There was at this period a general fashion for pessimism, melancholia, drug-taking, as a means of escape and for the composition of morbid lays and also an increase in the suicide rate among poets. Those who survived returned later, at the age of sixty, to the point they had left at twenty, facing the void of Europe where the old gods had died and where the old order, although decayed, was still clinging obstinately to its prerogatives.

In Italy and in Europe as a whole the writings and personal papers of the many poets who died so young, echo the pain, the indignation and sorrow which this 'lost generation' felt. Small wonder that suicide and madness took so large a toll!

'Life is bitter, filled with mortal nausea and full of a tedium in which nothingness gapes before man', wrote Leopardi. Equally indicative of the mouldering of the mighty Baroque establishment in the days when Austrian, French, and Papal troops were at pains to uphold the Old Order in Italy, was the refrain of Manuel de Cabanyes: 'What is ignorant man, poised midway between the infinite and nothingness? All things are born in nothingness and aim for the infinite.' The melancholy that enveloped Italian emigrants like Pellegrino Rossi, Rossetti, Sanvitale, the two Ruffini, Scalvini and Gioberti was shared by their Polish, Magyar, and Spanish colleagues.

'A cell was my cradle, the desert was my school,' sang Saavedra. Distress and despair spring from the pages written by political prisoners like Michelangelo Castelli, Luigi Pastro, and Confalioniere. Long before Dostoevsky's *The House of the Dead* Giorgio Pallavicion Trivulzio, Sigismondo di Castromediano, and the Frenchman Alexandre Andryane set their experiences in that framework, relegating Europe to the status of a dungeon and a penitentiary. The writings of Giuseppe Montanelli, Felice Orsini, Angelo Frignani, Luigi Martini and Carlo Bini furnish a small catalogue of prison memoirs. The title of Vincenzo Maisner's book, *From Venice to Theresienstadt*, bore significantly the name of the place where the hopes of so many prisoners of the Third Reich were to find their burial.

'Abandon hope, all ye who enter here.' Dante's inscription over the gates of hell indicates the bitter experience of European Romanticism, as well as of Italian thought and literature – the bitterness of *scender le scale d'altrui*, the ascent of unfamiliar stairs to beg for bread and shelter, the endurance of hope extinguished and trodden underfoot.

From this seed of bitterness sprang both national mysticism and revolutionary myth. Was not one's country, *la patrie, patria* – Italy, Poland, or any other – the pure maiden violated by strangers yet eternally virginal, and now rising up in the dawn of a new age? Breast bared, climbing the barricades: that was how Delacroix depicted Marianne. Was not one's country the 'small immortal maiden, Hope' of whom Charles Peguy, son of an Orléans basket-maker, sang on the eve of the First World War? Songs of dying and resurgent hope resound through Spanish, Portuguese and Italian Romanticism. Religious embers glowed in the hearts of exiles each of whom saw their particular nations in a Messianic guise, as Christ bearing the Cross. It was in the grip of this politico-religious emotion that Poland's poetic revolutionaries, gathered in Paris, composed their works.

In Italy Romantic religiosity and political Romanticism merged in Gioberti's singular vision of the Pope as standard-bearer of the Italian federation, fraternal arbiter, patron of freedom and culture and assuming the duties of that chivalric order of the Holy Ghost whose *duce* centuries earlier Cola di Rienzo had fancied himself to be. Mazzini's watchword,

'God and the people', became for Fabbri, Mameli, d'Azeglio, Gioberti, and Cattaneo that of the Risorgimento and was also adopted by Italian atheists.

Once around 1830 and again around 1848 it seemed that the split among European youth would be healed. Romanticism, 'liberalism', 'socialism', revolutionary fervour, and Catholic Reform met briefly on common ground, then went their separate ways. On both occasions revolt and capitulation, hope, anger, and disillusionment followed each other in quick succession.

In France a young generation sympathetic to monarchic principles but indignant at the reactionary, uninspired character of government under Louis XVIII and Charles X, turned its back on the Bourbons and entertained liberal and subsequently sociality, ideas. Chateaubriand inwardly parted company with the regime in 1824 and was followed by Victor Hugo. Balzac, himself a royalist, sketched the situation of *Jeune France* in 1830 when he wrote much later, 'These youngsters, feeling their way, uncertain about everything, blind and clairvoyant at the same time, were regarded as completely negligible by greybeards jealously preoccupied with keeping the reins of state between their own weak fingers. Had they retired, the Monarchy could have been saved by this French youth on which the old doctrinaires, these émigrés of the Restoration, today still expend their scorn.' How many more times in the nineteenth and twentieth centuries would a young generation be sacrificed and consumed by its elders?

Saturn devouring his sons. Between 1819 and 1823 Goya painted this titanic and dreadful theme, intrinsic to European reaction, on the dining-room wall of his country house. Victorian criticism accurately assessed its revolutionary content and horrifying disclosure when this fresco, transferred to canvas, was shown with his other *pinturas negras* at the Paris World Exhibition of 1878. Philips Gilbert Hamerton said that the collection:

> proved how Goya's mind grovelled in a hideous inferno of its own, a disgusting region, horrible without sublimity, shapeless as chaos, foul in colour and 'forlorn of light', peopled by the vilest abortions that ever came from the brain of a sinner. He surrounded himself, I say, with these abominations, finding in them I know not what devilish satisfaction, and rejoicing, in a manner altogether incomprehensible to us, in the audacities of an art in perfect keeping with its revolting subjects. . . . Of all these things the most horrible is the *Saturn*. He is devouring one of his children with the ferocity of a famished wolf, and not a detail of the disgusting feast is spared you. The figure is a real inspiration, original as it is terrific . . .

This demonstrates – and let the example serve as model for its predecessors and its successors, down to our own day – how traditional, reactionary art criticism, through its opposition to the disclosure of the infernos that exist in human society, can be essentially political. What Goya had dared to do was to expose contemporary cannibalism performed in the name of a monstrous God. *Two Men Fighting with Clubs* portrayed a struggle between men who, though sinking into a morass, are intent upon fighting one another to the bitter end. This was his interpretation of civil war which from that time on lay below the surface in all Europe's national wars, transforming them into the type where 'France stands on both sides', as Victor Hugo in 1871 had imploringly reminded friends and foes of the Commune. In 1824 Goya emigrated from the Spain of Ferdinand VII, with its reign of terror and 'Rehabilitation Tribunal', to Bordeaux.

Réponds-moi, Dieu cruel! This cry to God to justify Himself was raised by both Hugo and Lamartine. The latter demanded that He should rouse himself from His too prolonged passivity and, altering a heavenly order which had lost its power to appeal to man, act afresh. The frequently cited and highly suspect titanic qualities of these Romantic poets were symbolic of that young generation, and had their origin in the 'atrocious situation' and 'despairing hopelessness' to which Musset, Chateaubriand, Dumas and Vigny testified on the eve of the July Revolution.

Hope and hopelessness alternated in the decades before 1848. Of the total 1824 edition of fifty-six thousand copies of Paris newspapers no less than forty-one thousand expressed Oppositional views. In 1829 the adherents of Saint-Simon constituted themselves into a sort of church of the new era. In 1830 Romanticism conquered Paris in the shape of Hugo's *Hernani*. In 1831 Mazzini formulated at Marseille the programme of Young Italy. The new decade brought with it new names of poets who wanted to pass on the divine spark from God to man – Tennyson and Browning in England, Guerrazzi and Espronceda in Spain, Herculano in Portugal. In 1834 constitutional monarchy was proclaimed by royal statue in Spain. In 1836 the Septemberists introduced liberal rule in Portugal. But England's Reform Bill of 1832 with its limited franchise was a great disappointment, and the Oxford Movement, founded in 1833, combined liberal and reactionary traits to produce an ecclesiastical renaissance confined to academic circles and out of touch with the history, mass movements, and revolutions of its century.

1831 was the year of Towianski's emigration to Paris, where he evolved his belief that Poland in exile must suffer so that historic Poland might be resurrected and lay its fortunes in the hands of God. Poland as the Messiah of nations was a concept that Krasinski, inspired by Michelet, developed in his poem *The Dawn of the Third Day*. What Hölderlin, Schelling, and Schlegel had descried for the Germans, Krasinski with similar emotion foresaw for Poland – the coming, after the First Kingdom of the Old Testament and the Second Kingdom of the New Testament, of the Third Kingdom of the Holy Ghost, of freedom, of the awakening of peoples, of the awakening of the Slavs. In his poem *The Spirit of the Steppe*, Bohdan Zaleski, also making his way to France and Switzerland in 1831, saw the destinies of Poland and the Ukraine interwoven with that of the world.

During these years Greek, Serb, Croat, Rumanian, Polish, and Russian poets and writers blended national mysticism, Romanticism, political religiosity and Messianic beliefs into a compound which has been found since the Second World War in Africa and Asia. Under the spur of German and French Romanticism, dormant powers were mobilised in eastern and central Europe, forces deriving from the legacies of Bogomil and Hussite heresies and elements of religious movements suppressed for centuries in the Byzantine, Ottoman, Papal, Tsarist, and Holy Roman Empire's dominions.

National Messianism took root in the very old impulse of religious non-conformism. In the awakening peoples 'brothers' rose against 'fathers'. Around 1830 the notion took firm hold that the empires of Tsar, Sultan, Emperor, and Pope would soon tumble. Moses Hess introduced this doctrine into early Marxism, and Karl Postel, alias Charles Sealsfield, fleeing from Moravia and the Roman Church, first took this conviction with him to America and then returned with it to Switzerland. The poet Lenau was one of the earliest to see matters in their historic context – a chain of torch-bearers, from the Albigenses and Waldensians onward via John Huss, the Anabaptists and Thomas Munzer, carrying the light of a new day and fresh faith through a night of onslaught, repression, and eclipse.

The Austrians shot Constantine Rhigas, the Greek, at Belgrade but nothing could prevent the poets of freedom, revolt and revolution and with them the steady rebirth of their peoples, through religious and cultural revival, for emerging everywhere between 1830 and 1848.

There were the Poles – Towianski, Krasinski, Slowacki, Mickiewicz, Goszczynski, Norwid, Dzialyski, Kraszewski. On the heels of the Poles there followed Uniate Ukrainians, Slovaks, Croats, Irish, Flemings, Walloons and Italians, all trying to extract elements of change from Roman Catholicism in a new age. This was why the Poles in particular observed the stirrings in France that surrounded Lamennais in 1830 and the religious uprising in 1848 with such deep sympathy and felt implicated in their collapse.

Petar Preradovic, Croat grandfather of the Austrian poetess Paula von Preradovic, invoked the mission of the Slavs to teach mankind its brother-hood. Russian Messianism followed the call after its own fashion. The Serbs, Vuk Karadzic, Branko Radicevic and the rest, sundered from those Croats who adhered to the Roman Catholic culture of Preradovic, Stanco Vraz and Ivan Mazuranic, founded their first national cultural centres in exile at Budapest and Vienna. The Czechs Kollar and Nebscki, the Hungarians Petofi, Varosmarty and Arany, the Transylbanian Alexandrescu and his supporters (who fled to South America after the failure of 1848 and enlisted among the rebel troops of Jose Paez, Bernando O'Higgins, and Simon Bolivar) all illustrate the two-fold fate of the Romantic and post-Romantic generation between 1830 and 1848. On the one hand there was an inner emigration through which cultural research and scholarship, language and poetry established islands of national resistance and contributed the growth of national consciousness. On the other hand was an outer emigration, the paths of which led to the Americas and the assembly points of other emigrants – London, Brussels, Geneva, Paris.

'THE FRENCH FAUST'; SAINT-SIMON

A chacun selon sa capacité, a chaque capacité selon ses oeuvres.

This was the motto of the followers of Saint-Simon, that philosopher, planner and pioneer of the large-scale industrial society, the advocate of humanity in an age of technocracy who, until he was overshadowed by Karl Marx, was perhaps the greatest symbol of the nineteenth century as a whole.

Saint-Simon was not only a source of influence to communism and the father of Christian Socialism. He was, with his *Le Nouveau Christianisme* of great importance to both literary and political French Romanticism from 1830 to 1848. George Sand, Victor Hugo and Vigny all acknowledged their debt to him, and Hugo's famous aphorism, 'Romanticism and socialism are the same' referred to the Saint-Simonian interpretation of socialism.

Saint-Simon came from Picardy, the home of so many prophets and leaders. A peer of France and grandee of Spain, Claude-Henri de Rouvroy, Comte de Saint-Simon (1760–1825) spent a large part of his fortune assisting established and up-and-coming men in the fields of science and learning – men like Monge, Lagrange and Arago – while for years on end he led a poverty-stricken existence as a clerk and copyist. His favourite phrase was: 'The Golden Age lies in the future, not in the past.' His desire was to become a Charlemagne in the realm of the intellect; to bring to fruition the hopes of the eighteenth century for the progress of mankind with an improved distribution of food and other necessities in a united world based on world peace (achieved through the organisation of labour), a religious revival, international collaboration and economic coordination. Foreseeing the struggle of European nations for hegemony he pleaded for the early constitution of a Council of Europe. He died a pauper, after much suffering, although this destination and lingering illness was preceded by a brilliant career.

When hardly out of his teens, Saint-Simon had taken part as an officer in the American War of Independence. He was present at the battle of Yorktown and remained in the United States from 1779 to 1793, becoming a member of the Society of Cincinnatti whose president was George Washington. Back in France, he became a colonel at twenty-two but relinquished military life to devote himself to social and political studies. At the outbreak of the French Revolution he abandoned personal rank and title. His relatives emigrated. An entry in the minutes of the Municipal Council of Peronne for 20 September 1793 recorded that 'Citizen Claude-Henri Saint-Simon, *ci-devant* aristocrat, domiciled in this city, has appeared before the Council and declared his wish to have the stain of his original sin (descent) removed by republican baptism.'

He adopted the name Claude-Henri Bonhomme and surrendered his officer's commission, his medals and his civil distinctions. For centuries Jacques Bonhomme had been the popular nickname for the French peasantry whose *jacqueries* shook the country from the ninth to the eighteenth centuries, although historians have until the second half of the twentieth century overlooked most of these uprisings.

During the Reign of Terror Saint-Simon was for eleven months (1793–4) a prisoner at Paris in the Luxembourg, from which few emerged except in the tumbril rolling towards the guillotine. He never spoke of his experiences there but in a dedicatory letter to his nephew Victor (published as preface to his *Nouvelle Encyclopedie*) he narrated how Charlemagne had appeared to him one night and foretold that he would become a first-rate philosopher.

The French Revolution's gaols were a cradle to the nineteenth century. Within their walls outstanding literary works, such as those by Madame Roland and André Chenier, were composed. In the Luxembourg from December 1793 to November 1794, Tom Paine wrote the second half of his *Age of Reason*. Perhaps he and Saint-Simon met and discussed the two revolutions, American and French, in which both had played a part. Paine was released a month before Saint-Simon, eight months after Danton and Desmoulins (the latter with Young's *Night Thoughts* under his arm) had entered.

Revolution and Romanticism, imprisonment, longing for liberation and the true beginning of a New Age – these summarise the nineteenth century, for all the great themes debated in the decade 1790–1800 were resumed in the letters of those members of practically every European nation who were incarcerated and executed between 1918 and 1945.

Intoxication with life followed the end of the Terror. In liberated Paris Saint-Simon delighted in his share of the joy of living and tried his hand as financier, property speculator and entrepreneur, but he did not forget his mission. He took an apartment close to the École Polytechnique (that magnificent creation of the Revolution) in order to maintain close contact with its teachers and pupils. The New Age was to belong to technology, industry and a working society, so he attended lectures himself, particularly those dealing with natural science, physics and mathematics, acted as patron to poor but gifted students and in 1801 enrolled in the École de Medicine. Life, the unity of all living things, fascinated him. In his *Lettres*, dedicated to the First Consul, Napoleon Bonaparte, he foresaw the new society as ruled by mathematicians, scientists, chemists, physiologists and artists. Even in later years he did not abandon the hope of becoming Napoleon's expert on society's reconstruction – that dream as old as Descartes, Leibniz and Plato.

In 1804 he returned to Paris from Switzerland impoverished and was forced to seek a post as copyist in the state pawnshop. From there on he wrote only at night. A 'good Samaritan' provided him with a home and paid the printing costs of his *Introduction into the Scientific Works of the Nineteenth Century*, published in 1808.

At fifty he described his life as a series of falls and foundered endeavours which, however, as experiments, had been essential. In his view life as a whole was an experiment whose purpose, preparation of a better future, was achieved through constant failures as well as success. In the nineteenth century artists, poets, philosophers, inventors and Utopians did, by suffering and hard work, achieve the future. To disregard their experiments with new experiences and new tasks would be to ignore the century's greatness and its human quality.

In 1812, eighteen years before the appearance of Comte's *Cours de philosophie active*, Saint-Simon enunciated this 'positive' philosophy. By 1813 he was near complete breakdown, penurious and ill, afraid of lapsing into insanity. Yet in October of the next year he published a pamphlet *On the Reorganization of European Society, of the Necessity for Means towards Gathering the Peoples of Europe into a Single Political Body*. It proposed a European league of nations, a Continental parliament, a common European system of education and a unified system of communications (roads and major canals, linking the Rhine, Main, and Danube, as well as rendering the Baltic countries accessible by a link of eastern European waterways with inland Europe).

His assistant, August Thierry, a fussy, prosaic and sentimental 'idealist', a bourgeois with the faint heart of a pedant, shrank back as his master evolved ever bolder ideas and, in December 1816, founded the periodical *L'Industrie* to win supporters for his work of reform. Saint-Simon's fate was to be betrayed, denounced and subjected to ridicule by both his young pupils and assistants: first Thierry, then Comte, who in 1817 at the age of nineteen had finished his mathematical studies at the École Polytechnique.

The second volume of *L'Industrie* contained the *Letters from Saint-Simon to an American* in which the United States was taken as a model for the European society of the future. By 1817 his plans for the social system were perfected. They anticipated in many respects the ideas of Henry Ford and Walther Rathenau.

'Politics is the science of production.' 'Everything for and by industry.' The new society was to be in the hands of industrialists, technocrats and bankers. A 'Dictatorship of Men of Parts' would displace rulers, aristocrats, soldiers and priests. With Comte in 1817, Saint-Simon began his criticism of Christian theology. He understood what every thinker, reformer humanist deserving of the name was to see: a fresh society and a fresh age postulated a fundamental criticism of Christianity, its sovereign authority, its theology and its premises.

In 1819 he founded, again with Comte, the short-lived periodical *La Politique*, and then *L'Organisateur*. In the first issue of the latter on November 1819 appeared his famous letter on the future of Europe. Prophesying civil war in France, Britain, Germany, Italy and Spain if internal mismanagement under the old establishment was to continue, he illustrated his conviction with a parable about drones which constitutes one of the most significant political manifestos of the nineteenth century. Should France lose in a single day the services of its three thousand leading scholars, artists and workers (fifty each of engineers, artists, etc.) the loss would be irreparable. Should

France lose in a single day the thirty thousand people regarded as the most important in the state, including the King's brother, the Dukes of Angoulême, Orléans, Bourbon and so on, the marshals, cardinals and so on, plus ten thousand individuals of private means, no political calamity would be sustained.

> We have so many civil servants equal in calibre to our ministers, so many priests just as qualified as our cardinals, archbishops, bishops, apostolic vicars, and canons . . .

> Ignorance, superstition, laziness, and the enjoyment of expensive pleasures are the dowry of the leaders of our society while its capable, thrifty and hard-working members are simply used as underlings and tools. In a word, it is at every turn the incompetent who are entrusted with overseeing the competent.

> It is the major miscreants who are appointed to punish the misdeeds of the minor sinners.

The prevailing social system was immoral because the dominant class, compounded of vanity, ignorance, superstition, incomprehension and extravagance, was criminal. 'Until today mankind has proceeded along the road to civilisation with its back turned on the future. Its gaze had been customarily turned to the past; the glances thrown towards the future have been rare and cursory. Now that slavery has been abolished, it is to this that mankind must primarily devote its attention.'

On the eve of the Congress of Vienna Saint-Simon advised that assembly of his plans for the reorganisation of European society. He had in mind the formation of a United Europe by stages. The first would be an Anglo-French Union, the second that Union's association with Germany. Hereditary monarchy and a European Parliament were to give Europe a stability capable of preventing its self-destruction through war, civil war, and economic throat-cutting.

He saw the men of the Restoration obsessed by fear of revolution, yet knew that this new revolution could be frustrated only by the reconstruction of society and a revival of religion. To his mind the current political order, was topsy-turvy, a rule by inferiors, idlers and mediocrities. The lesson was to restore the normal order of things, and the way to do this was 'to put secular power in the hands of outstanding industrialists and to remove all political power from the aristocrats and rich idlers.' 'The moment of crisis is at hand.' 'This crisis will eventually lead to the establishment of a genuinely global religion and allow all peoples to adopt a peaceful social order consistent with their individual character.' What mattered was 'no longer military victories of the old sort, but scientific and economic progress.' 'The time of illusions is definitely past. Nations calculate their interests today very cold-bloodedly.'

In 1823 the publication of his *Industrialists' Catechism* began. The third number of the series appeared a year later under the title *Positive Polity* 'by August Comte, pupil of Saint-Simon'. Comte analysed the greatest impediment to society's progress as lying in the spread of the revolutionary spirit. His remedy was a scientifically positive social order and he pleaded for a dictatorship of industrialists.

Here was the beginning of a type of fascism. Saint-Simon became painfully aware of the disparity between his ideas and those of his pupil, Comte, and reproached him with disregard for society's religious foundations. But the fundamental reason for their estrangement lay in the fact that Comte was in spirit already a nineteenth-century savage, brutal, thirsting for success and indifferent to individual rights, whereas Saint-Simon never lost that respect for the individual which came as a matter of course to eighteenth-century thinkers. Positivism plundered intellectual property during the nineteenth century, just as a certain form of *Realpolitik* was to prove indifferent to the rights of 'small' or 'foreign' nations. Saint-Simon's work was to Comte simply 'material' which he exploited. For the manipulators of *Realpolitik* peoples were simply 'human material'.

This was precisely what Saint-Simon foresaw and his aim was to counteract this 'materialism'. The first part of his final publication, *The New Christianity*, appeared in April 1825 a few weeks before his death. The title was taken from an aphorism of Saint-Martin: 'God effects his work through centuries and He is getting ready a new Christianity.' Saint-Simon felt himself to be the prophet of this new Christianity, a universal religion which would unify all men in fraternity, pay special heed to the poor, the wretched and the exploited, and be in harmony with science and the age.

He well knew himself to be dying. He passed away on 19 May 1825, surrounded by his friends who listened attentively to his last words: 'Religion cannot disappear from the world, it can only be transmuted' and 'My whole life is contained in one idea: to enable all men to develop their capacities freely.'

THE SAINT-SIMONIANS

Immediately after Saint-Simon's death a group of his friends and disciples met to discuss the continuation of his works. The periodical, *Le Producteur, Journal de l'Industrie, des Sciénces et des Arts* was founded in 1825; a group of young men under the leadership of Barthélémy. Prosper Enfantin and Saint-Armand Bazard, industrialists, civil servants and many others of similar type, gave up their careers to serve the movement; schools and associations were founded to continue his work.

In 1831 the periodical *Le Globe* was acquired by the group. The words *Journal de la Doctrine de Saint-Simon* were appended to the title, and his own motto, *De chacun selon sa capacité, à chaque capacité selon ses oeuvres* was also added. The movement in the first place propagated the public works, road-building and the waterways communications programme and proposed to

Louis-Philippe the transformation of the army into an industrial organisation and training-school for the masses.

A flood of slander and denunciation engulfed the Saint-Simonians. The 'people' thought them ridiculous, outrageous, presumptuous, crazy and dangerous. The government viewed then as anarchists. Enfantin and Michel Chevalier were sentenced for 'illegal association', to a year's imprisonment at Saint-Pelagie (where Saint-Simon had lain in the days of the Terror). Their followers scattered, went as missionaries to Marseille, Toulon, Lyon and Rouen, became ordinary workmen or craftsmen, and tried thus to bring Saint-Simonian ideas nearer to common understanding. They continued none the less to be attacked and abused.

Around 1300 the persecuted Franciscan Fraticelli had fled to Africa, the Near East and Russia. The Saint-Simonians went to Turkey, Egypt and North and South America. It was they who drew up schemes for the Suez and Panama Canals. Ferdinand de Lesseps put into effect concepts conceived in prison by Enfantin, and it was the latter who in 1839, as a member of the Scientific Commission for the development of Algeria, soberly and prophetically analysed the future, the potentialities and the eventual self-dissolution of colonialism. In France Saint-Simonians were active as pioneers in industry, banking and railway expansion, set up credit institutions to help the small tradesman and prepared plans (used later by Haussmann) for a reconstruction of Paris.

The fascination of early Saint-Simonianism lies in its fusion of 'industry' and Messianism. 'Mankind is a collective organisation which matures over generations like the individual does over years. Its development is an upward one.' 'Comprehension of the law of human development includes tradition and prophecy. All social conditions of the past are coloured and those of the future revealed thereby.'

History, according to the Saint-Simonian philosophy, proceeded by means of alternating epochs, first an organic (religious, constructive) one and then a critical (irreligious) one. 'Progress in the power of moral education can . . . be regarded as the most important manifestation of the progress of freedom, which consists above all in loving and wanting what must be done.' 'Mankind's future is religious and its religion will be greater and mightier than any in the past. Its dogma will be a synthesis of all human creativeness and artistry: social and political institutions will, in an overall perspective, constitute a religious foundation.'

'*We are not a sect.*' 'The word "sect" implies an opinion which detaches itself, which we are not. Rather we are *approaching* a territory where no general, genuine and deep state of belief exists and we aspire to fill this gap.' The teaching of Saint-Simon had the power 'to unify all sentiments, all ideas and all interests that are today divergent because it is a doctrine of general application and because it is a religion.'

FOURIER

Charles Fourier (1772–1837) was the son of a prosperous Besançon tradesman who hated trade and eked out a living as an insignificant clerk. He is
interesting for his plan to establish small prototypes of a new society, a
phalanstery, in which he envisaged about eighteen hundred people of all
types and classes living together in 'phalanxes'. The links between them and
their fellow communities would be formed by industrial forces which would
carry out major projects of waterway construction, soil improvement, road
building, desert irrigation and afforestation.

Fourier further recognised that a new social order demanded a fresh
sexual morality and fresh forms of sexual association. He was against the
'prison' of marriage, and in many ways anticipated feminism, believing that
the freedom of women and social progress would develop together. He was
convinced that one of the reasons for the domination of Europe by men was
the fact that its rulers had never appreciated the value of women. He even
went so far as to say: 'To destroy the mastery of men there ought to exist for a
century a third sex, both male and female, but stronger than the male.'
The notion has gnostic and cabbalistic elements. German Romanticism
imagined a hermaphroditic personality as a primal Adam; Fourier projected
a vision of it into the future. This and his 'gospel of women' had a marked
influence on the Romantic and early socialist French feminist movement.

Fourierism continued to exist in Paris and other French cities even at the
beginning of the twentieth century. The spirit of its founder was a rich
source of inspiration to French socialism and contributed substantially to its
immunisation against Marxism. Jaurès, the great leader of French socialism
and champion of its concepts of peace, was also a disciple of Fourier. Another
was Godin, who founded a *familistère* at Guise as a sort of building and
co-operative society. Other followers founded phalanxes in the United
States in the form of quasi-socialistic settlements with sixteen hundred
members and five thousand acres of land each. In our own day Fourier's
theories are to some extent exemplified in the Israeli kibbutz and model
settlements in Africa and South America.

Another distinguishing trait of Fourier's thought became equally influential
– a harsh anti-Semitism which has affected social reformers in all European
countries. He attacked the 'despotism of commerce, this true satrap of the
civilised world' and enumerated thirty-six kinds of bankruptcy as methods of
practising fraud. 'Judas Iscariot arrives in France with 100,000 Francs
capital, earned in his first bankruptcy. . . . And people shout, so that its a
pleasure to hear, "Long live competition, long live the Jews, long live
philosophy and fraternity".' But the Jew, he continued, uses this craze for
tolerance to his own ends and co-operates only with other Jews. They,
'vagabonds without allegiance', are 'the secret foe of all nations'.

Friederich Engels translated these hypotheses about trade, bankruptcy
and Semitism. Published in the *Deutsche Bürgerbuch für 1846* at Mannheim,

they infected German *völkisch* ideology. Gottfried Feder, author of the first and only National Socialist party manifesto, and other early Nazi Utopians at Munich after 1918 adopted this line of Fourierist tradition – the worst in a rich, variegated, and important inheritance.

TROUBLED FRANCE

There were more than a dozen minor prophets and advocates of early socialism and political Utopianism living in Paris before and around the year 1848, and historically these figures, men such as Considérant and Becquer, have a threefold importance. In the first place they reorientated man's imagination. For thousands of years man had been preoccupied with the concept of heaven and hell, and the individual's relation to it. Man was now told to regard mankind's experiment to anticipating and planning the future. Secondly these Utopians had a considerable effect on French Romantic writers and thinkers. Thirdly, they made their mark, in France in the first instance, on the feminist and incipient working-class movements.

Rapid progress in industrialisation and the resultant poverty, coupled with the premonition that the Revolution had been merely the prelude to further unrest – these were some of the main causes of this change in attitude. There was a sense of standing 'on the edge of a volcano'. *Le Globe* was founded in 1824 by Paul Dubois and Pierre Leroux to associate current literature with liberal and Romanticist ideas. Romanticism was viewed as the continuation of the Revolution in literature and the arts. A significant swing was taking place among leading writers, who were veering from royalist ideas and political service to the Restoration regime to liberalism, socialism and a decisive alliance with the 'New Century' (a favourite title for periodicals) and 'the people'. Three important manifestoes of 1827–8 demonstrate this change: Sainte-Beuve's *Tableau historique et critique*, Emile Duchamps' introduction to his *Études françaises et étrangères* and Victor Hugo's preface to *Cromwell* with its declaration that 'Romanticism is literature's liberalism.'

In 1826 twenty million Frenchmen out of a total population of thirty-one million were still peasants. In 1839 fifteen out of twenty-five million adults could neither read nor write. The Bourbons sought to retard education of the masses. A panic fear of 'universities' led to the demand for their closure. Book production, it was also proposed, should be severely curtailed.

The introduction of the steam engine, railways and industry into French cities initially brought nothing but a deterioration of conditions. Social misery, as seen through the eyes of Victor Hugo and his young fellow-authors, derived from the following facts:

Of twenty thousand births in Paris in 1817 no less than ten thousand were illegitimate. In the same year there were registered seven thousand eight hundred abandoned infants. In 1832 only one-third of the French population ate meat. Between 1823 and 1848 ten years of comparative prosperity were followed by fifteen years of severe economic crisis. The working day, for both sexes and all age groups, lasted fourteen to fifteen hours. The approaches to factory sites were long; work began at five in the morning and ended at eight or nine at night; wages were forty-five centimes per day for a child between eight and fifteen, seventy-five centimes for one between thirteen and sixteen, two francs for a man, and one franc for a woman. The plants were dirty, cramped, unhygienic, anticipating the monumental ugliness of the nineteenth century. (In France, 'beauty' has always represented a political and social struggle as well as an aesthetic standard.) Tuberculosis, rheumatism, angina and all the diseases of poverty were a ruling factor. So were drunkenness and prostitution. The average age of workers was twenty-one, with the mass grave not far away. A report on the prevailing conditions, *De la misère des ouvriers*, was published in 1832 by Bigot de la Morogue, an aristocrat shaken to the depths of his being by what he had learned.

In 1833 France had one million, one hundred and twenty thousand paupers. Seven years later the Academy of Sciences (always somewhat behind developments) arranged an open competition on the theme 'Wherein does indigence consist? What are its hallmarks in various countries? What are its causes?' The people knew its indigence and the causes well enough and found its spokesmen. Since the Revolution a new readership had evolved for literature with a cause to plead – apprentices, soldiers, manual workers' women who shared in the purchase of Lamennais' writings and subscribed to *l'Avenir*.

Between 1789 and 1800 eight hundred newspapers began and ceased publication. By 1824 only thirteen newspapers were left in Paris: seven for the Government, six belonging to the Opposition. Their overall subscribers numbered five thousand six hundred. The censorship regulations had been strict before, but in 1827 a *loi de justice et d'amour* was imposed which was positively Baroque in the pompous paternalism of the language it used to cloak its harshly suppressive purpose. It was Press law, in fact, comparable to the sort that exists in Spain and Portugal today.

Poetry, classicist drama, loftily stylised expressions of thought and novels modelled on the rules of late antiquity or mediaeval verse epics had flourished under the old aristocratic regime. Now came the age of prose: the popular Press, the novel of contemporary life, the popular ballad, the romantic popular play, the pamphlet, melodrama and pantomime. The triumphal progress of vaudeville – comedy at the plebeian level – was a presage of the mass victory of the cinema. On 1 July 1836 the *Presse* appeared, the first newspaper designed for a large-scale readership, though soon to be rivalled by *Siècle*. Simultaneously the days of the highly-paid *feuilleton* began, directed at that section of the middle class which either had no interest in politics or was not allowed any. The *Presse* attracted George Sand, Madame d'Agoult and even Gérard de Nerval as contributors. Balzac observed that authors were now engaged in the production of consumer goods and no longer of works of art. The protest against the degradation of standards raised by certain poets was passionate but lonely.

On 4 January 1821 Stendhal noted that, 'It is essential that imagination should get to know the iron laws of reality.' More than three years earlier he himself had already begun methodically to cull stories from newspapers for use in subsequent works. For the first time incidents of the contemporary social scene became the novelist's raw material. Hitherto, heroes had been stately figures from an alien past. For the second edition of *Rome, Florence and Naples* in 1818, Stendhal planned to announce that 'the anecdotes I have entered in my journal are true as regards myself and my friends and the circumstances have been depicted with the most religious accuracy.'

The last phrase is revealing. A new religiosity and a new depth of emotion had taken hold of people, an emotion caused by awareness of the harsh reality of life as it was now being lived. The prophets of this reality were writers. They, as Victor Hugo proclaimed in the preface to *Odes et Ballades*, 'must move ahead of the people like a beacon. That is the mission of a genius. The Lord's elect are the sentinels whom He has left on the towers of Jerusalem; they shall fall silent neither by day nor by night.'

Jouffroy, in a famous essay of 1825, affirmed his faith in this younger generation. 'The hope of the new age rests on their shoulders. . . . They are the chosen apostles and in their hands lies the salvation of the world.' Stendhal commented that 'there is nothing in former decades for this generation to adopt, but everything for it to create anew'. Balzac adopted Hugo's view that:

> today the poet has taken the place of the priest. He plucks the light from the altar and brings it to the midst of the peoples. . . . It is *he* who consoles, damns, prays, prophesies. *His* voice not merely rings down a cathedral nave, but echoes from one end of the earth to the other. Mankind becomes his flock, hears his works, and ponders them. . . . The Pope over this terrible and majestic authority is no longer dependent on either kings or great ones of this earth, but has his mission from God.

Lamartine, in *Destinées de la poésie*, pronounced that 'Poetry has a new destiny to fulfil. . . . It must become one with the people and speak with their voice. . . . This is the kind of poetry which must be produced; the age demands it and the people crave for it.' The mystic union between St Francis and poverty – source of Franciscan verse and painting – was transformed here into a mystic union between 'people' and 'poetry' consecrated by the writer as spokesman for the Holy Ghost and the future of mankind.

The social, politically engaged and prophetic poetry of Paris and France between 1830 and 1850 anticipated what Mayakovsky and Bertolt Brecht, on the one hand, and 'people's democratic' poets in China and other Communist countries, on the other, were later, though at very different levels of excellence, to produce.

LAMARTINE

Alphonse de Lamartine (1790–1869), a man of aristocratic birth, was recognised from 1830 onwards as the mentor of the workers' poets, the champion of freedom and the spokesman of protest. Like Goethe, Shelley and Byron, he had searched for the reason for pain and suffering, calling in vain on God to provide the answer: 'Answer me, cruel God!' (*Méditations poétiques.*) Never receiving an answer, he had turned to Newton, nature, history and the Orient in the attempt to formulate his own.

The search for the answer to the questions besetting man at that time frequently took poets towards the East, but Lamartine himself was disappointed in his quest, although the voyage he made in 1832 was a decisive turning point in his life, transforming the previously narcissistic, egocentric poet into the advocate of the gospel of fraternity, the politician, the writer whose duty lay towards his people. He felt that his experience of the East had given him a greater awareness of the world and man in general and deepened his sense of responsibility.

Under the influence of Saint-Simonism in 1831 he had published *La Politique rationelle* in which he advocated a 'new policy' which would include the abolition of privileges and capital punishment, the separation of Church and State, the introduction of universal franchise and the expansion of the educational system to the advantage of all classes. After his visit to the Orient his devotion to politics became a more integral part of his poetical works. But he was no enthusiast. He knew that the future would be dearly bought with afflictions, disappointments, setbacks.

It was at this period that Lamartine began his manifold studies of popular education and the history of the Revolution. His eight-volume *History of the Girondists*, completed in 1847, which praised the principles of the Revolution but decried its excesses, was read, as had been his intention by a wide section of the population. During a speech at a banquet in 1847 he had compared the Revolution to the frenzy for the Cross, maintaining, however, that reason had been its motivating force.

Lamartine in fact rendered France considerable service, by paving the way for the fall of Louis-Philippe. He stood sponsor to the first 1848 Revolution, struggled against the rising tide of nationalism, implored parties of the left and right to preserve moderation in their dealings with each other, and to try and effect some sort of reconciliation; but these very activities ultimately caused his political downfall.

Sundered from the Catholic Church and that political Catholicism which at this period began to achieve a series of terrible and questionable victories which were to culminate in the Dreyfus Affair, he had a vision of Christ, a social Christ, who would bring truth, justice, tolerance, love and freedom to the peoples of the earth. Beyond everything else he wanted to divert the power and sincerity of the political left into channels which might be fruitful to France, and although he constantly experienced bitter disappointment at the end of his life, he never in any way abused his opponents.

VIGNY

It was of Alfred de Vigny (1797–1863) that Sainte-Beuve coined the phrase *tour d'ivoire*, in spite of the fact that French poets did not in fact retreat from life into a world of their own. It was only later, when pessimism took a real hold over him, that Vigny immured himself in his poetry, away from the barbarism of the times.

Poet, soldier and once a Christian, Vigny did not believe, as did de Maistre, that war was the answer to the problems of the world. On the contrary in his *Servitude et Grandeur militaires* (1835) he expresses the opinion that it is simply butchery, and as such destructive of freedom and joy.

It was not only on the subject of war that Vigny challenged de Maistre and his philosophy. In *Cinq-Mars* and *Stello*, where many of his ideas on society are expressed, Vigny, countering de Maistre's belief that the French Revolution had slaughtered innocent nobility, maintained that that nobility had, in fact, been slaughtered by Richelieu.

For Vigny the spiritual leaders were not those men favoured by his class, profession and generation, but Ballanche, the Saint-Simonian, Buchez, and the Quaker, Chatterton, whom he extolled in his novel of that name as an apostle of Christian Socialism.

One of Vigny's most basic beliefs was that man is lonely as the poet is lonely, and as Christ was lonely when deserted by God in the Garden of Gethsemane. He also had great faith in the poets, including himself, as people apart from society:

> The pariahs of society are the poets, men with heart and soul who are both nobler and more deserving of honour than others. Authority always detests poets because it sees in them judges who condemn it in the eyes of posterity. Authority loves mediocrity; it sells well and cheaply. . . . I believe in myself because deep down in my heart I feel a secret strength, invisible and indefinable, very similar to a presentiment of the future and a disclosure of the mysterious causes of the present time. I want to stretch out my hand to all men, comrades in the misery of this world.

It is this compassion that kindles the poetic spark in him. Human beings, all of them, are poor devils caught up in uncertainty, hallucination, false hope and false fear.

One of Vigny's early productions, *Eloa*, dealt first of all with poor devils – Satan and Lucifer, the Fallen Angel of Light. This resurrection of Origen's ancient theme, the redemption of Hell, made an enormous impression on Vigny's contemporaries. The Angel of Pity is moved by Satan's plight. Eloa, a sort of feminine Christ, rises against God out of love for man. Vigny was simultaneously at work on *Satan sauvé*, a miracle-play. It remained a fragment, but in 1837 he returned to the same theme.

He was a slightly built man and frail in health, but drew on the strength of a passionate indignation. In his journal he set down a vision of mankind at Domesday sitting in judgement on God who has to defend himself for everything wrongly suffered by the innocent since the Creation. The death of Vigny's beloved mother and a series of severe personal disappointments had released his long pent-up anger against Christianity and the Divine Judge Jehovah, although superficially the inspiration for *Le Mont des Oliviers* could be traced to Jean Paul's *Dead Christ's Harangue*. The situation of Christ in the Garden of Gethsemane was, to him, the quintessential pattern of man's situation in the world where, deserted by God, he is entirely dependent on himself.

Le Mont des Oliviers was written in 1837. During the two following years Vigny's experience of the politically active British upper class confirmed his conviction that he should play a political role in his fight for mankind. For three years, after his election to the Academy in 1845, he fulfilled this determination, although always remaining an individualist who never forgot that man, from first to last, suffers infinite loneliness. His hope, in March 1848, was that France would be able 'to establish a wise republic, like the United States'. He wanted to see a democracy headed by an intellectual and moral *élite*. When France was swept into the throes of civil war, he withdrew from the arena and devoted himself to preaching the inner regeneration of the individual as a prerequisite to the education of the masses.

GEORGE SAND AND THE FEMINIST MOVEMENT

> *'Her works are indeed the echo of our century. She will continue to be loved when it is no more, this poor nineteenth century which we traduce . . . '*
>
> ERNEST RENAN

George Sand (1804–76) was the illegitimate daughter of a laundress and an officer who came of very distinguished family (her grandmother was Madame Dupin de Francueil, cousin of Louis XVI and daughter of the famous Marshal Maurice de Saxe), and the conflict between the proletarian and the aristocrat in her was of prime importance in her life.

George Sand was born Aurore Dupin de Francueil, became on her marriage Baroness Dudevant, and later still, George Sand (her pseudonym). She had an unusually forceful personality, reminiscent of that of some of the Byzantine empresses. Thanks to her background she was unaware of any feelings of class, associating as easily with aristocrats as with the proletariat. She spoke for the hopes of the Saint-Simonians and for the unhappy, misunderstood women who were revolting against the bonds of contemporary society. She was deeply influenced by Pierre Leroux, Lamennais and Michel de Bourges. She read every new publication of interest and incorporated the material it contained, putting her own gloss on it, into her novels and articles. Her love affairs (with de Musset, Chopin and others) were blended into her writings in the same way. The ten volumes of her *Histoire de ma vie* reflect the purpose already shown in her first and highly successful novel, *Indiana* (1832) – that of a woman of powerful intellect and passion coming to terms with the ideas and movements of the French nineteenth century.

In her search for religious and social example, an idea incarnate, she turned in the first place to Lamennais, who rebuffed her, then to Leroux and Ballanche. Leroux she enabled to establish a printing-house and a Saint-Simonian agricultural co-operative. Throughout her life she helped poverty-stricken poets, socialist Utopians, political persecutees and penurious men and women of the people. After the *coup d'état* of 2 December 1851 she intervened bravely with Napoleon III to save sick prisoners, delay deportations and reprieve four young condemned soldiers from the firing-squad. The hundred books or so that she wrote during forty years brought her much money which she spent freely on charity and other forms of aid.

From 1832–48 her struggle was devoted particularly to the defence of women. In 1848 the feminist movement was crushed, together with the popular movement, and thereafter 'the men' won all along the political line. Their ideologies, their nationalism, their imperialism, their fears and their hatreds dominated Europe's expansion and its internal and external conflicts down to 1950.

'Lord God, Thou has sunk deep chasms into the womb of the oceans. Lord God! The griefs in the hearts of the women of our time would fill those chasms ten times over!' This was the theme of a Saint-Simonian pamphlet. What was the actual situation of women? They were underpaid, unprotected in their working-places, subject to the moods and lusts of their employers, without right of association and excluded from many professions and trades. Piece-work at home was done at starvation rates and maternity conditions were wretched. The struggle for the implementation of human rights (interpreted by nineteenth-century bourgeois democracy as the rights of propertied male citizens) really began with proclamation of the rights of women by Olympe de Gouges in 1792. After her execution, her work was continued by a few courageous women members of the aristocracy. Next Saint-Simon announced the great role allotted to womanhood in the peaceful society of the future, with Barrault following in his footsteps: 'Who, if not woman, has won battles for peace and love in the barbarous eras daubed with blood and tears?' Extreme Saint-Simonians adopted the cult of the 'Great Mother'. In March 1833 a party of them embarked at Marseille in the *Clorinde* to sail for the Orient in search of the messianic Great Mother, liberator of the peoples. As they cast off, they sang a hymn by Félicien David, *Compagnons de la Femme*, while from the quay there rang out a ballad by Vinçard: '*Chers Compagnons, précipitez vos pas, Le Peuple souffre et la Mère est là-bas.*'

A sharp contrast to these zealous male raptures is provided by the deeply felt but sober efforts on the part of women. In her *Ouvriers de Lyon* (1831), Delphine Gay appealed to liberal capitalists faced with a revolt against penury in that city: 'For egotism's sake, give bread today and work tomorrow to the toiling hand.' 'How badly, alas, are the people's needs understood in this century of big words and small minds!' She evoked a vivid picture of the babblers and phrasemongers of bourgeois democracy who, in the eyes of the revolutionaries, twice bought and sold France (in 1848 and 1871) and eventually were to drive their own and other countries into fierce rivalry and the First World War.

Womenfolk, the people, peace, freedom and genuine democracy. In the early years of the 1830s pioneers in the struggle for women's liberation appreciated very clearly the links between these points of reference. Women founded their own papers, where thoughtful contributions championed the economic, political and social equality of the female sex: *Appel à la femme* (1832), *Femme de l'Avenir, Femme Nouvelle, Tribune des Femmes, Journal des Femmes* (1833–6), *Citateur feminia* (1835), *Conseilleur des Femmes* (1833–4). There was also the *Carnet du Théogynodémophile* (1833), the final word in this title being a romantic verbal construction comprising a complete programme – friend of God, women and the people.

Supported by the Saint-Simonians, by Fourier (women must be freed from their social hell and man's selfishness), and by Cabet (women as the daughters of God will regenerate the universe), Frenchwomen of all classes fought for better female education and equality of rights between marriage partners.

One outstanding figure in this movement was Flora Tristan. She worked tirelessly for the emancipation of women and the working class as a whole during a life rich in experience of poverty, persecution, illness and misery. In her *Walks in London* she described the wretchedness of the slums. In her posthumously published *Emancipation of Women* (1845) she proclaimed her conviction that the education of women was essential to an advance in family standards and the political maturity of the nation. In her novel *Méphis* she declared it to be the destiny of woman to act as mediator between God and man.

The large and successful band of opponents to female emancipation (in Germany they were legion!) was led by men like Guizot (who objected to women's votes because 'Providence has apportioned to womanhood a domestic existence'), Louis Reybaud and Gavarni. Feminists were caricatured by Daumier. In *The Woman of Thirty* Balzac opined that 'to emancipate women means their ruin'. On the other hand Lamartine, Victor Hugo and Musset supported the cause.

George Sand was the movement's great patroness though she was well aware of its wider social implications. 'As long as official society constitutes a caste, so long will it give rise within itself to secret societies' (*Compagnon*, 1840). She demanded the right of all to work, to form trade associations, to set up agricultural co-operatives. It was this side of her activities in particular which gave her fame among Russian progressives and land reformers. Her influence, in any case, was felt by the European masses and élite alike. In England, Mary Ann Evans, adopting the *nom de plume* of George Eliot, chose the first half in her honour. She inspired a broad section of the Russian intelligentsia including Turgenev, Dostoevsky and Tolstoy. She was eagerly read in Poland, Bohemia, Rumania and even Germany.

For women, too, 1848 was the year of destiny and disappointment. In France they were refused the franchise and in July their clubs were already closed. Frenchwomen did not win the vote until 1945. One feature about a Western Europe where history continued to be made by men cannot be sufficiently emphasised. The increasing political neuroticism that developed in the second half of the nineteenth century was intimately connected with the disdain with which women were treated. Not infrequently its result was the strange 'revenge' involuntarily practised by ambitious women, like the wives of Napoleon III and Maximilian of Mexico, on their own husbands. At the start of the February Revolution of 1848, George Sand believed that she would see her hopes of fraternal communism come true, but realised only too quickly that extremists of both parties would destroy all hope for France. Like Victor Hugo and Lamartine, she fought for a reconciliation between the middle and working classes, and during the wave of denunciation, arrests and persecutions which followed, wrote: 'You may prosecute actions, but not convictions. Thought must remain free!' Finally, defeated at a political level, she retired to her château at Nohant, turning it into a place of refuge and consolation for the victims, and from that time on worked at the creation of a new class of individuals who would reconstruct the rotten institutions of the state, facing ridicule and slander all the time.

As a person and writer George Sand embodied the best and noblest traditions of political Romanticism and enlightenment in France, while always remaining aware of the difficulties facing the individual in an often hideous world. Her ability to understand life, her intellectual power and her range of sympathy earned for her, quite justifiably, the admiration of a younger generation and of such different personalities as Flaubert, Renan and Taine.

SATAN IN FRANCE: FIGHT OVER THE DEVIL

The mythologies of Old Europe had been first toppled and then restored by the French Revolution, but the generations in the years following 1789 were hungry for new myths and it was the task of the French poets and historians to search through Christianity, antiquity and Oriental philosophy to supply aptly contemporary motifs. From 1820 onwards there arose quite naturally a new myth. The people had never really accepted the defeat of Napoleon; peasants and workers continued to believe in him, never accepting the account of his death, and, like the late mediaeval German country folk expecting the resurrection of Frederick Barbarossa, awaited his return. It was because of their belief in this myth that they chose his nephew as Napoleon III.

In verse, legend and political pamphlet, Bonaparte came to be represented as the great rebel, genius, Messiah, quasi-religious and quasi-political Prometheus, saviour of the future and victor over death, distress and the Devil. And these were not superstitions which were confined to France. The notion permeated many countries in Europe, partially sustained by an even more deeply rooted idea which constantly recurred in French literature – belief in the devil's redemption.

The Devil had been both man's oldest enemy and his abettor in the struggle for, with, and against God. Should he return into the fullness of God, the history of the universe would become once and for all a history of mankind. This, the secret and yet manifest hope of nineteenth-century French Messianism, had for its background a gnosticism of the oldest kind, Origen's teaching, the hidden wish of the alchemists, and a subconscious awareness of the collaboration between opposing forces in the human psyche.

Satan as a cipher for the dynamism of history, progress and man's titanic, Promethean, Faustian powers arose in the first place as a defiant counterpart to the Devil, who, in the eyes of French Catholicism and royalism, could be seen in operation on all sides. De Maistre beheld the French Revolution as a 'work of the Devil'. Abbé Friard, in 1803, spoke of natural scientists as the lackeys of the Devil into whose hands they had delivered their country. Royalist and Catholic writings, from 1823 to 1890 and even beyond, pronounced the education dispensed by universities and secularist schools to be yet another extension of his influence. Indeed, he was responsible, among other things, for all the evils of modern times – republicanism, democracy, secular civilisation, the physical sciences and profane literature.

This deadly serious Devil had, however, to bear the brunt of competition from several dozen satanic manifestations in books, fashion and on the stage. It seemed on occasions almost as though these delicate, flighty and very fashionable little devils were going to spirit away everything that Europeans had for more than a millennium imagined and feared at the mention of the name of Satan. The Devil was to display a variety of faces during the nineteenth century and France was apparently to be an especially favoured arena for his sport.

There was a certain section of the French public which, excited by the bloody spectacles of the French Revolution and bewildered by the shocks of the Terror, wanted to relax, to be diverted, and yet not altogether to relinquish the fascination exercised by terror as such. Relegated to fiction it seemed harmless and acquired a certain attraction.

The waves of 'red terror' and 'white terror' were succeeded by a flood of 'black romances' imported from England. Crime and criminals were fêted. A craving for 'horror' seized the public mind, or at least a portion of it, and infected its imagination. To this was added a deep-seated anti-clericalism which took great pleasure in seeing the Devil in ecclesiastical garb, a monster in a cassock. M.G.Lewis' *The Monk* was published as early as 1797 in three French editions. The evil monk Ambrosio, who is not naturally evil but perverted by the unnatural ascericism of his calling, provided André Breton in his *Manifestos of Surrealism* with a major theme: 'Nothing is impossible for him who knows how really to venture his life.' This hero is fascinated by the spectacle of his own damnation.

A prominent feature of the chronicles of horror, the Devil and hell that played such a part in French Romanticism was the *école frénétique*. The phrase was coined by Nodier to distinguish sane and creative story-telling from extravagant ghastly tales. He coined the term on the lines of the English appellation 'satanic school'. Robert Southey, in the preface to *Vision of Judgment*, accused Byron of having established a 'satanic school' of writing which glorified religious rebellion and moral perversion, extolled arrogance and godlessness, and encouraged the practice of despair and progress along the road to nihilism. Nodier, an admirer of Byron, exempted him from his attacks – and himself became one of the pioneers of this movement in France.

The process by which the old arch-enemy and monster Satan became a hero and abettor of mankind is very significant. The Restoration was accompanied in the first instance by a revival in literature of the old belief in the Devil. The Vicomte d'Arlincourt, Gaspard des Pons, Marchandy and others served up the old varieties of hell and the stereotype Satan. The young Romanticists tended increasingly towards two schools, the 'Satanic' and the 'Christian'. An entirely original turn was taken by Alfred de Vigny who began to work on his *Satan* between 1819 and 1823. Strongly influenced by Byron's *Cain*, this new version of the Devil bore an unmistakable resemblance to its author. Here was a revolt against the pain and cruelty inflicted by God and the pointlessness of happenings in the world. This Devil proclaimed his solidarity with the unhappy, the suffering, and the defeated. He encouraged manifestations of strong feeling and took a stand against the *ennui du ciel*, the tedium of the Christian heaven.

About 1830 the Devil was used as a favourite symbol for the enjoyment of life, passion and wickedness. Operas, novels, paintings, lampshade silhouettes, periodical illustrations and poems acclaimed him. Romantic ladies said of their lovers, 'He has the eyes of Satan. I love Satan.' (*Figaro*, 2 November 1831.) The satanism of minor literary figures revealed, however, a certain ambiguity. God was being accused of all man's misfortunes while Satan's vindication was a direct attack on the philistine and Pharisaic nature of contemporary bourgeois official Christianity.

'Come, Satan, come, that I may embrace you and press to my bosom he whom priests and kings have calumniated.' Proudhon's notorious aphorism was derived directly from Romanticism. His premise, 'God is evil', was based on the argument that the traditional interpretation of the Godhead placed men squarely in their state of misery and left no room for progress. History was not a series of operatic scenes wherein God and the Devil fought one another, but a process of antagonistic principles. The Devil was freedom and decisively rejected the kings, priests and law-givers of the old world. This freedom, so wrongly called devilish, was the major force behind creative energy. 'Freedom, to you, is Anti-Christ, the Devil,' Proudhon wrote to the Archbishop of Besançon.

This was the courageous utterance of something which between 1830 and 1850 often cost French writers considerable anguish to admit – the incipient 'revaluation of all values', an awareness that man's creative powers lay rooted in that highly suspect subconscious which had so frequently been apostrophised as 'hell' or at least been condemned as coming from the Devil.

A very important part in this struggle over the reappraisal and under-standing of the Devil was played by the fact that his would-be redeemers were operating with old and even pre-Christian (gnostic, cabbalistic) as well as non-Christian (Manichaean) notions. It was still the incarnation of evil, the arch-enemy of God, who took up his stance in a last engagement against Him.

In 1840 the first edition of Alexandre Soumet's *La Divine Epopée* was sold out within a month. The basic ideas had preoccupied him for a quarter of a century and only religious scruples induced him to renounce his original title *L'Enfer racheté*. Contemporary criticism compared the work with Dante, Milton and Klopstock.

The scene of *La Divine Epopée* is set after the end of the world when there is simply heaven and hell. At that moment the devil, Idameel, impugns God as the arch-enemy of mankind, the vulture who devours His children or sends them to hell. Nevertheless, God the Father redeems Idameel, even though he has earlier thrust the lance of hate through Jesus' heart.

The real significance here is that redemption is attained without repent-ance. In effect Soumet tried the impossible – simultaneously to celebrate the revolt of man and to justify the authority of God. He professed himself a follower of the German school of philosophy.

In Paris and France around 1840 a restive public evinced a lively interest in mediaeval sects of Satan worshippers, Luciferians and those gnostically inspired. An outbreak of spiritualist manifestations competed for attention. Table-turning seances became the rage. The sacrilegious dealings of the *Societé infernale d'Agen* were presumably a mixture of psychic and neurotic fancies and sensation-mongering. At any rate, the bishop of that city had exorcisms performed, and a detailed inquiry into this satanic cult showed it to have been a case of fraud practised on miracle-worshippers and Devil-addicts.

Half-way through the century, after the catastrophe of 1848–9 the country was once more, as in 1800, in a general state of fear. Flaubert, fourteen years old, wrote a *voyage en enfer* whose *leit motiv* was 'This world is hell', a youthful impression reiterated in *Rêve d'Enfer* (1837), *Agonies, pensées sceptiques* (1838), and *La Danse des Morts* (1838). The Devil, in the fullness of his strength, invites Christ on a tour of the world and displays his victories. Christ can do nothing except weep, invoke God the Father, and pity mankind. He is totally impotent; Satan is the master and awakener of passions, the truly creative spirit who says to Christ: 'You can only cast down, but I effect birth and I cause them to love, these creatures! I dispose of the fate of empires and I rule in all the great affairs of state and the heart!'

The idea that the Devil is the world's animator is a gnostic concept variously encountered especially in France, from the eleventh century onwards. It permitted of two antithetical conclusions – on the one hand, condemnation of this world by way of an ascetic spirituality; on the other, a proud and audacious (though perhaps rather desperate) affirmation. Both inclinations could be seen at work in the minds of nineteenth-century French writers and thinkers.

Smarh, the hero of the still youthful Flaubert's novel of that name, published in 1839 and redolent of Byron's *Cain*, was taken by the Devil on a journey through the universe. What he learned was that the law of suffering and endless pain dominates the infinite cosmic expanses where God reigns over a creation palpitating with misery and grief.

In his long labours on *La Tentation de Saint Antoine* Flaubert elaborated the features of the Devil until they came close to those familiar to Mann's Adrian Leverkühn, C.G.Jung and depth psychologists. The book was dedicated to the memory of Alfred de Poittevin, a friend with whom the author had held prolonged philosophic discussions on Spinozist lines. Although impressed by the cosmic speculations of Pierre Leroux and Boucher de Perthes, he attached more importance to his personal experience. The ridiculous, the vacuous, the senseless and the idiotic exude a power of fascination and seduction that can grip the mind and the imagination. Who banishes the demon in his own breast? Who banishes the devils of the new age, rising from the depths of the subconscious, reminders of a dreadful prehistory in man? Flaubert's answer was 'Art'. To banish the devils tormenting him is the purpose of the artist's creation. Art is exorcism, notwithstanding that the artist initially experiences a certain sense of the uncanny. 'Beware of reverie,' he wrote to Maxime du Camp. 'It is a base monster that entices and has spoiled many a fine thing for me.'

In this strange, turbulent, tangled and so productive time, a group of young poets used to meet in Paris every Sunday afternoon. (Sunday is the day of the Lord and of *ennui*, disgust and *Weltschmerz*.) Their object was to read each other their verses, which, as one of them aptly commented, were 'of as diabolic, as anti-bourgeois inspiration as possible.' In short, the aim of these sessions was to scare the old fogies and to train their sights on, deride and score off the bourgeois, philistines, clericals, politicians and pedants avid for outlets of moral indignation. One of these occasions, in February 1846, was devoted to the recital of seven poems extolling the Deadly Sins. They were dedicated to Satan who was adjured to destroy the entire world.

BAUDELAIRE AND THE DEVIL

Did Baudelaire stand in any direct relationship to this semi-secret group of ecstatic satanists and angry young men. One of the group's poems, transmitted by Maigron, bears strong traces of his style:

> *Mon âme est un cloaque immonde ou, sans émoi,*
> *Se tordent enlacés les plus hideux reptiles;*
> *Et loin d'en avoir peur, mon Moi, mon sombre Moi*
> *Goute orgueilleusement ces délices serviles.*

Many of his contemporaries and enemies interpreted the satanism of Pierre-Charles Baudelaire (1821–67) simply as a pose. But whoever studies his features as reproduced in daguerrotype and then his work, *Les Fleurs du Mal* (1857), *Petits Poèmes en prose*, his translations of Edgar Alan Poe and his masterly critical contributions, will become aware that 'no author in the nineteenth century attached greater significance to the Devil than did Baudelaire'.

He knew that Satan lay deep within himself: 'I breathe him in and out' (*La Destruction*). He was, of course, very well acquainted with the satanic school (which had almost become a synonym for Romanticism), but went well beyond it. His importance for the cultural history of Europe and of France lies not merely in the discovery of 'new realities' and new sentiments, the conquest of new poetic realms and the effective exercise of technical control over the creative imagination, but also in the absorption and elaboration of the many contradictory satanic visions and concepts of this century.

Baudelaire was familiar with the notion of the Devil as man's benefactor, patron of the poor and abased, and as the lord and master of the destructive forces. Hope to him was a daughter of Satan and Death. As a pupil of Byron and Shelley he impeached God for not having kept His promises. *Abel et Cain* ends with the lines, 'Race of Cain, rise into the heavens, And throw God down upon the earth' (a theme taken up by Russian writers between 1860 and 1917). His blasphemies were uttered against a religion of which he had detailed knowledge. O'Neddy's assertion that 'blasphemy is an act of faith' was confirmed by Baudelaire in his remark to Théophile Gautier: 'Blasphemers corroborate religion.' He frequently reiterated the old argument that Satan's outstanding act of cunning was to induce the belief that he does not really exist.

De Maistre's pessimism made a deep impression on Baudelaire. He was conscious of having been moulded by Catholicism and felt his outlook to be distinctly Catholic. Nevertheless, he was just as keenly aware that there existed a yawning chasm between his intellectuality and interpretation of the Devil on the one hand and the Church's creed on the other. 'I yearn (how sincerely nobody except myself can realise) with all my heart to believe,' he wrote to his mother in May 1861. ' . . . But how does one attain this belief?' That was the crucial question for hundreds of thousands of individuals in nineteenth-century Europe. How could a person endowed with sensitivity, intellect and contemporary knowledge believe in the forms and content of the old faith?

VICTOR HUGO: THE NINETEENTH AND TWENTIETH CENTURIES

All of France's great hopes and fears during the nineteenth century were subsumed in the personality and work of Victor Hugo (1802–85).

His paternal ancestors came from Lorraine. His father, Leopold-Sigisbert

Hugo, was battalion commander at Besançon when Victor was born there on 26 February 1802. As a Jacobin, he signed himself *le sans-culotte Brutus Hugo*. In time he became a general in the army of Joseph Bonaparte, when he was King of Spain, and Count Siguenza. His son dearly loved Spain, which he got to know as a child, and all his life he wrote his diary in Spanish. He did not love his father, who had abandoned his mother.

Like Vigny, Lamartine and the most outstanding Russian writers of the nineteenth century, Victor Hugo had a strong maternal attachment. Only after the death of his mother in 1821 did he resume correspondence with his father and only saw him again eight years later in 1823.

His mother was a Breton from a home with Jacobin sympathies (which her son did not know) but, like Madame de Staël, turned royalist out of hatred of Napoleon and of her husband. Hers was a Voltairean royalism frequently encountered in the years 1810–15. 'My royalist mother did not care for priests.' This serious, strong-minded woman never entered a church, not on account of the Church itself, but because of its priests. She believed in God and the human soul.

At thirteen Hugo himself was passionately ultra-royalist. So passionately indeed that he failed altogether to notice how superficial, untenable and simply fashionable his militant, polemical and abstract royalism was. It was not until 1820 a final transition that he made from his mother's Voltairean royalism to Chateaubriand's Christian royalism. This so-called 'conversion' was exclusively a literary one, even though occasionally accompanied by Catholic concepts. This was, however, the earliest evidence of the religious trait in Hugo's personality. The 'champion of atheism' was a man of religion who, as he was subsequently to say of himself, needed prayer as a fish needs water or a bird air.

He first met Lamennais in 1821. What impressed Hugo about him was the manifestation of genius devoted to religion. He was already at this time preoccupied with what he felt to be the divine mission of poesy, and later went on to develop these ideas, describing the genius as a Messiah, a prophet. Each part of the definitive edition of his *Odes* began with a poem recalling the 'sacred mission' imposed on poets by God. The first volume of the first edition, published in 1822, opened with *The Poet in Revolutions* in which he saw the poet as the voice of God speaking out in successive revolutions, 'steps of God' and stages in mankind's progress. The poet, to him, was Orpheus, a 'ray of the divine spirit', having affinities with John the Evangelist.

His Messianic faith was from the outset tainted with dread and fear of death. On his wedding day his brother Eugène, whom he held in deep affection and who had been in love with his bride, went mad. In 1843 his dearly loved daughter Leopoldine was drowned with her husband in the Seine at the age of nineteen. His second daughter Adèle went to America and returned with the balance of her mind disturbed. These events inflicted permanent wounds on Hugo. Unless these things are remembered, his belief in freedom, fraternity and progress is unintelligible and his Messianism cannot be properly gauged. Every fresh upset subjected his faith to a bout of despair, and yet throughout his life, in poetry, politics and love, it was always resuscitated.

Lamennais was to Hugo a harbinger and pioneer of freedom in what he regarded as a torpid, senile Christian system and a Church that confined the spirit. In 1830 he wrote to him, 'You can do anything now. In the age in which we live genius constitutes a papacy.' He placed his hopes on Lamennais in the same way as Lerminier, who in 1834 told the latter, 'You sir, are engaged in this century's great task, to attain union between religion and philosophy, science and faith, the homogeneity of truth.'

From 1830 until 1849 the Gospel was for Hugo the guiding principle of his politics and social plans. In 1834 he declared in the Chamber that every constitutional charter must contain a version of the Christian creed. As deputy for the department of the Seine he fought for the abolition of capital punishment and invoked a vision of 'Christ, living and crowned, rising above the deeply stirred masses', should the measure succeed (5 April 1850). He invoked the Gospel 'to obliterate the chimera of a certain type of socialism'. A speech of July 1850 proclaimed, 'It is in His spirit that we must make provision for, and give public assistance to, the unemployed masses.' At the Académie Française, on 27 February 1845, he extolled the Jansenists of Port-Royal who 'wanted dutifully to reform Rome and to effect in love from within what Luther attempted in anger from without.' In 1846 his maiden speech as a Peer of France was on the theme that civilisation is none other than 'applied religion'. In the Upper Chamber on the eve of the Revolution, 13 January 1848, he welcomed the Pope as protector of the peoples and the persecuted verities.

His harsh, bitter struggle with the political representatives of French Catholicism, throughout the years 1848–72, constantly echoed his disillusionment that it should be they who desired to act as the apostles of hate, to be the exterminators of their opponents and the instigators of 'a second St Bartholomew Massacre'.

He took part in the events of the Revolution full of hope and anxiety. On 19 February 1848, three days before its outbreak, he had sat in a depressed mood in the Peers' Chamber, listening to the deputies of the 'haves', and noted down: 'Misery leads the people into revolutions and revolutions lead the people back into misery.' The fate of France and Europe lay in the hands of the National Assembly which was to be chosen. He foresaw two possibilities, the emergence of either a Jacobin, republic with terror and death in its train or a republic which 'will be the sacred communion of *all* Frenchmen living now and, one day, of all the nations of the earth in a genuine democracy.'

On 20 June he made a major speech whose theme was the urgent, unmistakable warning inherent in the misery of the masses, the unemployed, the workers' quarters where children ran naked around the streets, the old, the destitute, and the working girls reduced to prostitution. Four days later the civil war began. He rushed between the barricades to try and mediate.

With the election of Louis-Napoleon to the Presidency, Hugo evolved a comprehensive programme. For abroad, disarmament, a league of nations, construction of the Suez and Panama Canals, friendship with China, colonisation in Algeria. At home, the elimination of social distress through public works and aid, the expansion of industry, state promotion of crafts-manship, the sciences and the arts, special support measures for scientific research.

With growing horror he watched developments in the early months of 1849. What were they doing, his friends of long standing – aristocrats, the upper middle-class, Catholics? They were indulging in an orgy of hate and annihilation against the defeated. In May he was elected to the National Assembly. On 9 July, without previous consultation of his colleagues, he mounted the rostrum and implored the victors of the civil war to attempt reconciliation with their wretched, outcast, incarcerated foes. Now was the time to use victory and to create 'a well-balanced and complete framework of law, a great and prescient Christian code as well as of public succour, and, in a word, to obliterate the chimeras of socialism with the realities of the Gospel.' The speech released a tempest of rage, mockery, indignation, loathing and laughter which was never to be allayed and which would, after 1870, gain fresh momentum. At that hour Hugo broke with the Conservatives.

On 15 January 1850 he made a speech in the National Assembly that brought the hate of his enemies, the Catholics and the Liberal upper middle-class, to the point of incandescence. He attacked them both as the *grand parti de l'ordre*, an unholy alliance of God and gold, a sordid union between old Voltaireans and political Catholics.

> O I am not confusing you with the Church! You are the Church's parasites! You are the Church's disease! Don't mix up the Church in your deals! Don't call her your Mother in order to make of her your maid-servant! Don't identify yourselves with her! You render yourselves so little worthy of love that you will yet succeed in rendering her worthy of hate!

On 8 April he rose again, to protest against the deportation to Nukahiva of those convicted of political offences, declaring the measure an act of shame for France and mankind. 'Arise, you Catholics, priests, bishops, men of religion, members of this National Assembly whom I see sitting here among us! Arise! That is the part you have to play! What are you doing on your benches?' The *Moniteur* reported the reaction to this appeal as 'Laughter'.

In Hugo's eyes the combination of clericalism, chauvinism, and 'big business' meant suicide for France and death to a happier future. How that might look for Europe and the world he demonstrated in his opening speech at the Second International Peace Congress in Paris on 22 August 1849. 'The day will come when the weapons will fall from your hands, when war between Paris and London, St Petersburg and Berlin, will be just as absurd and impossible as it is now between Rouen and Amiens, Boston and Philadelphia.' That would be the day of European brotherhood, between Russia, Germany,

France and the other European peoples. 'The day will come when there will be no battle-fields other than the markets open to trade and the minds open to ideas.'

Meanwhile Louis-Napoleon, supported by the political leaders of Catholicism, was preparing his *coup d'état*. Its success did not deter Hugo from continuing to fight in his own newspaper, *l'Evénement*, against the Bonapartist assumption of power even after the two responsible editors, his sons François-Victor and Charles, had been arrested. When the paper was prohibited, he brought it out under the title *L'Evénement du Peuple*.

'They have got the Church, the Army and the Bank,' was his comment on the coup of 2 December 1851. He tried to organise resistance against the 'rebel' Napoleon III, founding a *Comité de Résistance* and volunteering his own armed services. On 4 December the fighters were mown down and massacred. The toll of those slain in Paris was officially four hundred. (Was it, in fact, twelve hundred or even two thousand?) Hugo, a proscribed refugee, roamed the streets of the capital night after night. At last, under the name of Lamin, he succeeded in escaping to Brussels. The nineteen years of his exile were to witness his greatest achievements.

Napoleon III put pressure on the Belgian Government to put an end to Hugo's hostile propagandist activities. The Belgians passed on this pressure and in August 1852 he crossed to Jersey. The protection he enjoyed there lasted until the alliance between Britain and France at the time of the Crimean War. In joint manifestoes the Archbishop of Canterbury and the Cardinal of Paris called for a crusade against the wicked Russians. Hereupon Hugo, in his periodical *L'Homme*, attacked Queen Victoria. He was forced to quit Jersey for Guernsey, where he awaited the collapse of the Second Empire.

By 1869 the political structure was cracking. The Emperor was forced to dismantle censorship, slacken police controls and prepare to take refuge in armed hostilities, as ever the last resort of nineteenth-century regimes and typical of the outlook behind them. *L'Appel au Peuple*, with the same editorial team as *L'Evénement*, appeared on 18 May. At the Peace Congress in Lausanne, on 14 September, Hugo made a belligerent plea for one last war and one last revolution as a prelude to the United States of Europe. On 3 September 1870 the Emperor capitulated at Sedan, on 4 September a republic was proclaimed at Paris. On 5 September Hugo returned to the city.

L'an terrible, 1870–71, began. Hugo at once composed his *Appeal to the Germans*. Three trips on the Rhine in 1838–40 had formed the basis for his book *Le Rhin*. In its preface he had expressed his love for and admiration of Germany, avowing filial sentiments for 'this noble and sacred mother country of all intellects' and adding that, were he not French, he would gladly be German. During the Franco-German crisis of 1840, when Becker was singing his song about the 'German Rhine', he had proposed to Prussia that France should obtain the river's left bank but Prussia, in compensation, should have access to the Atlantic Ocean and be allowed the incorporation of

Hanover, Hamburg and the other Free Cities. In 1870 he could therefore furnish adequate proofs of previous goodwill and claim a hearing for his argument that two nations, France and Germany, had built up Europe but that one of them, Germany, was now seeking to dismantle it. When the Germans laid siege to Paris, he declared that their aim was to degrade the Eurotas, the Nile, the Tiber and the Seine to tributaries of the Spree and for Berlin to take the place of Paris. On 13 February 1871 he fled with the National Assembly to Bordeaux, became parliamentary leader of the Left (those members grouped around Gambetta, Louis Blanc, and Clémenceau), and called on the France of 1792 to rise against Prussia-Germany.

France was now plunged into the civil war between the Provisional Government and the Paris Commune. Hugo took part in a repetition of the massacre of 1848. Now as then the 'new' National Assembly had an overwhelming Catholic majority. In 1871 the curtain went up again on the tragedy of June 1848. Thiers adopted the earlier tactics of Montalembert, leaving Paris in the hands of the 'Reds' in order, when they had fallen into the trap, to 'stamp them out ruthlessly'.

Hugo had friends in both camps who were killed or murdered. 'You who fight are slaying France! She is on the one side and the other!' Horrified he watched the atrocities of such reprisals as when the bourgeois Provisional Government despatched six thousand prisoners for sixty-four hostages shot by the Commune. His manifestoes against this suicidal hate and will to destruction, *Paris incendié, Les Fusillés, A ceux qu'on foule aux pieds*, belong to the grandest documents of this grand, murderous century.

C'est l'avenir qu'on rend à l'avance furieux was his constant theme during this period which split France right up to 1914 and beyond. Threatened, reviled and persecuted by both sides, his life several times in danger, the sixty-nine-year-old man fled his country to Vianden in the Grand Duchy of Luxembourg. He returned after the terrible year was over. When *L'Appel au Peuple* was permitted to reappear, he issued an appeal in the very first number for France to be put on her feet again so as to help in the re-erection of Germany, that Germany which was now of its own volition enslaved and must be saved by France. This was a view shared by the 1870 volunteer Friedrich Nietzsche.

In 1876, at the instigation of Clémenceau, the Senate of the Third Republic elected Hugo to its membership. There he strove for a large-scale amnesty and final liquidation of the after-effects of 1871, spoke out against Tsarist pogroms, pleaded against the implementation of death sentences at home and intervened on behalf of the persecuted all over the world. He became the 'French Tolstoy' and 'the old Orpheus' (as which the periodical *Don Quichotte* depicted him), a spellbinding bard of reconciliation who invoked gods and men to cease from slaughter. The Parisians made his eightieth birthday into a public holiday.

On 31 August 1881 Hugo revised the will he had made in 1860. He had previously affirmed, 'I believe in God. I believe in the soul. I believe in responsibility for our actions. I surrender myself into the hands of the

Father of us all. Since the established faiths are currently below the standard that they owe to God and man, I wish no priest to be present at my funeral.' Now he widened the terms to include a bequest of all his manuscripts to the Bibliothèque Nationale at Paris which 'will one day be the Library of the United States of Europe'. He added, 'I close my mortal eyes. My spiritual eyes will remain wider open than ever before. I decline all prayers on my behalf by the Church. I entreat the prayers of all.'

What was it that his spiritual eye saw? Man's mission, the progress of mankind, wading through seas of blood and tears, delusion, deceit and self-deception.

This nineteenth-century belief in progress was at its best neither so mean nor so ridiculous as its renegade followers would have us believe. For Hugo (and for not a few of those spiritually alien to him) it continued to be maintained regardless of a never ceasing awareness of gigantic dangers and catastrophes. Progress, to his mind, was the terrestrial human journey to the celestial and the divine. There were interruptions, to allow the weary to be brought in, and there were 'nights when it (progress) slumbers. It is one of the philosopher's aching fears to see the shadow cast upon the human soul and gropingly to invade the darkness without being able to wake the sleeper.' The aim of progress is man's spiritualisation. Hugo's hymns look back to the past of the Greek Fathers and anticipate Teilhard de Chardin.

Who are they that lead mankind through the hells and wastes of epochs to the shining heights to come? The poet-seers and scientists. The poet is the torch that 'in this century of adventure and hazards' casts a light ahead. His thoughts seem Utopian because they illuminate the hereafter. The poet-seer and all those spiritually related to him in whom the divine fire glows are in direct touch with God, 'for man makes priests, but God alone gives magical powers.'

'Peuples, écoutez le poète!' Peoples who listen to false leaders instead of heeding their poets will go astray on their fearful 'journey' through the cosmos, for man is a 'pitiable speck confronted by hostile infinity/And the universe his foe' (Les Ténèbres). The old anthropomorphic religions are not commensurate with the sternness of reality but drag down the Godhead and erect 'black altars endowed with a demonised God'. Men of stature, saintly and clear-headed, poets and scientists are needed who, by their experience of suffering will transform man (Toute la Lyre). The 'pale Christs' are not needed; 'I resist the melancholy old dogmas.' During his last decade Hugo's condemnation of established religion grew in severity. 'Every religion is a miscarriage/Of human dreams in the face of existence and heaven.' Progress was the desire of God; 'it is the great revolt, obedient unto God.'

What Nietzsche strove for, Promethean man's firm affirmation of his destiny, is found deep-rooted and realistic in Hugo. Not a word against the lonely eminence of lonely writers like Nietzsche and Kierkegaard who, aloof from humanity, sated and destroyed themselves in their opus. None the less, the utterance of Hugo was that of a man who had borne the full weight of his century and said, '*Soyons l'immense Oui.*' He believed in the transmutation of men through suffering, 'The human race is a medley of castigated demi-gods and reprieved monsters.' Precisely this monster, man, had the duty to help nature and every living thing in the conquest of misfortune and the acquisition of freedom and spiritualisation.

Dealing with God, Hugo assimilated all this earth's religions. The Christian God was succeeded in his view by the just God who is 'neither vengeful nor gentle', but is impatiently waiting for man to rise up to Him, clearing his way 'with great blows of knowledge, with great blows of the axe'. Man would attain God only by effort, science and suffering.

The task of God and man alike was to redeem Satan. *La Fin du Satan* (1854–60) had its origins in that period of preparation during which Hugo carried the load of his own griefs and the experience of mankind's sorrows through need, death, senseless violence and oppressions of every sort. For twelve years after the death of his beloved daughter Leopoldine he passed through harsh spiritual crises. To these were added the nineteen years of his exile. The ghostly discourses on Jersey led to the heart of this *crise mystique* (Maurice Levaillant) and were its clearest manifestation. With the seas dinning in his ears and overwhelmed by an inner loneliness to which the importunity of other exiles, with their worries, intrigues and tattle, lent a fotetaste of hell, during long autumn and winter evenings Hugo unburdened himself in exchanges with apparitions of the living and the dead, of animals and abstractions: Napoleon III, Marat, Robespierre, Napoleon I; Shakespeare, Aeschylus, Molière; Mohammed, Christ, Plato, Isaiah, Luther. That these exchanges were dialogues with himself palpable, but what was it that he learned?

The spirits of all men live in an eternal life where they gather all their doubts, their knowledge, their scepticism and their faith, a gigantic beehive in and out of which the bee-souls fly. Time and space are relative magnitudes, infinitely big and infinitely small, for 'Heaven has no calendar!' Every man is a complex ego beneath whose skin there are millions of living organisms, like the brain which alone is already an immense den of spirit-minds. Man, every man, is an enormous realm in which the crucified and the hanged, the souls of others, of plants, rocks and so on, are present. Man is an eternity, a colossal super-atom, who comprises all that there is. Should one day prodigious destruction overtake humanity, the plant world, the animal world, the world of living organisms, the world of petrification, and every other world, and but one grain of sand remain, God will smile, throw the grain of sand into space, and say, 'Arise, millions of worlds!'

Cosmogonic visions, insights into past millennia and the universe's millions of years, insights into the history of mankind and coming decades and centuries. The Angel of Death unveils to Hugo the effect of his verse in future crises, in the twentieth century, in 1920, 1960, 1980, and the year 2000. (Did he have a premonition that in the middle of the twentieth century the Bao-Dai sect, in Viet Nam, would venerate him as the founder of a universal religion?) Of one thing, as he told his son Charles and his daughter Adèle, the lonely man on Jersey and Guernsey was convinced: 'I am a priest. ... Every evening I pray. ... He who teaches about the invisible world is a priest.'

But his ghostly discourses came to an abrupt end and were never resumed. On 26 April 1860 he began work again on a subject that he had pondered for thirty years, first set down between 1845 and 1848, and now, in an ecstasy of inspiration, completed by 30 June 1861 – *Les Misérables*. Here he anticipated the fate of the deportees in the decade of Dreyfus and created the credible portrait of a saint, Bishop Myriel, an ultramontane and by no means a Leftist Catholic. For this character Hugo had made careful studies among contemporaries, and Monsignor Miollis, Bishop of Digne, served as model for a man who sincerely loves his flock and his God and lives for both.

'*Ce chiffre enorme: Dieu.*' This phrase, from the *Contemplations*, may be applied to both Hugo and the nineteenth century. 'This terrestial, mortal man Hugo, this son of the earth, was capable of creating a saint.'

The whole of nineteenth-century literature contained only three major saintly figures. All three were the creations of men who were either not Christians or, persecuted, stood on the brink of Christianity. Victor Hugo; Antonio Fogazzaro, with *Il Santo* (a novel which provided the programme for Italian modernism); and, chronologically beyond the nineteenth century but deeply indebted to it, Unamuno with his *San Manuel Bueno, mártir.*

5

A German Left

KARL MARX

To live in Dean Street, Soho, in the mid-nineteenth century was to live in one of London's cheapest and most squalid residential areas, a fact which a contemporary police report noted when describing the circumstances of a German and his family who were resident at No 786. Their lodging consisted of two rooms, one a living-room, one a bedroom. Neither contained a single decent or clean piece of furniture. Everything was torn and tattered, thick with dust. The large, old-fashioned table in the middle of the room was covered in manuscripts, books, newspapers, toys, dirty cutlery, and many other things, all in jumbled chaos. Visitors to the room had to grope through a haze of nicotine fumes, their eyes streaming. If they wanted to sit, there were two chairs, one with only three legs, which is why the other, despite all the apparel of childrens' games, was offered. But despite this, the tenant and his wife would be hospitable, launching into serious and interesting conversation in a way which made one forget all the domestic misery.

These surroundings, described by the same police as 'quite tolerable', were, for the tenants, living hell. Most of their possessions they had lost to the bailiffs in lieu of rent. Often, when all their clothes were in pawn, they would have to lie on the bed, together, without light or food. In 1858, on the death of his daughter, Marx could not even afford a coffin, and there was no money for a doctor or medicine. But he was most afflicted by the death of his son, Edgar, aged six. Replying to a letter of consolation he wrote:

> Bacon says that really outstanding men have such close ties with nature and the world and so much of interest to them that they can take every loss in their stride. I am not one of those outstanding people. I am shattered, in heart and mind, by the death of my child and I feel the loss just as keenly as on the first day. My poor wife too is completely overcome.

The 'poor wife' indeed went through every form of destitution with this man, and normally he had very little time for her, spending most of his days reading and pondering either at home or in the British Museum. Sundays were the only time he really spent with his family. They would walk up to Hampstead Heath and he would play with the children, telling them fairy tales of his own invention.

Reading and walking were Marx's favourite occupations. He loved poetry, and knew long passages of Dante, Shakespeare and Aeschylus by heart. In his old age he began to learn Russian and Turkish, in order to learn more about the agricultural conditions in those countries. He was then, at last, able to read Gogol and Pushkin in the original, although as a 'good German' he abhorre d the Russians as barbarians.

Marx was just one of the mass of European youth and exiles who came streaming into London in 1849 after the collapse of the '48 revolutions, that great catastrophe of nineteenth-century Europe. Mazzini, Kossuth, Louis Blanc, Ruge and Engels were only a few among the hundreds of émigrés, mostly destitute and glad of any invitation to Alexander Herzen's richly-laden table. A very different crowd from those other refugees, the aristocracy – Madame de Staël, Louise-Philippe, Metternich.

Marx died on 14 March 1883, to all intents and purposes a pauper in his own armchair, though spiritually he had died two years earlier when Jenny, his wife, had passed away after long and painful suffering with cancer. Only a small crowd of friends and labour representatives from abroad, eight in all, assembled around his grave in Highgate. The funeral speech was given by Friedrich Engels and is perhaps one of the best evaluations of the man.

Above all Marx was a revolutionary. To play a part, in this way or that, in the overthrow of capitalist society and the political institutions of the modern proletariat in whom he had created the consciousness of its own situation and needs, of the conditions for its emancipation – that was his real vocation in life. Conflict was his element, and he fought with a passion, a tenacity and a success as few have done. That is why Marx was the most hated and most slandered man of his time. And he has died venerated, beloved, mourned by millions of revolutionary collaborators, from the Siberian mines, across Europe and America, as far as California, and I can boldly assert: he may have had many an opponent, but hardly one personal enemy.

Thus spoke the first Father of the new Marxist Church who had himself done so much to build up faith in his friend and master, to expound him, and to reinterpret and reshape him in his own image – that of a German bourgeois of pietist descent.

Karl Marx had not the slightest regard for the 'Red mob', the 'Communist mob', the 'riff-raff' wanting to play at revolution. He kept himself personally at a distance from the workers of his time, holding neither their mental nor their political capacity in respect. With some justification he said of himself, 'All I know is that I am no Marxist.' Even Engels remarked to him, 'Neither the democratic, the red, or even the communist mob will ever love us.' In 1849 a German émigré listened stupefied to Marx's outburst of enthusiasm for Europe's traditional aristocracy and the enunciation of his vision of a new, historically potent aristocracy: an altogether new and dominant human type called 'the proletariat'.

Marx was not only to prove one of the greatest reverers of capitalism's historic mission, but also as one of the most persuasive promulgators of the splendid unity that existed in archaic, mediaeval society, an avowal which may be found right in the middle of *The Communist Manifesto*.

On his father's side Marx came from Europe's oldest intellectual aristocracy, generations of rabbis. Jews had come to Trèves, his native city, with Julius Caesar and Augustus. His father, Herschel Levi had entered upon a rabbinate that for the past hundred and fifty years had been almost an hereditary family prerogative. Among his direct ancestors were Joseph ben Gerson Cohen, Rabbi of Cracow at the close of the sixteenth century, and Meir Katzenellenbogen, who died as Rabbi of Padua in 1565. The university there counted him as one of the most illustrious minds of his age and had his portrait painted and hung in place of honour on one of the walls of its Great Hall.

Karl Marx's 'queen', the lovely Jenny von Westphalen, daughter of a Prussian Privy Councillor, was a direct descendant from the Presbyterian rebel, Archibald Campbell, Earl of Argyll, who ended his career by royal command on the scaffold of Edinburgh's market-place. Her paternal grandfather had been quartermaster-general to Duke Ferdinand of Brunswick.

Marx's thought combined the oldest European intellectual traditions and themes, with still older, archaic and non-European elements. In his view of history he adopted ancient gnostic and Manichaean ingredients. Via Aristotle he felt his way back towards Heraclitus, whose spiritual notions of fire were revived in the nineteenth century. From Heraclitus he moved to the Orient, towards the rock on which mankind's first great hero and martyr, Prometheus, was forged in suffering. These great traditions of European and pre-European thought were merged with knowledge of the eighteenth-century French Enlightenment, classical British political economy and the heritage of German Romanticism culminating in Hegel.

During his years of utter loneliness, the three and a half decades of London exile, there blazed forth from this wanderer between two worlds, between mankind's farthest past and farthest future, such fires as accompanied the passage of Moses's people. He broke out of the bounds of contemporary Jewry, those of the ghetto and of assimilated, Europeanised Judaism, back to Isaiah. In this century of prophets of all calibres, prophets of doom and salvation in so many forms, Karl Marx was the most fiery, most passionate, most biased, most radical prophet of them all. On his lips trembled the wrath of Moses against a recreant people. Woe unto him who incurred the judgement of this prophet, just as the excommunication imposed on friends, collaborators, disciples, or fellow travellers deemed too weak or viewed as suborners, sectarians, or misguided enthusiasts was pronounced with incomparable harshness. Ruge, Bauer, Kriege, Grün, Hess, Kinkel, Willich, Weitling, Schweitzer, Lassalle and many more were on the list. Arnold Ruge, 'his first confessor' (Schwarzschild), had said of him as a youth that 'Marx, gnashing his teeth and grimacing, will slaughter all who stand in his way.' What he wrote to Engels about Bakunin (whom Herzen called a 'Columbus without a ship and without an America') is typical of Marx's attitude; 'This Russian evidently proposes to become a dictator of the European labour movement. He had better take care. Else he will be officially excommunicated.'

The prophet was born in the beautiful city of Trèves, allotted to Prussia by the Congress of Vienna on 5 May 1818. A year before his birth Herschel Levi, his father, broke with his Jewish past, was accepted into the Lutheran Church, changed his name to Heinrich Marx, and became a passionate Prussian patriot and monarchist. This belief in Prussia made a deep impression on his son, just as he retained a lifelong affection for his beautiful birthplace.

His childhood and his schooldays were happy. He was fortune's favourite with his parents and to his death carried on him a photograph of his father. Good in class, he was 'equally liked and feared by his fellow-pupils, because' as his daughter Eleanor later recalled, presumably basing herself on her mother's accounts, 'he was always ready to participate in some new mischief, but jeered at his enemies in caustic verses'.

His school-leaving examination included two essays. In one the theme was to demonstrate the nature, reasons for and consequences of the unification of the faithful in Christ. His argument ran that unification in Christ represented a morality of a higher kind than any, including Stoicism and Epicureanism, known to antiquity. The other dealt with choice of profession. 'If we have selected that station in life,' he wrote, 'where we can act most effectively on behalf of mankind, burdens cannot bow us down. They are simply the sacrifices that we make for all. The pleasure we derive is not narrow and egotistic. On the contrary, our happiness belongs to millions, our actions remain quietly but continually effectual, and our ashes will be sprinkled with the glowing tears of noble individuals.'

His father introduced him to Voltaire and Racine, his future father-in-law to Homer and Shakespeare. According to his daughter Eleanor 'They remained his favourite authors all his life.' In 1835 he became a student at Bonn for a year, heard lectures by August Wilhelm Schlegel and associated with a circle of budding poets, thereby causing his father some serious alarm. His engagement to Jenny von Westphalen reassured the anxious parent. The girl's family was as desirable as any in Trèves and she herself very beautiful. After the celebrations her betrothed went to Berlin for five years, obtaining in 1841 a degree in philosophy.

In his first term at the university he listened to lectures on anthropology by Steffens and two years later by Ritter. Both of these academics, deeply influenced by Schelling, were protagonists of the Romantic interpretation of natural philosophy. Ritter believed that geography and geology were fundamental to the history of mankind. Here were to be found, in a spiritual wrapping, substantial rudiments of Marx's historical materialism. The Romantic interpretation of natural philosophy made a deeper impression on him, and subsequently on Engels, than he liked to admit. Engels' 'dialectical transition', the shift from quantity to quality, is a concept of evolution in nature just as familiar to the Romantic interpretation of natural philosophy as to Hegel. Lenin's article of faith that the electron is inexhaustible was rooted in German natural philosophy as transmitted to him by Engels. In his 1937 Yenan readings Mao Tse-tung linked ancient Chinese and German natural philosophy as transmitted to him via Marx, Engels, and Lenin, thus giving a common platform to archaic Asiatic and European experience alike.

Marx's literary bent was not abandoned at Berlin. Apart from a satiric novel (*Skorpion and Felix*) and a full-blooded drama (*Oulamen*), he wrote many romantic poems in pseudo-Gothic style, which once again revived his father's fears for his son's future. Again the anxiety was groundless. By the spring of 1837 he had turned his back on the idealism of Kant and Fichte in order to devote himself to Hegel, sealing the deed by entry into the 'Doctors Club'. This oddly-named association was composed of a set of free-thinking university intellectuals who met in beer cellars, mainly for the purpose of endless arguments about Hegel's theology. Their other activities included the writing of semi-treasonable verses and giving vent to vitriolic outbursts against kind, church, and the middle classes. Marx was very soon on a friendly footing with the principal members of the clique, the brother Bruno, Edgar and Egbert Bauer, as well as Köppen, a strange figure, who was one of the earliest investigators into Tibetan lamaism, and Max Stirner, author of a history of the French Reign of Terror and advocate of a special brand of ultra-individualism.

From 1839 onwards the Prussian authorities, both secular and ecclesiastic, observed these young men with the gravest distrust – and even one hundred and twenty years later right-wing German scholars poured biting scorn on these 'left intellectuals' who set out to alter the world's train of ideas.

None, however, exceeded Marx's acidity and derision as displayed in *The German Ideology*, a work written in 1845 at Brussels together with Engels and containing for the first time all the basic tenets of Marxism. Originally only *The Holy Family*, the portion devoted almost exclusively to an attack on the Bauer brotherhood, was published. Herein was levelled the reproach of slavish self-subordination to Hegel: 'This dependence on Hegel is the reason why none of these recent critics has even attempted a full criticism of the Hegelian system, for all that each of them so loudly claims to have gone beyond him.' Moreover 'all of German philosophical criticism, from Strauss to Stirner, restricts itself to criticism of (Hegel's) *religious* concepts.' (Marx's italics.)

GERMAN LEFT-WING INTELLECTUALS

The scorn and derision which Marx poured on the men connected with the Doctors' Club revealed only too clearly how disconcerted he was to realise that in Germany there did in fact exist a revolutionary train of thought which urged action, and had implemented a process of action, a way of thought in direct line of descent to man's earliest thinker, Prometheus.

The left-wing Hegelians of the Doctors' Club had tried to relight this

Promethean fire which had burned in Germany around 1780 and 1800, but, as Bruno Bauer wrote to his brother in 1840, philosophy is 'Prometheus bound', bound by the fetters of political reaction, and the fire was quenched by the deep resignation which affected the nineteenth century during its second decade.

At about this time a hitherto unknown author, Adam von Cieszkowski, published a scathing criticism of Hegel's 'anodyne' philosophy of history, demanding its replacement by a philosophy of action. The proper task was not to burrow comfortably into the past, but to anticipate the future. 'We must affirm from the outset that it is impossible to attain understanding of either organic and ideal totality or history's clearly established processes, without having perceived the future as an integral part of history which represents the destiny of mankind.' History was orientated towards the future. The task of the present remained, however, to place a brake on reaction, a start being made with the contrivance of a progressive government for Prussia. The trouble, as appeared soon enough, was the stout determination of Frederick William IV, the 'romantic on the royal throne' and initially great hope of the Young Hegelians, to preserve his Prussia as an enduring stronghold for the political and religious beliefs of his forefathers and to defend it against the modernist spirit. It was as an antidote to the 'athesitic' Hegelians that he summoned Schelling to Berlin, and who, in his inaugural lecture on 15 November 1841, promised that he would create a new fortress in which 'henceforth philosophy shall be able to dwell securely'.

Frederick William's step had been preceded by attempts on the part of Young Hegelians and kindred spirits (Bauer, Arnold Ruge, Feuerbach, Marx) to obtain a foothold in the university as teachers. Their political attack had been launched in the first place against the established Christianity of the state. Political enlightenment, as they appreciated, postulated religious enlightenment and a change in political conditions was impossible without change in religious conditions. With the academic door barred to them, they tried using newspapers and periodicals to bring about intellectual political ferment. When these were forbidden, they faced arrest, imprisonment and exile from Prussian territory, an inner and outer emigration before and after 1848.

In 1838 Ruge and Echtermeyer founded the *Halle Yearbooks for German Science and Art*. Their first campaign was against Görres and Leo, 'the Catholic and Protestant Jesuits'. Their manifesto *Protestantism and Romanticism* denounced the past fifty years as a retrogression from the Enlightenment. Ruge expounded this theme further in a sensational essay published on 1 November 1839, *Karl Streckfuss and Prussianism*, in which he alleged that Prussia had become Catholic and reactionary, having turned its back on the spirit of true Protestantism in the shape of a progressive, liberal and critical outlook. 'Here lies Prussia's weakness, here the danger for free Germany.' Ruge felt himself to be a Prussian to the core, and it was as a struggle for Prussia, for its religious and political faith and for its future that there began the great literary movement out of which Marx evolved and in whose toils he remained caught for the rest of his life, more deeply than in his scorn, he cared to admit.

If Marx, during the course of the nineteenth century, was undoubtedly the most inspired castigator of the Left then the same claim can probably be made on the Right for Heinrich Leo (1799–1878), flanked by Görres at Munich and later Louis Veuillot at Paris. This is probably true even though Leo, as self-willed as he was gifted, did not fit completely into any particular category, especially as far as his conservatism was concerned. For half a century the outstanding historian of Halle University and a brilliant journalist, he really awoke to his political calling in his fight with the *Halle Yearbooks*. To Ruge's and Echtermeyer's attack he replied with, *The Hegelingians*, a title typical of the verbal contortions with which he enriched the language. In this pamphlet he shows them and their associates to be 'enemies of the state, preachers of atheism and revolution'. The return salvo was fired by Ludwig Feuerbach in the *Yearbooks* issue on 3 December 1838. Earlier in the year he had already contributed an essay, *On the Criticism of Hegelian Philosophy*, in which he said, 'Philosophy is the knowledge of reality in its truth and totality; but the quintessence of reality is nature. . . . The most recondite secrets lie in the most straightforward, natural things which the fervently ontological speculator despises. Return to nature is the sole fount of salvation.'

The passage attracted Marx's keen attention, versed as he was in the theories and hopes of German natural philosophy. To the end of his life, and particularly during its last decade, he was to adhere to this tenet that man, reconciled with nature, would return to his point of departure free of all intervening alienation.

The young Prussian intelligentsia looked around for possible allies and its first glance fell upon France. On 13 April 1840 Ruge wrote in his *Yearbooks*, 'The more free France becomes' (matters were once more in flux there, since the July Revolution of 1830) 'the more urgent it is for Germany, especially Prussia, not to remain behind.' In 1841 Moses Hess, still only a Cologne publicist but soon to play the part of prophet to Marx's mission (though later his opponent), demanded in *The European Triarchy* a Prusso-Franco-British league against the two major reactionaries, Russia and Austria. German reformation and French revolution, he felt, belonged together. In sequel to Cieszkowski he wrote, 'The philosophy of action differs from the philosophy of history in as much as it includes in the field of speculation not merely past and present, but, alongside these two factors and deriving from them, the future too.' He proceeded to deal with the 'third revolution'.

Europe has already experienced two revolutions, the German and the French, because it was not prepared to accept peaceably the modern spirit. It has still to face a *third* one which will conclude the work of the modern spirit, beginning with the German Reformation. *This will be the practical revolution*, the one that, unlike the others, will have not merely a greater or lesser a relative, but an *absolute* influence on social life.

In March 1841 the Doctors' Club initiated its own small publication, *Athenaeum*, its title deservedly recalling the Schlegel periodical of 1797–1800, where the programmes for man's revolutions during the nineteenth and twentieth centuries were disclosed in lightning flashes of intellect. It was in this new *Athenaeum*, among whose contributors were Rutenberg, Köppen, Meyen, Bühl, Nauwerk, Engels and Hess, that Marx published some of his romantic poems. Köppen championed the Enlightenment and Frederick the Great: 'It (the Enlightenment) was the Prometheus which brought the light from Heaven to earth in order that the blind, the people, should receive illumination and be liberated from their prejudices.'

Athenaeum and the *Halle Yearbooks* were the forums for the intellectual vanguard of the German revolution. This was the time when Marx completed his doctoral thesis, with its defence of Epicurean 'idealism' as against the 'materialism' of Democritus. Bruno Bauer was urging on him their collaboration on a more radical periodical, the proposed title being simply *Archives of Atheism*.

Ruge's aim in his *Yearbooks* was to found a citadel of 'free philosophy' and knowledge which would liberate Prussia from the clutches of 'Catholicism', 'pietism', and 'cant'. He visualised himself as the legitimate heir to 'true Protestantism' and wrote on 2 May 1840 to a friend,

> You still continue to plague yourself with Christianity. To what end? Is there anything other than the truth of the spirit . . . ? All religion is nothing else than its incarnation . . . , the emotional force of the idea and submission to it. *And Divine Man is everyone who merges in the idea and in whom the idea merges.* . . . Idealism, not gratification, is what makes Divine Man, what makes religion. The ascent of humanness into divinity is no privilege, least of all that of Christ, Who indeed does not claim it and would not redeem us if in that way we attained forgiveness and love, and not through our own ascent, our own Ascension . . .

To attain an Ascension of self was the religious, philosophic, and political object of those whose sympathies lay with the *Yearbooks*.

In 1841 Ruge had to leave Halle. Shortly afterwards he told a disciple that the time of martyrdom for the *ecclesia pressa* was just ahead, and repeated that free philosophy was the Protestantism of the age. From 1 July 1841 until 2 January 1843, the date of final suppression, he published at Dresden the *German Yearbooks*. On 10 February 1842 Ruge received *Observations on the New Censorship Regulation*. It was a criticism of the recent Prussian censorship decree – and Marx's first political essay. And so he turned journalist. The case of Bruno Bauer whose licence to teach had been withdrawn in the early weeks of this same year by Bonn University, showed Marx that academic life held no place for him. Moses Hess had succeeded in persuading a group of liberal Rhenish industrialists to back the publication in Cologne of a newspaper, the *Rheinische Zeitung*, whose economic and political line was directed against the reactionary policy of Berlin. Marx became a staff member, then chief leader writer, thus gaining his first political experience as champion of the liberal economy of the progressive Rhenish middle classes. Berlin treated its newly acquired Rhine territories with a mixture of wariness and indulgence. It had no desire to irritate these Rhinelanders, who were in the process of building up an economic potential of real political importance. When the *Rheinische Zeitung* was banned without previous warning, the responsibility lay neither with the Prussian censors nor the landed proprietors, both of whom the paper had attacked, but with a fiery Russian protest. This is a facet which, from a contemporary Federal German perspective, does not lack a certain irony.

These Cologne days proved thoroughly fruitful for Marx. They were moreover his first, and almost sole, opportunity to address himself directly to German public opinion, one of his first moves was to print his *Observations* on the demoralising effect of Press censorship. It caused hypocrisy, he complained, a form of lie in regard to public affairs, and consequently self-deception on the part of the government because it confused its own voice in the Press with that of the people. 'For its part the people either sinks into political superstition or into political scepticism or, turning its back completely on political affairs, becomes a rabble unconcerned with public matters.' This analysis of artificial manipulation of public opinion is surely indisputable in not a few countries today.

Marx was even less kind in his treatment of German liberals: 'Germans are by nature the humblest, most submissive, most respectful of people. Sheer respect holds them back from ever turning ideas into practice.' It is understandable that suspicion of Dr Marx should be felt among certain Cologne citizens. The editor-in-chief of the *Kölnische Zeitung* condemned its rival as anti-christian and to this Marx replied that the true state was founded on reason, evolved via philosophical criticism, which served it as a guide. Genuine philosophy reflected social evolution. 'From the outset worldly wisdom, philosophy, seems to be better entitled to turn its attention to the application of justice in this world, the state, than is the wisdom of the other world, religion.'

In the summer of 1842 the publishers and editorial board of the *Rheinische Zeitung* formed a discussion group, 'Young Germany', which met once a week. The original members were Jung, Hess, Mervissen, Schram, Brüggemann, d'Ester; Marx joined them in October. Mervissen reported to the circle about his personal experience of the industrial movement in Britain and encounters with the Saint-Simonians in France. Hess, as the paper's French correspondent, gave an account of French Communist ideas, adding his own quota. He had already written an article on the subject (*The Riddle of the Nineteenth Century*) and was the group's only Communist. When the *Augsburger Allgemeine Zeitung* on 11 October 1842 accused the *Rheinische Zeitung* of being Communist, Marx could answer with perfect sincerity that he was as yet too unfamiliar with such ideas.

Hess was at that period Marx's first, and highly enthusiastic, disciple. 'You can prepare yourself,' he told a friend,

> to get to know the greatest, currently perhaps the sole, philosopher we have and will soon attract Germany's notice to himself. Dr Marx, which is the name of my idol, is still quite a young man (somewhere around twenty-four), but he will give mediaeval religion and politics the final push into the abyss. Along with the utmost philosophical seriousness, he has a most penetrating wit. Imagine an amalgam of Rousseau, Voltaire, Holbach, Lessing, Heine and Hegel, I say an amalgam, not merely a agglomeration, and there you have Dr Marx.

In the Rhineland Marx, brought up sharply against the harshness of economic and social conditions, gained his first experience of the rigours of reality, the prevalent structure of politics and society. The most important result of this was the end of his connection with the free-floating left-wing intellectuals whom Bruno Bauer, the dismissed theologian, had gathered at Berlin into his league of 'Freemen'. Aloof, extruded from social and political reality, the remaining members of the Doctors' Club degenerated into an intellectuals' union. Ruge's verdict, on 12 December 1842, ran, 'The "Freemen" are a frivolous, blasé clique. I have told them my opinion frankly and forcefully. . . . I tried to get them to dissolve, so as not to do more harm to the good cause.'

The circulation of the *Rheinische Zeitung* rose under Marx's efforts from four hundred to eighteen hundred subscribers and more than three thousand sales copies. Success came to an abrupt end in the spring of 1843. Marx, in a series of leading articles, had attacked the Russian government as a bulwark of terror, barbarism, obscurantism and the suppression of freedom in Europe. He openly advocated war against Russia, regardless of the fact that she was not merely in alliance with Prussia but the stronger of the two partners. Tsar Nicholas I happened to read one of these blistering polemics, put it under the nose of the Prussian ambassador, and issued an energetic protest in Berlin against this deplorable laxity of censorship. Immediate action was taken. The paper went down with flying colours. In its last issue 31 March 1843, the editorial board and Dr Marx bade their readers good-bye with a poem, *Farewell*, in which they compared themselves with Columbus: 'Columbus too was first despised, / His New World's dream yet realised.'

To Marx cessation of publication came as a relief. 'The atmosphere had become so oppressive,' he wrote to Ruge.

> It is unpleasant to perform menial services, even for freedom's sake, and to fight with needles instead of clubs. I was tired of hypocrisy, stupidity and brute authority on the one hand, and our bowing, scraping and word-juggling on the other. So the Government has set me at liberty again. . . . I can't make a fresh start in Germany, here where people falsify even themselves.

His first step, in April, was to marry Jenny von Westphalen, despite the opposition of her family. His next step was to emigrate to France, and there, in the years 1843–5, to undergo transmutation from the idealist philosopher and romantic poet Dr Marx, into history's Karl Marx. Not that he was an active revolutionary. On the contrary, he buried himself in books, especially the novels of Balzac. His most important activity was collaboration in the *Franco-German Yearbooks*, which Ruge initiated at this time. In them appeared his *Introduction to the Criticism of Hegel's Philosophy of Right* and *Review of Two Publications on the Jewish Question*.

'There are almost a hundred thousand Germans in Paris, more, that is, than in Dresden,' wrote Ruge to his brother in October 1843. The vast majority were, however, ordinary labourers, only a small minority being political refugees. Ruge's own object was to create, through his *Yearbooks*, a Franco-German intellectual alliance which would liberate France from religious subjugation to narrow-minded Catholicism and Germany from subjugation of a political kind. The project failed, though through no fault of Ruge's, and his friendship with Marx lasted barely a year. On 6 October 1844 he wrote to his mother, 'Marx is a thorough blackguard and an impertinent Jew.' It was curious that just at this moment the 'thorough blackguard and impertinent Jew' should, in the *Yearbooks*, have given evidence of a latent anti-Semitism; and all the more ironic that Bruno Bauer, the ex-theologian and wing Hegelian who was to become one of the most important ideologues of German anti-Semitism and two of whose pieces were the subject of Marx's *Review*, should claim that *he* was no Jew-hater.

This Paris period was the last time in Marx's life when he associated to any degree companionably both with those who agreed and those who differed with him in his ideas. He lived on the thousand thalers his Cologne friend provided and visited the cafés where German émigrés met, including the League of the Just which was to constitute the embryo of the Communist International. He was, however, beginning to sever his ties with Ruge, Feuerbach and the left-wing Hegelians in Germany, to withdraw even further from contacts with German and French Socialists and Utopians in Paris, with the Russians Annenkov and Bakunin. Finally he restricted himself to two friends only. One was the poet Heinrich Heine. The other was Friedrich Engels.

FRIEDRICH ENGELS

Friedrich Engels, 1820–95, was the son of a well-to-do textile manufacturer from Barmen; his family origins betrayed themselves throughout his life in a certain sermonising tone and a pedantic exactitude. His youth was marked by a severe internal struggle to break away from the pietistic background of his upbringing. Early on in his career he seemed likely to become a poet and man of letters, a fact which his father viewed with misgiving; and consequently he was packed off to England to learn the meaning of sober, harsh reality as it manifested itself in day-to-day, industrial and business affairs. En route for England he again encountered Moses Hess, who had already converted him to Communism. Although he had corresponded with Marx, it was not until two years later in Paris that he got to know this man, whose life-long friend he was to become.

Engels had started his literary-political career while doing his military service in Berlin. He had listened to Schelling's lectures, and immediately afterwards composed three pamphlets against him. Then, early in 1845, he published at Leipzig his *Condition of the Working Classes in England*, describing how the sight of this hell on earth had cured him of his 'philosophical arrogance' and German self-love. For much of his material he relied on the Press and on House of Commons debates, and he was convinced that Judgement Day, in the shape of revolution, was imminent. It is symbolic of the strength of his belief that at the end of his life, although over fifty years had passed, he still held this conviction.

Engels attributed to the Industrial Revolution in England the same significance as to the political revolution in France and the philosophical one in Germany. For the changes brought about by the Industrial Revolution were at least as great as those caused by the revolutions in France in 1789 and 1830. The most important outcome of the industrial upheavals had been the birth of the English proletariat. Social strife was to be found everywhere; on one side there reigned barbaric indifference and egoistic severity, on the other ineffable misery. Engels' description of Manchester at this time is particularly horrific. Existence in the world's then leading industrial city, as he describes it, is a vision of hell, with its poor cooped up in streets sunk in filth, feeding on rotten food, exploited in every way. Trade crises occurred all the time and the Poor Law Commissioners' reports assessed a 'labour surplus' in England and Wales of one and a half million. He was particularly incensed by the situation in the mines where men, women and children worked in bestial conditions and a foul atmosphere.

What Engels depicted was war, at the very début of a new age, among the people of one nation. Almost simultaneously there appeared *Sybil, or the Two Nations*, Disraeli's definition of the rift between the two classes. The strike of forty thousand miners in the north of England, who were finally dismissed by their employers, regardless of the conditions in which the measure left them, was symbolic of this war.

The conditions of the peasants on the land echoed the industrial misery. 1834 saw the repeal of the Poor Law of 1601, which had placed the onus of responsibility for the poor on parish authorities, and the passing of the new Poor Law, creating workhouses, which produced, in effect, concentration camps where five-year-old boys could be locked up for three nights in the mortuary for 'misdemeanors' and the dead were thrown into holes or bogs like dead cattle.

Engels quoted a leading article in *The Times* of June 1844, warning the rich of the dire outcome of current trends. Prominent Tories like Lord Ashley and Richard Oastler ('king of the factory children', whom children in industrial towns met in procession, to welcome as their leader and saviour) stood up for this proletariat against the Whig majority. Engels, the Rhineland industrialist's son, appreciated their efforts. But Engels, the Communist believer, thought it was too late for a pacific solution and that only out of revolution could the new paradise be born. 'The war of the poor against the rich will be the bloodiest that was ever waged.'

Engels met Marx at the right moment. Marx was cudgelling his brains with the problems of the alienation of man in modern society. Engels brought him the tidings that the new proletariat was destined to become the motive force of mankind's future development.

THE COMMUNIST MANIFESTO

In 1845, expelled from France, Marx went to Brussels. There with Engels he wrote *The German Ideology*. Apart from containing all the basic tenets of his revised outlook, it settled his account with the German intellectuals. In 1847 he and Engels crossed to England and in London reconstituted the German Working Men's Association as the Communist League. On its behalf he composed *The Communist Manifesto*, published in February 1848. Thus at the dawn of European revolution a bugle-call to action was heard:

> A spectre is haunting Europe – the spectre of Communism. All the Powers of old Europe have entered into a holy alliance to exorcise this spectre: Pope and Tsar, Metternich and Guizot, French Radicals and German police spies.
>
> Where is the party in opposition that has not been decried as Communistic by its opponents in power? Where the Opposition that has not hurled back the branding reproach of Communism, against the more advanced opposition parties, as well as against its reactionary adversaries?

> Two things result from this fact:
> I Communism is already acknowledged by all European Powers to be itself a Power.
> II It is high time that Communists should openly, in the face of the whole world, publish their views, their aims, their tendencies, and meet this nursery tale of the Spectre of Communism with a Manifesto of the party itself.

> To this end, Communists of various nationalities have assembled in London, and sketched the following Manifesto, to be published in the English, French, German, Italian, Flemish and Danish languages.

London was at this time the meeting-place for émigrés from half a dozen European countries and with half a dozen different sets of political views – liberals, nationalists, radicals, anarchists, socialists, democrats, republicans – all representatives of the awakening Europe of young nations. Marx's object with his League of Communists was to create the first and only International and to surpass the aims and aspirations of all these individuals and groups by the absoluteness of his prophecy that victory, reason, a happy future and true humanity lay only in the direction in which those marched to whom the future belonged.

'The history of all hitherto existing society is the history of class struggles.' With this opening sentence of the first main part of the Manifesto, Marx refurbished in his own way the age-old gnostic and Manichaean perspective on history as a fight between the Children of Light and of Darkness, a struggle between believers and unbelievers. Three eras, that of feudalism, of the bourgeoisie and of the proletariat, according to Marx, succeeded each other. A pattern of salvation based on the succession of three historical eras had already been a source of inspiration – to Joachim of Flora, Hegel, Schelling and Comte among others.

> The bourgeoisie, historically, has played a most revolutionary part. . . .

> The bourgeoisie, wherever it has got the upper hand, has put an end to all feudal, patriarchal, idyllic relations. . . .

> The bourgeoisie has, through its exploitation of the world market, given a cosmopolitan character to production and consumption in every country. To the great chagrin of Reactionists, it has drawn from under the feet of industry the national ground on which it stood. (Which, it may be said, was untrue of 1848, 1870, 1914 and 1933, but began to become a reality around 1960).

> The bourgeoisie, by the rapid improvement of all instruments of production, by the immensely facilitated means of communication, draws all, even the most barbarian, nations into civilisation. The cheap prices of its commodities are the heavy artillery with which it batters down all Chinese walls, with which it forces the barbarians' intensely obstinate hatred of foreigners to capitulate. . . .

> The bourgeoisie, during its rule of scarce one hundred years, has created more massive and more colossal production forces than have all preceding generations together.

The most imposing tribute to the historic performance by the 'bourgeoisie' and 'capitalism' during the nineteenth century was paid by their lifelong admirer, Karl Marx, in the Manifesto.

> For many a decade past the history of industry and commerce is but the history of the revolt of modern productive forces against modern conditions of production, against the property relations that are the conditions for the existence of the bourgeoisie and of its rule. . . .

> The weapons with which the bourgeoisie felled feudalism to the ground are now turned against the bourgeoisie itself.

> But not only has the bourgeoisie forged the weapons that bring death to

itself; it has also called into existence the men who are to wield those weapons – the modern working class – the proletarians. . . .

Of all the classes that stand face to face with the bourgeoisie today, the proletariat alone is a really revolutionary class. The other classes decay and finally disappear in the face of modern industry; the proletariat is its special and essential product. . . .

All previous historical movements were movements of minorities, or in the interest of minorities. The proletarian movement is the self-conscious, independent movement of the immense majority, in the interest of the immense majority. The proletariat, the lowest stratum of our present society, cannot stir, cannot raise itself up, without the whole superincumbent strata of official society being sprung into the air. . . .

The advance of industry, whose involuntary promoter is the bourgeoisie, replaces the isolation of the labourers, due to competition, by their revolutionary combination, due to association. The development of Modern Industry, therefore, cuts from under its feet the very foundation on which the bourgeoisie produces and appropriates products. What the bourgeoisie therefore produces, above all, is its own grave-diggers. Its fall and the victory of the proletariat are equally inevitable.

It is strange to observe how Marx managed to combine the qualities of a German professor and Hegelian, who sees the victory of his reason being brought to fruition in history, with those of the determination and strength of an Old Testament prophet who anticipates the coming of the Kingdom of God by way of the necessary fall of Jerusalem. In his great essay *Introduction to the Criticism of Hegel's Philosophy of Right* he had set out his arguments for a common bond between philosophy and proletariat. The problem was how Germany could be brought to the point of revolution. Marx, like Heine and, before that, Friedrich Schlegel, perceived a direct line of evolution between reformation, revolution, and philosophy, and therein the promise that 'radical revolution' would at the same time prove to be the 'universal human emancipation'.

The second part of the Manifesto treated the role of the Communists in the working classes and their future struggle for the dissolution of bourgeois society.

The Communists do not form a separate party opposed to other working-class parties.

They have no interests separate and apart from those of the proletariat as a whole.

The Communists . . . are . . . the most advanced and resolute section of the working-class parties of every country. . . .

Marx then disputed in detail a number of reproaches levelled at Communists, especially the one that they 'would introduce common ownership of women'. His circumstantial treatment of this point is interesting for many reasons, including the fact that he clearly wanted to dissociate himself from the communal possession of women propagated by religious 'communist' sects and enthusiast movements from the Middle Ages onward.

Does it require intuition to comprehend that man's ideas, views and conceptions, in one word, man's consciousness, changes with every change in the conditions of his material existence, in his social relations and in his social life?

What else does the history of ideas prove, than that intellectual production changes in character in proportion as material production is changed? The ruling ideas of each age have ever been the ideas of its ruling class. . . .

The Communist revolution is the most radical rupture with traditional property relations; no wonder that its development involves the most radical rupture with traditional ideas.

Marx emphasised that 'the first step in the revolution by the working class, is to raise the proletariat to the position of ruling class, to win the battle of democracy.

The proletariat will use its political supremacy to wrest, by degrees, all capital from the bourgeoisie, to centralise all instruments of production in the hands of the state, i.e., of the proletariat organised as the ruling class; and to increase the total of productive forces as rapidly as possible.

'Of course, in the beginning, this cannot be effected except by means of despotic inroads on the rights of property, and on the conditions of bourgeois production. . . .

Marx then postulated ten 'measures' which the working-class revolution would 'in the most advanced countries' immediately put into practice, closing this section of the Manifesto with the following sentences:

When, in the course of development, class distinctions have disappeared, and all production has been concentrated in the whole nation, the public power will lose its political character. Political power, properly so called, is merely the organised power of one class for oppressing another. If the proletariat during its contest with the *bourgeoisie* is compelled, by the force of circumstances, to organise itself as a class, if, by means of a revolution, it makes itself the ruling class, and, as such, sweeps away by force the old conditions of production, then it will, along with these conditions, have swept away the conditions for the existence of class antagonisms and of classes generally, and will thereby have abolished its own supremacy as a class.

In place of the old *bourgeois* society, with its classes and class antagonisms, we shall have an association, in which the free development of each is the condition for the free development of all.'

Initially the *Communist Manifesto* had barely any palpable effect or influence, a state of affairs which remained constant until the 1870s. As an historic force it did not gather pace until a restless section of the intelligentsia in Russia and countries which were certainly *not* among 'the most advanced, (and therefore not even the primary subject of the Manifesto's attention) instinctively grasped the quintessence of Marx's teaching, his doctrine of salvation and his message about the coming of the New Man, the New Society, the beginning of the truly New Age (which was the title henceforward adopted more and more by left-wing periodicals).

Marx himself was sparing with his delivery of impressive and illuminating indicators regarding his doctrine. On many important points, such as the constitution of society after the Communist victory, he remained completely silent. Yet certain hints were fascinating enough. First and foremost among these was the doctrine of man's 'alienation'.

Gnosticism of the most ancient type had dealt with man's alienation from, and release out of the One Godhead. Hegel's 'renunciation' and alienation were derived from Augustine's commentary on the Epistle to the Philippians, while his teaching about self-evolution and self-propulsion of ideas was rooted in Augustine's major work on the Trinity. In addition, Neoplatonists, Scotus, Eckhart and more recent gnostic mystics had concerned themselves with the same theme:

> The concept of alienation becomes ... from Hegel via Feuerbach to Marx, ever fuller in meaning. With Hegel it indicates a specific phenomenological stage of the spirit awakening to recognition of itself. Feuerbach uses the term already to subsume all sorts of speculative thinking. Finally Marx, in 1844, describes mankind's situation during the whole of preceding history as an 'alienation' of his 'true character' (Heinrich Popiiz).

Marx's interpretation of man is that of a working being who produces himself through his own work. During this process four forms of alienation occur: 1. the worker's alienation from the product of his work; 2. the worker's alienation from his work; 3. the self-alienation of man springing from wage-labour; 4. the alienation of the relationship between men which results in them being unable to regard their own relationship to the 'species', that is, to humanity, objectively and so appearing to each other merely agents.

To this state of affairs must be added a large number of facts which enhance Marx's historical importance. A major industrial society results in a mass of individuals who are lonely, feel alienated and uprooted, and look with deep distrust upon this society. In the first place they will be sensitive types, such as artists, intellectuals, brain-workers. Next are the masses of 'proletarians', followed in turn by the youthful intelligentsia in 'underdeveloped countries', and then those masses whom the suction of an utterly strange technical civilisation tears away from the bosom of their families, peoples, civilisations and religions. For all of these Marx has a road and an objective to offer. The road is that of history; the objective, 'the classless society'. To demonstrate the method, how to attain the lofty objective along the envisaged road, was left to his great successors: Lenin, Stalin, Mao Tse-tung. Through the Marxism-Leninism was to become 'the world's most influential political ideology'.

'For us there is but one single science, the science of history. Looked at from two different perspectives, history can be divided into natural history and human history. But these two perspectives are inseparable from time, and for as long as men exist the history of nature and the history of humanity are interdependent.'

History is progress along the road of nature's humanisation and humanity's naturalisation. 'Classes were to Marx the stuff of history's progressive process just as manifestations of national spirit were to Hegel' (Iring Fetscher).

Marx distinguished his own brand of Communism from that of the Enthusiasts as a:

> genuine assimilation of human nature, through and on behalf of humanity .... This Communism ... is the real dissolution of the conflict between men and nature and men and men, between existence and being, between objectification and personal participation, between freedom and sanction, between individual and species. It is the riddle of history resolved and it knows itself to be such.

In society as previously constituted everyone has a task and activity to perform which is forced upon him and which he cannot escape,

> whereas in Communist society, where no one is confined to an exclusive sphere of society, but can perfect himself in whatever branches he likes, society regulates production as a whole and thereby helps to make it possible to do this today and that tomorrow, to go hunting in the morning, fishing in the afternoon, tend cattle in the evening, and after dinner engage in criticism, just as it happens to please me, without ever becoming huntsman, fisherman, herdsman or critic.

That is the only passage in Marx's immense body of work which deals with the actual shape of future Communist society; but the intimation is a highly charged one.

On the one hand it is a 'reminder' of a condition of society, ancient and fundamental, to which the alienated masses and individuals will return through the maternal care of the Communist movement. Marx thought essentially in terms of the 'Great Mother' who, in the views he held about the material world, men in the mass and history, always hovered in the background. It is this concomitant and underlying appeal to an archaic world in Marx's philosophy of life and history that has rendered it inherently feasible to combine the 'national' Messianisms of Oriental and African peoples with Communist technology, economic principles, seizure of power and its vision of the future. At the same time, it evokes, in a few phrases suggestive of an ancient, primitive society where hunting, fishing, the care of animals, are the basic components of a free life close to nature and one's fellow-men.

Promethean solemnity as exemplified in German Idealism and German Romanticism attained its last flowering with Marx. 'In fact Marx tried to found a realm in which man would be at home wherever he went, would meet his equal everywhere, and would feel both self-confident and that he was receiving due recognition.' His aim, first and last, was to assist in the birth of the 'New Man'.

From this point of view Marx was utterly uninterested in technology (indeed, numerous remarks reveal an instinctive antipathy to it and equally little in economic problems). He hoped to have done with 'all this crap' within a few weeks or months, a time-table which had to be extended to decades to produce his unfinished masterpiece *Capital*. For all his absorption in the conflict between classical and post-classical British economic doctrine, he remained a religious philosopher.

As such, what stirred him most keenly was religious antithesis. His thought derived from essentially religious thinkers – Hegel, Feuerbach, Proudhon, and those much despised critics of Christianity, Bruno Bauer and David Friedrich Strauss. It is not mere chance that his attack and the impetus of 'Marxism' should have been directed with particular ferocity and dynamism against religion and Christianity. The very great effect of Marxist offensives against other older religions owed much to the religious fervour which inspired Marx himself.

In 1844 he proclaimed that:

as far as Germany is concerned, religious criticism, the premise for every kind of criticism, is substantially over.'

The basis of irreligious criticism is that man makes religion, not religion man. Religion is the self-consciousness and self-esteem of a man who either has not yet gained mastery over himself or had once again lost it. But man is no abstract being squatting beyond the world's periphery. Man is the world of men, the state and society. And it is the state and society who are responsible for religion, a topsy-turvy picture of the world, because they themselves represent a topsy-turvy world.

Religion is:

human nature as seen in imagination because human nature has no true reality.'

Religious misery is on the one hand an expression of genuine misery and on the other a form of protest against genuine misery. Religion is the groan of the cornered animal, and the disposition of a heartless world because it is the animating principle behind a senseless set of circumstances. It is the opium of the people. The abolition of religion as the illusory happiness of the people is the promotion of its real happiness. To demand relinquishment of a state of affairs which requires illusions. From religious criticism springs therefore criticism of the vale of tears whose halo is religion.

Religion is simply the illusory sun which revolves around mankind as long as it is not its own pivot. Consequently it is history's responsibility . . . to establish the truth about life on earth.

The criticism of Heaven thus transforms itself into criticism of this world, criticism of religion into criticism of justice, criticism of theology into criticism of politics . . .

Kierkegaard, who said 'Christendom is Satan's invention', wrote *First the Kingdom of God*, 'a sort of short story'. It concerned 'theology probationer Ludwig Fromm' who was in search of something.

And when you hear that it is a 'theology probationer' who is in search of something, then it requires no lively imagination to appreciate what he he must be looking for: the Kingdom of God, of course, which you should look for *first*. But no, that is not it. The object of his search is a royal appointment as parson. Moreover, as I propose to describe in a few short phrases, *first* quite a lot happened before he had got that far.

'First' came school, then attendance at a university, and thereafter the hunt for political patronage. 'He leaves no stone unturned, runs from pillar to post, puts his best foot forward with ministers and porters alike, and, in brief, is wholly engaged in the service of the Absolute.' After all these efforts to attain office, honour and funds, the theme of his first sermon is, 'Let first the Kingdom of God be your care.'

The purpose of this pretty tale, Kierkegaard affirmed, was:

to make it plain to you that the whole truth of official Christianity is nothing else than an abyss of untruth and delusion, something so unholy that only one single thing can truthfully be said about it: through your no longer participating in public worship in its present state (if so far you have done), you are permanently rid of one sin, and a major one at that – you don't partake in making a fool of God.

Insofar as you believe, and of course you do, that stealing, robbing, pilfering, whoring, slandering, and debauchery are offensive to God, the fact is that He finds official Christianity and its divine service infinitely more disgusting than these, seeing that man can fall into such brute stupidity as to dare to offer God a service composed entirely of frivolity, insipidity, and doltishness, and then venture to regard it as progress in Christianity.

First the Kingdom of God appeared in the series of pamphlets whose publication was undertaken by Kierkegaard in the last year of his life and with the last remainder of his fortune, in order openly to wage war against the National Church of Denmark.

Soren Aaybe Kierkegaard (1813–55) wrote the thesis (on the concept of irony) for his master's degree in the same year as Marx composed his doctoral dissertation. From 1843 date Marx's *Criticism of Hegel's Philosophy of Right*, Kierkegaard's *Either/Or*, Feuerbach's *Principles of Future Philosophy*, Bruno Bauer's *Christianity Discovered*, Weitling's *The Poor Sinner's Gospel*, Bettina von Arnim's *This Book is The King's*, and Proudhon's *On the Creation of Order among Humanity*. From 1844 date Kierkegaard's *The Concept of Fear* and Max Stirner's *The Ego and His Own*; from 1846 Marx's *The German Ideology*, and both Kierkegaard's *Unscientific Postscript*, and Malwida von Meysenbug's rejoinder *The Future of Christianity*.

The nineteenth century's three most influential critics of Christianity as well as their own age and society were Marx, Kierkegaard and Nietzsche. They did not read a word of each other's work. And that too is indicative of their time, a time when philosophers, artists, and poets could well be pulling in the same direction without knowing anything about each other, although their intellectual ancestry was identical. Kierkegaard, Marx and Nietzsche were the offspring of German Romanticism, German Idealist philosophy and German Protestant criticism of Christianity. They were all thoroughly familiar with Feuerbach and Strauss and in some degree too with those much derided unfortunates, Bruno Bauer, Ruge and the Berlin Leftists. Marx's and Nietzsche's attacks on and dissociation from Strauss and Feuerbach, just like the secret fascination Feuerbach exercised on Kierkegaard, intimate the stature of these men. They had many weaknesses, but also many qualities, and they displayed greater personal courage than most of this century's 'intellectual champions' have to offer.

DAVID FRIEDRICH STRAUSS

David Friedrich Strauss (1808–74) achieved in one moment international fame and total disruption of a splendid career (such as that open to theology probationer Ludwig Fromm) with the publication of *Life of Christ*, 1835. At the time he was an assistant lecturer at Tübingen, and the storm which broke out over his work was incredible, even bringing about the resignation of the Zurich cantonal government which had offered Strauss a professorial chair. Yet in later years Albert Schweitzer, a man distinguished for his practical Christianity, called Strauss the 'most truthful of all theologians' and the first version of his *Life of Christ* 'a work of literature' belonging to 'the finest that scholastic literature has to offer'.

Strauss was a product of Tübingen's famous theological institute, well versed in contemporary historical and philological studies. It was his pietistic conscience, combined with an incredible naïvety which compelled him to put on paper what thousands either knew instinctively, suspected or feared – that the gospels were a history with 'stories', that many fables and myths had been assigned to the historical Christ, that for many the human Christ was almost lost in his deification, and that the Johannine Gospel derived from a totally different intellectual and spiritual soil than did the synoptic ones. He wanted to face the truth brought to light by scientific approaches to theology, and loathed the fear which it induced in many theologians. Yet after thirty years of struggle he finally concluded that they were incapable of objective judgement because 'they are judge and interested party simultaneously' who 'see their own position as the spiritual class questioned. . . . But for every calling its own perpetuation is the highest law.'

Because Strauss had drawn this last conclusion from bitter experience, he published in 1864 a revised version of his *Life of Christ*. The first edition had been expressly intended for the clergy, not the laity; the second was 'for the German people'. 'I regard the German people as the people of the Reformation and the latter as a work that is not complete but which requires to be continued.'

Mankind, religion, Christianity and all they contained were, according to Strauss, an historical process: 'Through Christianity, mankind has become more deeply aware of itself than was previously the case.' But whoever would 'chase the priests out of the church must first do away with the miracle in religion'. He acknowledged his debt to his predecessors in biblical research, adding, 'The concept of a *Life of Jesus* is not simply a modern but a self-contradictory one.' Behind it lay the conflict between the Church's Jesus and the historical Jesus. The aspects of His divinity and humanity entered here upon 'a process of disintegration'. 'To that degree the notion of a life of Jesus is a portentous one. It comprises, as in a nut-shell, the whole of modern theological development. . . . The idea of a life of Jesus is the snare into which contemporary theology had to fall and which was bound to bring about its fall.'

This important passage needs to be understood as follows: it was the Protestant principle and the nineteenth century's scientific awareness which drove theology into this snare. Theology's self-destruction through dissolution into philological and historical disciplines, accompanied by the inner liquidation of the species of Christianity appertaining to and obeying this theology, was an 'inevitable' historical process which in the deployment of its positive and negative elements went far beyond the nineteenth century.

Strauss quoted, without giving his name, the outburst of an indignant theologian:

> If the Johannine Gospel is spurious, an interpolation, *then* our love is transformed into glowing hate, then it is no longer for us the spiritual Gospel which it was for Clement of Alexandria nor the one, tender, really main Gospel which it was for Luther, but the most tedious and most dangerous piece of botched work on the part of a muddle-headed fellow or a fraud.

This outburst conveys a glimpse of the subconscious psychological state of many 'orthodox' nineteenth-century theologians. Their minds stored a gigantic fear of, and defensiveness against, the disturbance of accepted ideas. Strauss' reply was that the author of the Johannine Gospel believed himself entitled to present his work as speaking with the voice of the Apostle because it was the lofty enunciation of a love, human and divine, which paid no heed to name, rank, or sect. The Johannine Gospel was '*the romantic* Gospel'.

Strauss had his own explanation for this element in the Gospels. 'I have in my earlier edition already proffered the concept of myth as the key to the tales of miracles, and much else in the Gospel accounts, which runs contrary to historical perspective. The origin of myths is to be sought in a 'production of communal consciousness on the part of a people or religious community . . . which may well be uttered by an individual in the first place, but is believed because he is only acting as agent for what amounts to a general conviction.'

'I cannot tell whether the supernatural origin which can be ascribed to Christianity does it more honour than if historical research seeks to show that it was the rich harvest of everything that up till then human endeavour everywhere had aspired to.' Its postulates were 'the marriage between East and West', the work of Alexander, and the pounding of Jewry 'in the mortar of history'. 'Had Alexander not preceded, Christ could not have come after.' 'For the rest, it is highly probable that Jesus' father was a carpenter and so belonged to the lower class of the people.' Strauss did not, however, go so far as Kierkegaard who, in sharp resistance to the 'edifying' Christmas festivities of middle-class Christianity, charged Jesus with having been an illegitimate child.

Two years before his death Strauss published 'a confession', *The Old and New Faith*, and categorically answered his own question: 'Are we still Christians – No!'

If we open our eyes and honestly face the consequences, we shall have to concede that the whole life and effort of educated contemporary nations is based on an outlook on life which is diametrically opposed to that of Jesus. Technology, industry and the arts furnished proof that this world was 'man's true field of endeavour, the essence of his aims'.

If a part of the workers in this field of endeavour still carries along with belief in the other world, it is no more than a shadow treading on their heels and in no way exercises any determining influence on their activities. . . .

Christianity never got beyond crusades and the persecution of heretics. It did not even attain tolerance, which, after all, is no more than a negative quantity in the scale of universal human love. . . .

If we don't look for excuses, if we don't want to twist and explain away, if we want 'yes' to mean 'yes' and 'no' to be 'no', in short, if we want to be honest and upright, then we must grant that indeed we are Christians no longer. . . .

The extent of the religious territory of the human soul resembles that of the Red Indians in America, which, however it may be regretted or condemned, is narrowed down by their pale-faced neighbours from year to year. But restriction, and probably transmutation too, does not amount to destruction. Religion is no longer to us what it was to our fathers. However, it does not therefore follow that it is extinct in us.

Strauss saw Kant and Goethe as Darwin's predecessors. As for the latter, his theory irresistibly attracts 'truth- and freedom-loving intellects. . . . (He) has opened a door through which a happier posterity can throw out the miracle for good'.

The cessation of belief in Providence, he concluded, does indeed count among the severest losses involved in renouncing Christian Church beliefs. Instead you see yourself standing inside an enormous, world machine with whirring gear-wheels and sledge-hammers and pile-drivers, not sure for an instant whether an unguarded movement in the deafening din will not find you seized and torn to pieces by a wheel or smashed to pulp by one of the hammers. . . .

'Initially this feeling of helplessness is truly dreadful. But our longing does not alter the world and our reason proves to us that it really is such a machine. . . . Our God does not take us up into His arms, but He does open to us wells of consolation within ourselves.' As compensation for 'the Church's doctrine of immortality' man has his 'activity on behalf of his family', his 'labours in his profession', his 'collaboration in the welfare of his people and humanity at large', and, by no means least, 'the enjoyment of beauty in nature and art'. This, and this alone, is 'the universal highway of the future, whereas all pains and costs expended on improvement of the old road must be regarded as wasted and lost.'

Plainly and ruthlessly, Strauss expounded a belief which held good for a section of the German middle class around 1872 and continued to be the philosophy of life of very many people until 1914 and even beyond. In the case of Strauss himself the belief had grown in a man who, formed by the Tübingen Institute, was at home in the world of Hegel and Romanticism, but who strode boldly ahead into the nascent age of industrialisation, technology and middle-class culture. In this man, who seemed to have rid himself of all illusions, one cannot help wondering what had happened to the age-old cosmic fear of the Germans. But in fact, Strauss was afraid, and said so openly and with great honesty. He was afraid of war, afraid for the German nation (Bismarck's Empire), of 'socialism', 'communism', 'the fourth estate'. The ancient religious, metaphysical, existential *Angst* underwent secularisation and was diverted into political and neurotic channels. Nothing so well reflects this process – so highly symbolic of the nineteenth century – as the work of Strauss' old age.

BRUNO BAUER

Nietzsche had no difficulty in unmasking and deriding Strauss in his middle-class personification as a 'cultural Philistine'. He was, however, startled to learn that a close sympathiser with Strauss had anticipated some of his own most characteristic ideas.

Bruno Bauer (1809–82) was not only of an age with Strauss, but also underwent a very similar fate. The son of a small china-shop owner, he began to teach at Berlin as a licentiate of theology in 1834, but only six years later, at the age of thirty-three, had his licence revoked. In that short time he had gone over from being a severe critic of Strauss' *Life of Jesus* to 'a development in the opposite direction'. Minister Altenstein, a man of traditional Prussian views and for a while patron of Ruge, had him transferred in his own best interests to Cologne and tried to obtain a professorial chair for him. The appointment of Eichhorn as Minister of Public Worship and Education put an end to that hope. The theological faculty of every Prussian university except Königsberg (Kant's own city) declared against Bauer, whereupon his teaching permit was withdrawn.

The gifted young man's reaction was one of overwhelming fury and as vigorous a determination to pursue with hard work the path he had chosen. After the victory of the forces of political reaction in 1848–9 he moved to Rixdorf, in the environs of Berlin, and lived there (as a friend reported to Nietzsche) in surroundings so desolate as 'only Gogol's most vivid imagination can picture'. He tilled his soil without reducing himself mentally to the level of a yokel. His library and study was in a former cowshed. As the years passed, he became known as 'the hermit of Rixdorf' and twice a week 'his patriarchal figure, in a suit he had patched himself, strode in high boots along the streets, his shoulders as unbowed as in the days of his youth and his eyes looking out from under the invariable peaked cap as calmly and penetratingly as ever.' Behind him he would be drawing a small barrow piled with the home-grown vegetables which he would sell at the market. 'Free as any monarch' and unbroken in spirit, he died at Rixdorf in 1882.

Bauer's initial aim had been to save 'the honour of Jesus' from Strauss' criticism. After his rejection by academic theology he noted that theological criticism lacked the liberty of genuine criticism: 'the prisoner may walk around his prison, but he may not leave it'.

He had maintained the view that Christianity, as an historical manifestation, had not originated in Palestine but at Alexandria and Rome; the Christian Saviour and the Roman Caesars, though hostile brothers, were products of one and the same historical force. When official theological scholars spurned his studies from beginning to end, Bauer was furious. Henceforth theology appeared to him as 'the dark spot in modern history' and he declared that 'No lie is evil enough for the theologian, in the panic of his soul, not to regard it as justified.'

In spring 1843 Fröbel, the Zurich publisher of Bauer, Herwegh and German left-wing intellectuals, paid a visit to his former patron, Alexander von Humboldt, at Berlin, having previously made a polite enquiry whether 'as a revolutionary bookseller' he would still be welcome. Fröbel had voluntarily abandoned his own academic career in order to turn publisher and bookseller: 'People are becoming more educated, education is becoming more popular.... On the potentialities inherent in this concurrence rest the potentialities of modern democracy, the potentialities of a new, popularly based civilisation.'

Fröbel, in the course of the talk, mentioned Bauer's *Christianity Discovered*. 'A dangerous title,' exclaimed Humboldt. 'Not that there is much to discover. A bit of artless cosmogony, a bit of mythical ancient history, a bit of dubious metaphysics and a cruder or more refined morality – those are the ingredients to be found in every religion and are obvious enough.' The comment mirrors the view of Christianity held at the top of the social scale by a member of the old Enlightenment.

Despite its immediate suppression after publication by Fröbel, *Christianity Discovered* not only played a hotly-disputed role in Zurich cantonal politics but had an explosive impact in Germany. Karl Marx, Friedrich Engels and Max Stirner all used its line of thought. The title was a counterpart to *Jewry Discovered*, a seventeenth-century anti-Semitic pamphlet. Bauer saw himself as 'a re-born Edelmann'. In his *Avowal of Faith* (1746) Johann Christian Edelmann had taught that Christ was pure, heaven and hell existed on earth only, there was nothing Christ wanted less than to found a religion, the clergy were responsible for killing Christ.

In the preface to his pamphlet Bauer brought up the question of the weaknesses of the French Enlightenment and the reasons for its defeat. The introduction closed with the statement that although he did not know what the work's fate would be, 'one thing is certain: Truth can say, like the Sybil, "Suppress, confiscate, burn as much as you like, the last page that remains – and *one* page will always remain – will cost as much as all that has been rejected and suppressed: a new world. The price stays the same and history will pay it." '

'Hell' was defined as consisting in the 'misery of religious conviction'. Religion was dominated by 'perpetual strife'. 'Religious differences ... are everlasting and cannot be harmonised.' 'The anathema of religious conviction is its *own* anathema.'

A sect (for Bauer 'sect' was the appropriate description for every Christian denomination) must 'go in perpetual fear of its adherents. It is never safe from treason (that is what thinking is called), nor from conspiracy (the name for scholastic research), nor from attacks by the desperate.' Regression will become fiercer 'the more the fear of sects grows and the danger that history will win becomes menacing'. The foregoing sentences illuminate equally happenings in France around 1830 and the struggle relating to 'Modernism' from 1890 to 1914.

Religion brought to perfection is the world's most perfect misfortune. The inner vacuum to which the Christian must aspire, the suspension of all tension, and the extinction of all inner fires result in either complete indifference and inertia *vis-à-vis* the state of the world or cowardice or the hypochondria with which empty Heaven harasses itself and those who keep it company. . . . Tyrants can safely rely on Christian inertia.

It was a startling picture of Christianity as a human disease and while most people will agree that it may not be totally accurate universally, it was accurate enough in regard to Christianity during the nineteenth century.

He pleaded for a 'healthy self-love': 'Whoever does not love and respect himself is either a rascal or is on the way to becoming one. In any case he must seem insufferable to himself and equally therefore to be a burden to mankind.' 'What else is the concept of God other than the consummated rejection of mankind, of victimised mankind, of man disavowed?' 'Fundamentally the pretence of the religious-minded man that he loves God is simply a confession that he hates mankind.' (On the Catholic side Péguy, Bernanos and Julien Green have put this point forward for debate.)

Bauer had no respect for theologians, their style or their temper. His charge of mendacity has already been quoted. To this was added the claim that inner instability of conviction produced instability of style. . . . Contradiction is unbearable to him.

He is the most irritable creature in the world. And that is very understandable! Since he does not adopt an untrammelled attitude towards matters in general and towards our own doubts, but can only oppose to us his narrow-minded outlook, he cannot but suppose that we are simply being obstinate, malicious and impenitent, and do not want to recognise the truth of what he says.

In *Christianity Discovered* Bauer carried out the first psycho-pathological examination of Christianity and the first phenomenological study of 'the Church's pathological social structure' in the shape of a 'closed society' in the way that a theologian of our day, Paul Schutz, has shown to be the case in *Parusia* (Heidelberg 1961).

His final sentence ran, 'Let us leave the Christians their enraged gods!' He adhered firmly to his atheism, but at the same time declined to leave the Church because he thought that the 'prison' should be worn away from within, not from without. His militant anti-christianity remained of a highly individual stamp. This is seen in his relationship to Max Stirner, the friend of his Berlin University days, and Ludwig Feuerbach. Each represented a different, in some respects, indeed, contradictory, form of atheism. Nevertheless all three were basically theologians pursuing tendencies and developments in German Protestantism. All three were of historical importance in the process of European Christianity's self-dissolution during the course of the nineteenth century.

These three contemporaries were subconsciously aware of their inseparable attachment to Christianity. In Stirner's eye Bruno Bauer and Feuerbach were 'dogmatists', meaning Christians, just as Feuerbach scented in Stirner's 'self-happiness' and 'ultra-individualism' a 'Christian individual blessedness'. Nineteenth-century atheists constantly reproached each other with Christianity or the remains of Christian piety and intellectual outlook. And they were quite right to do so, for it was only on the basis of this established ecclesiasticism, consisting of a professional theology and pietistic spirituality, that their Protestant Enlightenment could evolve.

LUDWIG FEUERBACH

Ludwig Feuerbach (1804–72) had studied theology at Heidelberg, philosophy under Hegel at Berlin, and qualified as a university teacher at Erlangen. Any academic future he might have had was, however, blocked by the publication of his *Reflections on Death and Immortality*, and it does seem that he was probably not suited to an academic career, for a series of lectures which he gave on religion in the winter of '48–9 at Heidelberg, disappointed his audience especially Gottfried Keller, because of the 'laborious, inferior manner of delivery'. He was possibly happiest living modestly and quietly at Bruckberg, associating with the country folk on equal terms, and indeed looking much like a forester himself.

To many of his contemporaries in Europe he seemed a great liberator, while to others his ideas were a source of ridicule because of their apparent triviality, banality and overtones of dogmatic Christianity. Today he is even regarded as a kind of Antichrist. But, as Friedrich Engels said of his book, *The Essence of Christianity* (1841); 'To have any conception of it you have to have experienced its liberating effect. The enthusiasm was general. For the moment we were all Feuerbach adherents. With what warmth Marx welcomed this new interpretation; the extent to which he was influenced by it can be seen from *The Holy Family*.'

To many tortured and timid spirits, frightened by the notion of the terrible and barbarically malevolent God Jehovah, Feuerbach with his glad tidings: 'All that matters is man', looked like a new Luther (whom he invoked in support of his arguments). 'The secret of theology is anthropology.' 'Religion is man's first, and indirect, awareness of himself,' a detour on the way to self-discovery. Man has created God in his own image. The positive evolution of religion consists in 'man finding ever less comfort in God and more in himself'.

'God was my first, reason my second, and man my third and final inspiration.' The Third Kingdom of the Holy Ghost, for which Hölderlin, Hegel and Schelling struggled, is present in this concept of man as the third source of inspiration at which point man dares to become wholly and completely man, recognising and avowing himself as such. 'The essence of man is the highest essence. . . . If the godhead of Nature is the basis of all religions, Christianity included, then the godhead of man is its ultimate purpose. . . . The turning-point in history will occur at the moment when it dawns on man that man's sole God is man himself. *Homo homini Deus*!'

The significance of Feuerbach as a pioneer along the road to the rebirth of piety is not difficult to appreciate if two points are borne in mind. On the one hand, he spoke as a theologian aware of the torments of conscience and spirit suffered by generations of men unable to make anything positive out of an alienated God. On the other, he spoke (around 1848) as a contemporary who had the courage frankly to state that Sunday Christianity was no more than 'a settled idea which stands in glaring contrast to our fire and life insurance companies, our railways and steam-carriages, our picture galleries and sculpture exhibitions, our military academies and polytechnical schools, our theatres and natural history collections.' Life was dominated by 'hypocrisy' because men wanted to be 'Christian' and 'pious' and could no longer be so. Feuerbach wanted to help such people by providing them with a new kind of piety by way of a fresh self-awareness where reason, love and strength of belief could rest on a foundation of man's trust in man. He envisaged man irradiated by the light of divine strength. 'In the eyes of the Israelites a Christian is a freethinker. That is how things change. What was religion yesterday does not count as such today, and what is today regarded as atheism is tomorrow's religion.'

It is no wonder that Feuerbach, genuinely naïve, did not survive the harsh realities of 1848. Nevertheless the impression he made on Marx, Engels, Nietzsche, in Russia, Britain and the world over, where men were concerned with remoulding religion, demonstrates how much he corresponded to the needs of his day.

MAX STIRNER

'Man is for man the highest being, says Feuerbach. Man has now been found, says Bruno Bauer. Let us take a closer look at this highest being and this find.' These three sentences begin Max Stirner's book *The Ego and His Own*.

Johann Kasper Schmidt (1806–56), who adopted the pseudonym Max Stirner, was a friend of Bruno Bauer from the Berlin Doctors' Club, and like many others of this small group of theologians and other freethinkers, he dared to say and write what more important individuals (for example Alexander von Humboldt) only uttered in private conversation, and many others would not admit at all. And if these men stooped at time to a certain vulgarity and triviality, or to a belief in the resurrection of the German intellect in Bismarck's Empire, this is understandable in the context of their loneliness and isolation.

> Thousands of years have overshadowed for you what you are and have led you to believe you are not egoists, but called upon to be idealists. . . . Don't look for liberation in 'self-denial', which is precisely what robs you of yourselves, but become egoists, each of you an *almighty ego*. . . . Recognise what you really are, give up your hypocritical exertions. . . . I say 'hypocritical' because you have none the less all these thousands of years remained egoists, but somnolent, self-deceiving, cracked egoists, you self-tormentors.

Nietzsche's struggle against a morality which had degenerated into cant is already found here as the focus of Stirner's effort to free men from the idols, ideals, delusions and phantasmagoria, which for thousands of years had risen in their minds as a result of the fear in their hearts.

Stirner asks why man allowed himself to be put into fetters for so long, from ancient antiquity down to the most recent clerics in the shape of Saint-Just and Robespierre, and likens Christianity and middle-class morality to a ghost world, where bourgeoisie, liberals and communists alike continue to weave a yarn which provides the self-made noose for man's self-destruction. He goes on to maintain that no one can release these tormentors from themselves, nor any external force or idea, political or intellectual movement. This liberation is something which only the ego itself can achieve: the individuality.

'I champion neither an idea nor thought, for "I", who is my point of departure, am neither an idea nor do I subsist in thinking. The realm of ideas, of thought, and of the intellect founders of me, the ineffable.'

Neither criticism nor atheism is enough, although Stirner had no objection to 'Christianity' if it helped the ego to gain control over itself. But a future also had to be secured.

The future is restricted to the words, 'The world of things is mine and the world of the mind is mine'.

What, then, is man? I am he! Man, the end and outcome of Christianity, is as *I* the beginning of history anew and the raw material to be exploited by it, a history of pleasure after the history of sacrifice, not a history of man or mankind, but – *mine*.

At the entrance to the new age stands the 'God-Man'. Will at its egress only God in God-Man be sublimated and can God-Man really die if it is only God Who dies? The question was not considered and all was thought complete when the work of the Enlightenment, the supervention of God in our day, had been brought to a successful close. It was not observed that man had killed God so as now to become 'sole God on high'. The *beyond external to us* has truly enough been swept away and the great undertaking of the Enlighteners accomplished; but the *beyond within us* has been transformed into a new Heaven and summons us afresh to assaults on Heaven. God has had to give way, not to us but to Man. How can you believe the God-Man to be dead without Man also having died?

Disdainfully and firmly Max Stirner declared, 'I, as an ego, set myself against the chimeras with which man in our time besets himself. They are religious, political, philosophical figments of the imagination and must be scattered by the will and the penetrative clarity of the ego which knows I am alone in the world, dependent on myself alone and the creative powers, that are within me.'

KIERKEGAARD

Kierkegaard was a master of deception and self-deception, a master of mystification. In assessing his work and personality, there is therefore some advantage in considering firstly certain points of reference in his philosophy and life.

He was in close sympathy with early German Romanticism, and consequently as in the Jena period of Schlegel, Tieck and Novalis, 'the borders between aestheticism and religion become . . . blurred' (Georg Luckàcs). He remained all his life under the spell of the German idealist philosophers and critics, while still wishing to transcend them. He was, in fact, fundamentally a despairing reactionary: 'My entire work is the defence of the existent.' And the greatness of his reaction corresponds to the greatness of his despair, God being, as he himself says, the postulate of those who despair.

Kierkegaard considered that history was useless for a knowledge of Christ because nothing could possibly be known about 'Christ'; 'he is a paradox, the subject of a belief, only there for belief'. He was aware of the critical investigations taking place in his day into the history of early Christianity, but saw clearly 'that on the basis of even relatively methodical scholarly examination the traditional apostolic approach to history and the traditional apostolic factual historicity of Christ can no longer be upheld'. He disparaged historical apprehension as a whole, for 'historical knowledge is a deception of the intellect as it is only an approximation to knowledge'.

There is a radical division between ethics and history. Ethical matters take place at a purely individual and inwardly directed level: 'The more man evolves ethically, the less he will bother about history'; and so Kierkegaard skipped eighteen hundred years of Christianity and with his religious nihilism resolves past and present, all historical developments, society, political institutions and Christianity itself for the sake of one single thing: to recover the Christian quintessence: 'An effort must be made to re-introduce Christianity into Christendom.' And only the individual can do this. 'Politics in these days are everything. On earth politics are put in hand for earthbound purposes. Religion sets out from on high to transfigure the terrestrial and then exalt it heavenwards.' Again the individual is alone capable of this exaltation, for he is a category of the spirit to which there is no greater antithesis than politics, and also a crucial Christian category.

Kierkegaard thought of his age as one of decay and insurgence, with Christianity buried under a mound of human lies, and envisaged himself as the harbinger of a new and nobler type of Christian who would emerge from this fresh category of mankind, the 'individual'. But he never held himself to exemplify the new type, being at once too aware of his own ambivalent relationship to Christ and that, not merely incapable of love, he was, indeed, in danger of being choked by his loathing of himself and mankind. Yet although he was convinced that no 'individual can help or save an age, he can only indicate that it is going under', he did, in a unique way, bear witness to a Christian conscience which vigorously opposed Christendom's disintegration, and condemned his own, disbelieving, despairing self.

His childhood was an unhappy one. He was born the last of seven children when his parents were already elderly, and was the son of his father's second marriage, a marriage which seemed to the latter to be some sort of fornication for which, like a new Abraham, he must try to make redress through the sacrifice of his youngest offspring. Kierkegaard never mentions his mother, hating her in a way gifted men often do who fear and suppress the feminine streak in themselves. (Yet it was probably the cheerful nature he inherited from her which saved him from suicide.)

His father, originally a shepherd, became a successful, self-made man, retiring from business at forty, and concerning himself with his books, his Bible and the education of his seven children. Even when an old man, however, he was preoccupied with a sin of his youth: he had cursed God. Consequently, as a form of atonement perhaps, he tried to make his youngest son a pietist, teaching him to abjure the world, to fight against sinfulness (of the flesh) and, as a Christian, to endure suffering (for his father the very essence of Christianity). It is not surprising that at a later stage, still under the spell of his father's influence, Kierkegaard wrote: 'To live God is to suffer.' In the boy's mind the father stood for an awe-inspiring God, and although he learnt to be sceptical about most things in this so-called sinful world, he could admit to doubt as to the reality of this father whom he hated, loved, looked up to, feared and in his innermost self perhaps abhorred. He was torn between this vision of God and Christ, but had one consolation: at least he was able to regard the abnormal sensibility which plagued him as a sign of being God's elect.

It is a result of his complex attitude to religion that Kierkegaard made paradox the axis of his thought. God is at a great distance and quite near. A Christian should hate what he loves and love what he hates. He was tireless in the exposition of paradoxical situations. 'The paradox is the subject of belief.' Behind this conviction lay the struggle in his mind, as a child, between 'father' and 'mother' and the effort to love what he loathed. For in his subconscious he loved with every fibre of his being his mother, the world, carnal pleasure, gladness and Regina Olson, while hating his father, his Church and his God.

Torn this way and that, he saw but two alternatives for himself: 'either the world to its utmost fearful limit – or the cloister.' (*Either-or* was the title of his first publication.) He was a master at lighting on and demonstrating deadly serious alternatives. His power of attraction, not merely for nervous intellectuals who wish to flee into a mentally refreshing Christianity, is displayed in the force with which he tries to render his hallucinations mandatory.

Faith, he wrote in 1849, was a delusive contest on behalf of a possibility. But what possibility did he think that men had? The precious one of becoming creative through their fear. He undertook what was perhaps the first attempt at an analysis of neurosis. 'The whole of existence frightens me, from the smallest gnat to the secrets of the Incarnation. . . . I feel polluted by the whole of existence, most of all by myself.' Nietzsche, his spiritual brother, was to speak of neurotic fear as 'a European sickness'; Kierkegaard was its harbinger. 'Repress the present and the outcome is fear of the future.' That was precisely what happened in the late nineteenth century.

Materially he had everything requisite to a well-to-do middle-class life. But he lacked two 'small things': love and faith. His greatness consisted in his inability to console himself for the absence of these two 'small things' without which many thousands of people fancy that life can be sustained quite satisfactorily. 'Had I had faith, I would have stayed with Regina.' He interpreted his life as atonement for the guilt of his father who had conceived him in sin, a sin multiplied by his own inability to love.

He met Regina Olsen in May 1837. He was twenty-four, she fourteen. He fell in love with her, they became engaged, and the beautiful young girl and slightly hunchbacked young man were the talk of the town. He felt like an old man beside her, regarded her as a 'beloved child' whose sex was almost irrelevant. In truth he was terrified of womanhood and marriage. His father died in August 1838. On 12 January 1841 he preached his first sermon. On 11 October of the same year he dissolved the engagement with Regina, apportioning all blame to himself, left for Berlin, and attended Schelling's lectures. He returned eighteen months later and, apart from two brief trips to Berlin in 1845 and 1846, never again left Copenhagen. He preached twice more, in August 1847 and September 1848, before finally abandoning a theological career. In January 1854 the bishop who had been his father's friend died. Less than a month later his essay '*Was Bishop Mynster a witness to truth?*' was published. Its target was Bishop Martensen, who personified for him the overall falsehood of Christendom, the established Church, and the clerical estate. Martensen's revenge was frightful. For decades after Kierkegaard's death he falsified him into an orthodox Lutheran who for the remainder of the nineteenth century was revered in Scandinavia as a sort of saint, a defender of the faith, author of 'improving' addresses, and teacher of a pietistic and perfervid Christianity.

In fact, Kierkegaard was a rebel who 'conducted a most radical struggle against the Church' (Karl Jaspers) and proclaimed, 'I am no Christian – and unhappily I am in a position to reveal that others are not either, indeed even less so than I.' None the less he was one of the nineteenth century's great Christians, just as, incapable of love, the love in his heart was conspicuous. Regina remained in his mind until he died and he left her his works. This enemy of matrimony wrote some of the finest pages in modern literature about married love. Like a new Isaac, he offered himself voluntarily as his father's sacrificial victim and could say that Abraham 'became great through that love which is hate of self'. And with his aphorism of absolute hate of self, he disclosed the terrifying secret of a Christendom which exists essentially in self-disgust, leads to hatred of neighbour and mankind, and ever again produces wars and civil strife.

His fear of his father, the dread Divinity, himself, woman and the 'filth' of the flesh were concentrated in his terror of the masses and a Communist revolution. In Communism, which so frightened him, he perceived the ingredient of Christian religiosity, and out of the immense vacuum and falsehood permeating his contemporaries he foresaw the rise of false prophets. Like Marx, he sensed in contradiction to the coming of revolution, the Reformation; this political movement would he thought turn into a religious one. At that moment new martyrs and new saints alone would be fit to rule the world. They would be spiritual ministers who could discriminate among the masses and transform them into individuals, ministers who would not want to dominate, ministers with insight into the hearts of men, ministers capable of enduring patiently and imperturbably the misdemeanours of the sick, 'for mankind is sick and, taken spiritually, sick unto death'. The mortal sickness of European Christendom was his deep conviction.

6

Germany Awake!

THE TRAGEDY OF GERMAN LIBERALISM

'The truth of the matter is that at the beginning of the nineteenth century Napoleon was, quite unintentionally, the pioneer of German Liberalism. By his reorganisation of German affairs he paved the way for the equality of all before the law, for fresh political procedures, and for a constitutional and unitary German state.'

(OSKAR KLEIN-HATTINGEN, 1911, *first historian of German liberalism*).

At face value this view seems to be incomprehensible to the casual student, for in Germany in the years following the French Revolution and the upheavals caused by Napoleon, a resistance to all Western, and particularly French, political ideas, and a repudiation of all European traditions began to make itself felt with a vehemence which lasted right into the twentieth century. And yet there is, nevertheless, much truth in the comment, for in the last decade of the eighteenth and the first decade of the nineteenth centuries the violence of this reactionary feeling was partially concealed by the amazing achievements of Prussia. Here men like Stein, Hardenberg and Wilhelm von Humboldt, profiting from the experience of recent history, started to work for a reform of the state, based on its own and on Western European tradition which, for those few years, created a basis of political thinking and planning which was bolder and more liberal than at any other time throughout the hundred years that followed. But the great beginning could not succeed. Stein, Hardenberg and Humboldt represented the enlightenment and a Protestantism based on conscience and good sense; their voices were drowned by ever more numerous ones from below, raised against enlightenment, princes, the Weimar of Goethe, yet still talking of the German nation. The new masses, a German people compounded of the middle and lower classes, students, artisans, apprentices and minor bureaucrats, not capable of understanding the significance of the revolution abroad, industrial or political, preferred the language of dreams, hatred and fears to that of good sense.

The most powerful of these spokesmen of the people was the son of a bond peasant at Rügen, who obtained his freedom after the birth of his son,

Ernst Moritz Arndt. By means of a pamphlet, *Attempt at a History of Villeinage in Pomerania and Rügen*, the young man succeeded in persuading the King of Sweden to abolish serfdom in those territories. Arndt was endowed with the talents of a plebeian leader and demagogue and, although dismissed from his professorial chair, was later of great significance to nineteenth-century thought, being in fact responsible for the myth of hereditary enmity between the French and Germans which poisoned the atmosphere of the whole century, as well as teaching the masses that the mission of mankind finds fulfilment in that state of exalted hate with which those nations regard each other. Popular rancour against the wealthy middle classes, against strangers, against Jews, had been rampant in Europe since the Middle Ages; but, under Arndt's tuition, it was revived and took the form of hatred of everything possible, of the French, the Jews, the Poles, the Russians, the Turks, the German princes, the Churches, Weimar and Romanticism, foreign clothing and words. And in Arndt lies also the roots of German aims in the First and Second World Wars, for he aimed at a greater Germany, which was to include Holland, Switzerland and Poland, stretching from Dunkirk to the East.

Just as significant was Friedrich Ludwig Jahn, the *Turnvater*, a 'noisy barbarian' (Treitschke), who divided the nation into good Germans and bad Germans and in his writing and speeches championed the cause of the German nation, exhorting German poets 'to inspire the Fatherland's arms and chant its victories'. And yet there was a plebeian enthusiasm and extravagance about him which was in many ways more genuine than that of the twentieth-century plebeian, Adolf Hitler.

It was Jahn who said that bad books were more dangerous than bad food, who inspired the students in their fanatical burning of books and the rejection of everything that was dissolute like Weimar. In fact, however, the Duke of Weimar had encouraged the occasion at Wartburg when books had been burnt by students, for it was there that preparations were set in train for the foundation at Jena of the *Allgemeine Deutsche Burschenschaft* in October 1818, in which three very different elements were represented: a radical right wing, a radical left wing and a wide, relatively unpolitical centre. Members of the Arnold Ruge type became energetic democrats and 'radical' republicans, providing an important leaven in the 1848 movement, and giving spice to the national-liberal trend of the middle classes in the later nineteenth century. Part of the radical right wing grouped itself at Jena, around Jakob Friedrich Fries, a pupil of Fichte who had a considerable following among the young at that period.

The question of greatest importance, however, and which Goethe voiced was: had the German people really woken up during the process of the Wars of Liberation? 'Germany Awake!' It was a grand theme and could be put into practice in so many different ways: as a summons to national-liberal German freedom and unity (giving primacy to freedom), or as a summons to national unity in freedom, or as popular summons to the formation of a nation in arms selected for and bound to the purpose of changing the face of the earth, starting with the map of Europe.

THE AWAKENING OF THE SCHOLARS AND PROFESSORS

In the nineteenth century in Germany the spectacular rise to significance and power of the scholars and professors is an inseparable link in the chain of the German tragedy.

During the eighteenth and early nineteenth centuries German scholars had always been regarded by the rest of Europe as 'semi- or utter barbarians', clumsy, lacking in confidence, incapable of spontaneity and in many ways overbearing and irate, but as the century progressed they rose, more than any other class in Germany, to a position of world standing. Indeed, they were highly regarded as leaders in scholarship and intellect, outstanding as organisers of new academic disciplines, admired as speakers at international conferences, and generally revered by the world.

The change in status was the work of a few men during the difficult decades of the first half of the century, when the rise to the position of a national spokesman was inextricably bound up with a rise in social status. Thus the scholars, men of learning, finally achieved their Golden or Heroic Age in the years around 1848, afterwards withdrawing into splendid isolation. Indeed to cite two personalities of a very different calibre, neither Bismarck nor William II wished to let these men have an acknowledged say in their new *Reich*, although they naturally still required their faithful service.

Lorenz Oken exemplifies the rally of the scholars to a new awareness for themselves and a new attitude towards their time. Born in 1779 in Baden of peasant parentage, he was a doctor and natural philosopher, as obstinate as he was talented. In 1816 he founded *Isis*. By 1848 he had expanded this periodical into an encyclopedia of the physical sciences and medicine and a forum for the expression of German views on these subjects. Seeing that open political activity was no longer possible after 1817, Oken decided to undertake the organisation and political education of German scholars within the narrower field of his own disciplines. In 1822, following the Swiss pattern, he founded a German doctors' and natural philosophers' association. At its first meeting in Leipzig, a very modest affair, many participants were sufficiently afraid of their political authorities to ask for their names not to be recorded for in April of the same year a Prussian Cabinet edict had forbidden all university teachers to enter upon political discussions. Penalty for disobedience was dismissal. Yet a quarter of a century later the number of members belonging to Oken's association had grown from twenty to six hundred and fifty.

These doctors and natural philosophers constituted the first national organisation of German scientists at the outset of the industrial age and the association was fortunate in having in its initial stages the beneficient spiritual patronage of Alexander von Humboldt's liberal and cosmopolitan outlook. At quite a different intellectual level were also the assemblies of German philologists and scholars organised under the aegis of Friedrich Thiersch, playing the role of Oken in another field. His paper *The Fresh Attacks on German Universities* was preparatory to the first of these meetings, held on 20 September 1836, where from the first a nationalist and fervently patriotic tone was adopted.

Ten years later at Frankfurt the first of the 'Germanists' Transactions' took place. (This was followed in 1847 by the second, and last, at Lübeck.) The opening speech by Jacob Grimm set the key. There was to be no discussion of politics, no acknowledgment of differences between North and South Germans, and no strife between denominations, the ancestors of all concerned having been Germans before conversion to Christianity.

The initial 'Transactions' convention revealed how closely nationalism in this section of the middle class was related to its struggle for political emancipation. When a participant declared that historical study should serve as 'a prophet of the future', it was obvious what sort of future was being anticipated – a Germanic one, and free, resting on German language and German law (as opposed to 'latin and the Napoleonic Code').

Jacob Grimm himself opened up significant perspectives. In times to come, he insisted, the German language would unite the German people, regardless of all boundaries. Two years later, in his *History of the German Language*, he expressed his regret that Lorraine and Alsace, Switzerland, Belgium and Holland should have been 'alienated' from Germany. (Odd to see Hegel's and Marx's 'alienation' recurring with this meaning!) Not, Grimm continued, that this severance should be considered 'irrevocable'. Consistent with the tenor of his vindication of the Germans and their language, Grimm dealt with German emigrants to the United States and demanded the institution of a commission for the preservation of their nationality. Instruction and practice in German abroad should serve actively to maintain national identity.

His suggestions and proposals lay in the air. The publication *Germania* had made its first appearance in 1845. Its founder was also the author of a book about the distribution of Germans throughout the world. For the first time, on the eve of 1848, the *Volksdeutsche*, members of the German ethnic group who after 1918 and 1933 were to be summoned to lofty service on the *Reich*'s behalf, were addressed by a true-blue Germanist.

Grimm compared the relationships to Germany of Germans abroad with that of ancient Greeks in Greek colonies to Hellas. In his eyes emigration and colonisation were closely linked. Germany was a mighty oak, its roots deep in Europe, its acorns strewn over the whole world.

What he said in 1846 presaged the description of Germany's eastward colonisation given by the Breslau historian Stenzel and the comments on 'Germany's eastern mission' provided by Ludwig Konrad Bethmann to the effect that the past was a summons to a still greater future and that there should be an 'unbroken chain' of German colonies to the Black Sea and beyond.

Thus in 1847 the language of the Germanists reached a comparatively restricted circle. In 1848–9, the same pronouncements, made at Frankfurt to the German public at large, were to be even more emphatic.

1848

On 18 May 1848 the German National Assembly met at Frankfurt.

> There is no question but that it was an estimable assembly which took up its deliberations within the bare circular walls of the Paulskirche. There had never been a better educated parliament. Present were more than a hundred professors as well as over two hundred learned lawyers, with writers, clergymen, doctors, mayors, senior administrative officials, manufacturers, bankers and estate owners to complement them, not to mention a few master craftsmen and smallholders – though no workers. Greybeards from the Napoleonic days and youngsters who would still experience the twentieth century; small-town notabilities, well-beloved and famous poets, rhetoricians, historians, politicians. An abundance of idealism was gathered there which, having had to tread softly throughout Metternich's Germany was about to become very vociferous. . . .
>
> A few thousand fine speeches, a few thousand dead and a few thousand legal proceedings – that was the harvest of 1848 and 1849. Of the great and hopeful agitation nothing appeared to remain except disillusion, shame and mockery' (Golo Mann).'

1848 was Bismarck's and Marx's year of apprenticeship. In March the former had wanted to organise a *coup d'état* and counter-revolution. Fourteen years later he said in that well-known speech which was taken so much amiss, 'Neither speeches nor majority resolutions are going to decide the major questions of the age – that was the mistake of 1848 and 1849 – but blood and iron.' Marx drew his own deductions: the revolution of 1848 is to be continued, with utmost rigour of intellect and arms against those responsible for its failure, namely, monarchs, the middle classes and *petite bourgeoisie*.

As a result of the uprising of 1849 no less than eighty thousand people, more than a twentieth of the population of the small territory, emigrated from Baden. The number of emigrants from Germany as a whole rose to some two hundred and fifty thousand a year after 1849, whereas in the 1840s it had been only about a hundred thousand and in the year of revolution had sunk to half that. Those who took the step into the unknown were the nation's most active and courageous, including born leaders of men who subsequently gained an honoured place for themselves in American public life.

This drain of an *élite* is something which affected Germany far into the twentieth century.

The Frankfurt Parliament lacked real power. The armies, the police, the state finances and the bureaucracies remained in the hands of those who in March 1848 underwent 'a momentary loss of nerve'. The Parliament of the Empire created by Bismarck was equally ineffectual. Bismarck and his pupil, Emperor William II, could ignore this 'watering-can of phrases' (Bismarck's nickname for Heinrich von Gagern the first president of the National Assembly), intractable. The Parliament of the Weimar Republic, soon denounced as merely a place for idle chatter, acquired no more actual power than either the Frankfurt Parliament or the post-1871 *Reichstag*. But what did prove real and thoroughly effective were the fears and personal interests of the middle class represented in all three of these 'parliaments', a middle class which, thanks to its horror of the masses, the Slavs, the 'corrupt West' and the 'wicked East', became caught in the toils of a hectic nationalism, inwardly capitulated, and was glad that the wars which it had itself in part evoked, not to mention the harsh, dirty business of exercising power, should be carried out by the strong men above. The failure and the destruction of the high hopes of 1848 none the less does not entitle its successors – who have done no better themselves – to scoff, but rather to show sympathetic understanding.

The German liberation movement of 1848 was compounded of four disparate elements – liberal, democratic, anarchic and communist trends, with the two last (numerically insignificant outside of the Frankfurt Parliament) straining for popular revolt. 'Liberals' and 'democrats' of very varied categories were at one with the conservatives and many, basically non-political people in ardently desiring German unity while holding very different views about German freedom. It is no accident that whereas sixty-eight per cent of the National Assembly's delegates were officials, only twelve per cent belonged to free professions and two and a half per cent were businessmen. Officials instinctively seek 'order'. At Frankfurt it was no revolution they had in mind (they shrank back before such a thing), but a constitutional monarchy with a strong army which would ensure peace at home and lend force to the claims of the united nation abroad. Foreign political cares and temptations (the Schleswig-Holstein question, France, Russia, Poland, the problem of Austro-Hungary) came to the fore and soon usurped the place of the one essential priority, the creation of a constituent assembly, demanding instead the arrogation of premature executive powers. The National Assembly included more than six hundred speakers among its members. The most energetic of them wanted speedy action – with the sword. For them foreign policy was the heart of politics and furthermore provided a distraction from internal difficulties. At Frankfurt left, right, and centre, a torrid nationalism made itself heard compared to which Bismarck's policy, let alone Metternich's, sounded almost pacifist. One sample of a type of left-wing nationalism will suffice: Ferdinand Freiligrath, appointed to the editorial staff of the *Neue Rheinische Zeitung* through the favours of his friend Karl Marx, extolled the glories of the coming German fleet.

Nationalism on the right was accompanied by panicky fears of the masses, 'socialism' and 'communism'. The evidence can be traced in many speeches, for example, in the following extract from the plea of Heinrich Ahrens, made on 1 August 1848: 'The issue here is that of civic equality, and not that of brutal, materialistic, communist equality which desires to repeal all natural distinctions of intellectual and physical faculties and to eradicate their consequences in regard to work and acquisition of fortune.' It is significant in this context that the middle class was already petrified so long ago with that nightmare of 'red egalitarianism' which will eventually throttle all individuality.

The most significant defeat sustained by the left was in the discussions on Polish affairs. In the first place, its motion to admit provisionally the Polish delegates from Posmania was defeated. Then, in reply to the Berlin revolutionary leaders' condemnation of the partition of Poland, Wilhelm Jordan, author, Germanist and professor, rose to his feet and fiercely attacked the move to recognise Polish nationality and to provide Prussian Polish territory with a separate constitution. It was time to abandon,

> Germans gushing about Poland. . . . I say that the policy which calls on us to set Poland free regardless of cost is a short-sighted, self-forgetful policy, a policy of weakness, a policy of fear, a policy of cowardice. It is high time that we awoke from that dreamy self-forgetfulness in which we have enthused over all sorts of other nationalities while ourselves suffering a humiliating lack of freedom and a subjection at the hands of the whole world, awoke to a healthy national egotism . . . which sets the welfare and honour of our country ahead of everything else.

Here, in 1848, was the reaction to the Treaty of Versailles, 1919. Here was the bellicose opposition to the 'surrender' politicians and against the 'cowardice' and 'weakness' of all who did not avow 'a healthy national egotism'. Here already is the vocabulary and the mentality of those who in 1871 rendered it impossible for Bismarck to come to a constructive arrangement with France, insisted in the First World War on holding out until 1918 for a 'peace with victory', and to this day stand in the way of a genuine German-Slav reconciliation and compromise.

Herein lies perhaps the greatest tragedy of the German liberation movement. After 1848 and what happened at Frankfurt, Europe no longer believed in 'German freedom' because an oratorical majority of the National Assembly first announced this to be freedom against the freedom of other peoples and then lent it supporting action.

In 1953 Friedrich Wilhelm Foerster, eighty-five years old and living as an émigré in New York, tried to defend himself against attacks on his attitude during the Second World War by circulating a letter to 'liberal' German newspapers. It was not printed. Foerster, a relative on his mother's side of the

1870 commander-in-chief Moltke, had in 1895 addressed the German Emperor in his publication *Ethische Kultur* in the following terms: 'You, William II, are leading the German nation into war. You, William II, King of Prussia, are spreading through Europe the poison of Prussianism.' Now, in 1953, Foerster recalled an incident dating back to 1918.

Permit me to quote an illuminating avowal made by the late Prince Albert of Prussia, regarded in Hohenzollern circles as an *enfant terrible* on account of his utterly independent views. It was at the end of the First World War and the recipient of his confidence was my friend Leo Frobenius, the African explorer, who told me of it shortly afterwards. 'Listen carefully, my dear Frobenius,' said Prince Albert, 'for one day you will recall what I tell you now. Prussia is finished. There is nothing to be done. That happens to nations. For centuries we trampled on the Slavs. Now they are rising up again. The day of the Slavs is dawning. Open your eyes, my dear Frobenius. I repeat, the day of the Slavs is dawning! That is our fate, and richly we have earned it. There is such a thing as justice, in the life of nations too, and justice is mightier than the German propaganda which tries to stand everything on its head.' Leo Frobenius was a great patriot and it cost him much to repeat this to me. He did so, because the story incessantly plagued him.

The men of the right and centre at the Frankfurt National Assembly were fundamentally neither fanatics, nor 'militarists', nor 'imperialists', nor in the main Prussians. Without experience of politics, without familiarity of international affairs, without knowledge of the self-destructive potentialities accompanying the Industrial Revolution, they mouthed big words and toyed with perilous daydreams and illusions.

In Spring 1849 a deputation from the Assembly proffered Frederick William IV of Prussia the German imperial crown. The King declined with a stirring speech. He refrained from telling the gentlemen from Frankfurt to their face that he thought their imperial crown tendered by the people 'an imaginary hoop composed of mud and clay', a 'sausage roll', a 'pig's crown', a 'crown by grace of butchers and bakers', a 'dog-collar'. His conviction was that 'Only soldiers help against democrats.'

They did. First Vienna fell, then Berlin.

'THE SANCTITY OF WAR'

During practically the whole of the nineteenth century the 'sanctity of war' (Fichte) was a dogma defended unanimously by many, very different groups – idealist philosophers, left-wing Hegelians, national liberals, professors and theologians – only a few Old Prussians, conservatives and Catholics adopting a more cautious attitude, which merely earned them isolation from their political friends.

The nature of this disturbing belief can easily be seen from a few quotations:

'Germany needs a war, on its own, in order to become aware of its own capacity' (Jahn, 1831); 'the hope of banishing war from the world is not only senseless but thoroughly immoral. If realised, it would necessarily stunt many vital and glorious forces of the human soul and transform the world into a pantheon of selfishness' (Trietschke); but it could as well have been said by Wilamowitz, Eduard von Hartmann or Harnack. In his *System of Political Science* (1857), Konstantin Rössler writes: 'Violence and struggle are man's point of departure' a theme taken up by Adolf Lasson in his *Principles and Future of International Law* (1871), which was inspired by the 'great victory' of 1870–1: 'the powerful state is the better state, its people is the better people, its civilisation is the more valuable civilisation. . . . The dream of a legal order above and between states, born of cowardice and false sentimentality, is muddle-headed and nonsensical.' Fifteen years later, in *Civilisation, Ideal and War*, his lesson was that 'a so-called petty state is no state at all, but simply a tolerated community which, in a ridiculous way merely pretends to be a state, without being able to exercise the most intrinsic function of a state, that of being able to parry with force every kind of pressure.' Lesson, like many theologians, professors, and publicists, believed that his fight was against 'superstition', 'as though a nation's state of civilisation could be more clearly and more positively demonstrated than in war. . . . A government which, to satisfy formal justice, surrendered the interests of its citizens or the state as a whole would be downright guilty of treason. It would be self-abasement for a nation to allow the sacred substance of its nationhood to be imperilled for the sake of outward legalistic form.'

While neither Bismarck nor the professional soldiers, the Old Prussians nor the old conservatives, thought along these lines, this did represent the general outlook of national liberals from 1810 onwards. Heinrich von Gagern merely expressed the common view when he said: 'I understand the vocation of the German people to be a great and globally dominant one.'

Complaints have often been levelled at 'Prussian militarism' but in fact, although this existed, its limits were narrow, and it was a tendency inspired not by military sources, but by those 'idealists', 'philosophers', theologians and publicists of 'liberal' and 'national' quality who, in the great vacuum following 1848, wanted to mould 'the nation of poets and thinkers' into one of heroic warriors.

If one is to appreciate the full extent of the tragedy of German liberalism it must be observed operating at the highest, not lowest, intellectual level among its adherents. As outstanding and widely cultured a historian as Karl Lamprecht went into raptures about the Germanisation of Europe. Hans Delbrück, a man of independent character and (rightly) highly esteemed, allowed himself to become befogged by the Navy League propaganda. Friedrich Naumann, last bloom on the stem of liberalism, could happily pronounce, 'I am a Christian, Darwinist and imperialist.' Even the left-wing liberal publication, *Neue Rundschau*, forum for the whole of Germany's young élite (Gerhart Hauptmann, Thomas Mann, and so on) in 1907–8 gave Erich

Dombrowski space to preach a gospel of conquest over Russia, south-east Europe, and western Asia, a pious wish often repeated since 1860. At the time of Dombrowski's contribution, liberals were talking openly about a partition of Russia and Paul Rohrbach, representing liberal imperialism, expressed the belief that in the German colonies a freer and more democratic type of German would develop, who would have a favourable effect on the mother country.

A straight line of development extends from 1848 to the petition in 1915 by three hundred and fifty-two professors, clergymen, judges, teachers and businessmen to the Imperial Government, 'In the name of the spirit of Germany and German civilisation', requesting the incorporation into Germany of the industrial areas of northern France and Belgium, the Baltic provinces, British naval bases and suitable colonies. It had been drawn up by Alfred Hugenberg who wrote: 'We must not hesitate, out of any kind of false humanity, to encumber France as massively as possible.' At the same time it demanded evacuation of the population currently domiciled in large parts of Russia.

Such was the language of Heinrich von Gagern and his political friends. It was, as Victor Hugo and Ernst Renan had already said in 1871, a foretaste of the future. 'When the Poles in 1945 drove all Germans out of the territory east of the Oder-Neisse line, they did none other than what German alumni had proposed in 1915' (Friedrich C. Sell, *The Tragedy of German Liberalism*).

FANTASTIC NATIONALISM

As Klein-Hattigen pointed out when reviewing the history of the National Liberal Party from 1807 to 1911, German liberalism was never a unified movement, and as time went by it turned ever more to militarism, even formulating, in a wave of 'fantastic nationalism' the so-called Polish Laws which aimed at the propagation of Germanism in Western Prussia and carried their cult of Bismarck to the point of self-denial and self-emasculation'.

'Fantastic nationalism': an apt and comprehensive phrase, indicating clearly a process which, proceeding well beyond the limits of National Liberal circles, between 1866 and 1914 infected the German middle classes who, proud of their culture, possessions, and Empire, untrained in the analysis of home affairs of foreign policy, were easily misled. This was natural since the German middle class – indeed, the German people as a whole – had no say in national policies, which lay firmly in the hands of Bismarck and later in those of William II's Imperial Chancellors. It is not surprising, therefore, to find more and more extra-parliamentary circles and associations, like the Pan-German Union and the Navy League, absorbing the middle classes and, with an irresponsibility fostered by radicalism, and helped by every variety of publication, creating an enthusiasm which was intended to influence those in power.

One document, the pamphlet, *Germania Triumphans*, 1895, will serve as more than adequate evidence of this 'fantastic nationalism'. It propounded as targets for a truly German policy the conquest of the Baltic provinces, Poland, South Africa, South America, Mexico, Borneo and New Guinea, not to mention other territories. These targets were to be attained in the first place by a war with France, then by a war of the Western Powers with Russia, and thirdly by a war against Britain waged by an allied Germany and the United States. These matters are dealt with in even more detail by General Friedrich von Bernhardi in his publication, *Germany and the Next World War*, 1912.

The relevance to home affairs of such political imagination run riot becomes evident in a piece written in 1907 by the chairman of the Pan-German Union, Heinrich Claus, under the pseudonym, D.Fryman. *If I were Emperor* demanded suspension of universal franchise, expulsion of the Social Democrats, restrictions on freedom of speech and the press (much of which Bismarck and William II had considered), loss of civil rights for the Jews, and so on. And since these noble aims were only to be realised after a victorious war, Claus-Frymann demanded the annihilation of France and the incorporation into the German Empire of Holland and Belgium.

Basically this Pan-German programme contained the substance of Hitler's 'New Order', as Sell points out: 'The seed had been sown earlier and all the mass sequestrations, mass expulsions, mass murders of the Second World War had been envisaged by Pan-Germans three or four decades before.'

Spreading through industrial circles and via them to individual politicians, as well as by means of a growing literature, ideas of this type became widespread in the decade preceding 1914, survived 1918 and completely undermined the Weimar Republic, the poisonous effect of which still took its toll of many leading politicians. One of them, Alfred Hugenberg, a founder of the Pan-German Union, subsequently leader of the German Nationals, played a sinister part in the intrigues which brought Hitler into power. Another, Gustav Stresemann, star of the policy for a Franco-German *entente* had also been very prominent in the Union which, together with the Navy League, started an inflammatory propaganda campaign against Britain which was supported by major industrial figures who stood to earn handsomely from naval construction and armaments.

The Wiemar Republic was a republic without republicans, a democracy without democrats, with a parliament which had no political power. The tragedy of this state, which foundered on self-betrayal, lay broadly speaking in the narrow nationalism of its statesmen and politicians, who, while availing themselves of current sentimental, humanitarian and democratic phraseology, never really departed inwardly from the policy they had followed prior to 1918. Statesmen, politicians and party leaders, who were certainly anything but National Socialists, acted as cover for the illegal 'black' *Reichswehr*, the secret rearmament, the biased judiciary and the oppression and persecution of those true democrats, republicans and others who attempted to halt the self-destructive tendencies of their nation. It was Ebert, leader of the majority socialists (eventually the victim of one such trial) who guided the Social Democrats along this carefully concealed path of inner capitulation to reaction in the first instance by means of his slogan, 'I hate revolution like sin.'

BISMARCK AND WILLIAM II

The age of Bismarck and William II, 1866–1914, constituted an extremely close-knit unity – one, in fact, which orthodox believers in the former and enemies of the latter, are still, as they were fifty years ago, at pains to hide. In the course of this procedure Bismarck is praised to the heavens and William II, convicted of having grossly disrupted the work of the revered master, damned to hell. In point of fact, however, as Bismarck's closest collaborators were shocked to see, he himself, as an old man in the long years before his dismissal, had begun to destroy his own work.

While the Emperor showed him filial devotion and disregarded his father's ideas, Bismarck had loved him dearly and regarded him very much as his spiritual heir. But the unhappy, weak William II, handicapped both by his physical impediment and by an inferiority complex, could not bear the constant intellectual strain on him, whether it was imposed by the super father-figure, Bismarck, or by his actual father, Frederick. In addition to this, both he and Bismarck were outrageous eccentrics, bound to regard any whose views differed from their own as mortal enemies. Both of them lived in a state of perpetual civil proceedings and *lèse-majesté* court cases against such 'traitors'. They regarded ministers literally as servants and did not hesitate to use to the hilt their friends and collaborators. They were surrounded by yes-men, no one ever being sure of their favour, irrespective of the services rendered. They lived in a state of pompous ceremony and of dogmatic, biased opinions, hating socialists, taking great pleasure in threatening war, in bluff, and in the fear of war they spread by way of speeches, newspaper articles and diplomatic manœuvres.

Apart from these similarities of character, the strongest tie between the two men was their heartfelt fear for the future of the Empire, a fear which would often keep Bismarck awake at night. Indeed, this fear of downfall was both a personal drama and the tragedy of the Empire, for it signified that neither of them lived in the nineteenth century proper, the century of industrial revolution, of the new popular masses, of experiments in architecture, painting and writing. On the contrary everything new filled them with a deep disquiet, and they would retreat into their own refuges, Bismarck to his horses, William to pageantry, festivity and military parades, which never failed to irritate his relatives. It is certain that this fictitious world in which they lived was transparent, even at that period, to all political opponents.

At this point it must be made clear that these comments are not the product of the Austrian author's resentment against Prussia, for in fact the historic Prussia as it really stood had little or nothing to do with the 'Prussia' of pageantry constantly invoked. Bismarck's Prussia was his own invention, and however skilfully he had foisted it on the former Emperor, grandfather to William, William II never succeeded in achieving anything reminiscent of that bygone military world.

Another prefatory note, giving recognition to the human dignity and personality of Bismarck and William II, is also appropriate. Bismarck was one of the nineteenth-century's most charismatic and fascinating personalities. William II was quick-witted, had outstanding oratorical talent, and was steeped in genuine goodwill. This Emperor who was so fond of talking about shining armour and who gave offence to the whole world, wanted at the bottom of his heart to live in peace and friendship with everyone (even with the wicked Social Democrats, and especially with his Jewish friends).

BISMARCK

William II once said of Bismarck, 'the prince lies like a mighty granite boulder in a meadow. Turn it over and you'll find only worms and dead roots underneath.' 'A *red* reactionary, out for blood', was Frederick William IV's description. Bismarck himself, however, believed he had something of the 'Teutonic devil' in him, a demonic element which he did not find surprising – after all the ancient Germans had worshipped thunder and lightning, not the sun.

There was a great deal of truth in all three comments, for there was something of the archaic in Bismarck, something of the ancient Germanic and pre-Christian. He had great belief in the salutary power of trees, loved the forests and was a keen rider. He also had that avidity for possession and acquisition of land, the need to cling to the property one possesses with childish tenacity, a quality encountered east of the Elbe but not among the descendants of Western German aristocracy. There was also the 'feudal' quality in him which made him so loyally attached to the king.

Warfare had always been a principal tradition among the aristocracy (to whom he would have liked to belong), being in a sense a natural extension of hunting and the chase. And Bismarck's attitude to the wars he planned was exactly that of a huntsman: a brilliant series of political stratagems. It was not that he felt any enmity towards the antagonist, and particularly not towards Napoleon III, with whom he had many traits in common, but despite this he played him off to his own ends and out-trumped him. At the end of the Franco-Prussian War Bismarck remarked that he was calculating on four wars which the Prussians would be able to wage successfully, and when the Crown Prince Frederick feared the 'onset of a series of wars which could be the beginning of a bellicose century', Bismarck accepted the possibility with equanimity. War was the business of the nobility.

Bismarck himself was no militarist or soldier. In fact, he looked down on most generals and professional officers, yet he loved wearing uniform. He fancied himself an ancient Germanic or mediaeval warrior, passionately pursuing his feuds; whether at home or abroad made no difference. He spared neither previous allies nor social equals. His vendetta against Crown Prince Frederick (who reigned briefly as Emperor, though mortally sick) was fought with all the lust and ferocity of the protagonists of Shakespeare's royal dramas.

He was animated by an elemental, straightforward cruelty. In the campaign against France he declared that no prisoners ought to be taken, because corpses did not need rations.

The archaic element in him refused to recognise any legal obligations. Right was what happened to serve him at that moment, a fact which went for foreign policy as much as for taxes, which he refused to pay. (After his downfall he took legal advice as to whether, on his own estate, he might defend himself with pistols against bailiffs and police.) His maxim was that whoever was against him was an enemy of the state.

He cared little for tradition and honest dealing. In his intimate circle he liked talking about the 'legitimacy swindle', the 'nation swindle', the 'German colonial swindle', the fraudulent Empire. For he held in no higher esteem the 'mummery' (as the Prussian General Staff called it) of the proclamation of the Empire in the Hall of Mirrors at Versailles on 18 January 1871 than did the principal participants against whose will he forced it through. They regarded it rather as 'poor theatre'.

Three days after this rare spectacle, at which not a single civilian was present, he wrote to his wife:

> It is terribly long since I have written you. Forgive me, but this imperial birth was a difficult one and kings at such a time have strange desires, like women before they give the world what they can't keep anyway. As male midwife I wanted desperately more than once to be a bomb and to explode, making the whole place go up in the air. Essential business fatigues me little enough, but when it is inessential it embitters me.

To the end of his career he recurrently thought of putting an end to this 'abortion' of 1871, the German Empire, and never abandoned his theory of its 'constructive dissolubility'. He who saw William II as 'the certain ruin of the Empire', knew himself to be the perpetrator of a miscarriage. As late as 1896 Prussian generals and men about the court of Berlin thought and spoke of the necessity of a *coup d'état* by Prussia against the Empire.

In his diary the Emperor Frederick gave a priceless delineation of the debate, which was conducted for three hours in 'an overheated room', between King William, the Court Minister von Schleinitz, Bismarck and himself, as Crown Prince, about the title 'German Emperor'. This was the form that Bismarck had already agreed upon with the King of Bavaria, after procuring (with monies from his Reptile Fund) that indebted monarch's signature to a letter requesting King William to become German Emperor. But William if he had to swallow the bitter pill, wanted to be known as 'Emperor of Germany'. In helpless outbursts of rage he compared his future titular situation to that of a Prussian 'character major', an honorific description conferred on retirement on Prussian captains deemed incapable of holding staff appointments. Furiously he asserted that he did not care a fig for the whole affair and 'would stick only to Prussia'.

On the evening of this strange day the new Emperor wrote to his wife that his strongest inclination was to abdicate and make everything over to Fritz (the Crown Prince). On the day of the imperial election he declined to give Bismarck his hand, spoke not one word to him, and at dinner refused to look at a draft for the new imperial coat-of-arms with a 'Pah, what matter?' A Prussian nobleman, who enjoyed talking French and to pretty ladies, there rose in him a deep, genuinely instinctive resistance to Bismarck's unnatural creation. His son Frederick felt no less sceptical about this extraordinary imperial foundation which would not but bewilder the whole of Europe, not least the Germans themselves. Bismarck's own wrath was vented against the Potsdam court chaplain who used the occasion of the festive sermon on the proclamation for a polemic against Louis XIV. 'More than once I thought to myself, "Why can't I ram this cleric?"'

With his departure from office Bismarck left behind a hopeless situation. That is, hopeless if seen only through his eyes and the means he was accustomed to use – the employment of force, at home and abroad. The tragedy of his successors as Chancellor and of William II was their inability to free themselves from his outlook and his narrow political imagination.

WILLIAM II

Hinzpeter, William II's tutor, described his charge as ambitious, alert, of no more than average talent, imaginative, extremely self-willed, undisciplined, averse to methodical thought, unreliable, ungrateful, impetuously subjective and hungry for the exercise of power. This amounts to a caricature of Bismarck, with all the faults and none of the abundant qualities of strength inherent in the latter's personality.

In 1911 Klein-Hattingen, the historian of German liberalism, drew a picture of the Emperor as:

> a ruler ... lacking the restraint normally practised in the civilised world and the modesty resulting upon awareness of one's limitations ... (a) propensity for gloss and glitter, pomposity of surroundings; an inclination for embellishment unsupported by sound taste. ... (He) wants to be the deciding factor, regarding his people as not mature enough for self-government. He, who makes so many mistakes and commits so many gaffes simply because he is no hero in the art of keeping his mouth shut, fancies himself mature – 'my course is the right one!' ... William the Multifarious ... is a semi-modern, a strange case of dynastic atavism personifying a variety of absolutism. ... He is the incarnation of militarism and the sworn opponent of parliamentarianism.

His critic went on to express the hope that 'William II may appear more favourably in the eyes of posterity than he can at present in those of his contemporaries.'

Fundamentally this weak and vacillating man wanted to please everyone and to get on with the whole world. At heart he simply wanted to frolic; he meant no real harm. In fact his pranks were the cause of much anger to the Tsar and the King of England in their personal encounters, and his speeches alarmed the world at large. When his military advisers (under whose influence he fell completely) introduced him to the gigantic toy of a German war fleet, things began to look serious.

'We have bitter need for a strong Navy!' With this clumsily phrased sentence, uttered on the occasion of the launching of the battleship *Kaiser Karl de Grosse* on 18 October 1899, the Emperor announced a naval construction programme not merely prematurely but even against the wishes of Tirpitz, Hohenlohe and Bülow. During the preceding years, the parliamentary Opposition had vainly fought against this 'naval frenzy'. On 14 December of the same year, during the debate on the proposal for an enormous naval support programme to run until 1917, a speaker exclaimed: 'Here we have the characteristic feature of current policy, with the Government's gaze fixed almost hypnotically on the Navy and all other requirements receding into the background.'

The 'new naval era' (Walther Hubatsch) of the Great Powers began around 1890 and involved the United States, Britain, Japan and Russia. As far as Germany was concerned, the first indication was the reactivation of the 1848 project for a German navy, revealing yet again how closely everything in the intellectual, political and social spheres of Europe and Germany was linked, whether directly or indirectly, to the events of that year.

There was, however, one specifically German aspect which differentiated the Empire's participation in the 'naval frenzy' from that of other nations. The propaganda of the Navy League, the Pan-German Union and certain industrial circles met with such approval because a 'strong fleet' was an almost erotically operative symbol for power, manhood, freedom and 'international policy'. To a male world become neurotic, mentally constricted and perplexed, it presented the prospect of escape from the traps and blind alleys of Bismarck's later European policy. It seemed to hold out the promise of a future painted in radiant colours: light, white ships, armed with symbols of the highest masculine strength, sailing out to sea. Since the days of Egyptian hieroglyphics the sea has been a cipher for freedom, death and redemption which especially at critical times, has had powerful impact on the deeper levels of individual personality.

The spell cast upon spectators by the sight of the German Grand Fleet was recalled as late as 1950 by Walther Hubatsch, historian of the Tirpitz construction programme.

Put together with the greatest zeal, intelligence, skill, patience and love, the German navy of the Wilhelmine period was, apart from the British, the only one 'in Europe worth anything'. Who would have wanted to shun the force of the impression made by the big, light-grey vessels of the battleship squadron pounding through the North Sea, with decks cleared for action, gun-barrels trained high, and turrets belching smoke, while black torpedo-boats, at terrific speed and ... forecastle and bridge showered with the white foam of the surging waves, ... raced towards their target – who, of those who experienced this, would ever want to forget?

These proud ships were erotic symbols in the highest degree, and William II, inwardly cramped and physically slightly crippled, felt truly liberated only when he could sail in his yacht across the seas which 'his' navy was to throw open to 'his' Germany.

In all the years before 1914 the Emperor evinced himself a prisoner of his fears, his phrases and his court clique, while still managing thoroughly to alarm the world. On 8 November 1898, visiting Damascus, he assured three hundred million Mohammedans that 'at all times the German Emperor will be your friend'. On 27 July 1900 he addressed to the troops sailing from Bremerhaven for China his 'Huns' speech:

The task which the old Roman Empire of the German Nation was unable to solve the German Empire can fulfil. The means which render that possible is our Army. . . . No quarter will be given. Prisoners will not be taken. A thousand years ago the Huns under Attila made a name for themselves which, in narrative and tradition, still reflects their power. In the same way, and through you, the name of Germany must be established in China in such a way that never again will any Chinese ever dare to look askance at a German. . . . Open the way for civilisation once and for all!

On 8 September 1906 at a Silesian celebration the Emperor invoked the memory of Frederick the Great and demanded that all those who disagreed with him should leave Germany. 'I will not put up with pessimists. Let him who is not suited to the task in hand drop out and, if he prefers, let him seek a better land.'

Even his best intentions were turned to misfortune. To improve relations with Britain the Emperor gave an interview for the *Daily Telegraph*. Its publication on 28 October 1908 caused a storm of indignation in Britain and Germany alike. His wooing of the British included comparing them with March hares run mad and scolding them as treble dolts for succumbing to suspicions unworthy of a great nation. He sought to dispel fears regarding the German navy by explaining that Germany was a young, up-and-coming world power which needed a strong fleet to protect its constantly increasing global trade, interference with which would not be tolerated. Germany was forward-looking and held a broad horizon in view. He proposed a naval alliance against China and Japan.

The interview nearly caused the Emperor's abdication. In the few years left before the First World War he became aware of plans to put him under restraint on the plea that he was 'ill'. He clung fearfully to his Divine Right. His speech on 25 August 1910 had as its tenor that, regarding himself as an instrument of the Lord, he would not be diverted from his path.

German editorials on 16 June 1913, the twenty-fifth anniversary of his reign, were in part servile, in part very critical, reflecting the views of a nation itself divided. Many Germans hoped that the anticipated war would rehabilitate the nation and cause a renaissance of intellect and spirit. Others feared the worst.

When war came the Emperor, unused to regular occupation and flinching from responsibility, took refuge in hunting, social occasions, a multitude of hobbies and trivialities oddly reminiscent of Himmler's wayward historical speculations during the Second World War. In June 1916, he became interested in decipherment of the Hittite tongue. When someone remonstrated, he flared up, 'What more important things! Decoding of the Hittite language is at least as important as the whole war. Had the world concerned itself more actively with the Hittites, war would never have occurred because France and England would have realised that danger always comes from the East and would never have entered into alliance with Russia!'

The Emperor interested himself in linguistic researches in British prisoner-of-war camps, the progeny of Zebu bullocks and a long exposition by Professor Förster of the university of Breslau regarding the eagle as a heraldic animal (January 1917). 'I don't care a jot for the mood of the people!' (August 1916). To a speech by the mayor of Homburg (February 1918) he replied that war was a divine expedient for the education of mankind. Not that God always had luck with such measures. He had tried it with the Romans and was now making one last attempt with the Germans, whose task was to see that order prevailed in the world. Utterances of this kind oppressively recall Hitler's table-talk in his air raid shelter during 1943–5.

In 1917–8 the Emperor referred in conversation to the following as a part of the peace-terms: the incorporation into Germany of Lithuania and Courland; a Poland tied to Germany by a military convention; a Belgium under German control forced to cede Liége and the Flanders coast (23 April 1917); payment by the enemy of a hundred milliard marks reparations (11 May 1917); and 'I shall demand Malta', 'We shall throw the British out of Calais', 'I have given orders for a march on St Petersburg as soon as we have settled things in the Ukraine' (2 February 1918).

The dreams of a madman in his 'cement den' (as he called the spa hotel at Bad Kreuznach) or in his court train? Not at all. Right to the end the Imperial Government and also the federated, component German governments adhered to conditions for a victorious peace which were both exorbitant and fantastic. German political imagination was rotten through and through. The one great chance – peace with Russia – was squandered disastrously. 'Why don't they simply shoot Trotsky at Brest-Litc vsk? He does nothing except stir up our people. Napoleon would have had that done long ago!' (2 February 1918). Germany's extravagant demands not only imposed a 'Versailles' on Russia, but anticipated and went far beyond the limits of any exactions imposed by the West at Versailles.

An unhappy prisoner of the years 1914–18, the German Emperor, was constantly under pressure from Hindenburg and Ludendorff. On 11 April 1925 the former declared that 'I have never lost faith in the German people and the help of God. . . . I stretch out my hand to every German with a national outlook. . . . and I appeal to every German to help me in the resurrection of our fatherland.' Hindenburg had not the slightest intention of avowing allegiance to the Republic, saying that he did not alter his political convictions. On 25 February 1932 he wrote to Herr von Berg, 'There is bad blood being made against me in the right-wing Press and at meetings by saying that I had accepted my candidature for re-election from the Left or a black-red coalition. This assertion is an absolute lie! . . . I shall, however, defend myself with every means available to me against being described, contrary to the truth and the better knowledge of those concerned, as a candidate of the Left or a black-red coalition.' On 30 January 1933 he appointed Hitler as German Chancellor.

The link between 1870 and 1933 remained unbroken. The young Hindenburg was present at the Imperial proclamation in the Hall of Mirrors at Versailles. The matured Hindenburg personified the myth of patriotic leader, the defender of his country, the representative of victory in the years 1914–18. The aged Hindenburg handed over the reins of state, which had devolved on him, to Adolf Hitler, the 'unknown soldier' of 1914.

Engels, in his percipient publication *The Franco-German War*, foretold the frightful fruit of the hostilities of 1870–71:

> For Prussia-Germany no war other than a world war is any longer possible and, at that, a world war hitherto undreamt of in extent and intensity. Eight to ten million soldiers will wring each others' necks and, in the course of these proceedings, eat Europe bare like a swarm of locusts. The destruction within a period of three to four years will equal that of the Thirty Years War and will stretch across the whole of the Continent. There will be famine, epidemics and a barbarism inspired by the needs both of the military and the popular masses. The confusion in the artificial mechanics of trade, industry and financial affairs will be irremediable and will end in general bankruptcy.

Karl Liebknecht saw these consequences arising from the annexation of Alsace-Lorraine as clearly as Engels had in 1871.

THE DRAMA OF THE CENTRE AND SOCIAL DEMOCRATIC PARTIES

On 13 March and 10 April 1932, Hindenburg was elected president by ballot by the 'black-red coalition' which he so loathed, and one wonders why the Centre and the Social Democrats, the two parties which had been for so long the strongest both during the Empire and during the Republic, were not able to avoid the disaster. This is, however, not the place to deal with this question and a few indications must suffice.

The Centre's great days had been under the leadership of Ludwig Windthorst, who had had the courage to fight against Bismarck and Pope Leo XIII simultaneously. When the pope tried to influence him in the direction of Centre support for Bismarck's Emergency Law, he had declined.

The Centre party could claim to be the pioneer in parliament of 'true liberalism'. It held the fine traditions dating back to the first political and ecclesiastical concentration of German Catholicism in 1848. The programme of the Catholic election committee gave support in the political field to that freedom in all spheres which the liberal movement in Europe demanded. Wilhelm Emanuel von Ketteler, subsequently Bishop of Mainz and author of *The Labour Question and Christianity*, which criticised social questions of the day, had welcomed the 'downfall and death of the deplorable police state'.

In its heroic days the Centre fought against Bismarck's anti-socialist laws, for Poland and Alsace-Lorraine, against war and the armaments madness. Nevertheless, during the decade preceding 1914 these signs of deterioration and transformation, preparatory to its capitulation before the anti-democratic Right, had already become visible. Franz von Papen, the man who introduced Hitler to Hindenburg, purchased the Centre's principal paper, *Germania*, and Heinrich Brüning, the last outstanding Chancellor before Hitler's assumption of power, felt himself as a former officer, politically in bond to Hindenburg. A single incident shows how deeply rooted this upright man was in certain rightist-national ways of thought: Brüning, forced to flee the country, reproached Hitler for his 1934 pact with Poland as a betrayal of German interests. A contributory factor to the Centre's decline was its abandonment, under the leadership of Monsignor Kaas in the 1930s, of its 1848 traditions, regarding itself instead as the representative of the Curia's interests in Germany.

No less problematical was the evolution of the Social Democratic Party. Under leadership of a Prussian non-commissioned officer's son, August Bebel (1840–1913), it proceeded in a strictly disciplined manner towards development into a mass party of nationalist sympathies. Bebel, of weak physique, originally wanted to become a soldier. As a co-founder of the Social Democratic Workers' Party (1869) he played a principal part in the heroic struggles of the Bismarck and Wilhelmine eras and spent no less than six years in prison. He died just before the outbreak of the First World War. Yet there can be no doubt that, together with the other leaders of the party, he would have staunchly delivered the German working masses to the battlefield.

CONTAMINATION AND BARBARISATION OF THE GERMAN IMAGINATION

The widespread contamination of the German mind, deriving from inside and outside the individual, was given considerable encouragement by the extravagant emphasis laid on certain public festivals as well as by a degeneration in the standards of academic ethics. It was a pollution of the imagination begun in 1848 and still continuing in 1933.

Among secular red-letter days the anniversary of the victory at Sedan took the lead, inspiring positively frenzied emotions. Paul de Lagarde in 1890 described the 'domineering hatred' systematically inculcated thereby. 'It is savagely brutal to remind a neighbour-nation again and again how it sustained defeat at our hands. If a person in private life behaved towards his fellow-humans the way that Germany carries on against France every 2 September, he would incur the exact opposite of esteem and affection.' The participation of universities, he thought, should be forbidden. As for schools, 'they are not the appropriate breeding-ground for so-called patriotism. The current dissemination of certain political and historical views under that name is sheer pollution of youthful minds. To take sides and to kill the capacity for truthfulness and conscientiousness serves only to produce a slavish or, if you prefer, menial mentality.'

In 1900 Theodor Mommsen interceded for the abolition of Sedan Day. The great historian (1817–1903) spent the last decades of his life in a state of ever increasing inner loneliness. He was overcome by 'despair at our public and moral state of affairs'. A true patriot, he scolded the German people for being 'contemptible' (1893), 'contaminated' (1895), 'rotten' (1892), 'base and spineless' (1897) with Teutonic servility in its blood (1887) because 'the individual, even the best, cannot get over an inborn submissiveness and political fetishism' (1899). This last aphorism, to be found in his will, remained unknown until 1948. 'Let my grave be marked by no word or image, not even my name. I want to be forgotten by this spineless nation as quickly as possible and would regard it as no honour to remain in their memory.' (1885, letter to his wife.)

Academically speaking, it was the Germanists and the historians, who contributed most to the pollution of political imagination. Because its unbroken continuity is traceable almost to the present day, 'The Fall of the Germanists' has been hotly disputed. Nevertheless it is a 'fact, all too frequently passed over in silence, that most German governments, certainly since 1848, distributed largesse from secret funds in order to persuade the Germanists to accommodate themselves to the officially desired "public opinion".' Prussia was conspicuously active in this respect, to such a degree, in fact, as to provoke as early as 1866 the protest of Wuttke against such practices.

Supervision of the professorial body, again in Prussia, played its part in retarding the formation of freer political opinion. A law of 1898 put unestablished university lecturers within the field of discipline of the educational authorities. In 1899 Delbrück was fined five hundred marks for criticism of governmental policy towards Denmark. Civil proceedings were undertaken against Quidde on account of his pamphlet *Caligula*.

The wide influence of the pupils and venerators of Treitschke, who in their capacity as teachers, incited youngsters at secondary and primary schools in Germany and the German-speaking areas of Austria-Hungary, has been unforgettably depicted by Adolf Hitler in his reminiscences of his schooldays. It is significant that not only men like Treitschke (an interesting renegade) but also eminent figures in the world of historians, supported the cold war against Britain and anticipated the actual hostilities which they held to be inevitable. From 1895 on historians openly discussed a coming world war, seeing in 'the Russian danger' the *raison d'être* for future German power. Max Lenz in 1900 foretold the downfall of the British Empire and was convinced that 'we hold the balance in our hands'. As Ludwig Dehio has shown, there existed no difference between the train of German thought and expression and that of the most outstanding historians, including Lenz, Delbrück, Hintze, Marcks and Meinecke. Their ideal on war and peace (a victor's peace after war) were the same, except that the scholars' language was more humane and possessed a greater range of style than did Pan-German propaganda.

The barbarisation of, and the political twist to, the German imagination can clearly be seen in two processes: firstly, in a particular kind of Germanist philosophy and secondly, in the evolution of racial biology and eugenics. Both processes found an intellectual point of departure in Goethe's *Faust*. This becomes evident if we pick out certain threads from Act Five of Part Two; they bring into startling focus certain temptations and catastrophes which the nineteenth century was to hold for Germany.

Faust, though in extreme old age, is still driven by an insatiable appetite for whatever life has to offer. His immediate undertaking, with the help of labour placed at his disposal by Mephistopheles, is the reclamation of land from the sea. But there is a piece of adjoining territory which he covets, occupied by two old people. Philemon and Baucis (they are symbolic of Old Europe) are aware of the position:

> He is godless, long has lusted
> To possess our home and glade;
> Let the vesper chimes be tolled.
> We'll kneel and pray, in sunset's glowing,
> God revering, as of old.
> Faust is irritated by this Accursed chime, all solace ending,
> ... The bell condemns as incomplete
> My high estate, the cottage brown,
> The crumbling church, the lindens sweet,
> Are things I cannot call my own.

The nineteenth century was to witness plenty of old churches and houses being torn down and replaced by hideous new structures for a multitude of 'reasons'. Frequently enough 'expansion' was merely an excuse to rebuff and to hide fear of another world that was felt as an intrusion.

The Three Mighty Fellows arrive with rich booty from far lands. 'War, trade, and piracy are one,/An indivisible trinity.' Privateering, British and Dutch colonialism and mercantile strife, buccaneering and the pillage of foreign countries practised from the sixteenth century onwards, merged and were camouflaged in nineteenth-century imperialism. 'The open sea sets free the mind' could be a prophetic vision of the German fleet after 1848, while 'You catch good fish or catch a ship' suggests intuition of the maritime rivalries of the past and those of the future between 1890 and 1918.

Mephistopheles' promise to the Three Mighty Fellows that Faust will 'royally entertain/The fleet', which has brought a rich and colourful cargo from overseas, evokes a mental picture of the regattas, naval reviews and yachting festivities at the end of the century, notable especially for William II's familiar and uncouth behaviour towards his British and Russian cousins.

Faust nevertheless remains morose because:

> Yon aged couple ought to yield,
> The lindens still I have to gain,
> The clustering trees above the weald
> Mock and destroy my wide domain.

He longs to view from the knoll where the two old people live:

> The triumph of the human mind,
> That carried out fair wisdom's plan,
> And added living-space for man ...
> ... The chime, the scent of linden-bloom,
> Confines me as in aisle or tomb.

Mephistopheles encourages this destructiveness the victims of which will be this remnant of unsullied nature and the old couple:

> Then why on scruples choose to dwell,
> Since colonising's served you well?

A glimpse at nineteenth-century colonisation shows a gigantic process of destruction of old civilisations and uprooting of ancient peoples, precipitated by the colonisers' spoliations.

Faust's mind is made up: 'Go move them out, make this your care.' Mephistopheles, with an ear-splitting whistle, summons the Three Mighty Fellows.

> Come, and obey the Master's call,
> Tomorrow Sailors' feasts for all.

The next scene, deep night, begins with the song of Lynceus, the Keeper of the Tower, chanted from his watch-post.

> A look-out born,
> Employed for my sight,

To tower-service sworn,
The world's my delight.
I see what is far,
I see what is near,
Moon, planet, and star,
The wood with its deer,
In all things perceiving
The charms that endure,
And, joy thus achieving,
My own joy is sure.
Dear eyes, you so happy,
Whatever you've seen,
No matter its nature,
So fair has it been!

This song concisely mirrors the old world, its calm perspective and contemplativeness, a world free of jealousy and self-disgust (which ails the man of the new world), its happiness resting on a contentment found within, yet a world unable to defend itself and doomed.

Aghast, Lynceus sees hell erupt as the Three Mighty Fellows burn down the hut and chapel. Baucis and Philemon perish in the flames.

Must these eyes, this far discerning,
Look upon such sights of woe? . . .
All that won the fondest gazing
Gone, with ages long ago.

Faust, despite his imperious egotism, had not intended harm to the old people and still dreams of giving them ground elsewhere:

A new homestead now I raise,
That they fell my grace enfolding
All the sunset of their days.

Mephistopheles disillusions him:

We quickly sent the couple packing;
They, with a suffering brief and slight,
Gave up the ghost and died of fright.

Four Grey Hags enter – Want, Guilt, Need, and Care. The first three disappear again, but not before Faust, lonely as he now is, has glimpsed them:

There came here four, but only three went hence;
. . . I'm left to struggle still towards the light:
Could I but break the spell, all magic spurning,
And clear my path, all sorceries unlearning . . .

The words recall a thousand years of magic and poetry pervading Old Europe.

Faust – Man – is alone in the world except for Care and Mephisto the Devil.

> Full well I know the earthly round of men,
> And what's beyond is barred from human ken.

Man's only chance is to attend to his daily task and to follow his own road.

> Why haunt eternity with dim surmise?
> Things he perceives are his to realise.
> So may he wander through his earthly day;
> If spirits gibber, let him go his way;
> In forward-striving pain and bliss abide,
> He finds them who is never satisfied.

An altercation with Care ensures. Faust rejects her warnings:

> No more! You get no hold on me,
> I spurn the folly that you say.
> Get hence! Your wretched litany
> Might lead the shrewdest man astray
> . . . 'Tis hard, I know of daemons to be rid,
> The spirit-bond is difficult to sever;
> But you, O Care, in stealing action hid,
> Creep with a power I will acknowledge never.

Care replies,

> That power more potent you may find
> As with a curse I go my ways,
> For mortal men through all their life are blind,
> Which you, my Faust, shall be to end your days.

She breathes on him and Faust is blinded. But he is not to be deterred.

> Deep falls the night, in gloom precipitate;
> What then? Clear light within my mind shines still;
> . . . To end the greatest work designed,
> A thousand hands need but one mind.

The apothegm is redolent of Bismarck.

Faust's orders are obeyed a last time. He staggers into the outer courtyard of the palace, groping by the door-posts.

> What joy the clash of spades now brings to me!
> Thus toil my people for me without cease;
> They make, that earth may find itself at peace,
> A frontier for the billows of the sea,
> Committing ocean to a settled zone.

The robot-like labours of the Lemures, with Mephistopheles as overseer, create new land. Faust's energy remains undimmed:

> A marshland flanks the mountain-side,
> Our gain would reach its greatest pride
> If all this noisome bog were drained.

His sightless eyes are on the future:

> I work that millions may possess this space,
> If not secure, a free and active race . . .
> Ay, in this thought I pledge my faith unswerving,
> Here wisdom speaks its onal word and true,
> None is of freedom or of life deserving
> Unless he daily conquers it anew . . . Such busy,
>   teeming throngs I long to see,
>
> Standing on freedom's soil, a people free.
> Then to the moment I could say:
> Linger you now, you are so fair! . . .
> Foreknowledge comes, and fills me with such bliss,
> I take my joy, my highest moment this.

He sinks back into the arms of the Lemures, who lay him on the ground, dead.

THE FAUST EQUATION

What Goethe saw as illusion, wish-fulfilment and dangerous self-deception German commentators without exception took as an exposition of destiny: German man, as the true Faust, is called upon to establish world dominion in the sphere of intellect and civilisation.

As early as 1825 Hermann Friedrich Wilhelm Hinrichs, professor at Halle, not content with claiming that in *Faust* there was manifested the German people's superiority to all others, added: ' . . . all other nations must recognise the German nation as their master and judge in matters of science. . . .'

In 1836 Heinrich Düntzer thought that 'German joviality, German profundity of mind and German speculativeness, German grasp of intellectual beauty, German enthusiasm for genuine human dignity, German perseverance and energy, all these components of German life' were to be found embodied in Faust.

Then in 1848, academics of a nationalist turn of mind clad Faust in Wotan's cloak and at the same time perceived in him a second Siegfried. By 1850 the ideology of the destiny of the German, as the true Faust, was fully and richly matured.

In Vienna and Munich there was some considerable resistance among the Roman Catholic and orthodox Protestants to the Faust personification, but with the victory of Sedan the idea took a triumphant hold which remained uninterrupted until 1914. The notion of identity between Faust and the German man conquering the world, gripped the hearts and minds of the people. Guilt became greatness, as a dozen Faust commentators, professors and preachers agreed: 'Faust's true guilt and, at the same time, his greatness, lies in his struggle against the limits imposed on human nature.' The name of Faust became a spur to national self-help and self-liberation, national self-consciousness, arrogance and national zeal. At the same time it became the by-word of a Western civilisation of German origins, since in Germany alone was to be found the necessary intellectual high-mindedness (Hans Schwerte). Thus Goethe's *Faust* became the 'Domesday Book of German man' (Th. A. Meyer).

This traditional perversion of *Faust* was upheld by the Faust enthusiasts around Houston Stewart Chamberlain and Spengler, as well as those preachers who invoked Faust on behalf of a German world mission, from 1918–45. They made, in fact, of a great and solitary figure the exponent of a Germanic global mission wherein culture, civilisation and politics were blended like Wagnerian visions.

RACIAL CURRENTS

German Folk-Songs about Doctor Faust, (1890), *The History of German Christmas* (1893), and *Faust Fragments in the Literature of the Sixteenth and Eighteenth Centuries* (1889–99) were all three the work of Alexander Tille, lecturer in German language and literature at Glasgow (1890–1900). Tille later became a senior industrial executive at Berlin and in 1903 was appointed legal represenative for the Saarbrücken chamber of commerce and industrial associations, during which period he became friendly with Baron Stumm-Halberg, the major industrialist and member of the *Reichstag* to whom is ascribed the achievement of changing William II's attitude from sympathy for the working classes to a passionate hostility to the Social Democrats.

In 1895 Tille published yet another work on the Faust theme, *Darwin and Nietzsche, a Book of Evolutionary Ethics*, which merged Faust, German industrial matters, Darwin and Nietzsche (reinterpreted on very 'Germanic' lines) into an ideology which contained elements subsequently found in Himmler's racial breeding theories and practices. He also attacked men like A.J. Balfour (the British statesman and Christian), putting into their mouths the following evil trains of thought:

> Your morality, great Nature, is different. That is why, according to our wee morality, you are immoral. Well now, what we want to try and do, we tiny mortals, is to squeeze you for once into the straightjacket of our wee morality. No matter whether it is to the detriment of the human race ... so long as we help our wee morality gain the day.... You practise the survival of the fittest, we that of the unfittest. We have

special institutions for coddling the crippled, blind and crazy, as well as the syphilitic and consumptive, so that they shall be able to transmit their troubles to generations to come. . . . '

Man, Tille continued, is 'biological material' which requires appropriate utilisation. The future belongs to the fittest only, and they, in the first place, are those men of business who, in the harsh struggle of economic competition, have evinced themselves as genuine national leaders. Their 'iron self-discipline' in the fight for money and material position shows them as being best suited to the conditions life has to offer, the fittest in fact, 'far ahead, for example, of the academic whose meagre capacity for asserting himself puts him far down the list.'

Nature is mercilessly cruel and inexorable in the sacrifice of individuals on behalf of the species. Man must follow suit.

It is *right* of the stronger race 'to annihilate the inferior', for everywhere in nature the higher vanquishes the lower. That had already been proclaimed by Wilhelm Jordan, the nationalist professor of 1848 and one of Tille's principal authorities. The victory of higher German civilisation over the lower variety of other nations was consequently inevitable. Not that Tille advocated war. He trusted that German industry and political manipulation would suffice in a sharp power conflict to achieve its triumph without resource to arms. A stronger country has quite simply the right to 'take' another. Tille's use of an idiomatic vulgarity demonstrates the close connection, long before Hitler, between a vulgar, deeply neurotic political ideology and practice, and a vulgar sexuality.

The absolute criterion of man is work. 'Those races' (meaning pygmy tribes of central Africa) 'of whom the British missionary said that he could manage to regard them as brothers are *not human beings in our sense* (Tille's italics) . . . and *cannot* be such, for they are ignorant of labour.'

Returning to the theme of the fit and the unfit, it is socially indispensable that 'as long as it is decided not to kill the unfit, there should be a level to which they can sink'. A forerunner of Tille, Schallmeyer, had already suggested the establishment of compulsory 'colonies' for the inferior.

A first rule of self-preservation is the elimination of 'racial desecrators' (Tille employed this dreadful term in a very wide sense), the unfit and the idlers. 'Let us sacrifice the cripples, the sick and their descendants so that room shall be left for the healthy and the strong.' Sentence by sentence Tille speaks for Himmler and Hitler.

'Hereditary capitalist' must be abolished in order to forestall degeneration in the third and subsequent generations of heirs to wealthy economic personalities. Celibacy is undesirable. Instead there ought to be 'love marriages' and an abundant excess of procreation, thereby ensuring a healthy national potential in the competition with other peoples. Tille went into raptures over the Chinese, because in his eyes they were an instance of a thousand years' successful popular breeding. Fixed boundaries are altogether wrong since a ruthless economic policy must adopt as its aim incitement of 'other nations against one another, wait calmly, and work steadily so as eventually to gain the benefit'. Wars are unserviceable for the purpose of sorting out the *élite* since popular breeding and the constitution of a new and pugnacious aristocracy of economic specialists will ensure a sound future.

'There is nothing abnormal about one nation from time to time taking a slice of territory from another.' 'Large regions can be *taken* without a shot being fired.' 'If we Germans beget more fellow-countrymen than our neighbours, we need more land to feed them and must have it in order to maintain the total population at a tolerable level.' The foreigners acquired in the process will have to be deported. 'Every historic right is untenable as against the right of the stronger.'

'When will it at last be understood that a war between France and Germany is no more than a storm in a teacup' compared with the prodigious struggles between the human races which occur without proclamations and uniforms, without princes and cannon. 'Shoot-and-slay patriotism' has fallen behind contemporary ethical evolution. Tille was a real revolutionary who, as such, vulgarised his venerated Nietzsche.

'The world could today well belong' to the German people, 'as it does to our Anglo-Saxon cousins, indeed to an even greater extent,' if it had managed its procreative capacity economically instead of 'squandering it'. Were this the case the 'members of our race' would be in a far better position to assume for themselves a dominant situation all over the globe and to chase their competitors out of the field.

Christianity is to no small extent responsible for the German nation's tardiness, the negative dogma of that Nazarene rabbi who fell into the hands of Roman justice on account of communist agitation. It is regrettable that Germans should still 'bring junior education to a standstill by spending enormous sums on outdated religions'.

Tille was waiting for the man who would 'carry the masses along with him and inspire them with the new ideal'. Obviously he had in mind some major figure in the economic world with a strong political urge. Possibly Baron Stumm-Halberg, for an edition of whose speeches he was responsible.

It proved a very different economic personality who displayed an interest in the problem of how Germany was to obtain sufficient human material to be able to cope with the wars and exertions of the future.

In 1889 Haeckel made an approach to Heinrich Ernst Ziegler. 'A patron of science', he was told, had allocated a large sum of money for an open competition on the theme 'What have the principles of the theory of heredity to teach us in respect of the internal evolution and legislation of nations?' Haeckel was a zoologist and proponent of the theory of heredity. The patron who requested that his name should be revealed only after his death, was Alfred Friedrich Krupp.

The first prize was won by the Bavarian medical man and independent academic Wilhelm Schallmeyer for his book *Heredity and Selection in the*

History of Nations, a Study in Political Science based on Modern Biology. Schallmeyer had first brought himself to public notice in 1891 with his publication *On the Menace of Physical Degeneration among Civilised Mankind.*

Eugenics progressed by leaps and bounds during the last decade of the nineteenth century, drawing upon and quoting in its support British and French precursors. What made the German interest in it so exceptional, however, was the radical and political turn given to the science. Otto Ammon wanted to rear 'heroes in mind and deed'. Schallmeyer entered a plea for a 'racial service' and would have liked to prepare the German people biologically for the struggle for existence between states.

It is remarkable too, how this version of eugenics, and later racial breeding, was pursued with particular keenness in southern Germany and the German-speaking parts of Austria-Hungary. Christian von Ehrenfels, a highly honourable man and a professor at Prague, concerned himself with the 'fundamental perniciousness of monogamy' and advocated artificial insemination. This was a good starting point for Wilhelm Hentschel and his Mitgart League, which after 1901 advocated the breeding of a white, Aryan race.

Mention must be made in this connection of Lanz-Liebenfels, whose publications Hitler devoured during the period of his youth he spent in Vienna. This ex-Cistercian raised the first swastika banner over a castle in the Danube valley.

As for Hentschel and his Mitgart League, Walther Darré drew directly upon them for his *New Aristocracy from Blood and Soil* (Munich 1936).

In 1895 a book by Alfred Ploetz was published in Berlin, entitled *First Principles of Racial Hygiene,* with the sub-title *The Fitness of Our Race and the Protection of the Weak, an Experiment in Eugenics and its Relationship to Humanitarian Ideals, especially Socialism.* Ploetz described his work as 'a sort of eugenic Utopia'.

A strong man is good, a weak one is bad. War creates the splendid opportunity to exterminate the 'bad' varieties as cannon-fodder. That is why the following maxim should be adopted: 'In the course of a campaign it would be a good thing to transport the specially assembled bad varieties to a spot where the need for cannon-fodder is great and where individual fitness does not matter so much.'

Poverty has an excellent function to fulfil, that of a 'weeding-out machine'. It exterminates in a natural way the weak and the unfit who are incapable of a strong life.

Needless to say these German eugenicists were passionately anti-Socialist and generally too of an anti-christian frame of mind.

'Eden lies ahead of us'; mankind is 'susceptible of infinite improvement'; a long stretch of evolution is yet to come. And for these views Alexander Tille cited Nietzsche in his support.

7

Another Germany

The will to freedom, the spirit of freedom, so much the current theme of poets at the time, is embodied in Germany in the nineteenth century by three people: Bettina Brentano, Heine and Nietzsche. And although the last of these has been quoted by eugenicists and would-be racial breeders in the last decade of the century, one should not allow this fact to mislead one. He, like the others, must be apprehended in the intellectual tradition of early Romanticism. Here, in these three we find for the last time that spirit which inspired the youthful Goethe and his associates. All three, lonely and misunderstood, fought for a fuller, truer, richer life, opposed to the lies of contemporary society and of established religious beliefs.

Bettina Brentano (1785–1859) grew up in the aura of Romanticism. Her family were on terms of friendship with Goethe; her brother, Clemens, her husband, Achim von Arnim, and her brother-in-law were all outstanding figures in the German Romantic movement. During the decades of political reaction, when Arnim withdrew to his small property near Berlin, avoiding the Prussian capital, Bettina stayed among the people. During the cholera epidemic of 1831 she cared for the poor and sick and issued an appeal to the King that he should postpone the building of his projected cathedral and build instead homes for the starving Silesian weavers. Her all-embracing humanity was based on her own motto: 'My happiness is that of others, my life is based on that of others.' Her *salon* was the last refuge of freedom in the 1840s in Berlin, and because she lacked that nineteenth-century sickness, self-disgust, because she had faith in herself, she was able to believe in others: 'I am inspired by confidence in myself. . . . The manifestation of God is eternal in every moment, and so man is eternal too, for God manifests Himself in his being.'

When Bettina wrote *Günderode* (1840) and *Clemens Brentano's Vernal Chaplet* (1844) with their political and quasi-political themes, she was trying to remind the youth of that fourth decade of the spiritual impetus which had inspired the preceding generation – that of freedom, the future in God. 'And then I say to myself, Who is God? – *God is the future*! . . . World events that look dangerous for peace and the contemporary state of affairs, are simply a spiritual torrent pouring between political banks, peoples by dismal dolts, towards the divine, that is, freedom-begetting God.'

On the eve of 1848, at a moment when the God of freedom seemed near, Bettina published her *Ilius Pamphilus and Ambrosia*, pseudonyms for the authoress and for Philipp Nathusius.

Nathusius, born 1805, was the son of a big industrialist. He started his career as an idealist and enthusiast who translated Béranger and wrote *Ulrich von Hutten* as a counterblast to Görres' *Athanasius*. Following the events of 1848 he turned reactionary and as early as '49 took over the *Volksblatt für Stadt und Land*, which was to become the most popular paper in 'Christian' circles. It published bitter attacks on communism and socialism, while his associate, Heinrich Leo, wrote violent criticisms of the *Halle Year Books*.

To return to the fictional exchange of letters between Ambrosia and Pamphilus, we find a theme which was much used by earlier poets: 'the spirit is fire'; God is fire; life is fire. And against this threefold fire contemporary Christianity was opposing itself, a foe to God and mankind.

> The Church fathers, Augustine, Calvin, yes, and even Luther seemed to be possessed of the idea, surely demonic? that whoever wishes to rule over the spirit of man must frighten and crush him. . . . That's where the Gordian knot is tied! Whoever wants to cut it must disregard these distracting portrayals . . . purposefully touched up by these brokers in religion who for their own secret designs cheat us of Christ's gentle spirit. . . .

Bettina pleaded for reason, enlightenment, and love, condemning the despotic churchmen who surrounded the Prussian throne: 'Deformed, hunchbacked, false, hectic, rickety, lazy, bilious, befogged souls they are. . . .' A false and superficial education was alienating the young from their true nature: 'Education is an abominable deceit.' In the person of Ambrosia she sought to prise her young friend away from a form of Christianity that consisted of fear, hate, narrow-mindedness and superstition. 'I see an abyss opening before you. . . . ' On the eve of 1848 Bettina begged German youth not to surrender to reaction, nationalism and the Churches' arrogant claims. 'Do not flee from me, Pamphilus, for know that I speak not for myself, but for the future.'

Bettina was not content just to tear away the masks and reveal to youth the false religion and false education they tried to hide. In *This Book is The King's* she turned to the highest authority in the land, Frederick William IV, with whom she had been on terms of friendship before his accession to the throne in 1840. For the monarch's political advisers, however, including her brother-in-law, Savigny, who was Minister of Justice from 1842 to 1848, she had nothing but contempt. On this occasion she chose to be published anonymously, but sent the King a copy of the book, her covering letter acknowledging authorship and containing the magnificent phrase 'Politics, to be the real thing, must be inventive'. That was in July 1843. She took for her motto: 'Freedom alone produces spirit, spirit alone produces freedom.'

She set her scene as a conversation piece between Goethe's mother, as a mouthpiece for German freedom, and her own parson, a representative of religious and political reaction. To assume the guise of the former suited her well, seeing that she and the good lady were both offspring of the free Imperial city of Frankfurt which for centuries had admitted and protected freethinkers and Nonconformists. Bettina, like Strauss, Ruge, Marx, Heine and Kierkegaard, knew that political criticism presupposes criticism of religion. Consequently she struck straight at the root of the religious and political faith of contemporary rulers – their belief in the Devil. The parson is thoroughly shocked:

'What, madam, you want to lay hands on our Devil, without whom there can be no stability in religion? No, no, we can't afford to lose him. There would be gaps all over the place.' *Frau Goethe* recalls the Inquisition in Goa about which she had just been reading. Her parson comes to the conclusion that the woman has not the slightest fear of the Devil nor the least regard for her soul's salvation in the beyond. 'Virtue,' she maintains, 'is a matter of here and now, not some time in the future. Virtues knows no law of barter and no court of law where it can enter proceedings. It does not plead for itself, but is simply and wholly a celestial and creative force. Care for the future is outside its scope and everything beyond that is a mere bogy to scare children.'

Frau Goethe, Bettina's mouthpiece, condemns the Inquisition and 'your established religion'. 'Faith is what you call disbelief and disbelief is your compulsory faith.' The Creation was not ended on the seventh day but is still going on. It is 'God's worship' wherein 'He labours incessantly'. 'Your sermons, Parson, are drained and find no echo in men's hearts. You yourselves are saturated with the entire Church procedure. If you didn't have the Devil as the father of lies and self-deception to help you weave superstition, whims, follies and, indeed, the vagaries of world events into the tyrannical red tape you pass off as Christianity, you would be at your wits' end.' Christians are completely immured in 'illusions', a 'dream-life'. Their distorted 'faith fantasy' is an opium, a dangerous sedative. She would like to tempt the 'pyramid-believer', the parson, out of his 'pyramidal fortress' and into 'the freshness of my meadow where the winds of the universe blow'. 'It is with the hidden talent of man's free spirit, which is lost to him because you make no use of it, that we must storm the gates of Heaven.' ' . . . The free spirit is the road to immortality and he who cannot find his way to it renounces after-life.'

'I ask you, Parson! In the name of the Pharisees, answer me. With what right do you profess Christ Whom you belie in your Philistine states?' 'You bewail the Redeemer's painful death and crucify dependent humanity. You pray to the afflicted Mother of the Lord and dedicate the mother of humanity to intolerable pain. And religion? A wretched cloak for malignant disease.' 'This religion of yours is and always has been madness, crime, and murder.' 'You never rest, and fancy yourselves always free to pull up spiritual freedom by the roots although the scent of its blossom acts as balsam.'

At this point the discussion becomes political and the conversation is joined by the Mayor.

Capital punishment is the regime's (every reactionary regime's) pivotal point. Consequently the Mayor and the parson are all for it. 'Anyone would think,' remarks *Frau Goethe*, 'that you had only invented the Last Judgment so as to pass the poor sinner on there from your own.' 'The felon is always a bad mark against the state.' They weep crocodile tears over him, the loyal servants of the state and the priests, because a poor devil must needs be executed; but it is they, 'the felons', who ought to pay the penalty. 'The sons of dust . . . find no other road except from life to death.' Appalled, the Mayor demands to know whether she should spare the scum which is always on the brink of revolt, unteachable and totally unappreciative of every sacrifice made on its behalf. Of what sacrifices can the state boast, the woman retorts. These 'dregs' 'provide good fodder for enemy cannon'. The masses as cannon fodder was the 'solution' to the social question that in Germany, France, and Russia, from 1848 until 1914, was recurrently studied, discussed, planned – and practised.

This proletariat, continues *Frau Goethe*, that you both damn for now and hereafter, has a deeply inherent honesty, courage and greatness of its own. She quotes court records about thieves and professional criminals, and demonstrates their immanent morality. She describes, with the aid of contemporary reports, prison conditions and the barbaric judicial processes which are the tools of a class and caste; the poor are doomed from the outset. Only a system, protests the Mayor, can save us from the chaos of this criminal world. A system, asks *Frau Goethe*, 'Is that not despotism of conscience? The worst thing conscience can imagine is to accede to a system! It is blind faith in a system you want?'

The Mayor has his chance to be heavily derisory. 'Rascals, thieves, vagabonds, convicts, whose proper place is in the city corral. A fine flock they would make, trailing at our ruler's heels!' This is in reply to the suggestion that it is precisely out of this 'scum', the underground of the people in which potent forces are consigned to damnation, that a regenerated nation could be drawn. 'I would train men of sense and practical ability, men destined for fame and the position of heroes in history, out of this herd.' Here, deep down, lies a potential, the truly creative potential of humanity that is churlish and malcontent, but also undeveloped. By rearing these unkempt, penurious masses 'the sanctity of national feeling in its pristine vigour could be restored'.

Mayor and parson are obdurate in their opinion: The rabble is incorrigible and incapable of being taught. *Frau Goethe* in turn becomes severe: You dare not teach your brothers because 'Fear is rank within your soul and the fetters on your spirit are heavier than those in your jails.' In these your brothers you slay the future, for 'Man is not yet, he is but coming. Man is not born, he is but in embryo. Man is yet in the womb and his mind is but the sleepy such of the unripe foetus.' Enormous, positive and creative reserves which could prove fruitful for the arts and sciences, political and economic life, are stored within these malefactors. There should be established a sort of delinquents' university: 'The penitentiary a sanatorium!'

'The people,' says *Frau Goethe*, 'would understand my aspirations, for they see themselves in the offender,' but the 'judge too must see himself in the offender and sense his potential,' just as princes and regents must. An alliance between the lower classes and the ruler could revolutionise the world. 'Nor do I know what advantages you have over the criminal in comprehension or in imagination! He might well prove energetic in ridding himself of his fetters, by which I mean achieving freedom in the sciences, where in your minds adhere blindfoldedly to the old rite.' 'Maybe we have already beheaded the Seven Wise Men of our age or hanged the Four Evangelists, and perhaps we are simply making do with the dross of generations and cannot produce geniuses any more. All that are left to us are aristocratic scamps, gone soft and decadent!' 'Were we ourselves mentally sound, it would be out of the question that we did not heal transgressors.' Society's sick condition finds expression in the sick situation of its offenders. Ailing, inwardly unfree men 'above' result in ailing masses 'below'.

In 1852, when she was almost seventy, Bettina published the second part of her 'royal book', *Talks with Demons*. Its dedication was to 'the spirit of Islam in the person of the magnanimous Abdul Medjid Khan, Emperor of the Osmanlis' and, through the mediation of General von Webern and the Turkish embassy at Berlin, a copy was in fact presented to him. Not a single subject that had been taboo since 1849 was left untouched, but the authoress herself left continual gaps to indicate what, if openly expressed, the censorship authorities would have cut.

The Demon stands by the couch of the sleeping King. He wants to win him over to the emergent peoples and to be their champion. Heavily, still in his sleep, the King replies, 'You talk of the rising of the peoples, of the abolition of human plagues, of doing away with war. How do you propose to gain the upper hand over these sources of eternal strife?' The Demon: 'Were you able to assimilate the spirit of revolution within yourself, you would be the people's inspiration, taking the initiative and being the fount of law that fructifies the spirit.' The King: 'You mean that you think reform could alter the course of the world?' The Demon: 'Most certainly. Kings, as heirs to Cain, rule by crime and fratricide. . . . What the peoples want, everywhere, is common brotherhood and faith.' The King remains sceptical, maintaining that the peoples are incapable of rising above themselves because they always give way to their passions and plunge down to their own undoing. The Demon argues that there are revolutions which purify peoples and charges monarchs with levity in the treatment of their subjects. 'All military action against popular revolt is wanton. . . . What have you done with the peoples' future? What with your own? A dragon's head of discord springs from every drop of blood that flows towards the Furies.' Kings seek to exterminate nations 'under the cloak of Christian religion'. (The authoress never named the fateful date 1848, but the inference was obvious enough.)

The King continues to moan his slumber song: 'The peoples are of boorish wit. . . . Insolent when things go well, but crawling, venal, when their luck is out. Their speech is the lowing of herds, their features a rallying-point for vile lusts.' He fears world revolution and the overthrow of all things. The Demon agrees: 'There are difficult times ahead. I see written in the stars, "The era of the sheep will become an era of wolves".' 'Is there not already an era of wolves? This tumult of revolt and deceit, these crafty attacks emanating from desperate schemes, all directed against me . . . ' The Demon: 'The great man's calling is to find the way where even dissonance constitutes the essential note in transition. . . . And then the King will head his people's revolutions.'

Now the spirits of the awakening peoples – the Poles, Italians, Magyars, Germans and the rest – approach the couch of the sleeping King and tell him of the resurrection of slain nations. 'God, Who transforms the age of destruction into the ages of regeneration, is with us.' The spirit of the common people urges the King to set himself at their head: 'Revolutions are not crimes, but the consequences thereof.' Still the King persists, 'I grasp all, yet impossible, it seems to me to make common cause with the people.' While the pleading spirits slowly depart, he groans, These visions will drive me mad, The spirit of Islam utters the final warning: 'Vouchsafe, while there is yet time. For the time will come where you will want to make concessions and find none to accept. The answer will run, *"Had you come but yesterday. I have no need of you today."* '

Bettina's voice sounded the calls of Romanticism and revolution. In Warsaw, Budapest, Vienna, and Paris of 1848 her tones would have been well understood. But she was speaking to a drowsy Prussia, a slumbering Germany. By autumn 1856, four years after its publication, not one copy of *Talks with Demons* had been sold. It had been totally hushed up.

HEINE

Heinrich Heine (1797–1856) was one of the most influential of German poets, the effect of his works reaching widely throughout Russia, Italy, Poland and France. A direct descendant of Goethe, Hegel and Hölderlin, he prepared the way for Nietzsche and was a source of inspiration to Wagner. For his work was concerned with the recreation of myth in the modern world. (In this he anticipated Stefan George, Rilke, Freud, Gerhart Hauptmann, Jung and Joyce.)

Heine had one of the most brilliantly alert and penetrating poetic minds of the century, and he certainly had no illusions about his countrymen. He foretold the German revolution with the words 'the civil war (was) in my breast'. He bore in his own heart so many of the century's problems: he was both Jew and German, Christian and heathen; he felt the death of Jehovah and of Christ, the resurrection of gods and man; above all, he had a deep consciousness of the cosmic Christ. He was familiar with the 'Two nations' in every state and knew the innermost links between revolution and tradition. He was socialist, communist and traditionalist; claimed to be tired of Europe, yet died an ardent European patriot. But, above all else, Heine was a German who thought day and night of Germany, and of the way its people had been deceived and betrayed: 'Never was a people more brutally insulted by its rulers', preface to *French Affairs* (1832). In this work he also accused those who had drafted that summer's Federal Diet resolutions of 'high treason towards the German people', even going so far as to accuse 'His Majesty, Frederick William, Third of the name, King of Prussia', of perjury. He continued with the following warning: 'But do not rely on our helplessness and fear. The cloaked man of our time, as bold of heart as he is ready of tongue, who knows the great word and can speak it, may already be standing beside you' . . . and then, bitterly, he adds,

> have no fear. I am only jesting. You are quite safe. . . . The great fool will always protect you against the little ones. The great fool is a very great fool . . . and his name is the German people. . . .
>
> If a good friend speaks of his suffering with sympathy, or even suggests a household remedy, he becomes enraged and strikes at the counsellor with his iron weapon. He is particularly angry at those who wish him well. He is the most bitter enemy of his friends, and the best friend of his enemies. O, the great fool will always remain faithful and obsequious; he will always amuse your little Junkers with his giant pranks; for their delight he will repeat his tricks every day; balance innumerable loads on his nose; allow many hundred thousands of soldiers to trample on his belly. But have you no fear that some day he may shake off your soldiers – and in an excess of buffoonery squeeze your head with his little finger so hard that your brains will spurt to the very stars?
>
> Fear not. I am only jesting. The great fool remains obsequious and obedient – and should the little fools want to do you harm, the great one will strike them dead.

(Passages quoted from *The Poetry and Prose of Heinrich Heine*, selected and edited by Frederic Ewen, The Citadel Press, New York, 1948.)

Heine perceived likewise the decay of Christianity in millions of hearts, regardless of the façades maintained by 'Christian states'.

> Our heart overflows with deepest pity – it is old Jehovah Himself who prepares for death. We have known Him so well, from the cradle up, . . .
>
> We have seen Him in touch with Assyrian-Babylonian civilisation, and then emigrating to Rome. . . .
>
> We have seen Him becoming more and more spiritual, whimpering meekly, a loving Father, a friend to mankind, a do-gooder, a philanthropist – it was all of no avail –
>
> Do you hear the tinkling of the little bell? Kneel down – a dying God is receiving the last rites.

Heine's complaint against Christianity was its incapacity to exercise any longer a salutary influence.

> The eventual fate of Christianity depends therefore on whether we still need it. For eighteen hundred years this religion was a blessing to suffering mankind; it was providential, godly, hallowed. All that it did for civilisation, by curbing the strong and strengthening the weak, by linking peoples through identity of sentiment and speech . . . is insignificant even beside the great consolation that it offered mankind. Eternal glory is due to the symbol of the suffering God, the Saviour with the crown of thorns, Christ crucified, Whose blood was (so to speak) the palliative balsam that ran down into the wounds of mankind. . . .

But, he added, neither the German masses nor German philosophers nowadays believed any longer in this Saviour. Instead the philosophers wielded cudgels in the evolution of their ideas and the masses yielded to the ancient, underground forces which Christianity had for so long held in check.

> Your German revolution will be no gentler or milder because it has been preceded by the *Critique* of Kant, the transcendental idealism of Fichte and even the philosophy of nature. These doctrines gave birth to revolutionary forces which only wait for the day to erupt and fill the world with terror and amazement. The natural philosopher will be terrible indeed because he has allies in the forces of nature, because he will be able to invoke the demonic energies of old German pantheism, because that ancient love of war which we find among the old Germans will awaken once more in him . . . Christianity – and that is its greatest merit – has somewhat mitigated that brutal German love of war, but it could not destroy it. Should that subduing talisman, the cross, be shattered, the frenzied madness of the ancient warriors, that insane, berserk rage of which Nordic bards have spoken and sung so often, will once more burst into flames. The talisman is rotting. . . . When that day comes, beware your neighbours' children, you French people, and do not meddle in our German affairs! For verily, harm may befall you. Beware lest you fan our flames, and take good heed not to quench them. You might easily burn your fingers in the fire. Do not smile at my advice – the advice of a dreamer who warns you against Kantians, Fichteans and philosophers of nature, or at the visionary who anticipates the same revolution in the realm of the visible as has taken place in the realm of the spiritual. Thought precedes action as lightning precedes thunder. German thunder is, I admit, thoroughly German – not very nimble – it is somewhat slow in coming but it does come. When you hear its crash, which will be unlike anything before in the history of the world, you will know that German thunder has at last hit the mark. At the sound the eagles in the sky will drop dead, and lions in farthest Africa will draw in their tails and slink away into their

royal caves. A drama will be enacted in Germany which will make the
French Revolution look like an innocent idyll. . . .

And that hour will surely strike. As on the tiers of the amphitheatre,
nations will group themselves around Germany to witness the great
gladiatorial combats. I warn you, Frenchmen, keep very still and, on your
life, do not applaud. . . . I wish you well; that is why I speak the bitter
truth. You have more to fear from a Germany set free than from the entire
Holy Alliance with all its Croats and Cossacks. . . . I don't know what you
are reproached with. Once, in a beer-hall in Göttingen, I heard a young
Pan-German declare that Germany must avenge Conradin von
Hohenstaufen on the French, who beheaded him at Naples. You have
surely forgotten about that, long, long ago. We, however, forget nothing.
So you see, when we finally feel the need for battle with you there will be
no lack of good reasons. In any case, I counsel you to be well on your
guard. No matter what happens in Germany, whether Crown Prince of
Prussia or Dr Wirth comes to power, always be on the alert, remain at
your posts quietly, weapons in hand.

Heine published this prophecy in *Religion and Philosophy in Germany*. His
reference to Dr Wirth, the organiser of the Hambach Festival in 1832, shows
that he foresaw the same danger of brutalisation in German national
liberalism as in other spiritual and political trends. Frederick William iv's
reactionary policy was epitomised for him by the completion of Cologne
Cathedral, the physical manifestation of a political Protestantism directed
against France. His incisive intelligence told him that where religious and
spiritual substance was fast running out, a certain German patriotism would
make itself the spokesman of a hot-blooded nationalism the slogans of which
would be 'Germany's world mission', with German civilisation, Luther and
Protestant principles serving as battle-cries against Frenchmen, Russians,
British and others. Ten years later, in *Ludwig Borne: a Memorial* (1840), he
recalled an experience which foreshadows precisely the tenor of discussions
at Vienna around 1900 and at Munich around 1920, not to mention
Himmler's 'cares' for the breeding of a Teutonic race:

In a beer-cellar at Göttingen I once had occasion to marvel at the
thoroughness with which my Pan-German friends prepared the proscrip-
tion lists for the day when they would come to power. Whoever is descended, even in the seventh generation, from a Frenchman, Jew or Slav
would be exiled. Whoever had uttered the slightest word against Jahn or
had written anything whatsoever against the absurdities of Pan-Germanism
could anticipate a death sentence.

Heine's greatness becomes visible, however, only when the depth of his
insight into yet another aspect of this vast process is appreciated: his awareness of the reawakening of ancient elemental long-buried forces in the

Germans and in other peoples of the world. He knew and loved this subterranean Germany, this Germany of pre-history and fairy-tales, of Paracelsus,
of a mythical and magical knowledge of the soul's secrets and veiled elemental
spirits.

'They say that there are old people in Westphalia who still know where the
icons are hidden. On their death-beds they tell their youngest grandchild,
who then carries the precious secret within his taciturn Saxon heart. In
Westphalia, ancient Saxony, not everything is dead that's buried.'

In his *Travel Pictures*, following comments on Sir Walter Scott, Heine
referred to the

> great grief felt at the loss of national characteristics which dissolve among
> the similarities of modern civilisations, a grief which now plucks at the
> hearts of all peoples. The heritage of national memory lies deeper than is
> generally supposed. Dare to bring forth the old tokens again and over-
> night the blossoms of old love will have sprouted again. That is a fact,
> not a figure of speech. A few years ago, on the day after Bullock had
> excavated an old heathen statue in Mexico, he found that during the
> night it had been ringed with flowers. This happened in spite of the fact
> that Spain had destroyed the old Mexican beliefs with fire and the
> sword, and for three hundred years had fiercely uprooted and ploughed
> the minds of the inhabitants and sown in them the seeds of Christianity.
> Flowers of that kind also boom in Scott's poems. Indeed these poems
> themselves rouse the old feelings. In Granada men and women used to
> rush out of houses with cries of despair when the song of the entry of the
> Moorish king was heard in the streets, so much so that its chanting was
> forbidden on penalty of death. In the same way the tone of Scott's poems
> had painfully shattered a whole world. Their tone resounds in the hearts
> of our old aristocracy who see castles and escutcheons decaying. It
> resounds in the hearts of our middle class who watch the cosy old habits of
> its forefathers being thrust aside by far-reaching, distasteful modernity.
> It resounds in Catholic cathedrals whence faith is fled and in rabbinical
> synagogues whence even the faithful flee. It resounds in the most distant
> banana forests of Hindustan, where the mourning Brahmin foresees the
> withering of his gods, the destruction of their ancient cosmic order, and
> British victory all along the line.

In a few brief sentences Heine compressed the effect of the enormous
process that evolved with the twentieth century, the painful reawakening,
under the impact of modern civilisation, of archaic substrata, whether in
Europe, Asia, Africa, or South America. Old wounds break out anew under
the pressure of civilisation's coordination. At a time when negroes were
looked on as but half-human, creatures to be shown in circuses together with
animals, or as a commercial proposition, as slaves, Heine had perceived in
them brothers who, on the other side of the Atlantic sang their songs of
lament for Africa, their lost mother. Like the young Friedrich Schlegel, he

recognised in India the infinite continent of the soul, the source of mankind's most ancient wisdom. He saw the gods being resurrected from the soul's primeval depths.

Heine was aware of these things because he experienced them within himself as German, as Jew, as Christian. He was all three of these and with a stricken intensity matched by few Germans, Jews, or Christians of his century. He pilloried the New Germans and Old Germans, the Christianised middle-class Jews, and the bourgeoisie that fancied itself 'Christian'. At one and the same time he was working his way painfully back to that old Germany which was the haven of the soul and of mankind, back to that Jehovah who had led the prophets through the deserts, and back to Jesus Christ.

> At night I think of Germany,
> And then there is no sleep for me:
> I cannot shut my eyes at all,
> And down my cheeks the hot tears fall.

With deep emotion he looked back on the history of Jewish persecution and intuitively realised the fate that was yet in store for the children of Israel. A passage in his unfinished tale, *The Rabbi of Bacherach*, sets out his views:

> My noble lord, if you would be my knight, you must fight whole nations, and in this battle there are few thanks to be won, and even less honour. And if you would wear my colours, then you must sew yellow rings on your cloak, or bind a blue-striped scarf around you. For such are my colours, the colours of my house, the House of Israel, the house of misery, which is despised and scorned in the streets by the children of good fortune.

What was the burden that a Christian must assume if he wanted to become a true Christian? He must boldly wade through the litter and trash piled up by the churches and the denominations, bearing his cross for himself.

Heine's own faith was rooted in cosmic evolution: 'Stones become plants, plants become animals, animals become men, men become gods.' He believed in a great and good future for mankind, one where man and God would be united in gladness:

> I've lighted your way in the darkness, and when the fight began, battled ahead in the front lines.

Here round about me lie the bodies of my friends, but the victory was ours. The victory was ours, but here round about lie the bodies of my friends. Amid the wild paeans of triumph sound the chants of the funeral rites. But we have time neither for grief nor for rejoicing. The trumpets sound anew, fresh battles must be fought –

I am the Sword, I am the Flame.

WAGNER

Heine's physical collapse began at Paris in May 1848. Nietzsche's ultimate mental collapse occurred at Turin in December 1888, ten years after he had finally broken with Wagner, the main link between Heine and Nietzsche. The former made Wagner a present of *The Flying Dutchman* and presented him with a multitude of themes in *Lohengrin, Tannhäuser, Götterdämmerung* and *Tristan und Isolde.* Man set free through woman, the dying God (Wotan), the victory of God the Son over God the Father, Siegfried as symbol of the uprising of the Teutonic gods in Germany – all were concepts derived from Heine. The composer began by acknowledging his debt in part, but subsequently concealed even that.

Richard Wagner (1813–83) was, for three generations of adherents, the expression in music of German revolution. The ninth son of a police registrar, he was a child of the people, knew penury, hunger and the desire for better things. His career as musical conductor at Magdeburg, Königsberg and Riga was interrupted by his flight, on account of debts, via London to Paris in 1839. He resumed his career in Dresden three years later. There he remained until 1849 when, owing to his participation in political events, he once more had to make his escape, this time to Switzerland. Amnesty did not follow until 1861, but was succeeded shortly afterwards, in 1864, by Ludwig II's summons to Munich. This Bavarian monarch had the desire to erect his own 'temple of the Muses', far from both Vienna and Berlin, but once more there was disagreement, and again Wagner found himself an exile in Switzerland.

With the Empire Wagner finally achieved fame. Princes and patrons answered his call for a new form of art for the new *Reich*, and he himself was summoned to provide it. Between 1872 and 1876 he built his Bayreuth festival theatre. In 1868 in his *German Art and German Politics*, he had adjured German Princes not to allow German art to perish, yet again, in poverty and pointed out that in France culture and politics were allied and that continued neglect of this factor by German rulers 'would therefore represent the triumph of French policy'. He continued, on a slightly menacing note: 'Should the German princes not evince themselves the faithful standard-bearers of the German spirit, they will, deliberately or not, be the abettors of the French Revolution's victory over the German spirit which they themselves failed to heed. Their days will be numbered, whether the blow comes from there or here.'

'Their days will be numbered' and the blow will come from the man of the people, the *duce*, the salvation-bringer, the champion of the Third Kingdom. In *Rienzi*, as early as 1842, Wagner had drawn with the insight of a demagogue, the figure of Cola di Rienzo, the leader of the masses whose charisma awakens the slumbering spirit of the people. Hitler was absolutely right to make his appearances at Bayreuth. Bismarck, on the other hand, declined to go there, this sort of popular leadership and enthusiasm being utterly abhorrent to him.

Art and Revolution and *Future Artistic Production,* early publications by Wagner, echo the views of revolutionary Romanticism. [Shelley and Byron, Poles and Magyars, Italians and, above all, Frenchmen proclaimed that poets and people, people and art, art and revolution belonged together and should in future be joined in holy alliance.]Wagner's German revolution was, however, counter-revolution in the fullest sense of the word: counter to Britain, counter to France, counter to 1848. With a sure eye for a change in circumstances, with a firm instinct for power and readiness to play the dictator (one man, and one alone, would be in charge at Bayreuth), with an iron will which broke the resistance of friend and foe, Wagner went the way he chose. None the less his inner nature was torn by passion, ambition, disgust, ennui, contempt for his fellows and self-loathing. He was perhaps one of the very few great artists whose self-loathing bore creative fruit, because he expressed it in the guise of the downfall of his heroes – gods, men, Teutons.

'My nights are practically sleepless. I get out of bed feeling tired and sick to face a day that will not bring me a ripple of pleasure. Intercourse with people only torments me and I withdraw from it merely in order to torment myself again. I am overcome by loathing for whatever I put my hand to. – Things can't go on like this. I don't want to endure life any longer!'

These sentences, and those that follow, could well have been written by Hitler during his youth in Vienna before 1914. In fact they were written in 1852 by Wagner to his friend Liszt, whom he advises to give mankind the kick it deserves and then go with him out into the wide world, even though it means being 'merrily dashed to pieces down some chasm'. Loathing for everything and everyone is everywhere: 'The real reason for my suffering lies in my exceptional relationship to the world and my surroundings, which are incapable of offering me any satisfaction any more. For me all is martyrdom and torture – insufficiency. How I have been infuriated on this journey, amidst the beauties of nature, by this rabble of mankind! It revolts me constantly, and yet how I long for people!'

The simultaneous loathing for and attraction to people is a distinct link between Wagner and the 'writer' (his official professional description right down to the seizure of power in 1933) and 'artist' Adolf Hitler. Mankind must be beguiled and led, if not voluntarily, then by force. Wagner was moreover absolutely serious in his determination to coach and lead a new mankind. Despite the exaggerations of Bernard Shaw's interpretation of him as a major Socialist, and of the *Ring* as a piece of Socialist mythology in which the twilight of the gods stands for the eclipse of the capitalist era, Shaw did clearly and correctly perceive one point. Wrapped in magic and sentimentality, Germany mythology and history, Wagner's work did make an impact on the spectator which subconsciously conveyed its creator's intention: to demonstrate German revolution in action, a revolution of the masses and a revolt by the individual, victory over false preachers (as of artistic canons, in *The Mastersingers*) or false conventions or false power. His *Allkunstwerk*, his own phrase for an overall artistic totality, was an astounding achievement and enabled him to fulfil an admirable objective. For, through it the German middle classes, after 1848 and again after 1870, could observe – and enjoy with every fibre of their body and soul – the spectacle of the German revolution on stage – in the presence of the 'victors', the princes and the highest and mightiest in the *Reich*. Yet this was not altogether masochistic for the great music dramas showed not simply 'victory': the days of the old gods were numbered. Wagner's works intimated what was also palpable to sensitive spirits like Nietzsche and Burckhardt: that in the strange creation of the Empire of 1871 lay the seeds of its decay.

Wagner, one of the outstanding experts on the mind and temper of the Germans of his day, had purgation of yet another kind to offer. Contemporary political neuroticism was closely linked with the rising pressure of contemporary sexual repression. If the outbreak of war in 1914 was greeted by so many as a form of release, then the reason for this was to be sought in the liberation it brought from the immense burden of subjugated, inhibited, proscribed erotic emotions.

One of Wagner's earliest operas bore the revealing title *Liebesverbot*. His love stories constitute a positive uprising, more or less manifest, of liberated ardour. Veiled in *The Flying Dutchman* (1843), bursting forth in *Tannhäuser* (1845), veiled again but at the same time also unveiled by the 'Swan' motif in *Lohengrin* (1847), passion was finally given free rein in *Tristan und Isolde* (1859) (*Translator's Note:* The composition of *Lohengrin* was completed in March 1848, but its first production was delayed until 1850. Similarly Wagner had already begun work on *Tristan und Isolde* when he fled from the complications of his love affair with Mathilde Wesendonck to Venice in August 1858, but the first production did not take place until 1865.) Wagner himself was all too familiar with the upsurge of physical ecstasy and had the courage to depict it on the stage. This was the greatest revolution effected by his revolutionary temperament. Thousands upon thousands of Germans afflicted by forced continence found release in the spectacle of Eros feeding upon the enticements and beauties of forbidden fruit. Indeed, Wagner dared to go even further. He ventured to parade Sigmund Freud's tragic themes: What is the human family other than in incestuous community wherein unchaste relations subsist between the Wotan father and daughter, and as must be suspected, every man may have some relation to every woman?

Dressed in Teuton and Christian myth (Wagner tailored both 'materials', without scruple and as being of the same value, to his respective requirements), Wagner presented in the manner of a psychologist the historic and sexual complexes affecting German, Christian, Western man, omitting none of the delusive, mortal, fascinating elements inherent in their union.

SCHOPENHAUER

Arthur Schopenhauer (1788–1860) died proudly and with serenity, secure in the knowledge that he had been the best known philosopher of his day. Yet during the eleven long years of his teaching post at Berlin University he gave only one lecture, the first, for he suspected a conspiracy of the German intelligentsia against him and with stubborn pride continually arranged his lectures to coincide with those of Hegel, and in fact never gave them. His principal work, *The World as Will and Idea*, was published two years before this appointment, in 1818.

His status as philosopher and, in particular, as philosopher to the German middle classes was first determined by the catastrophe of 1848. He had been only too ready to lend even his opera-glasses to the Prussian officers conducting an operation against the rebels from his apartment window, and hated the 'Paulskirche fellows' as he called the supporters of the Frankfurt Parliament right to the end of his life.

Revolution was for him a personal threat for he was the son of a banker who trembled for the fortune he had so agilely saved from a banking-house bankruptcy. And intimately linked with this fear of revolution was a fear of women and of the future. It was, in fact, this trinity of fear which made him the fashionable philosopher of the middle classes with their slightly shame-faced opportunism. There was also yet another, even more important, reason for Schopenhauer's fame in the Germany of his century: he expressed the 'pessimism' which hung so heavily in the contemporary air.

Like so many other men of the late nineteenth century, Schopenhauer was possessed of an immature, uncouth sexuality (possibly due to his hatred of his mother). Symptomatically, he adored actresses, though very unsuccessfully. The greenness of his sexual appetites corresponded to his gluttony which moved the owner of his favourite tavern to raise the prices on the menu for him.

He was positively riddled with fears, even cowering before the postman in case he should bring bad news and in his will writing in Latin the directions to secret drawers where he kept his securities. Yet he was not the only man to gaze in fear on the future. Kierkegaard and Nietzsche, like him living on the perimeter of society with some private means, felt the same. And as with them the outward impression he gave – that of boor, ironist and eccentric old bachelor – hid a sober intellect and sensitive spirit. His outward appearance was perhaps merely a defence against being deceived by anyone, whether by established authority, the Churches or German philosophers.

One of the main problems he considered was how man could find redemption, while he possessed that brutal resolve to domination and self-preservation which symbolised evil will that rules the world. Schopenhauer's answer was simple: the individual must be extinguished.

Schopenhauer discovered for himself not only Buddhism and an early Christian mysticism, but also asceticism and pity, itself sensational in denunciation of pity had been preached for two hundred years: since the Calvinists in the sixteenth and seventeenth centuries. He himself was descended from a line of Dutch parsons, and the Calvinist fears and Calvinist rebelliousness against a ruthless, frightening God, ran in his spiritual veins. In this common religious background lay one reason for his early influence in England and the United States.

It was a problem for a member of the new German Empire's middle class, however, to achieve redemption without actively practising asceticism, Buddhism or compassion, each one impossible in this particular society. But there was one great aid to the extinction of individualism: art. The urge towards redemption on the part of the new middle classes could be met in the new 'temples' of art, the concert halls, opera houses, theatres, museums, festival centres, and in particular at Bayreuth, through Richard Wagner.

NIETZSCHE I

'I loved him and no one else. He was a man after my heart.' Dressed in the white robes of a priest and lying on the divan in his sister's apartment at Weimar, during the long years of his mental twilight Nietzsche would always say, whenever Wagner's name was mentioned, 'I loved him very much'.

As for Schopenhauer,

> I saw in every line that cried renunciation, denial, resignation, a mirror reflecting with dreadful grandeur the world, life and individual spirit. Here I was faced by the utterly impersonal, luminous eye of art and I could see sickness and salvation, banishment and refuge, hell and Heaven. I was powerfully seized by the urge for self-recognition, yes, self-laceration . . . .

Influenced by Schopenhauer and sharing his disappointment with the nationalist aims of 1870–1, he foresaw a terrible future:

> The waters of religion ebb; they leave quagmires and shoals behind. Nations once more part in vicious enmity; they covet each other's destruction. The sciences, prosecuted without moderation, but constant with blindest *laisser faire*, erupt in all directions; every dogma dissolves. The cultured classes and states are swept away by an egregiously despicable financial economy. Never had the world been more worldly, never poorer in goodness and love. The learned professions are no longer beacons or havens amidst the tumult of secularisation; they become daily more restless, more mindless, more heartless. Everything, including the present arts and sciences, serves the approaching barbarism . . . .

> Certain forces are at work, colossal but savage, elemental, and totally merciless. . . . For the past century we have been prepared for a series of fundamental upheavals. Recent effort to counter this most ingrained

modern tendency towards destruction with the so-called national State's integral strength can, for a long time to come, merely result in an increase in the general insecurity and state of menace.

'Everything on this globe', Nietzsche grimly suggests, 'will be determined by its crudest forces, the egotism of those out for gain, and military despots.' 'Revolution, and the atomic one at that, is inevitable. . . . We live in the atomic age, the era of atomic chaos.'

He anticipated the feelings of the succeeding generation – the pain of youth in an age of such great inner decay and dilapidation, which, with 'all its weakness and still with the best of its power, places obstacles' in their way. 'The erosion of uncertainty is peculiar to this age. Nothing is based on firm foundations and staunch belief. . . . The ice which carries us has become distinctly thin and all of us feel the uncannily warm breath of the westerly breeze. Soon no one will be able to go along the ground which is now beneath our feet.'

It was across precisely such a stretch of ice that European youth felt itself to be walking in the years around 1900, 1910 and 1913. And yet the man who had gauged so accurately the emotions of this doomed generation had himself spent a very sheltered childhood and youth, and when he was appointed to an academic chair at Basle before he was even twenty-five, he seemed set for a successful career.

Since his birthday had coincided with that of Frederick William IV of Prussia, Nietzsche's father, a pastor who looked on that monarch as his benefactor, christened his son after him. Later, after the death of his father, he was nicknamed 'the little pastor'. A school teacher also compared him to the young Jesus in the temple, and his classmates stood in absolute awe of him. At the age of twelve he had a vision not only of 'God in his glory', but of God and the Devil together, 'a queer trinity, namely, God the father, God the son, and God the Devil'. Later as a student he again experienced a sort of satanic vision: 'What I fear is not the dreadful presence behind my chair, but its voice. Not the words uttered, but the horribly inarticulate, inhuman tone of that presence. Ah, if it only spoke as men speak!'

Nietzsche felt himself suffocated by vulgarity at every turn, the vulgarities of Christians, Anti-Semites, academics, the bourgeois and the Philistines, and suffocated by the ugliness and arrogance of Germany as it had evolved around 1870. In defiance of German nationalism he called himself a Pole. In protest against the Sedan anniversary celebrations he composed paeans on the French intellect which he contrasted with German pretensions to power. In the face of Teutonic anti-Semitism (aggressively propounded by his sister and brother-in-law Förster) he proclaimed himself pro-Jewish. Scorning Establishment Christians, he championed Jesus, the Man Who was crucified by Church and state, while supercilious German idealist philosophy drove him to side with the pre-Socratic philosophers, Heraclitus, and the spirits of fire supported by Aristotle and Hegel.

What was it that Christ rejected? Everything that goes today by the name of Christian.

Germans know immediately what I mean when I say that philosophy is corrupted by the theological strain. The grandfather of German philosophy is the Protestant parson and Protestantism itself its Original Sin.

Protestantism can be defined as Christianity's one-sided paralysis – *and* reason's too. . . . Only the two words 'Tübingen Institute' need to be spoken to understand *what* German philosophy basically is – an *insidious* theology . . . The Swabians are Germany's best liars, they are innocent liars. . . . Whence the cheering that Katn's appearance roused in the German academic world, three-quarters of which parsons' and teachers' sons. . . . A crooked path back to the old ideal lay revealed. The concept of 'the *true* world' and the concept of morality as the world's *essence* (the two most malign errors that there are!) were once more, thanks to a clever scepticism, if not provable, at least no longer refutable . . . .

The Church had licked Christianity into the shape of an artificial system, a system in which the ecclesiastic's fear and thirst for power, the masses' urge to redemption, fictions, resentments and lies had, for nearly two thousand years, been cunningly interwoven with one another. Nietzsche saw it as his role to destroy this system, and had hoped to gain support in this from Wagner.

Nietzsche had the courage to say what many thousands of men in the years after 1848 and around 1870 knew, and of which many others were painfully aware: the epoch of Christianity was coming to an end, although, during the process of its decay, it would still be capable of causing wars and internal dissensions.

Anyone familiar with science and possessed of an academically rained, awareness of things can hardly believe any longer in a personal God. Man stands infinitely alone in an immeasurably large and intrinsically senseless cosmic space, existing within a cycle of mortality and fresh life that carries within itself the seed of death. Man, infinitely alone as he is, comes together in masses, peoples and collectives, so that nationalism and imperialism look like despairing efforts to maintain some position in the merciless fight for survival. God is dead and Christianity, during the course of its own evolution, has provided man with the intellectual equipment and spiritual strength to recognise, with honest sobriety, that there is no God, no personal God. Jesus' cry from the Cross – 'My God, my God, why hast Thou forsaken me?' – was interpreted by Nietzsche as man's shriek of dread recognition as he hangs between Heaven and earth on the cross of reality.

In proximity, closest proximity, to nineteenth-century Christianity, Nietzsche pondered the historic situation of man after the death of God and after the end of Christianity. In this he found the support of a true friend, who was subsequently to bring him home from Turin by then mortally sick in mind. This was Franz Overbeck, a theologian who early on had fully realised the exceptional seriousness of man's situation.

Our twentieth century apparently lacks time (preoccupied as it is with civil and national wars) to face the vital perceptions, insights, and questions which were invoked by so many courageous men in the nineteenth century. Intellectual and spiritual bravery are not among the virtues of our age. When they do occur, as in the case of Alfred Delp, Dietrich Bonhoeffer, Karl Roman Scholz (three theologians pursuing their thoughts in the shadow of the scaffold), and Reinhold Schneider, they are in near fraternal vicinity to Nietzsche and are at once hushed up by their survivors.

Nietzsche's criticism of Christianity and of belief in a personal God are encountered at their most unalloyed in his relationship with Franz Overbeck; in their exchanges he found himself and illuminated his own thinking.

OVERBECK

Franz Overbeck (1837–1905) was by origin what Nietzsche would have liked to have been – a 'good European'. His mother was a Roman Catholic Frenchwoman. His paternal grandfather emigrated from Frankfurt-on-Main to England. His father was a merchant in Russia with British citizenship. He himself was born at St Petersburg, spent his early childhood in Paris, and spoke Russian, English, and French before starting to learn German at Dresden when he was twelve. He was powerfully influenced in his youth by his friendship with Heinrich von Treitschke, from whom he acquired, in his own words, 'the art of venomous criticism'.

Study of theology at Leipzig and Göttingen was followed by an academic career. The young lecturer, in the interest of pure scholarship, did not hesitate to deliver a six-hour address to a student audience of one, and the description of him as 'a monk mortifying himself on behalf of learning' was an apt one. In 1870 he was given a chair at Basle University. His lectures, prepared above all for his 'own thorough information', evinced great conscientiousness and the students admired his veracity and objectivity.

His lifelong friendship with Nietzsche was without a break and for five years, until his marriage, they had their lodgings in the same house. They felt themselves to be at their best in each other's company, a feeling rooted in their common dislike of becoming utterly absorbed by their academic appointments. They were at one in rejecting the contemporary lunacies of anti-Semitism and 'Parsifal Christianity' and both became increasingly critical of developments in Germany after 1870: 'The real corruption of man is the state' (because it debases scholarship, religion, and morality by using them to its own ends).

Overbeck was familiar with the works of Tolstoy, Turgenev, Ibsen and Zola, discovered early Strindberg, Hamsun, Léon Bloy and Adalbert Stifter, and in music championed Hugo Wolf. He was an agnostic and a sceptic unable to find the purpose of life in nature or history. Death came slowly upon him, after long suffering, but he faced it with equanimity. His funeral, he requested, should be very quiet and at his grave-side there should only be spoken 'a prayer for the repose of his soul'.

He remained a teacher of theology all his life, despite the fact that Christianity and his sense of what was true did not correspond. 'I had not been a student for a year before I abandoned my childhood habit of saying the Lord's Prayer every evening and I have not resumed it since.' Whoever designated himself a Christian should choose a way of living appropriate to the challenge provided by Christianity. The latter was 'far too lofty a matter for it to be so easy, in a world wholly alienated from Christianity, for the individual to identify himself with it without more ado. In fact, with the exception of theologians, nobody does so nowadays.'

Despite the fact that he himself had renounced Christianity, he nevertheless felt a deep respect for the true Christian. He made a sharp distinction between theology and Christianity, however, maintaining that theology, as an academic discipline, could equally well be taught by a non-Christian.

In 1873 he published *On the Christian Character of our Contemporary Theology*, which thirty years later he admitted to have been autobiographical, illustrating how 'right in the centre of Christendom a teacher of theology had not merely, on principle, renounced his own Christianity, but had disputed all of theology's claim to represent Christianity'. But there was absolutely no reaction to his publication, a fact which increased his inner conflict as a theologian even more. He never again mentioned his apologia, but continued to feel uneasy that he was unable to act as religious adviser towards his students, and finally relinquished his post. It was, however, the only work he ever published.

'I may say that Christianity has cost me my life,' runs a note among the thirty boxes of papers that he left behind and which constitute an exact report on the course of his experiment with life. The external tragedies and dramas of many nineteenth-century poets, artists, inventors, doctors and people in public affairs are familiar enough. Comparatively little is known about the tragedies of its many, and often outstanding, theologians and clergy who inwardly bled to death. Among them Overbeck has a special place. Arguing against attempts to summarise and assess contemporary history, he wrote 'The real events in any period are generally the least known, with but few men fully aware of them.'

His little book had been inspired by Paul de Lagarde's *On the German State in relation to Theology, Church and Religion*, published earlier in the same year, and by David Friedrich Strauss. It addressed itself to theologians only, not laymen. In the preface to the second edition, thirty years later, he acknowledged that Nietzsche had been his 'co-author'.

The principal question he posed was whether theology could ever be entitled to the attribute 'Christian'. The antagonism between faith and knowledge was irreconcilable; 'Consequently any action on the part of any religion which results in contact between faith and knowledge is in itself and in conformity with its structure intrinsically *irreligious*.' 'No conviction, for example, is more essential to any one religion that that it alone is the true one. On the other hand, there is none of which knowledge will more surely rob it.' Scholarship recognises immediately 'that no religion can oppose another without harm to itself, a fact for which classical Christian polemics against heathenism furnish the best proof.' 'Theology is simply part of Christianity's secularisation, a luxury that it permits itself, but which, like every luxury, cannot be had for nothing.' 'Theology, insofar as it is a branch of learning, does not possess any cognitive principles of its own. Therefore, being in no position to dictate such to other branches, it can only accept them from these. It cannot even continue to indulge in the fancy that it is a Christian science.'

Protestant pastors, he proposed, should confine themselves to being the priests and spiritual shepherds of their flock not troubling them with their personal and scholastic convictions. Such sacrifice in the service of the community would bear rich fruit and curb the intolerable cant which issued from the close union between the office and the individual who was expected constantly to 'bear witness'. The sole qualification should be love for one's fellow-men. Providing he had this, a theologian could act just as well as parish priest, even if his personal tenets 'had not one jot in common with the faith of his parishioners'.

He ends with a moving appeal to the Protestant ecclesiastical authorities 'not to exacerbate, but, in every way at all permissible, to mitigate the conflicts to which the clergy, especially its younger members, . . . are currently exposed. Few emerge whole from their ranks; the defeated are broken men.' That was the fate reserved for many of the finest spirits and minds in Roman Catholicism during the decades preceding 1914.

During the last thirty years of his life Overbeck pondered ever more deeply on the history and character of Christianity. 'History cannot be set bounds by Christianity. On the contrary, history reaches beyond the bounds of Christianity on all sides. That is why history is an abyss into which Christianity has cast itself with utmost reluctance.' The lengthy history of Christianity is itself an argument for accounting it dead. That history constitutes 'the best school for learning to despair of the existence of a God as navigator of the world's fate'. The Gospels are stranded between poetry and history. 'The Church Fathers are men of letters despite themselves.' The catastrophe in the history of primal Christian literature is its canonisation, for with that all works of the New Testament ceased to be understood. Once they were elevated to the level of a perpetual criterion, a thick veil was drawn over their origin.

The God of Christianity is the God of the Old Testament. The outlook of the Old Testament is superior to that of Christianity because it does not attempt a theodicy. Early Christianity was eschatological, concerned with the beyond, and containing a profound negation of the world. An honest argument between Christianity and the world has not taken place since the days of Constantine. The turn taken then 'decided that nothing would ever be attained other than a cultural Christianity which would have to content itself with imagining it had conquered the world, whereas in reality it had been conquered by the world.'

Christianity's crisis is curdled by theology, a thoroughly irreligious manifestation. 'Theology can be called the Satan of religion.' Its task is to quell certain eternal truths which convey all too clearly the ultimate problems of human existence and the difficulties facing life. Christian theology, in particular, is 'a very early corruption of Christian religion'. This professor of Protestant theology regarded Protestantism as a totally subordinate facet of Roman Catholicism, by whose grace it existed and whose downfall it would not survive.

He admitted but one single form of apologetic, the conduct of a man's life. 'We live, it is said, in infidel times. That may be so, and it is up to us critics to prove it. No less so, though, for our apologists. For the judgement of a future age may estimate them as proving it even more thoroughly.'

'My day will come, though I may not live to see it.' The nineteenth-century's theologians passed Overbeck by in silence. Karl Barth, however, has declared that his change of front between the first and second editions of his *Commentary on Romans* (English translation of the sixth edition, *The Epistle to the Romans*, published 1932), was caused in part by his study of Overbeck, this 'uniquely pious man'.

NIETZSCHE II

There are similarities between Overbeck and Unamuno's San Manuel Bueno, *mártir*, the parish priest of a poverty-stricken country district whose community reveres him as a saint while he has long lost his faith in God and Christianity. Overbeck was appropriately destined to be Nietzsche's true friend, for it is in the perspective of Overbeck that the mortal seriousness of Nietzsche's conflict with Christianity and his conviction (God *is* dead) becomes evident.

... the most serious Christians have always been well disposed towards me. For myself, an opponent of strict Christianity, I am far from bearing a grudge against the individual for what has been the misfortune of thousands of years. With me the Christianity of my ancestors comes to its close – austerity of intellectual conscience, reared by Christianity and now sovereign, turns on Christianity. Perhaps we are today the most thoroughgoing atheists because it is we who have longest resisted becoming so.

The birth of a (religious!) atheism out of the processes of growth and disintegration of two-thousand-year-old Christianity can be observed in the dramas of Overbeck's and Nietzsche's life. A passage in Friedrich Hebbel's diaries serves to bring into focus their contemporary situation and the direction in which their thoughts were leading.

Ours are evil times . . . the 'Insight into Nothingness' used to be under lock and key. Now every child and youngster can get at it! Yes, and will the eagle fly any higher when it ceases to believe that it can reach the sun? History has a colossal task. Hell's fires are damped and its last flames have seized on Heaven and consumed it. The concept of the Godhead no longer suffices, for man has humbly recognised that God without ballast, that is, without a mankind to cradle, suckle, and render happy, can still be God and blessed. Nature is to man what a musical theme is to its variation. Life is a convulsion, a fit of the vapours, or an opium hallucination. Yet where will history find an idea that will make up for, or outdo, that of the Godhead? I am afraid that, for the first time, it is not up to its task. It has ground a lens to catch the idea of a free mankind which, like the King in France, is incapable of death on earth. History *concentrates* (Hebbel's italics), it concentrates rays for a new sun. No, indeed, a sun does not come into being just by holding out a cap for alms.

Nietzsche knew that too. The new sun, the godliness of the new man, the superman, could be won only by suffering. His search for the sun, the mountain-top, the open skies and the open seas, was both literal and metaphorical. He sought them in Italy and in the valley of the Engadin. He needed the new 'noon' and 'summit' in order to emerge from the sickness, the ugliness, and the mendacity of past centuries and a reeking present. To assist in the birth of the new man, he evoked the pre-Socratic Greeks, Hölderlin, Christ, and Dionysus. ' . . . the world is still rich and undiscovered, and even to go under is better than being stunted and malignant. Our very strength forces us to take to sea, there where hitherto all suns have gone down.' Tired, unproductive man believes in what *is*; creative man believes in what *will be*. His 'experimental philosophy' was an attempt to instil a consciousness of the colossal tasks of the 'possible'. It was in this sense that Henri van de Velde and other young artists, architects, and 'adventurers over the sea of life' understood Nietzsche as prophet of new potentialities. Twentieth-century art, as examplified by Klee and Chagall, Joyce, Musil, Broch, Camus, and Sartre, should be regarded as polychromatic and polymorphous experimentation in accord with Nietzsche's summons.

New men and new gods are not merely possible; they are essential. Nietzsche wanted to stimulate man's moral imagination into inventing a new ethical code as part of the art of a higher life. The concept of guilt and punishment was to be retracted and God was to be purged of the traits of vengeance and his socially useful power to punish. Christians had 'wanted to invest God with a right to revenge'. It was now necessary to fight for the right to a new life for both God and man. 'You call it God's disintegration, but it is simply His desquamation – He sheds his moral skin. And soon you will see Him again, beyond good and evil.' In the guise of Zarathustra, he was the advocate of a 'new God' on the model of those creative spirits who are 'great men'. 'And there is room for many new gods!' But Nietzsche was well aware that new forms of asceticism, fasting, seclusion, pain and struggle were requisite to the birth of the race of men, a point overlooked by his followers. At the same time he rejected the old wars of the old world, the hostilities born of hate and fear that were launched by the Christian states of his own day. 'Christianity is still possible at any moment and is bound to none of the shameless dogmas which have embellished themselves with its names'; 'He who would say, "I don't want to be a soldier, I don't care about the tribunals," he would be a true Christian' (*The Will to Power*).

Nietzsche's philosophy was in line of descent from the early Romantics. Many of his principal ideas seem like 'translations' from the language and experiences of Baudelaire, Rimbaud, and those others who delved into the abysses of the human soul. His thoughts have served the artists, poets, architects, city planners, painters, designers and fashion creators of the twentieth century. It was a dreadful error on the part of his contemporaries and subsequent followers to think that they could interpret his enunciations on the new beauty, the 'will to power', the venture into the freedom of the open seas (after God's death) as a justification for their own power politics.

'At last the horizon appears clear again, even though sombre as yet. At last our ships can be outward-bound again, regardless of all danger . . . the sea, *our* sea lies open once again, or perhaps there has never been such an "open" sea as yet.' In this tone we have a foretaste of Saint-John Perse and René Char. Since prehistoric days the sea has been the symbol of freedom, ecstasy, and man's divinity. That was the way in which Hölderlin and the Greeks saw it, and Nietzsche shared their emotions. After their own fashion the men of the Navy League and Emperor William II had also tried to break out of the stuffiness and constriction of their time and to 'harness' the sea to the Grand Fleet. This was where the fatal misunderstanding of Nietzsche's 'will to power' began, a misunderstanding that lay in the air, was promoted by his sister, and which he himself furthered to a certain extent by the lack of restraint in his speech. Its range covered every aspect of soul, intellect, and politics.

I am an emissary of glad tidings, such as there has never been. I know tasks of such loftiness that hitherto there has been no term for them. Only with me do hopes spring afresh. I am withal, and must be, the man of destiny. For, when truth steps into the lists against the falsehood of millenia, convulsions, earthquakes, and displacements of mountains and valleys such as have never been dreamt of, will occur. Notions of politics will then be wholly merged in a war of the spirit and all power structures of old society will explode, for, one with another, they all rest upon the lie. There will be wars again, the like of which the earth has never seen. Only with my coming will there be *great politics* on the earth.

New wars, great politics – it was natural enough to think of the approaching world war as such. But in fact Nietzsche had greater conflicts in mind, those involving the destruction of the thousand-year-old structure of morality, custom, and society. As the philosopher with the hammer, the iconoclast, as an explosive force ('I am not man, I am dynamite'), he wanted to clear the paths of men into the good future, which would come when man took responsibility for the history of his fellow-men.

Confidence and frankness! would characterise the 'noble man'.

Inability to take his enemies, his mishaps, and his misdeeds seriously for long – that it the hall-mark of a strong, full-blooded nature. . . . (A good example in the modern world was Mirabeau, unable to recall the insults proferred and the mean actions done to him and unable to forgive only because he – forgot.) Such a man shakes off with a jerk the vermin that crawl beneath the skin of others. In his case alone is it possible, supposing it to be possible at all, to really *love* ones enemies. How great is the respect that a noble man has for his enemy, and such respect already contains a bridge to love. . . . He insists on having his enemy to himself, as his personal distinction, and could not tolerate an enemy other than one in whom there is nothing to despise and *much* to hold in honour. Imagine on the other hand 'the enemy' as the man of rancour envisages him. This being his own action, his creative deed, he conceives 'the wicked enemy', the *'evil one'*, a basic concept which he is then able to contrast with its counterpart, the 'good one' – himself!

From 1870 to the present day we can trace an unbroken tradition of murderous vulgarisation and neuroticization of the concept of the enemy, making it impossible to see a foe in any other way than as 'the wicked enemy' or to speak of him other than slanderously. French Catholics, spokesmen of the Curia, German Protestants, and, in 1918–20, prominent German Catholics and Protestants, talked in terms that word for word anticipated those used by the *Führer* in 1933. Nietzsche was aghast to hear the use made of such speech by Christians, theologians, anti-Semites, and Teutomanes. He was unable to convey, even to imitate, his own greatest discovery: a new sort of conflict, void of hate and at a level beyond clubs and cannons; not the high priests' and generals' sort of conflict, but the struggle for a new and higher life.

Henri van de Velde wanted to erect at Weimar a Nietzsche stadium. He and his friend Count Harry Kessler were two of the most prominent Nietzsche enthusiasts in Germany around 1900. Their wish was to 'serve art and peace'. It was also with this motto that Kessler sought to enlist sympathy in Britain, France and Germany. Yet when, between 1910 and 1913, he put forward a plan for a Nietzsche memorial at Weimar, he was greeted with the fanatical resistance of nationalistic and reactionary German artists. An international subscription fund was to be established. For this purpose Kessler again sought help abroad. To his support came André Gide, Anatole France, and

Henri Lichtenberger in France; Gabriele d'Annunzio in Italy; Gilbert Murray, H.G.Wells, Walter Raleigh and others in Britain. Aristide Maillol would have worked on the sculptures, van de Velde would have been the architect. Van de Velde's own inspiration derived directly from Britain: from Ruskin and Morris.

8

Trends in Britain

'*The consequences of Darwinism (which, incidentally, I regard as correct) are frightful*'

NIETZSCHE, 1872

The impact Charles Darwin had on his contemporaries was that of a mental sledge-hammer – both hard and sharp. In Germany, Russia and America he was regarded as the originator of a new perspective on life and the founder of a scientifically-based religion, of a new, universal church of believers in science, progress and the struggle for existence.

Darwin himself was totally disinterested in this reaction. He was, quite simply, the product of nineteenth-century England, the England of grim class conflict and the Industrial Revolution, where the words 'Class', 'Industrial Revolution', 'Two Nations' were more than mere neologisms, where they discovered the searing experience of innovation, destruction of beauty, and of slums.

Industry, meaning the growth of factories, was in the first place practically synonymous with cotton (and thus with the slave trade and colonialism). However, despite recurring economic crises from 1793 onwards, it soon took hold of all aspects of trade, flourished, until, by 1848, it dominated the world market. At the same time the growth of the railway (the 'child of the coalmine') covered England with a new network of communications, and the Agrarian Revolution forced many hundreds of landless peasants into industrial centres, where endless filth, ugliness, disease, hunger, and exploitation awaited them. Child women labour formed an integral part of the picture, with men constituting only one third of the cotton industry's labour force.

We have already discussed the pain and sorrow of Blake at the prevailing conditions, and the anger of the great generation of poets between 1798 and 1824, of Byron, Shelley, Keats, Coleridge and Wordsworth. This was the Britain from which these men sought refuge in the creation of their poetry.

OWEN

Robert Owen, like Friedrich Engels, had initially been engaged in the cotton industry, but whereas the latter belongs to the history of the international labour movements, Owen embodies British genius in the field of reform.

Born in 1771, Owen began his career at eighteen as the maker of spinning machines, became a cotton spinner and, on 1 January 1800, took over the factory at New Lanark which, through years of hard work, he turned into a model enterprise. In spirit he followed the thread of John Beller's ideas (Colleges of Industry, 1695) and the demands for social reform of the dissentient religious movements, which, however firmly suppressed, still continued to find adherents. The most bitter opponents of such ideas were members of the Established Church. As leaders of religious opinion, these men, mainly the sons or protegés of leading aristocratic families, constituted an important reactionary element in society and politics. The drive behind social reform came almost solely from nonconformists such as Wesley's evangelists. The Bible Society, founded in 1804 for the purpose of placing the Bible in the hands of the masses, the abolition of the slave trade in 1906, the abolition of whipping for women convicted of crimes – all these were the work of nonconformists.

Like many other eager individualists who were unable to find an outlet for their aims in England, Owen went to America. In April 1825 he bought Harmony, a settlement in Indiana belonging to a German communistic sect called Rappites, rechristened it New Harmony, and tried to establish a fresh kind of community there. The scheme was a failure mainly because he so often had to be absent on unavoidable business. Returning to England, he founded the London Labour Exchange (1832–4) and in 1833 put forward a plan for the first English trade union organisation which was intended to introduce a new social order. In that same year many workers' leaders were arrested and transported to Australia as 'conspirators and traitors'. The Chartist Movement was called into being by Owen's followers. Six hundred years after the barons of England had obtained their rights in Magna Carta, the People's Charter was drawn up demanding political and social rights for the common folk. The Movement began heroically, but petered out, for in the struggles of 1838–48 it failed, as a purely workers' movement, to get the support of other lower and middle-class groups.

Karl Marx drew the lesson from the Chartists' débâcle that Owen had declined to accept: the workers had to have political power in their hands before a new social order could be established. He was by then living in exile in England among the infidels – those Socialists who did not believe in the Marxian tenets. Their successors took Owen as their model in organising social reform movements like the Fabian Society (the group around Bernard Shaw, Beatrice and Sidney Webb, H.G.Wells) and Keir Hardie's Labour Representation Committee. Hardie's tract (he was the founder of the Labour Party) *Can a Man be a Christian on a Pound a Week?* was motivated by the same sense of fraternal responsibility towards the poor, the working classes, and humanity at large as Owen's had been.

Owen's first important publication (*A New View of Society: or, Essays on the principle of Formation of the Human Character*) appeared in 1812–3. His main work, *The Book of the New Moral World*, was published in eight parts between 1836 and 1844. His autobiography (up to 1830), *The Revolution in the Mind and Practice of the Human Race*, came out in 1849, a document that mirrors half a century of thought, action, effort, British tenacity, and an indomitability of soul and mind that no number of failures and defeats could discourage.

In the first of these works Owen wrote, 'Any general character, from the best to the worst, from the most ignorant to the most enlightened, may be given to any community, even to the world at large, by the application of proper measures; which measures are to a great extent at the command and under the control of those who have influence in the affairs of men.' '. . . the poor and working classes of Great Britain and Ireland have been found to exceed fifteen millions of persons, or nearly three-fourths of the population of the British Islands. The characters of these persons are . . . formed without guidance or direction, and, in many cases, under circumstances which *must* train them to the extreme of vice and misery, thus rendering them the worst and most dangerous subjects in the empire.' 'Half-naked, half-famished,' masses, their numbers waxing hourly, they constitute ever increasing danger.

He raised his voice against the fatalism.

These Essays are intended to explain that which is *true*, and not to attack that which is *false*. For to explain that which is true may permanently improve, without creating even temporary evil; whereas to attack that which is false, is often productive of very fatal consequences. The former convinces the judgement, when the mind possesses full and deliberate powers of judging; the latter instantly arouses irritation, and renders the judgement unfit for its office, and useless.

How much longer shall we continue to allow generation after generation to be taught crime from their infancy, and, when so taught, hunt them like beasts of the forests, until they are entangled beyond escape in the toils and nets of the law? when, if the circumstances of those poor unpitied sufferers had been reversed with those who are even surrounded with the pomp and dignity of justice, these latter would have been at the bar of the culprit, and the former would have been in the judgement seat. Let feelings of humanity or strict justice induce you to devote a few hours to visit some of the public prisons. . . . They (the inhabitants) will tales unfold . . . that will disclose *sufferings*, *misery* and *injustice* . . . which, previously, I am persuaded, you could not suppose it possible to exist in any civilized state. . . .

In his *New View of Society* Owen made a detailed report on his New Lanark experiment and maintained that:

These principles, applied to the community at New Lanark, . . . persevered in for sixteen years, effected a complete change in the general

character of the village, containing upwards of two thousand inhabitants
. . . In this progress the smallest alteration, adequate to produce any good
effect, should be made at one time; indeed, if possible, the change should
be so gradual as to be almost imperceptible, yet always making a permanent
advance in the desired improvements . . . .

This is social reform through empiricism or sociology in day-to-day
practice. Recent American social science, which has taken for its field of study,
group constitutions, group conflicts, inter-racial tensions, and social developments in Asia and Africa, and is trying to use science, empiricism, economics
aid and education, for its own purposes, can look on Robert Owen as its
forerunner.

He was concerned to achieve the total reform of British society. In the
address prefixed to the Third Essay in *New View of Society*, he asked businessmen ' . . . will you not afford some of your attention to consider whether a
portion of your time and capital would not be more advantageously applied
to improve your living machines?' And in the Third Essay itself:

Hitherto indeed, in all ages, and in all countries, man seems to have
blindly conspired against the happiness of man, and to have remained as
ignorant of himself as he was of the solar system prior to the days of
Copernicus and Galileo.

Hitherto, however, the tide of public opinion in all countries has been
directed by a combination of prejudice, bigotry, and fanaticism, derived
from the wildest imagination of ignorance; and the most enlightened men
had not dared to expose those errors which to them were offensive,
prominent, and glaring.

It is much to be regretted that the strength and capacity of the minds of
children are yet unknown: their faculties have been hitherto estimated by
the folly of the instruction which has been given to them . . . .

The nineteenth century was one of great teachers and great reformers in
the methods of teaching. Simultaneously it was one of tyranny over, and
malformation of, children on the part of neurotic fathers and schoolmasters
who infected them with fear, hate, and sexual complexes. In Britain,
moreover, the adolescent criminal was trained in the very institutions which
the offspring of the poor were compulsorily sent. Owen condemned this
desecration of the young long before Dickens' moving protests.

It is beyond all comparison better to prevent than to punish crimes.
A System of Government therefore which shall prevent ignorance, and
consequently crime, will be infinitely superior to one, which, by encouraging the first, creates a necessity for the last, and afterwards inflicts
punishment on both. That government then is the best, which in practice
produces the greatest happiness to the greatest number; including those
who govern, and those who obey.

As for ignorance,

... destroy this hydra of human calamity, this immolator of every principle of rationality; this monster, which hitherto has effectually guarded every avenue that can lead to true benevolence and active kindness. ... Yet ... to this day the British Government is without any national system of training and education, even for its millions of poor and uninstructed!!

Even the recent attempts which have been made are conducted on the narrow principle of debasing man to a mere irrational military machine, which is to be rapidly moved by animal force.

Owen was a resolute opponent of Malthus, whose acquiescent, deeply pessimistic dogma about excess population and the inevitable famine and misery of the masses (only to be 'eliminated' by way of disease, destitution, and war) was to find so fatal an echo in the nineteenth and twentieth centuries and commented '... but he has not told us how much more food an intelligent and industrious people will create from the same soil, than will be produced by one ignorant and ill-governed. It is, however, as one, to infinity.'

... there is not perhaps a stronger evidence of the extreme ignorance and fallacy of the systems which have hitherto governed the world, than that the rich, the active, and the powerful, should, by tacit consent, support the ignorant in idleness and crime, without making the attempt to train them into industrious, intelligent, and valuable members of the community; although the means by which the change could be easily effected have been always at their command!

'The rich, the active, and the powerful.' Between 1066 and 1918 power in Britain, although continually infiltrated by outsiders, was in the hands of state, church, and the upper classes. Whatever caste happened to be in power, the dominion of the ruling class was always harsh. In 1783 the Tories under Pitt the Younger came to power and remained there until 1830, thanks to the governing class's reaction to the French Revolution. Between 1809 and 1822 laws against freedom of public opinion were of the utmost severity. Writers were transported, thrown into prison, fined.

On the other hand British liberalism found a representative in Jeremy Bentham. In a publication by Joseph Priestley, pioneer of modern chemistry and friend to the French Revolution, he found a phrase which cast a spell over him: 'The greatest happiness of the greatest number.' Happiness, he believed, was an objective in life; happiness was welfare, freedom in moderation, work for fellow-men, reform.

In the opening years of the nineteenth century, Britain was without freedom of speech, freedom of assembly, freedom of association. Then a number of liberal-minded men set out to change this. One of them was Henry Brougham, a contributor to the *Edinburgh Review* (the voice of political liberalism from

1802 onward), a supporter of popular education, and a leading figure in the foundation of 'Godless' University College, London. In 1808 he met James Mill. Together they formed a circle of men, a small but zealously impassioned minority, which challenged an overpoweringly hostile majority.

JOHN STUART MILL

James Mill, son of a Scottish country cobbler, abandoned a theological career in Edinburgh to practise that of a free-lance journalist in London. By industry and tenacity he rose to a senior post in the East India Company, as his son John was also to do.

John Stuart Mill (1806–73) was 'the greatest work of his father'. With iron discipline and inflexible purpose, James undertook the boy's education in a way reminiscent of Leopold Mozart. At three, John began to learn Greek. At six he was doing eight hours' study a day. At seven he was reading Aesop, Plato, Herodotus, and Xenophon in the original. The father impressed on the son a deep belief in the power of education and institutions to alter society as a whole. John was deeply attached to his father, and his greatest happiness lay in winning his approval.

In the circle of Bentham's friends, where James was a leading figure, John listened to the atheistic and politically radical discussions which were as far ahead of their time as those of the Fabians would be half a century later. For recreation he read history and collected plants. When he was fourteen, he spent a year in France with the Benthams. German he learned from Sarah Austin, the member of a progressive Unitarian family.

From 1823 to 1826 he acted as his father's assistant. At sixteen he composed a devastating, sixty-page criticism of Sir Walter Scott's *Life of Napoleon* and contributed frequently to the radical Press. Until he was twenty, he was intellectually no more than the product of his father's training. Then, during ten difficult years, overshadowed by bouts of melancholy, he broke away from the rationalism which had been instilled into him. Later, however, he was able once more to come to terms with his other trains of thought and went on to become one of the most open-minded British thinkers of his age. He sought to fulfil Goethe's injunction of versatility and zealous reading of German, French, and English literature furthered his efforts to achieve inner freedom and emancipation.

In 1830 he met the twenty-three-year-old Harriet Taylor, the first and only woman in his life. For the first time he experienced the beauty of a woman. Henceforth he was convinced that woman's task was the beautification of life and that all her gifts of intellect, body, and soul should be devoted to spreading beauty, elegance, and grace.

Her husband was a Unitarian and hence belonged to a group which, thanks to the Tories and the Established Church had many links with Radicals. Thus the wife of his political ally became Mill's Beatrice, his spiritual guide. From 1831 onwards none of his work was printed without previous submission to her. She influenced his thought and his style, making him sturdier, more decisive, more critical. The more famous he later became, the more he relied on her and wrote for her sake only. In April 1851, after the death of her husband, he and Harriet could at last marry. She had aged considerably, and was partially lame as well as suffering from tuberculosis. He was sickly and weak. Both were exhausted from decades of intellectual and spiritual effort. Harriet died, during a wintry journey, on 3 November 1858 at Avignon, and was buried there at the cemetery of St Veran. John spent the major part of his final years in a weekend retreat close to her grave, which he visited at least once a day. The epitaph, composed by him and carved on her tombstone, proclaimed that:

> Her Great and Loving Heart, Her Noble Soul
> Her Clear Powerful and Original
> Comprehensive Intellect
> Made Her the Guide and Support
> The Instructor in Wisdom.

Her life, work, and example lent hope that 'The Earth would Already become/The Hoped-For Heaven'. This is one of the nineteenth century's most impressive testimonies to belief in mankind.

Towards the end of his life Mill's thoughts were concerned with life after death. His faith rested in a benevolent, finite, but certainly not all-powerful Godhead. He affirmed once again the Manichaean-based conviction held by his father that the universe is the scene of a contest between two opposing principles, with man on the side of God. His last, fevered words, to Helen, Harriet's daughter, were, 'You know that I have done my work.' He died at Avignon on 7 May 1873 and was buried beside his beloved wife.

Anyone who is unable to see the greatness of John Stuart Mill, lacks the capacity to appreciate the greatness of British genius. German derision of Mill's 'insipidity', 'superficiality', 'shallowness', and 'phrase-mongering' is merely a symptom of the growing Anglophobia in Germany in the late nineteenth century.

Spiritual, philosophic, political, and religious thought was an indivisible unity in Mill's intellect. His basic principle was that man is responsible to man. He lent Carlyle, for his history of the French Revolution, the rich mass of material he had collected. He supported Auguste Comte for a long time with regular remittances. As early as 1831 he favoured the transformation of southern Australia from a convict colony into an area for normal colonial settlement, thereby drawing down on himself the wrath of Government and Church alike. He pleaded for adoption of a new policy towards Canada and he pioneered the concept of the British Commonwealth as an association of self-governing dominions. As a member of the Commons (1866–72), he spoke for the working classes and defended the Irish, which cost him much respect and earned him bitter enmity, but also gained him the friendship of John Morley, at that time struggling for a living as a free-lance journalist.

Morley subsequently continued Mill's political heritage, acknowledging his debt to him as his source of intellectual inspiration.

Enormous excitement and indignation was engendered by Mill's publication, in 1869, of the *Subjection of Women*, a volume dedicated to the memory of Harriet and attacking the ever more male-oriented, rancorous, and domineering spirit, which even in Britain, infused the second half of the nineteenth century. Its thesis was that social freedom and freedom in the future depended on the liberation of women. The work became the Bible of the feminist movement not only in Britain, where the fight for female suffrage had already begun, but in many other countries, forbidden though its circulation might be. In translation it passed secretly from hand to hand and exercised widespread influence on the slowly altering attitude of mood and mind.

Preoccupation with the status of women and with freedom naturally caused him to direct his gaze towards France, whose political and intellectual strife between 1830 and 1848 Mill followed with keenest attention. In de Tocqueville's *Democracy in America* he found ample proof for one of his own favourite themes namely, that the terror of 'public opinion' could effect more brutal suppression of the individual than many a tyrant's act. He saw Britain flooded with German intuitional philosophy and perceived in it as renaissance of magical thinking, prerational as well as irrational. It was against this German line of thought and against sacerdotal dominion that he composed his *System of Logic*. Its appearance in 1843 coincided with that of Carlyle's *Past and Present*, Macaulay's *Essays*, Ruskin's *Modern Painters*, Dickens' *Martin Chuzzlewit*, and Bulwer Lytton's *Last of the Barons*.

Mill wrote proudly to Comte, after its publication, '*Désormais on pourra choisir; on ne sera plus rejeté vers le camp allemand faute de trouver ailleurs un système philosophique nettement formulé . . . Je commence à espérer que ce livre pourra devenir un vrai point de ralliement philosophique pour cette partie de la jeunesse scientifique anglaise qui ne tient pas beaucoup aux idées religieuses.*' He had in mind an Anglo-French intellectual and scientific alliance against the German school of innate ideas and 'magical' philosophy, as well as against superstition, wherever the latter might be encountered.

Twenty-five years later he summarised his conviction in the following terms: 'If it were possible to blot out entirely the whole of German metaphysics, of Christian theology, of the Roman and English systems of technical jurisprudence . . . there would be talent enough set at liberty to change the face of the world.' Even in old age he continued to be disturbed by the notion of strength of intellect and spirit being blocked by religion in its various manifestations and by philosophies of intuition. Many of his British opponents, including Gladstone, Carlyle (his former friend), Ruskin and Matthew Arnold, upbraided Mill for his alleged materialism. He was, on the contrary, a religious thinker, through and through. His three essays on religion (1873) testify to the faith he received from his father – God may well exist, but He needs man's cooperation; Jesus Christ, the Son of Man, can set us an example of this. The French Revolution, Mill believed, had brought too close the era of sentiment and heroism. The dawning era of democracy, introducing a new epoch for Europe and the world at large and superseding man's previous adventurous course, required a scientific and social development shaped according to a carefully formulated plan. Responsibility, in his eyes, was poetry in action, spirit and imagination finding expression in a religion of mutual service.

Mill had always been fascinated by Greece. In 1855, in Rome, he remembered a suggestion of Harriet's that he should write an essay on Freedom, and from this came *On Liberty*, a work which has been translated into practically every language, and read by men of every nation. Indeed, it is illuminating that this book has nearly always been banned by countries with a totalitarian or semi-totalitarian regime.

The motto of Mill's essay was a maxim of Wilhelm von Humboldt's which intimated the importance of allowing individuality to develop in its richest diversity. The two outstanding themes are the tyranny exercised by majorities, and the general tendency the world over to increase the power of society and reduce that of the individual, a trend becoming ever more formidable and dangerous. He writes: 'If all mankind minus one were of one opinion, and only one person were of the contrary opinion, mankind would not be more justified in silencing that one person, than he, if he had the power, would be justified in silencing mankind.' 'But the peculiar evil of silencing the expression of an opinion is, that it is robbing the human race; posterity as well as the existing generation; those who dissent from the opinion, still more than those who hold it. If the opinion is right, they are deprived of the opportunity of exchanging error for truth. . . . ' 'All silencing of discussion is an assumption of infallibility.'

'It is a bitter thought, how different a thing the Christianity of the world might have been, if the Christian faith had been adopted as the religion of the empire under the auspices of Marcus Aurelius instead of those of Constantine.' Very great positive developments in Christianity had been thwarted by permanent suppression. ' . . . the dictum that truth always triumphs over persecution is one of those pleasant falsehoods which men repeat until they become platitudes, but which all experience refutes. History teems with instances of truth put down by persecution.'

'To speak only of religious opinions: the Reformation broke out at least twenty times before Luther, and was put down. . . . Even after the era of Luther, wherever persecution persisted, it was successful. In Spain, Italy, Flanders, the Austrian Empire, Protestantism was rooted out; and most likely would have been so in England, had Queen Mary lived, or Queen Elizabeth died.'

In 1857 Mill complained that 'harsh prison sentences' were still being imposed for 'unorthodox expressions of opinion concerning Christianity'. What was often praised as rebirth of religion, he went on, was frequently nothing but a fanatical outbreak of bigotry. Broad strata of the British people were deeply intolerant below the surface and this tendency was ready to break out at any time. (An analogous trend occurred in France and Germany between 1870 and 1914.)

Mill also attacked all persecution of so-called heretics: 'The greatest harm is done to those who are not heretics, and whose whole mental development is cramped, and their reason cowed, by the fear of heresy.'

'No one can be a great thinker who does not recognise that, as a thinker, his first duty is to follow his intellect to whatever conclusions it may lead. Truth gains more by the errors of one who, with due study and preparation, thinks for himself, than by the true opinions of those who only hold them because they do not suffer themselves to think.'

In recent centuries Europe had had experience of three vitally forceful intellectual movements: 'Of such we have had an example in the condition of Europe during the times immediately following the Reformation; another, though limited to the Continent and to a more cultivated class, in the speculative movement of the latter half of the eighteenth century; and a third, of still briefer duration, in the intellectual fermentation of Germany during the Goethean and Fichtean period.' Since then, Mill felt, European thought had become paralysed.

The renewal of barbarism in this world of up-and-coming masses was being promoted by Christianity.

By Christianity I here mean what is accounted such by all churches and sects – the maxims and precepts contained in the New Testament. These are considered sacred, and accepted as laws, by all professing Christians. Yet it is scarcely too much to say that not one Christian in a thousand guides or tests his individual conduct by a reference to those laws. The standard to which he does refer it, is the custom of his nation, his class or his religious profession.

Christians had the bad habit of condemning in argument all who thought other than themselves as evil and immoral. 'I believe that other ethics than any which can be evolved from exclusively Christian sources, must exist side by side with Christian ethics to produce the moral regeneration of mankind.'

Mill visualised the coming of a world of mass classes and machines, a world where houses would be built, corn sown, battles fought, churches raised, and prayers said by machines. That is, automatons in human form. But, he protested, human nature was not a machine constructed on a single pattern and appointed to a prescribed task; it was a tree that wanted to grow and spread in all directions in accordance with the trends of its inner laws of vitality.

The masses, and the instincts of the masses, now enjoyed supreme power. In Britain and the United States the governments were their agents. This being the situation, the few individuals left must be encouraged to behave other than the masses. 'In other times there was no advantage in their doing so, unless they acted not only differently but better. In this age, the mere example of non-conformity, the mere refusal to bend the knee to custom, is itself a service.' 'That so few now dare to be eccentric marks the chief danger of the time.' Accommodation to the lowest common factor had become the rule. 'The greatness of England is now all collective; . . . But it was men of another stamp than this that made England what it has been; and men of another stamp will be needed to prevent its decline.'

'It is individuality that we war against: we should think we had done wonders if we had made ourselves all alike; . . . We have a warning example in China', where extreme collectivisation and dictatorship of 'custom' had exhausted creative energy. (It is as well to recall the Mill was issuing this warning to his countrymen in 1858.)

The modern regime of public opinion was, in unorganised form, what Chinese systems of politics and education were in organised form. If individuality were not able to assert itself successfully against this yoke, Europe, for all its aristocratic ancestry and generally proclaimed Christianity, would show a tendency to become a second China. Europe was 'decidedly advancing towards the Chinese ideal of making all people alike'.

M. de Tocqueville, in his last important work, remarks how much more the Frenchmen of the present day resemble one another than did those even of the last generation. The same remark might be made of Englishmen in a far greater degree. The circumstances which surround different classes and individuals, and shape their characters, are daily becoming more assimilated. Formerly, different ranks, different neighbourhoods, different trades and professions lived in what might be called different worlds; at present to a great degree in the same. Comparatively speaking, they now read the same things, listen to the same things, see the same things (Again, Mill was writing a hundred years before mass television), go to the same places, have their hopes and fears directed to the same objects, have the same rights and liberties, and the same means of asserting them . . . .

Education, political change, improvement in the means of communication and industry were constantly promoting this assimilation. 'If the claims of Individuality are ever to be asserted, the time is now, while much is still wanting to complete the enforced assimilation.'

If resistance waits until life is reduced nearly to one uniform type, all deviations from that type will come to be considered impious, immoral, even monstrous and contrary to nature. (Mill foresaw this development eighty years ahead of the perfected products of conformist societies in East and West.) Mankind will speedily become unable to conceive diversity, when they have been for some time unaccustomed to see it.

The contemporary generation had a great responsibility towards the rising generation. If the process of social decay continued, 'it can only go on from bad to worse, until destroyed and regenerated (like the Western Empire) by energetic barbarians'. Mill did not specify which barbarians, but it was in this sense that Lamennais and his friends alluded to the external and internal barbarians, the Russians and the proletariat respectively.

Mill went on to issue the warning that once the highways and railways, banks and insurance companies, major industries, universities, welfare societies, and other such institutions had been nationalised, when all local administration was simply a department of the central bureaucracy, and when all men were ultimately employees of the government, then all the freedom of the Press in the world, all law-making, and every function in Britain or elsewhere would be able to confer 'liberty' only in name. The dictatorship of an all-powerful bureaucracy was thrusting ahead. Even today (in 1858:) the Tsar 'himself is powerless against the bureaucratic body; he can send any of them to Siberia, but he cannot govern without them or against their will'.

One of the most difficult tasks of a liberal government consisted in not allowing all its best capacities to be absorbed by its own bureaucracy. 'A state which dwarfs its men, in order that they may be more docile instruments in its hands even for beneficial purposes, will find that with small men no great thing can really be accomplished.'

CARLYLE

Just as Mill's *On Liberty* had been a warning to Britain, first and foremost, but also to the world at large, not to allow the forces of liberalism to decline or be suppressed, Carlyle's *French Revolution*, his greatest work, had, twenty years earlier, broken the spell cast over the British perspective by Burke.

Thomas Carlyle (1795–1881) was the son of a mason, a member of a sect of seceders from the Kirk. He himself, although not a Christian, was a puritan at heart, and he was deeply affected by the materialism which he saw at the root of the Industrial Revolution in Britain. One of his achievements, in the first half of the nineteenth century, was to free Britain from a wave of enthusiasm for the German spirit, and, in the second half, to infect many Germans with his enthusiasm for Frederick the Great and 'men who make history'.

Distressed at the mendacity of social circumstances, Carlyle became, beyond anything else, a critic of political, social and religious affairs. His novel, *Sartor Resartus* (1831) is based on the concept that civilisation rests on the wearing of wrong clothes, that is attachment to false conventions. He maintains that the British have crumbled into two classes, dandies and drudges, the rich and the poor, and that one day these two sects will probably share out the country between them.

This malicious notion was, with its modicum of truth, probably at the back of Disraeli's mind when he wrote *Sybil, or the Two Nations* (1845). The key passage comes when one of the strangers, talking to Egremont says, 'Yes, two nations; between whom there is no intercourse and no sympathy; who are as ignorant of each other's habits, thoughts and feelings as if they were dwellers in different zones ... who are formed by different breeding, fed on different food, are ordered by different manners, and are not governed by the same laws.' 'You speak of', said Egremont hesitatingly, 'the Rich and the Poor.' Disraeli wrote novels whose purpose was to awaken young aristocratic interest in the need to take over the leadership of both these nations. As Prime Minister he, who in his early days was clear-sighted enough to testify that the age of colonialism and imperialism was historically already obsolescent, was to render this era of Britain's most brilliant.

This was the era of Queen Victoria, who, ruling from 1837–1901, gave her name to an age signifying riches and splendour for a governing class that attained power through the electoral reform of 1832. Before that date the franchise was limited to 400,000 electors; afterwards to some 900,000 out of a total population of more than twenty million. The Victorian Age signified deepest content and gravest discontent; the mendacity of conventions (against which social critics and novelists, as well as Carlyle, protested) and a lonely, intensive struggle for truth, the battle between science and an antiquated, ecclesiastical perspective; ugliness, brutality, Puritanism, combined with longing for beauty of body and soul; imperialism and colonialism at their harshest, and the beginning of a universal longing for world peace; conservatism, Christian liberalism and Christian democracy; rule by an oligarchy which, within the confines of its family life, fancies itself a democracy.

Carlyle made it his aim to attack the hypocrisy and irreligiosity of the leading circles, with their riches and 'democracy', who 'talked' while the masses were disintegrating in penury. He was both reactionary and revolutionary in one. National Socialists, Fascists and Left intellectuals were all able to cite him. For example, in *The Nigger Question* (1853) we learn that slaves should stay slaves. In *Past and Present* (1843) we learn of the peace, humanity and beauty of a mediaeval monastery is compared to the hideous factory of the present. Scott's enthusiasm for the Middle Ages, the Oxford Movement, the romanticism of works from Coleridge to G.K. Chesterton and Hilaire Belloc – all are related to and reflected in the ideas of Carlyle.

Reading through Carlyle it is possible always to see the thorough reactionary, the writer of extravagances, injustices and dangerous half-truths. It is, however, probably better to see a great man, who in loneliness and sorrow, as critic and interpreter, sought to close the gap which existed in the nineteenth century, between literature, art and the public.

FROUDE, RUSKIN, ARNOLD

Carlyle's mental drama and his religious struggle are illuminated by the life and work of his friend and pupil, James Anthony Froude (1818–94). He was the son of a Tory and clergyman, the brother of one of the leaders of the Oxford Movement. He himself rejected the movement with the phrase, 'Oxford Counter-Reformation', and resigned his fellowship at Oxford after his novel, *The Nemesis of Faith*, had been publicly burned in the lecture room of Exeter College in 1849. The novel dealt with the discrepancy between day-to-day reality and the fictional faith in which young gentlemen of the times were educated, and described the mendacity which existed in both the established churches. In fact it portrayed, as Froude himself maintained, that 'the one great Bible which cannot lie is the history of the human race'.

Civilisation and religion had, according to Froude, become deeply dubious. Religion was always an undecided battle. Whenever, after victory, it congealed into an institution, it lost its vitality. Ceremonies and avowals of faith possessed strength as long as they created spiritual crises, and represented an actual exertion in the struggle against a specific evil and on behalf of a specific good (*The Cat's Pilgrimage*, 1850).

Froude became the outstanding historian of the English Renaissance and Reformation. As editor of *Fraser's Magazine* (involving close association with Carlyle), he exercised from 1861 to 1874 considerable influence on upperclass opinion. At this later stage of his career he was the clear-eyed, critical friend of youth, revealing the deep inner crisis affecting religion, intellect, culture, and society. His conviction was that both Churches, that of England and that of Rome, were utterly lifeless except as subjects for theological speculation. Froude, a man of refinement and an open, sensitive nature, had a delicate appreciation of Newman, and was very familiar with the Middle Ages – though this was, to him, a strange, distant world.

In his later years John Ruskin (1819–1900) claimed to be a pupil of Carlyle. His genuinely Quixotic fight against the steam-engine, and his abhorrence of London, may well be reminiscent of Carlyle's invectives. But Ruskin, despite his veneration of the Middle Ages, his cult of Gothic (he believed in its possible rebirth), and other manifestations of enthusiasm, was a different 'modern' type. His father was a prosperous businessman and a staunch Calvinist. His own aim was to conquer and transform the ugly, evil world, and, in order to implement this change in social conditions, he proposed to use the medium of art. He saw art as 'a passionate and wholehearted endeavour to fathom the mysteries of the deeper things of life; not only of beauty, but also of truth and goodness'. It had a social, an allembracing dimension and was closely linked with the future. *The Seven Lamps of Architecture* (1849), *Lectures on Architecture and Painting* (1853) and *The Stones of Venice* (1851–3) reveal his belief that architecture is expressive of a people's entire social existence. From a writer on art he became a Socialist and social reformer through his understanding of art as a problem of humanity. *Essays on Political Economy* (1863), *Time and Tide* (1868), and *The Political Economy of Art* (1875) were milestones along this road.

Together with William Morris, who consciously related his efforts to their social framework, Ruskin realised that beauty in art demands a healthy society, and he tried to create ways for European man to climb out of the straits in which he found himself.

Despite the difficulty of comparison between a Continental Power and a maritime one with possessions in all four corners of the world, it is not impossible to compare the realm of the Emperor Francis Joseph (1848–1916) with that of the Queen-Empress Victoria (1837–1901) insofar as the percipience of alert minds among their respective subjects are concerned.

Ludwig Wittgenstein came to Britain for the first time in 1908. He was concerned with aeronautical experiments, at the Kite Flying Upper Stratosphere Station, near Glossop in Derbyshire. He returned in 1929, became a professor at Cambridge, and during the Second World War was a medical assistant at Guy's Hospital, London. Later he worked in a medical laboratory at Newcastle, dying at Cambridge in 1950. 'The philosopher' (he states) 'treats any question like an illness', and for him the aim of philosophy was 'to show the fly the way out of the fly-bottle'. The purpose that lay behind Wittgenstein's philosophical labours was the same that preoccupied outstanding Victorian personalities: how was it possible to ease the way for sick members of a sick society, out of a pompous, ornate ghetto-like existence where man duped himself with false faiths, feelings, concepts, and conventions?

On 24 October 1865, in a letter to his mother from Zurich, Matthew Arnold expressed the fear that Britain could become a small power like Holland 'for want of perceiving how the world is going and must go, and preparing herself accordingly'. In 1872 Disraeli made his great speech about the Empire, an avowal of faith in imperialism. Two years later this man, an admirer of Bismarck came to power, and from 1874 until 1901 Conservative rule was characterised by a basically imperialist policy.

Disraeli, the principal spokesman of this imperialism, had formerly held different opinions. In 1852 he wrote, in a private letter, that the 'wretched colonies', which would anyway be independent within a few years, were nothing but a millstone around Britain's neck. The Benthamites had advocated the Empire's dissolution. But the leading colonial reformers all died early. By 1855 none were left and imperialism could rush into the fray of colonial conflicts, economic belligerency, and finally war.

Matthew Arnold (1822–88) recognised the spirit that accompanied this and despondently divided British society into three groups – barbarians, Philistines, and rabble – all equally self-centred and equally incapable of doing anything constructive for culture, freedom, or the future. Himself the son of the great educationalist and headmaster, Thomas Arnold, he was, besides being a poet, a literary, social, and religious critic plagued by deep-dwelling doubt about everything that he saw around him. Oxford showed him the men of science and learning sundered from the contemporary world; London the men of affairs severed from the past and the future. He discerned discontinuity between the inner and outer structures of society. As a government inspector of schools, he observed closely the social miseries of the time. In *Culture and Anarchy* (1869) he wrote that Britain was suffocating in an anarchy of prosperity and the belief in a permanently undisturbed functioning of the business, earnings, and income machine. The nation needed an aim which would cure it of this anarchy. And this aim would be culture, which he defined as 'a disinterested endeavour to learn and to propagate the best of that which is known and has been thought in the world'.

Arnold wanted an open-minded Britain, receptive to creative foreign influences like Goethe, Heine, the French essayists, and George Sand (whom he visited at Nohant in 1849). Like Ernest Renan, he thought his countrymen would do well to take an example from Prussia. This was the theme of *Friendship's Garland* (1871), in which a Prussian noble visits England and smiles at the backwardness of its institutions, its happy-go-lucky methods, its optimism.

Arnold had in mind the free Germany of Goethe and Humboldt. It was in their sense that he wanted to master the multitudinousness of intellectual, religious, and cultural aspirations. In his view culture was possible only in a healthy nation and self-improvement attainable only by helping others. The overriding problem for him, and for his friend, Arthur Hugh Clough, who in his search for existential truth and an individual, free faith, chose the bitter path of poverty and loneliness, was how man, in this age of bewildering contrasts, choking with abundance and poverty alike, could possibly find his own true self. How he could return from self-alienation to that possession and understanding of the self which one characterised by candour and dignity.

> To see if we will poise our life at last,
> To see if we will now at last be true
> To our only true deep-buried selves.
> Being one with which, we are one with the whole world.

To achieve complete understanding of and communion with the world, a total understanding of self is necessary. Yet this was impossible because of the miserable state of religious life, which Arnold held to be the root of all evil in contemporary social conditions. The form which it took in practice seemed to him to preclude any extension of man's knowledge of himself and would have liked to reform the English Reformation. As a young man he had been inspired by Newman. After reading Locke, in 1850, he was convinced that reason was 'the only rock of refuge to this poor, exaggerated, surrecited humanity'.

Here he comes close to Browning, who believed that religion was essential, but not in the form in which it then existed. Tennyson also expresses the torment of an age to whom nature appeared harsh and cruel, and sings the praise, in *Locksley Hall*, of unrestricted progress, of a universe wide open to the free, creative energies of man:

> 'For I dipt into the future. . . . Saw the vision of the World and all wonder that would be. . . . In the Parliament of Man, the Federation of the World.'

DARWIN

The Victorian Age is characterised by the great cleft which ran right through the creative personalities of the time, a cleft between belief and unbelief, scepticism and the will to surrender to something great and pure, the knowledge of which lay in heart and brain alike. It was precisely this cleft which produces socialists like Frederick Denison Maurice and Charles Kingsley who, through their own lives, taught a Christian democracy of which the clergy were incapable, and into this turmoil of great hope and great fear, of security and insecurity, that Darwinism exploded.

In 1859 Fitzgerald's *Omar Khayyam* appeared, together with Samuel Smiles' *Self-Help*, the first great novels of George Eliot and George Meredith, and *On the Origin of Species by Means of Natural Selection or the Preservation of Favoured Races in the Struggle for Life*, by Charles Darwin.

The last of these has been called 'the most important book of the century', and certainly it was one of the most influential. Its themes, the conclusions it invited, unleashed the impending storm. From the day of its publication it became impossible for many to believe any longer in the personal God of the Church's teachings. Its significance was even greater than that of Copernicus' *De Revolutionibus Orbium Coerestrium*, which has penetrated popular consciousness only in this age of space exploration. It started a controversy between scientists and theologians which lasted until 1900, and was used by men all over the world as the battle-cry for an anti-religious campaign which accused dogmatic Christianity of being the impediment to man's progress and knowledge.

Now, a century later, it is fashionable to smile at the vehemence with which theologians reacted to Darwinism, for antagonism has been overcome and evolution is declared to be a magnificent manifestation of the Godhead. Indeed the twentieth century is even incapable of appreciating the grandeur of the conflict. But however lightly present theologians describe Darwinism as a step 'long overdue', Christians of the time knew that its teaching and its consequences could not be combined with the world view presented by the Bible, nor with the traditional interpretation of God, man and history. For the whole meaning of life turned on the creation of the world by God, and on the human race as descendants of Adam and Eve; on the idea of original sin and redemption. This was the world view credited by Newman, one of the purest and most cultured Christians in Britain and Europe at the height of the nineteenth century. In 1879, twenty years after the appearance of *Origin of Species*, he was nominated a cardinal.

The first great public clash occurred on 30 June 1860. Bishop Samuel Wilberforce, an extremely successful Church of England preacher and speaker, rose at the meeting of the British Association in Oxford to deliver an annihilating onslaught on Darwin's work. Like many other persuasive enemies of Darwin even long after, he was more familiar with the contents of the book from what others said about it rather than through actual reading; that rendered him the surer of his victory. At the close of his speech he turned to Huxley and enquired whether it was through his grandfather or his grandmother that he claimed his descent from a monkey?

The Bishop sat down to thunderous applause. Then Thomas Henry Huxley (1825–95) spoke. This zoologist, a teacher at the Royal College of Surgeons, and the man who applied Darwin's theory of the origin of species to the human race, was grandfather of Julian Huxley the biologist. Calmly, he explained Darwin's theories. Turning to Wilberforce, he closed with the words that he was not ashamed to have a monkey for his ancestor, but would indeed be ashamed to be connected with a man who used great gifts to obscure the truth.

The gauntlet was down. To his life's end Huxley maintained his conviction that the downfall of Christianity was ensured beyond all doubt.

'You know, all is development. The principle is perpetually going on,' says Lady Constance, in Disraeli's *Tancred* (1847). It was a notion that Robert Chambers, an 'indefatigable populariser of knowledge', had supported in his *Vestiges of Creation* three years earlier. Lord Monboddo, a Scottish judge, had suggested in a book published in 1780 that man had originally been a monkey.

A certain educated sector of society had long been conversant with ideas that presupposed the biological evolution of all living matter and evolutionary differentiation between the species. For thousands of years mystic and non-mystic, scientific and speculative presentiments and surmises about a major process of evolution had lain in the air – from the pre-Socratic philosophers and Aristotle to Kant, Linné, Erasmus Darwin (1721–1802, grandfather of Charles Darwin), Lamarck, Saint-Hilaire, Diderot, Von Buch (1773–1853), W.C.Wells (1757–1817), and J.C.Pritchard (1786–1848). German Romanticist naturalism abounded with ideas on evolution. Goethe pronounced it to be the new major purpose of natural research. On 13 February 1829 he remarked to Eckermann that highest reason could attain to the Godhead by research: 'The Godhead is in what becomes and what transforms itself, but not in what has become and is dead.'

For twenty years Charles Robert Darwin (1809–82) hesitated to publish the account of his researches and theories. This caution has been explained as consideration towards his wife's religious beliefs and, more especially, his own innate timidity. His famous grandfather, Erasmus, and his father, Robert (two doctors), both stuttered and were extremely sensitive and nervous; his uncle Erasmus committed suicide; a line of eccentric female relatives heightened the emotional tension of his nature.

All his life he was delicate and frequently ill. He himself ascribed his valetudinarianism to deprivations he had suffered when, at twenty-two, he began his journey around the world in the *Beagre* (1831–6). In fact his state of health was largely a question of psychogenesis. He tried, by means of a strictly regulated working-life ('My life goes like clockwork'), devotion to his family (of ten children), and pleasure in country existence to relieve the intense pressure that so weighed him down mentally. For he knew that for many of those who read and took him seriously there was no longer any way back to their God of the Bible, God the Father who provides for each and all personally. Darwin knew (as Nietzsche, for his part, did) that he had initiated the destruction of Christian consciousness.

It had been anything but his intention to abandon his faith. He simply lost it, gently, smoothly, imperceptibly, in the three years following his voyage around the world: 'Disbelief crept over me at a very slow rate.' Publication of his discoveries and theories struck him at first as being like murder, not indeed a slaying of God but of the faith of his fellow humans. As a non-Christian, he had a highly developed Christian conscience. In 1876, at ivy-covered Downe House in Kent, where he lived from 1842 until his death, he began his autobiography and avowed, 'I believe that I have acted rightly in steadily following and devoting my life to science. I feel no remorse from having committed any great sin; but have often and often regretted that I have not done more good to my fellow-creatures.' And he thought this 'a poor excuse'.

'I am not the least afraid of death,' he avowed. And Darwin died richly blessed with children and earthly possessions, working to the end, and was buried, with permission of the Dean, in Westminster Abbey.

The *Beagle*, equipped by the Admiralty, put out to sea on 27 December 1831 with instructions to go round the world. Since the sixteenth century, naturalistic studies, mathematics, astronomy, and medicine had been closely connected with British maritime interests. Darwin, happy neither with medicine nor theology, was invited to participate in the journey as an unpaid naturalist observer.

During the next five years the sickly but highly-observant young man saw things that astonished and shocked him – manifestations of nature not merely alien to man but totally indifferent to him. (One of the fundamental beliefs of Christian middle-class members of society and seventeenth, eighteenth and early nineteenth-century adherents of the Enlightenment had been that God had performed the Creation entirely for the benefit of man, whom every insect served and to whose advantage every seed grew, to the eternal praise of the Creator.) In South America Darwin found fossils and on the Galapagos Islands encountered astonishing prehistoric animals which seemed to have sprung straight out of hell. Pitiful human beings too, had more affinity with beasts of the field than with the Victorian gentleman.

He was taken aback, astounded, but always scrupulously, anxiously observant, level-headed and sympathetic. The unity of all living things on earth became apparent to him, and there was an element of the religious in his experience. In his first note-book (1837–8) Darwin wrote that 'if we choose to let conjecture run wild, then animals, our fellow brethren in rain, disease, death, suffering and famine – our slaves in the most laborious works; our companions in our amusements – they may partake of our origin in one common ancestor – we may all be melted together'.

That last phrase is of far-reaching significance. The 'back to nature' movement had begun in the eighteenth century, both before and during Rousseau's life, when 'homeless' man had been beset by a longing for his ancestors, sought through primal language, the primal family, and primal experience, the beginnings of society, the matriarchs, and the origin of all life. Utopian socialists and early socialists invented the family of man, a primal communism. This was the background to Darwin's protracted and hesitant retrospection into the times when the brethren of man, his relatives in the realm of life, had been evolved and had evolved in ramification.

In October 1838 Darwin read Malthus' *Essay on Population* in which the author had derived his concept of the 'struggle for life' from Erasmus Darwin's *Zoonomia*, a work which his grandson had previously read without any marked enthusiasm. In this context it meant that the fittest animals (later humans) survive in the struggle for life and thus, through their combative zeal, extol the selective Godhead. This Calvinistic image of pre-destination was soon to become secularised, turned to naturalist purposes, and find economic application.

Bertrand Russell and other British authors have suggested that Darwin's theory was in the main an extension to the animal world of *laisser faire* economics and the practice of Mancunian liberalism. Darwin wished to see the harshness and brutality of the struggle for existence as a more merciful process, taking place over infinitely long stretches of time, the stages of a discriminatory but constant process, which gradually transformed the species. The transformation was accomplished with the same generous flexibility that conservative – and liberal-minded enthusiasts of progress would have liked to see the transformation of British society. The constitution of the state of nature, in the eyes of the intellectually and politically conservative Darwin, displayed many of the virtues of the constitution, unwritten but practised, that governed British society.

Darwin closed his book with 'a curiously Victorian combination of cautious statement, honest conviction, diplomatic respect for the piety of others, calm realism and vague optimism', although the first edition (sold out in twenty-four hours) lacked the subsequent reference to the 'Creator':

> Thus, from the war of nature, from famine and death, the most exalted object which we are capable of conceiving, namely, the production of the higher animals, directly follows. There is grandeur in this view of life, with its several forms, having been originally breathed by the Creator into a few forms, or into one; and that, whilst this planet has gone cycling on according to the fixed law of gravity, from so simple a beginning endless forms most beautiful and most wonderful have been, and are being, evolved.

This conciliatory ending did not conciliate his contemporaries. The outcry in Britain was furious. Darwin ignored the many attacks made upon him and continued his work. But he was deeply wounded by the criticism of the Rev. Adam Sedgwick, his former professor of geology. Sedgwick, calling Darwin a lunatic and a criminal, accused him of demoralising mankind, degrading it to barbarity, and doing everything to break the bond between physical nature and the metaphysical will of God thus, were it possible, reducing mankind to a lower condition of abasement than ever before in the course of history.

In his autobiography Darwin had described how, in the course of his life, his Christian faith had dwindled away. Soon after his return from his voyage around the world he had realised that all sacred writings were mythologies, a part of the development of the peoples to whom they belonged. 'The Old Testament was no more to be trusted than the sacred books of the Hindoos.' His rejection of it, he emphasised, was not only on account of 'its manifestly false history of the world' but because of 'its attributing to God the feelings of a vengeful tyrant'. Here was an underlying theological fact and slowly he had become an 'agnostic' (the word invented by his friend Huxley). The clearest enunciation of his religious development is to be found in his correspondence with his American champion Asa Gray. The latter was a botanist, lawyer, writer, theologian, and physical scientist. Out of Darwin's ideas, theories, and researches he evolved an American version of Darwinism. On the Continent, Ernst Haeckel created a German Darwinism that, much to Darwin's own astonishment, took the form of a new religion.

HUXLEY

'The progress of society depends not on imitating the cosmic process, still less in running away from it, but in combating it'
EVOLUTION AND ETHICS

Huxley was convinced that the nineteenth century needed a new religion corresponding to the reality of nature, society and the evolution of all living things. Man had to assert his qualities with care, in this process, since every error would be dearly paid for; he was confronted with a merciless, mechanical cosmos, but had to face both past and future, since man was capable of being taught, and science would show how he might live.

The creed of this new type of man was expressed by Huxley in a letter he wrote in answer to Charles Kingsley's condolences upon the death of his child: 'truth is better than much profit. I have searched over the grounds of my belief, and if wife and child and name and fame were all to be lost to me one after the other as the penalty, still I will not lie.' These were the words of the scientifically educated man who believed that man's prime duty was the search for truth: 'my business is to teach my aspirations to conform themselves to fact, not to try and make facts harmonise with my aspirations. Science seems to me to teach in the highest and strongest manner the great truth which is embodied in the Christian concept of entire surrender to the will of God. . . . I have only begun to learn content and peace of mind since I have resolved at all risks to do this.' He did not believe in retribution, but in the fact that, with every moment of our existence, we pay for the actions we perform: 'In short, as we live, we are paid for living.'

Huxley was imbued with a deep and strong faith of his own which he described to Kingsley in terms of chess. Perhaps God was the invisible player on the other, invisible, side of the board, which was the world. The pieces were the phenomena of the universe, the rules of the game the laws of nature, and ourselves the players on this side of the board. 'We know that his play is always fair, just and patient.' '*Sartor Resartus* led me to know that a deep sense of religion was compatible with the entire absence of theology. Secondly, science and her methods gave me a resting-place independent of authority and tradition. Thirdly, love opened up to me a view of the sanctity of human nature, and impressed me with a deep sense of responsibility.'

In the light of his discomfiture of Bishop Wilberforce, who had evinced himself an overbearing but inferior opponent, Huxley warned Kingsley that if 'this great and powerful instrument for good or evil, the Church of England, is to be saved from being shivered into fragments by the advancing tide of science, it must be by the effort of men who, like yourself, see their way to combination of the practice of the Church with the spirit of science.'

This was an appeal to the special British genius for facing up critically, soberly and toughly to austerely tough, though honourable opponents. Again and again he called on his countrymen to come to friendly terms with science and the future. Whether or not this was possible in Britain 'depends upon how you, the public, deal with science. Cherish her, venerate her, follow her methods faithfully and implicitly in their application to all branches of human thought, and the future of this people will be greater than the past.'

His patriotism was his motive for joining the Metaphysical Society, a discussion club that was founded in 1869, lasted for eleven years, and included among its members the most prominent national figures like Gladstone, Manning, Tennyson, Ruskin, and Ward. Only three people of any importance refused to join – Newman, Spencer and Mill. This was the arena where Ward and Huxley met as hard-hitting but fair adversaries, in debates of a type which were only possible in England in the nineteenth century, save from time to time in private arguments between Protestant and Catholic adversaries in Tübingen.

Huxley had originally wanted to be an engineer, but at the age of thirteen changed to medicine. He was also greatly impressed, even as a youth, by German intellectuality, an admiration common to English, scientifically-biased, youth before 1871. For example, John Tyndall, scion of an old nonconformist family with scientific leanings, had studied at Marburg and Berlin. And even in Huxley's own life there was an element of the Germanic.

His masterpiece, *Evidence of Man's Place in Nature*, was published in 1863, and was the best possible propaganda for Darwin's theories. Its principle theme was that man can anticipate unlimited biological evolution for himself. But both feet firmly planted on the ground, he saw a number of impediments in Britain's way, in the first place in the shape of Germany and the United States. He became an active supporter in a revised plan of education which would enable Britain to compete with the armed and industrialised potential of post–1870 Germany, and summed up his beliefs in his famous speech on 'Scientific Education', saying that Britain, in its struggle for existence, had the need to provide scientific and technical training, thus endowing Darwin's 'struggle for existence' with a political, topical and, later, militaristic slant.

Huxley launched his campaign for technical education in 1877 under the motto, 'only a scientific people can survive in a scientific future'. But even while, in 'University Education', an address in which he congratulated the United States on 'the enormous actual, and almost infinite potential' of their cities, and prophesied a great future for the country, he added, 'size is not grandeur and territory does not make a nation. . . . The one condition of success, your sole safeguard, is the moral worth and intellectual clearness of the individual citizen.'

In later years he became deeply impressed by Indian religion and philosophy, as well as by Buddha's atheistic religiosity. Man's task, it seemed to him, was to call into being a small, but rational and friendly world of fellowship in a hostile and formidable universe. One of his last censures of Christianity reprimanded its followers for being too egotistically concerned with their highly private spiritual salvation and not caring for society as a whole. On his tombstone he had inscribed three lines from a poem by his wife:

> Be not afraid, ye waiting hearts that weep,
> For still He giveth His beloved sleep,
> And if an endless sleep He wills, so best.

This too is Victorian Britain, a Christianity dissolving in post-Christian stoicism.

Huxley's belief in progress was latterly gravely troubled by his awareness of the unrest in the air and the barbarisation of the masses. On what course were Britain, France, Germany set?

In the 1894 edition of his main work he included three essays, the last of which, 'The Aryan Question', written in 1890, regardless of earlier cautious attitudes and efforts at evasion, he linked Aryan language with Aryan race.

COUNTER-CHRISTIANITY AND IMPERIALISM

As always in a time of uncertainty and change, new names – particularly those of men from abroad – brought fresh ideas. Returning from India in 1872, where his experiences had convinced him that force alone could maintain a ruling civilisation, Sir James Stephen produced an argument to counter those of John Stuart Mill in his *Liberty, Equality, Fraternity*, which were further developed by Sir Henry Maine, also of the Indian service, in *Popular Government* (1886). Likewise William Lecky, in *Democracy and Liberty*

(1896) stated that liberty was suitable only for supermen, and that democracy was a foolish dream.

The hour was ripe for the introduction of a certain facet of Nietzschean thought into Britain, and as Bernard Shaw observed, no name of a foreign contemporary was so frequently encountered as that of Nietzsche. The cult was, in fact, mainly the work of writers of second and third rank, among them Thomas Common, with his biennial publication, *The Good European* (1903–15), and O.Levy, who published the first authorised, complete edition of Nietzsche's works in English.

Bagehot's *English Constitution* (1865) expresses one aspect of this development: fear at the rise of the masses and of new types of demagogic politicians. The fact also that by the 1850s and 1860s broad sectors of the population had ceased to believe in a personal God was the subject of much controversy. For example, A.R.Wallace and his friends formed a group to discuss whether God could or wanted to ward off evil.

The notion of a finite God was becoming ever more acceptable, Tennyson being one of the supporters, Thomas Hardy (1840–1928) another. This man, a trained architect who turned author, achieved early success, and made a great deal of money. As a young man he knew Mill's *On Liberty*, almost by heart, had been one of Darwin's earliest supporters, and was a confirmed pessimist. His poems *God's Funeral* and *God-Forgotten* were composed long before the First World War. He was utterly sceptical of the revival of Roman Catholicism in Britain, avowing instead his faith in a Prime Cause which could not be morally comprehended because it was 'loveless and hateless'.

Britain's outstanding poets, Swinburne and George Meredith among them, stood in open rebellion against Christianity, championing freedom, and the power of the intellect. Anti-clericalism was rampant throughout the country, and in the 1880s the weight of discontent among the masses, whether in Britain, France or Germany, was ever more marked. This was the period when the popular press began to attain power. Between 1866 and 1882 some six thousand newspapers existed in Europe. By 1900 the number was doubled. The *Daily Telegraph* was the first of the really large-scale popular papers, then the *Daily News*, followed by the Paris *Matin*, the *New York Herald* and *New York Times*, the Berlin *Neueste Nachrichten*, the Paris *Le Petit Journal* and *Le Petit Parisien* and Scherl's *Lokal-Anzeiger*. On the heels of the Penny Press came the Halfpenny Press, with the *Daily Mail* and *Daily Express* in the lead.

The masses, putting it briefly, were against the liberalism and humanity of the older upper and middle classes against 'weak tolerance', foreigners and Jews. They were for strong policies, strong words, strong men, and pride in imperialism. Their spokesmen were army officers, naval men, colonial officials, academics, and globe-trotters.

Greater Britain, Sir Charles Dilke's imperialist programme, was inspired by the author's journey around the world. A gigantic success, it ran into sixteen editions between 1869, the initial year of publication, and 1885.

Paul Leroy-Bealieu, a leading French political economist, 'answered' Dilke in 1874 with his *De la Colonisation chez les peuples modernes*. Five years later Friedrich Fabri asked (and answered in the affirmative) *Does Germany Need Colonies?* In 1881, a year before the foundation of the German Colonial Society, Wilhelm Hübbe-Schleiden demanded *German Colonisation*. Two years later Professor Seeley held his famous series of lectures on the 'Expansion of England'. When published, they sold 80,000 copies within a short time. The same year witnessed the foundation of the imperialist Primrose League. The politicians began to follow the lead of the professors.

At first there seemed, for Britain and France at any rate, an enormous booty in sight. Most of the explorers, in Africa and elsewhere were of military origin, and imperialism took the form of crusades, sustained by a fiery nationalism of laymen and clergy alike. Cross was confronted with cross and Christian with Christian, overseas now, as once in Europe.

In 1895 Paul Claudel, a junior French diplomat, was posted to Shanghai, and arrived to find a China torn by corruption and civil war, seemingly succumbing to the pressure of Christian powers. Commenting on the role of religion at the time, Carl J. Cruckhardt notes: 'Camouflaged behind the Christian missions came economic prospectors, and behind them fleets and expeditionary forces.' He goes on to add the reminder of an official French report dated 1900: 'by not giving adequate attention to our patronage of Catholic missions in China and thereby surrendering the most important means to extend our influence in the Far East, we allowed it to happen that in 1882 the Italian Franciscans in Shantung yielded their task to priests from the diocese of Münster in Westphalia.' Burckhardt adds, 'The consequence of this deal is familiar, consisting in the occupation of the Bay of Kiaochow by the German Empire.'

Anti-Christian and Christian missions worked hand in hand in pacific and bellicose colonisation, subduing whole areas of Africa and Asia. In France anti-clerical governments fought Church, clergy and political Catholicism, while simultaneously intervening in Africa, the Middle East, and the Far East on behalf of their 'white fathers', the French missions. France sent more Christian missions abroad than all other European nations put together. Around 1900 the overall establishment of Christian missions in Africa, Asia and Oceania, composed of mutually hostile contingents, consisted of forty-one thousand Roman Catholics and eighteen thousand Protestants.

In this way the web of Western European imperialism contained, besides economic, political, and military elements, strong extra-Christian and Christian ones whose motto could well be taken as 'God helps those who help themselves'. The feeling of being entirely self-dependent, of having to fight one's own battle, alone, brought the concomitant 'God with us!' *Gott strafe England!* was not far removed.

The most impressive combination of Christian and non-Christian elements may be found in Rudyard Kipling (1865–1936), the great bard of British imperialism. This 1907 Nobel prize-winner wrote more than three hundred short stories, the famous *Jungle Book* (1894–5), a few outstanding novels like *Kim* (1901), and a larger number of unimportant ones. Son of an Anglo-Indian official, he came to England when he was five and returned to India immediately after his schooldays. Unable to do military service on account of the weakness of his eyes, he still possessed sight enough, as reporter for an Allahabad newspaper, for cynically acute observation of the life of British officers and civil servants in India. At twenty-two he became world famous, initially in English-speaking countries, for a collection of short stories, issued in seven cheap volumes after previous publication in Indian newspapers.

> We don't want to fight, but, by Jingo, if we do
> We've got the ships, we've got the men, and we've got the money too.

His nationalist songs unleashed waves of emotion in the masses. The *Barrack Room Ballads* (1892) enjoyed colossal popularity. His military lays (*Mandalay, Fuzzy-Wuzzy*) were his most original and his best. There was something of Malraux, Camus, Saint-Exupéry, Ernst Jünger, in this man who twirled the rapier of his eloquence to champion a life of risk, daring, fighting and dying. He was an imperialist and anti-intellectual ('what do they know of England who only England know?') who hymned the British as God's chosen people bound to assume 'the white man's burden'. God had intended the 'lesser breeds' to be so. With the God of battles, the God of the Old Testament, whom his songs invoked, he summoned up the ancient hate of nation against nation. He saw the possibilities for exploiting fears and hopes with the help of modern means of organisation. He also saw how, not least in the train of his own ballads, a torrid nationalism grew from year to year. He prayed, in one of the finest of his poems, to the Lord of Hosts for forgiveness, forgiveness for arrogance and a false super-nationalism, and that the gift of humility should imbue the British: 'Lord God of Hosts, be with us yet – Lest we forget – Lest we forget.'

Kipling's 'Take up the White Man's Burden' anthem, the summons to dominion over savage peoples, 'half-devil and half-child', was dated 1899. The occupation of Africa had not taken long. In 1875 less than one tenth of this continent had been under European sway; in 1895 less than one tenth remained untouched. The enormous booty of Burma and Indo-China fell in addition into British and French hands. The new militant naval policy found the perfect instrument in Captain Alfred Mahan, US Navy. No country, he maintained, could uphold its greatness and global economic position without the possession of big battleships. His book, *The Influence of Sea-Power upon History* (1890), quickly translated into the language of those nations ambitious for world-prestige, was highly successful. In 1894 Britain founded the Navy League for the promulgation of his theories, and Germany followed with the *Flottenverein* three years later. Admiral von Tirpitz confessed that he had 'gulped down' Mahan. With the irrational symbols of 'warship' and 'ocean', imperialism and economic nationalism conjured up from the spiritual deeps the glistening and aggressive ensigns for new wars.

A fiery nationalism infected Europe. Developments in Germany after 1870 have already been noted. Treitschke now preached that for large national states weakness was the worst sin; that a Great Power must eliminate minorities; that Catholics and Jews must be dealt with severely. In Russia and France there was a close alliance between nationalism and anti-Semitism.

The aggressive French Right found fluent spokesmen in Taine, Déroulède, Maurice Barrès (*Scènes et doctrine du nationalisme*, 1902). In Russia Michael Katkov, the leading publicist and a minor world power in himself, gave Déroulède in 1886 a vociferous welcome. While Roman Dmowski pugnaciously argued the case for a Greater Poland (*Polonia Magna*), Count Tisza contended that in Hungary all other nationalities should submit to the Magyars. In Italy Francesco de Sanctis, Bertrando Spaventa, and Gabriele d'Annunzio whipped up a nationalist fervour through which the young editor Benito Mussolini, after an apprenticeship among the workers, would win his first spurs.

The hour had come for a political twist to be given to the racial notions which, since the eighteenth century, had preoccupied only academics, etymologists, novelists, and lone Utopians. The period 1870 to 1900 witnessed its adoption by the Swede A.A.Retzius, Vacher de Lapouge and Gobineau (who made greater stir in Germany than in France), L.A.J.Quetelet, P.P.Broca, and dozens of others. On the eve of Hitler's birth in the German-speaking portion of Austria, insidiously pervaded by racialist beliefs and racial fanatics, L.Gumplowicz attained prominence with his *Race and Nation* (1875) and *Racial Conflict* (1883). For practical purposes racial conflict in the first place signified anti-Semitism (and not only among Gentiles). In 1886 Edouard Drumont issued a call for a final decisive act of extermination against Jews in Europe (*La France juive; La dernière bataille*, 1890). From 1892 on his newspaper *La Libre Parole* incited civil war. That was precisely ten years after Tsar Alexander III had authorised a rigorous anti-Semitic policy accompanied by pogroms. In 1891 alone three hundred thousand Jews left Russia.

The British waxed enthusiastic about the 'subjugated peoples' of the Continent and simultaneously looked down with utmost contempt on the inferior Irish race. 'Home Rule' was defeated in 1886. In the same year the Conservatives and National Liberals in the Reichstag pressed for increased Germanisation of the three million Poles in Posnania and West Prussia. Katkov and Aksakov popularised and propagated a severe Russification of non-Russian peoples in the Tsarist realms while the Ministers Dimitri Tolstoy, Plehve, and Pobedonostsev (the *éminence grise*) preached the doctrine 'One law, one language, one religion'.

9

Utopianism and Pacifism: Constructive Political Sanity

Europe was in the grip of hate and fear, and the search for a way out of this dilemma, through utopianism and pacifism, derived from Anglo-Saxon inspiration. Utopias are, as Raymond Ruyer notes, 'an expedient against the tyranny of rulers and the lack of imagination and inertia of the ruled', and constructive political sanity finds scope, first and last, in the realm of utopianism. Following in the footsteps of Thomas More and Francis Bacon, Lord Erskine wrote *Armata* (1817) in which man, at the request of God, sets out to reconstruct the world with the aid of a newly discovered force which enables him to harness powerful new machines to his purpose.

The first half of the nineteenth century was dominated by the utopian fancies of Frenchmen. In the second and technological half, the outstanding figure was Jules Verne, who, while keeping within the framework of current realities and contemporary science, compiled 'an encyclopedia in novel-form'. He was a great admirer of technicians as pioneers of a new world and in his romances they were usually British.

1889, the year of Hitler's birth, saw the publication of three outstanding Utopian stories: Verne's *Robur the Conqueror*, in which the hero is the symbol of progress, Theodor Hertzka's *Freiland*, where man is the master of creation, and T.R.Stockton's *The Great War Syndicate*, in which a body of scientists takes over hostilities, and thanks to an automatic missile, achieves a quick victory for the United States followed by an alliance between the two paramount Anglo-Saxon powers which ensures world peace.

F.A.Fawkes writes of the same subject: 'I believe that the speed of communication achieved through steam and telegraph has contributed more than all the books and newspapers, more than all the religions, to destroy the old, melancholy era of wars and to produce a new, sound morality. . . . ' The effect on the world of the natural good sense of science and technology is, however, not a new theme, having been shared by Leonardo, Galileo, and many other generations of doctors and scientists at Padua University.

H.G.Wells in his book, *The Time Machine* (1895) describes man's adaptation to every kind of radical change. He treats time as a fourth dimension, and sees man as evolved into two types, a civilised kind descended from the leisured classes and a bestialised proletariat living underground and literally living off the helpless, elegant, degenerate members of the other. This prognosis of the future seems to be based on the London inferno described from his own experiences by George Gissing (1857–1903). This man was a true *déraciné*, as described by Maurice Barrès in 1897 in his novel of that name. Scenes of ghastly misery in London's underworld, drawn in *The Unclassed* (1884), *The Nether World* (1889), and *Born in Exile* (1892), foreshadowed the broken existences which can be found today in the giant cities of South America and Asia. Gissing was a forerunner of Louis-Ferdinand Céline.

In *War of the Worlds* (1898) Wells, recounting the evacuation of London in consequence of an invasion from Mars, anticipated the 1940 London blitz. *When the Sleeper Wakes* (1899) was an account of the world, fully mechanised and industrialised, under political dictatorship, and engaged in a mortal struggle between capital and labour, two hundred years hence. In *The Time Machine* Wells' explorers, taking another leap forward of a million years, lit on outsize crustaceans as the highest form of life.

A rosier picture was painted by T.B.Russell in *A Hundred Years Hence. The Expectations of an Optimist* (1905), where he showed contemporary expectations fulfilled in the year 2000: radio, television, coloured and three-dimensional sound films, revolutionary progress in medicine, floating cities, wireless power transmission, and super-weapons rendering wars senseless because they kill war. Two years earlier Godfrey Sweven, an American, had portrayed in *Limanora, the Island of Progress*, a more highly-developed type of human society whose members had brought their bodily spiritual, and intellectual faculties to a far higher pitch and calmly awaited the physical termination of their prolonged lives by way of a geological catastrophe, quite certain that the purest form of energy within themselves was immortal. 'God – so they felt – was the perpetual maintenance of animation.'

Raymond Ruyer has called Nietzsche's *Thus Spake Zarathustra* a utopian experiment in Darwinism, and the subject of mankind's ability to survive or otherwise was a theme initiated by important British and French exponents of utopianism. H.G.Wells trenchantly took it up again after the First World War (*Men like Gods*, 1923), demanding the transformation and improvement of the human race. Here he followed in the footsteps of Ernest Renan. With the Franco–German conflict in mind, this 'Pope of atheistic science', as his Roman Catholic enemies labelled him, demanded of that same science a rectification of man, bodily and in his intellectual and spiritual hereditary factors. Divinity would emerge from humanity, as man had emerged from animals; creatures would come into being who would use mankind as mankind uses animals (Philosophic Dialogues, written 1871, published 1876). In the same year as *Men like Gods*, J.B.S.Haldane, the well-known British biochemist, foretold that already by 1950 the first ectogenesis would probably take place, while by 2070 only a minor proportion of children would be born in the normal way as artificial generation would facilitate the breeding of more suitable human types.

Probably the most eminent explorer in the world of utopianism has been William Olaf Stapledon, born 1886 and lecturer in industrial history, philosophy, and psychology at Liverpool University. *Last and First Men – The Story of the Near and Far Future* was published in London in 1930 and brought out in a fresh edition in the United States after 1945. The author examined the potentialities and tasks of mankind during the span of five hundred million years. The first human species, *homo sapiens*, is extinguished after a series of bloody wars in a natural catastrophe which leaves only a small residue of survivors to hand on the sacred fire. A similar fate befalls the second, third, and fourth human species in their respective ages. Not until the fifth species does mankind attain truly human proportions of body and mind, a civilisation which to us, the first species, is incomprehensible on account of our insufficient intellectual and spiritual capacities. The expectation of life among the fifth species will, thanks to the biological improvement in constitution, amount to three thousand years. The process of maturation will last for one third of that time. During this long period of adolescence, children will live in segregated areas, enabling them to overcome all the stages of political immaturity represented by wars and revolutions. After the fifth species there begins a deterioration in human evolution caused by a cosmic catastrophe and necessitating a resettlement of the human race, first on Venus, then on Neptune. Only with the fifteenth species does it prove possible for man to resume his progress under his own propulsion. The eighteenth species is that of the 'Last Men' who succeed in achieving an ultimate climax of intellectual capacity through the association of individuals in a 'group mind' and the entire group in a 'racial mind', the sort of concentration of physical, intellectual, and spiritual energies in a collective super-species on which Teilhard de Chardin trained his sights.

For Stapledon the world, whatever it stages of evolution and whatever the catastrophes it sustains, remains a world of incompatabilities, at once beautiful and terrible. Were the intellects of all the planets and all the universes beyond our own space-time continuum to merge in a divine intellect, perfection would be attained. That final step is, however, incapable of consummation. Before the onslaught of the last catastrophe, the inhabitants of Neptune fling nuclei of living matter into cosmic space so that life there shall have another chance.

Between 1889 and 1915 fifty-five books written in English dealt with planetary travel. From 1926 on technical and scientific utopianism, much of it published in periodicals, made gigantic strides in Britain and the United States. By 1954 science fiction counted some five hundred thousand regular American readers and its authors were headed by such highly-qualified personalities as Julian Huxley, grandson of 'Darwin's bull-dog', and the mathematics professor E.T.Bell, writing under the pseudonym John Taine.

The modern inventors of Utopia have based their writings on the premises of the Copernican cosmos and disbelief in a personal God, God the Father of Bible and Church alike. Hence the ardent opposition with which these Utopian dreams were greeted in Christian and conservative circles. Christians were not first content with making fierce protests; they even presented Counter-Utopias, generally of a terrifying character. This shock treatment is something quite different to the glorification of horror which plays so big a part in contemporary mass-produced fiction, cartoons, and some science fiction. True, both methods technically derive from the eighteenth and nineteenth century – tales of horror and Baroque bogy propaganda, but the divine and human terror of the Counter-Utopia is rooted in metaphysics and religion, whereas in 'horror' productions the shock apparatus has a psychological function, both stimulating and cathartic. In American cartoons it serves to detract from fears of nuclear warfare.

The Counter-Utopia probably began with Jean Paul's *Monarch of Machines* (1783–4) and came to maturity with E.T.A.Hoffmann. The Breton writer Emile Souvestre, son of an engineer, may in part have been working off his hatred of his father when, in 1846, he described in *The World to Come* the universe in the year 3000 dominated by machines and with profit and money for its gods. His Christianity induced him to doom this technocracy by divine intervention, thus providing a truly representative symbol of that fear of 'godless' technology, modern civilisation, and an incomprehensible intellectuality and social outlook which haunted Christians in the nineteenth century.

In *The Coming Race* (published in 1871 and running into six editions in the same year) Edward Bulwer-Lytton, a Liberal politician turned Conservative, drew a gruesome picture of a subterranean realm where everything was perfect but imagination dead. The inhabitants of this mechanical inferno were stunted creatures who simply lived, loved and died.

The fear felt by Christians on behalf of their Church and in regard to the future is illustrated by R.H.Benson's *The Lord of the World*, a novel about anti-Christ not only much read on publication (1907), but even today reprinted and translated into various languages. Benson, whose father was Archbishop of Canterbury, was a Catholic convert, and the book was a result of his own experience. But his condemnation of the modern world as anti-Christian is somewhat modified in *The Dawn of All*, published four years later in Rome, in which the Last Judgement finally puts an end to the satanic ferment in which science, technology and the drive of modern man have conspired against God.

Both World Wars naturally generated abundant Counter-Utopias. More interesting, however, is the drawing by Robida for *La Caricature*, 1883, entitled *La Guerre au vingtième siècle*, which anticipates aerial, bacterial, chemical and submarine warfare, as had H.G.Wells' *The War of the Air*, ten years before.

In 1912 a woman's warning against a type of war different from any which had occurred up till then was published: *The Barbarisation of the Air* by Bertha von Suttner. In this instance utopianism and pacifism combined to fight the age-old fear, the fatalism of centuries, the belief that wars will and always must exist because man's original sin creates them and this is God's punishment. This is a doctrine which has ever been a part of Church dogma and against which modern optimists have maintained a running battle, a continuous fight for peace, and for Christ, the Prince of Peace.

Nonconformism of religious inspiration, which exists primarily in Britain, and there only by virtue of centuries of struggle, persecution and suppression, constitutes today the firm, vital core of European pacifism. The hopes of a Bertrand Russell and a section of the British Labour movement have their roots in nonconformism, just as Christian pessimism and Christian war dogma derive from Augustine, who taught that man might hope for himself but not for his neighbour. As Hans Urs von Balthasar comments, 'this sentence blockaded the evolution of a theology of hope for fifteen hundred years'. Wyclif attacked the political theology of *Civitas Dei* in his *Trialogus*. Pacifist groups among the Albigensians, Waldensians, Lollards, and Paulicians condemned the bellicose teaching and practice of the mediaeval Church and Luther, in his younger days, was sympathetic to their outlook. In the days of the Reformation its sponsors were that wing of the Anabaptists which had links with the Mennonites in Holland and through them with Britain. In Germany the pacifist heritage of Erasmus and Sebastian Franck was only revived with Herder and Kant. The second of these coined the term 'League of Nations' which rang so strangely, so redolent of Western hostility, in the ears of Weimar Republic Germans.

Heirs to the pacifist ideas of the Bohemian Brethren, the Brownists, the Simonians, the Socinians, and the Mennonites, were the Quakers, who from 1660 onwards lived and suffered for their conviction that Christians must not wage wars. It was in 1660 that George Fox and eleven fellow-believers published the famous declaration against civil and international warfare. Thirty-three years later William Penn, Quaker and son of the heroic Admiral Penn who served Charles i, Parliament, Cromwell, and Charles ii, brought out his plans for the future peace of Europe: an international court of justice, composed of ninety representatives, was to meet annually. His treaty of 1682 with the Indians enabled the founder of Pennsylvania to establish the first unarmed government in the world. His tenets were good faith and goodwill, openness and love, and 'We are all one flesh and blood'.

For the early nineteenth century Jeremy Bentham was, with his *Principles of International Law and Peace* (1786-9), the pioneering pacifist. He proposed two main policies: the reduction of the armed forces of Europe, and the emancipation of their colonies. Bentham told his countrymen that it was for them to set an example, and change their habits. Distrust of their own politicians led to even greater distrust of those of other nations. The Press was corrupt and convinced the masses of nothing better than a narrow, nationalistic possessiveness for their own interests. Every sort of repressive act and crime was rendered respectable here, if only it could be shown that it had to be performed in the national interest. He maintained that the secret diplomacy and secret funds in Foreign Office control were a danger to peace and the future of the country. He saw how fear could be manipulated for political ends and of terror and panic encouraged by a propaganda of hate.

Bentham's views were shared by Immanuel Kant, a nonconformist on his mother's side, and with Scottish blood in his veins. Kant was familiar with Western pacifist thought and held it in high esteem, particularly as expounded by Saint Pierre and Rousseau. Like Bentham he was against every form of colonialism and saw the most evil manifestation and abuse of the power principle in the utterly lawless imperialism of the Maritime Powers. As Kurt von Raumer remarked, Kant's plea against forcible intervention in the affairs of another state is an epoch-making challenge to ideological warfare, whether directed towards the spread of religion or the imposing of a political or social doctrine. He complained that gladness should be an emotion which should never be felt on victory, but rather repentance, and openly exposed the presumptuousness of man in laying claim to providence in matters of war, the word, 'Nature'. 'Use of the word nature is more appropriate too for the limitations on human reason when, as here, hypothesis (not faith) is at stake ... and more modest than the assertion ... that we can recognise' the signs of 'providence'. In the same way he despised the Christian belief in punishment by God for original sin. One of his first quarrels had been with that penal outlook which upheld the Lisbon earthquake, with its thousands of female and child victims, as a just judgement of God.

Kant's most remarkable work is his great treatise *On Perpetual Peace* (1795) in which he insists that the problem of governmental organisation is essentially solvable. Given a large group of rational beings demanding a set of laws for general compliance, each individual would be secretly inclined to exempt himself from their observance. The answer, as he saw it, was to fit these people into a constitutional pattern where the mutual opposition of their private interest so acted as a brake upon one another that their public behaviour would be the same as though such antipathies had never existed. The problem must be solvable because it was not a matter of mankind's moral improvement but the working of human nature. If this was applied to settling the factiousness inside a community by inducing its members to force each other to accept the yoke of legal sanctions, a state of peace, in which the rule of law was operative, would inevitably follow. Kant showed considerable courage in seeking to establish, in the face of a twisted theology and an 'idealist' philosophy, that peace is a technical problem. The issue was not to make men 'good', noble, moral, unselfish beings, but to collaborate with the working of human nature.

On Perpetual Peace passed through twelve editions during its author's lifetime, another twelve between 1805 and 1914, and many more after the First World War. Derived from Western trends of thought, it was unsuccessful in awakening any effective pacifist movement on German soil. In fact, the first pacifist movement in Europe grew out of the Peace Societies in Britain and the United States between 1815 and 1867. English Quakers, invited by Alexander I to spend fourteen years in Russia propagating their beliefs, were able to spread the concept among the Nonconformist underground of the Tsarist empire. The first peace congress took place in 1842 in London, where since the preceding year a certain bond had developed between the pacifist movement and protagonists of free trade. In the United States fifty pacifist associations had merged as early as 1828, into the American Peace Society. Six years later its outstanding personality, William Ladd (1778–1841), pleaded in his *Advance of Peace* for the establishment of an international court of justice.

After the London Congress, the first international pacifist assembly was held in December 1848 at Brussels. The following year Victor Hugo opened the Paris Peace Congress with a speech in which he called for a United States of Europe.

The first tangible effort to prevent an outbreak of hostilities was undertaken by British Quakers in 1853 on the eve of the Crimean War. The people had been summoned to participate in the military action by the Archbishop of Canterbury and the Cardinal of Paris, in language appropriate to that of a crusade. The resolution of the Third International Peace Congress, passed at Frankfurt on 24 August 1850 and appealing for the education of youth through the Press, at school, and from the pulpit in the will to peace, had been in vain.

Between 1867 and 1870 the European pacifist movement continued in France under the leadership of Frederic Passy. In the Austro-Hungarian and German parliaments proposals for disarmament were introduced between 1875 and 1878 by important pacifist figures. Two Austrians, Anton von Schmerling and Adolf Fischhof, made an active attempt to institute an inter-parliamentary union.

The last decade of the nineteenth century was of great significance to the pacifist movement. In Britain and the United States in particular the sympathies of wide circles and prominent personalities were engaged. Two works, *Lay Down Your Arms* by Bertha von Suttner and *The Role of War* by the Russian, Johann von Block, made so deep an impression on Nicholas II that he caused his Foreign Minister Count Muravieff to circulate to all diplomatic representatives at the Court of St Petersburg a memorandum which resulted in the convocation of the First Hague Peace Conference in 1899.

The Tsar's 'manifesto' bore the date 24 August 1898 and was thus in day and month identical to that of the Frankfurt appeal. Armaments, it declared, consumed the physical and intellectual strength of the nations. 'Hundreds of millions are expended on the procurement of frightful machines of destruction which are today regarded as science's last word and are fated tomorrow already to lose all value on account of some fresh discovery in this field.' Armaments were leading to catastrophe. The Tsar proposed an international peace conference which 'would, with God's help, be a favourable prognostic for the coming century. It would unite in one mighty league the efforts of all states honestly striving to let the great concept of world peace triumph over all elements of discord and dissension.'

The words echoed resonantly in the Anglo-Saxon world. The Second Hague Peace Conference in 1907 met at the instigation of President Theodore Roosevelt. The agreement reached there on 18 September regarding the peaceful settlement of international disputes is still valid today. Downright mockery, however, was all that the Conference gained from the German Emperor.

In the hate-racked world of Central Europe one woman fought for peace: Bertha von Suttner. Of aristocratic Austrian blood, she was born in Prague in 1843 and related, on her mother's side, to the fighter for freedom and poet, Theodor von Körner. It was not until her marriage with Baron Artur Gundaccar von Suttner that this spoilt young countess began to appreciate responsibility towards one's fellow human beings. Then, with the words, 'the world and I, we are one and this world needs me and my love', she took up the cause of humanity. Her novel, *Lay Down your Arms* (1889), was translated into every conceivable language, including Russian and Japanese. Acting as Alfred Nobel's secretary, she persuaded him into endowing the Nobel Peace Prize, which Henri Dunant, founder of the Red Cross and instigator of the Geneva Convention, was the first to receive in 1901. In 1891 she founded the Austrian Peace Society. A year later, with her young collaborator, the publisher, A.H.Fried, she brought out at Berlin the first issue of the monthly periodical, *Die Waffen Nieder*. In 1908 it became *Friedenswarte*, and still continues, but like all pacifist publications in Central Europe is confined to an indigent existence.

In Europe Bertha von Suttner spoke at hundreds of meetings on behalf of the pacifist movement. In the United States she gave more than a hundred lectures on the subject, won the understanding of President Roosevelt, and in 1910 moved Andrew Carnegie to found his Endowment for International Peace. In 1905 she was the first woman to receive the Novel Peace Prize; her collaborator Fried was given the award six years later. German and Christian circles attacked, derided, and abused her as a crazy fool, 'peace fury', 'peace slut'. In 1899 she ventured a prophecy: 'The twentieth century will not come to an end without human society having done away with the greatest scourge, war, as a legal institution.'

She died, completely exhausted in Vienna on 21 June 1914. Exactly a week later the assassination of the Heir Apparent at Sarajevo set the First World War in motion. 'God with us' was the unanimous cry of Catholics in France and Protestants and Catholics in Germany who interpreted the struggle as a crusade on behalf of their respective nations and civilisations. During the course of the hostilities a very famous theologian mounted the pulpit of Notre-Dame Cathedral at Paris and delivered a sermon against the lonely fighter for peace at Rome, Pope Benedict xv. In 1915 Bishop Michael von Faulhaber, the subsequent Cardinal of Munich, wrote, one year after the occupation of Belgium, 'It is my conviction that as a matter of martial ethics this campaign will become for us the text-book example of a just war.'

Pope Benedict xv's peace appeal of August 1917 sank in a sea of hate and rejection; it failed to reach the bulk of Christians. The only memorial to this pacifist Pope was that erected after his death by the Mohammedan Turks. Similarly when the first (and, soon after, the second) atom bomb was dropped on the Japanese, not a single official comment was made by the Roman Catholic hierarchy of the United States (as a Catholic American historian has noted).

Bertha von Suttner published *The Barbarisation of the Air* in 1912. The barbarisation of the masses in the nineteenth and twentieth centuries in Europe and the contamination of hearts and minds is inextricably bound up with the concomitant evolution in the Christian systems and creeds during the same period. It would seem that a science of peace, an amitology ('applied science of amity and unselfish love') of the kind promoted by the Russo-American Pitirim A. Sorokin and sponsored by the Harvard Research Center in Creative Altruism established 1949 can only strike root beyond the confines of Europe and its major Churches.

10

Problems of Protestantism

When one is considering the nineteenth century one fact of outstanding significance must be borne in mind: although many Christians belonged chronologically to this age, accepting its technical advances into their way of life,
they never really accepted either the spiritual or intellectual changes that
accompanied them. They were not simply unfamiliar with this side of their
own century, but reacted towards it with deep fear and hatred, which they
particularly directed at the epoch's specifically satanic symptoms – its
science, art and technical progress. Goethe was still regarded with aversion
by German Roman Catholics as late as 1900 because they had never
accepted the Protestant spirit; French Catholics saw the Republic as an
'atheistic science'; Ernest Renan and his supporters saw the Jewish Captain
Dreyfus as a conspiracy against Holy France and the Holy Mother Church.
Papal encyclicals demonstrated a remoteness from contemporary developments seeing them rather as heretical machinations, much as Metternich
represented them to his emperor, Tsar Alexander 1 and the Popes.

'Doubts come from the devil', proclaimed Court Chaplain Stöcker, and
rarely has a single sentence more aptly revealed the secret source of ecclesiastical and political reaction. That such reaction leads to murder, war and
extermination of all doubters, was revealed only too clearly during the course
of the nineteenth century. In 1900 Friedrich Naumann (1869–1900) wrote
with admirable frankness in his *Letters on Religion*, 'we are either wolves or
lambs. We side either with Bismarck or with Tolstoy. Either with the Gospel
of the mailed fist or the gospel of brethren of communal life.'

Hermann Kutter, a Swiss Protestant pastor uttered a similar remark in
1907:

> Our entire Christianity is an unremitting compromise with the Powers
> of this world. It hobbles in both directions, serving God and mammon.
> Look at the 'Christian' governments and states, 'Christian' society,
> 'Christian' private life, and you will constantly witness the same menda-
> cious spectacle. . . . The Gospels condemn war as an abomination. Jesus'
> teaching forbids every war. But the 'Christian' state uses precisely the
> preaching of the Gospels to imbue its soldiers with courage and martial
> rapture. . . . In its savage perfection of power the 'Christian' state lags in
> no way behind any heathen entity. Violence and tyranny are its hall-

marks. *Everything* is subordinated to it. Woe unto him who resists it in the name of Jesus! But . . . *who* faces up to this lie, *who* is heartsick at it? This all-corrupting compromise on the one hand cripples Christianity beyond recognition and on the other enables the secular power under the 'cover' of Christianity to heap all the more confidently one misdeed upon another . . . . Our faith has become something specifically *spiritual*, a spiritual abracadabra whose formula is composed of Bible verses.

Kutter underlined the fatal division between externals and inwardness. This:

enables even the most earnest Christian to serve both God and mammon without noticing it. It is *that* which has deleted the name of God utterly from real life. It is *that* which is responsible for precisely the 'faithful' being incapable of imagining Heaven, the throne of the living God, other than in the shape of a celestial assembly room glittering with gold and diamonds. It is that, and *that alone*, which is to be held accountable for the fact that today not merely the most imperative postulates of the Gospels but the most commonplace demands of humanity are turned down out of hand as impossible and nonsensical by Christians themselves and that the world faces convulsions that will make all revolutions and wars that have taken place hitherto seem like child's play.

This outcry from the conscience of a Protestant pastor in 1907 was republished in December 1961.

A study of the frame of mind of young theologians and clergymen who volunteered for military service at the beginning of the two World Wars has yet to be made. Many, no doubt, hoped that the front-line fire would bring a solution to the problems besetting them, would, in some way, purify Christianity and the Church. The attitudes leading to the splendid missionary movements of the nineteenth century, attitudes of men, nonconformists, individuals breaking away from the orthodox churches of the day, personalities such as Schweitzer, have still to be recorded. Schweitzer himself had earlier described the most daring undertaking of German Protestants – research into the life of Christ – as one of the revolutions of the nineteenth century which stands comparable to the other revolutions which took place between 1789 and 1950, as constituting, with them, the revolution of mankind marking the beginning of man's new epoch.

Political revolutions cause a far deeper unrest in nations than is intended. On the heels of intellectual revolution, represented by the Romantic era, came the excitement of scientific discoveries such as scientists themselves did not always want to believe. The discovery of the neanderthal man was one such event. In the nineteenth century men strained their minds back thousands of years to gain a better understanding of themselves, but at every turn a strange story blocked their efforts: the story of Jesus of Nazareth.

WHO WAS JESUS?

Copernicus and Galileo had envisaged the world as a small planet in an infinite cosmos. Darwin and his friends had seen man in the environment of his cognates in the animal world, growing to maturity there and, in the process, surpassing his relations and ancestors. In the same spirit of the need for truth, German Protestant theologians searched in the rubble of history for the *man* Jesus, who during a thousand years' evolution of theology and popular piety, had almost disappeared in the divinity of Christ, the Second Person of the Godhead. The Word had absorbed the man Jesus, as the sun absorbs dew. One day these men stumbled on the rabbi Yeshu mi-Nasrath, a man of uncannily familiar traits, a Pharisee, but a foreigner belonging to a strange people, from whom many paths led back into even earlier civilisations, but from whom came no lead into the social, spiritual, political and mental situation of the nineteenth and twentieth centuries. In this period of historical research on the part of German theologians two authors may be quoted.

In 1937 Walter Nigg wrote: 'All great criticism, though it may not be immediately evident, is inspired by a creative power. Its inmost intentions derive from a desire to be productive', and such was the case, in his opinion, with regards to the critical activity of German Scholarship at that period.

'The phenomenon of research into the life of Jesus is unique,' wrote Werner Picht in 1960.

Nowhere else in history is there to be found a religious self-determination of this sort where research into the history of dogmas goes hand in hand with thorough investigation into canonic writings so as to track down the historical appearance and address of the founder of the religion Who is venerated as a divine being. The premise for that was collision between a belief based on revelation and a scientific manner of thought setting out to be the custodian of truth in the conviction that 'true' and 'untrue' should be decided according to scientific criteria and that truth must be ascertained by scientific means.

As the result of great exertion, research managed to demonstrate that the Gospels – viewed as historical source material – were compilations on which many men had been at work. Certain phrases and passages were elucidated as 'genuine words of Jesus', whereas the great symbols 'Matthew', 'Mark', 'Luke', and 'John' were seen as having a bearing on various communal traditions, trends, and aspirations of the first and second-century communities. Nevertheless the personality of Jesus became ever more unfamiliar and elusive. The result was twofold. By 1900 the energy behind research was sapped; some of those engaged reached the conclusion that Jesus was no more than a myth, a constructive fancy of early Christian communities.

PROTESTANT CASES

The honour and dignity, the human and Christian greatness of German Protestantism in the nineteenth century is inextricably linked with the many disciplinary actions, condemnations and depositions of theologians and clergy carried out by a Church leadership which saw its role as policeman of God and emperor. Martin Rahde said of this period:

Trying to enumerate the cases individually is like stepping into a large cemetery studded with crosses. They began in the forties of the last century when Restoration theology was no longer prepared to tolerate the deviationist opinion in teaching and a Rupp, a Wislicenus and an Uhlich were dismissed from their appointments, a move which did the Church no good because it resulted in the blood-letting effect of the free religious movement.

Walter Nigg has described a dozen such cases, mostly occurring before the First World War, but even some after. It was a 'witch-hunt', a persecution of dissenters by the Church equal to that in the political and party political field. Christoph Schrempf, one of the better-known cases, told his accusers firmly: 'Under prevailing ecclesiastical and theological circumstances the instructional and liturgical discipline of our Church is a breach of morality ... the demand that individual clergymen shall unconditionally comply with it is morally highly dubious.... The customary duty of a Protestant clergyman puts a noose round his conscience.' The consistory replied to this with Schrempf's instant dismissal and loss of pension rights.

Carl Jatho, a preacher with a charisma of his own, had held appointments at Bucharest and Cologne before, at the age of sixty, in 1911, a board of thirteen theologians and lawyers forbade his further activity within the Protestant Church, and his defending counsel, Professor Otto Baumgarten of Kiel, was shocked by the callousness and lack of interest with which this 'warm-hearted, benign preacher' was treated.

Gottfried Traub, the passionate protagonist of a free Protestantism, author of the phrase 'party church', wrote of the marble cross which stood over the table of the consistory's president, 'A downright dreadful sight. Have this cross removed in future! Enough had to be borne already. There ought to be sufficient spiritual good taste within a Christian to prevent his standing under the Cross on which Jesus forgave everyone and opened the gates of Heaven to the thief and announcing, "According to Paragraph So-and-So the position of A.B. is such that ... ".' Pain-wracked, Traub cried out, 'Long live the tribunal! Death to Protestantism!'

In 1892 Schrempf had requested the senior Württemberg church authority to dispense clergymen from the obligation of consummating the act of baptism in conformity with the text of the Apostolic Creed. Too many of the clergy, he argued, could no longer believe in the Immaculate Conception and the physical Resurrection and Ascension; they were consequently forced into lying. Jatho was convinced that the Biblical view of the universe was destroyed beyond recall, making it essential to try and evolve a religious concept which is compatible with scientific knowledge. 'I believe in the immanence of God in the world because I believe in an infinite and eternal world.'

The argument about the Apostolic Creed, rendered topical by Schrempf, eventually involved the leading Protestant theological historian, Adolf von Harnack (1851–1930). A group of his Berlin students asked whether, together with students of other universities, they should file a petition with the High Consistory for abrogation of the Creed. Harnack rejected the proposal, but, orally and in writing, broached the subject thoroughly with them. Very many Christians, he contended, still believed in the Creed. The Church must not abrogate it unless it had succeeded in producing a new creed which surpassed the old in form and force. 'Recognition of the Creed in its literal terms is not the test of Christian and theological maturity. On the contrary. A mature Christian, educated in understanding of the Gospels and Church history, must take exception to it.' But a small publication on the subject, issued in order to calm people's minds had the opposite effect of loosing a storm of indignation.

Court Chaplain Stöcker launched vehement attacks on Harnack, garnishing his polemics with such epithets as 'an ecclesiastical Catiline'. The tempest grew ever more violent and for a moment, with the leading men of the Church ranged on one side and the outstanding figures of scientific theology on the other, it looked as though Harnack's own position would be at stake. He himself adhered firmly to his previously assumed position: he had no wish to rob the masses of believers of their faith in the literal terms of the Creed, but neither he nor the well-educated of his day and outlook could continue therein.

WHAT IS CHRISTIANITY?

What is Christianity?, a series of lectures given by Harnack at Berlin University in the winter term, 1899–1900, is one of the most famous documents of German Protestantism of our time, and has been translated into many languages. People have derided it, but for honesty of statement, by a scientifically trained conscience it has no equal.

Harnack urges the study of the Gospels, for in Christ is to be found faith in the higher evolution of His religion after Him. 'What is unintelligible to you, have no hesitation in putting aside.' 'What is at stake is not the matter of the miracles, but the decisive question, whether we are helplessly harnessed to an inexorable inevitability, or whether there is a God Who rules and Whose power to subdue nature can be solicited and experienced.'

Jesus dealt with three themes: 'First, the kingdom of God and its coming. Secondly, God the father and the infinite value of man's soul. Thirdly, the higher justice and the command of love.' 'There is nothing in the Gospels which tells us more surely what gospel is, and what outlook and disposition it produces, than the Lord's Prayer.' Jesus proclaimed no social programme, but 'I do not doubt that the time will come when comfortably living ministers will be as little tolerated as domineering priests. We are becoming more sensitive in this respect, and that is a good thing.'

Harnack opposed 'Church politics' and 'political parties' which developed a 'terrorism inside the Church'. Likewise, Christology was a 'dreadful story. On the basis of "Christology" men have turned their religious teachings into fruitful weapons and have spread fear and horror. It is an attitude which still continues. . . .' There follows Harnack's much quoted and much attacked pronouncement of faith: 'Not the Son, but the Father alone, belongs to the Gospel as preached by Jesus.' The sentence, 'I am the Son of God' was not put into His Gospel by Jesus Himself, and whoever places it as a sentence among others there adds something to the Gospel.'

Harnack then continues, 'The Roman Church is the most inclusive and the mightiest structure, the most complicated and yet the most homogenous, that history as so far known to us has brought forth. All the forces of human intellect and soul as well as all the elemental powers of which man is possessed have laboured at this structure.' And this was indeed a compliment paid to the fear-inspiring opponent of nineteenth-century Protestants, who steadfastly imagined that the Church of Rome was preparing to strangle freedom of spirit, Protestantism, science and the German nation.

Yet Harnack was perfectly frank. In his opinion the Roman Church was a continuation of the Roman Empire, the pope a 'sacerdotal Caesar'. He felt that the inner piety and its expression as found in Roman Catholicism was purely Augustinian, and whereas once Christians had died rather than worship Caesar, they now, while not actually worshipping an earthly ruler, 'have subjugated their souls to the authoritative commandment of the Roman papal monarch'. He continues 'Roman Catholicism as a secular church, as a régime of privilege and power, has nothing to do with the gospel and indeed contradicts it fundamentally.' He considers both its inner pauperisation and its outer accretion of power an 'enormous retrogression'.

He stood out just as boldly against the link between Protestantism and the state, saying that it had often been attempted 'to bring the Church within the reach of the police and to use it as means for the maintenance of secular order'.

Harnack closed with a reference to a great problem 'wherein the Christian sense of brotherhood has yet to prove itself in a way wholly different to that in which it has given this problem recognition in earlier centuries' – the social problem. If this task is fulfilled, 'we shall be able to answer the most recondite question of all, *the question, what is the sense of life*, the more satisfactorily.' (The words italicised here were set in heavy type in the original.)

Adolf von Harnack in 1900 looked gravely and hopefully into the future. His son Ernst (1888–1945), a senior official, was executed as a member of the Social Democratic group of the German Resistance Movement, together with the men of 20 July 1944. The two Harnacks embody, each in his own way, a German Protestant truthfulness which has become exemplary for Europe and beyond. They possessed a degree of conscientiousness in thought and research which had grown and matured through many generations of theologians. They had the research worker's love of truth which painfully sets aside its own theories and, finding what he has neither sought nor wanted, sacrifices the convictions that have become dear to him. Protestant research workers demonstrated this truthfulness for the first time in a unique fashion in the nineteenth century when they destroyed the most cherished heritage that a dozen preceding generations had bestowed upon them, the sacrosanct, imperturbable, pure words of God as found in both Testaments of the Bible, sundering them into conglomerations of varying origin, varying age, and sometimes patently varying quality.

The effect of the destruction on the 'destroyers' was matched by the horror of many churchmen who protested against the 'uprising of the anti-Christ' amidst Protestant theology. Orthodoxy too, the conservative Protestant world, has its hidden dramas, tragedies, and cross-roads.

11

Problems of Catholicism

The state in which European Catholicism found itself on the eve of the First World War was just as catastrophic as that of Protestantism. Many thousands of Catholics had but the scantiest knowledge of their faith; French Catholicism was permeated with a pathological dread of Germans, Jews, Freemasons and the Third Republic; German Catholicism was riddled with slogans and appeals leading straight to the battlefields of the First, and then Second World War. Intellectual and spiritual comment was firmly silenced, and genuine academic, Catholic *élite* was excluded from it.

To understand the problems confronting European Catholicism in the nineteenth century it is necessary, however, to appreciate that a large section of its adherents had scarcely changed their outlook over a period of a thousand years. The Industrial Revolution had only slowly taken the peasants away from their accustomed communal life, in which the daily round alternated with days of feasting and worship – an existence which, while limited, was yet a firm framework in which the simple man could live at ease.

As the Industrial Revolution made itself felt throughout society, however, primitive instincts were released which asserted themselves with destructive energy in times of war and civil strife, and, in times of peace, produced spiritual dreariness, tedium, cynicism and nihilism. The Catholic Church did, in fact, make a real attempt to retrieve the earlier pattern of existence, and the many congresses, pilgrimages and other Catholic occasions, were intended to give cohesion to the masses who threatened to disintegrate into frightened individuals.

In order to maintain this belief in the Church, it was important to demonstrate to the body of believers the redemptive power of the priesthood. Young priests were issued with a book of meditation which maintained that the priest has the power to bring God to earth during the act of communion, a power of which the Prince-Archbishop of Salzburg commented, 'Where in Heaven is there such power as resides in the Catholic priest! ... Mary brought the Divine Child into the world once, yet, behold, the priest does this not once ... but ... as often as he officiates. The Catholic Priest is able not merely to invoke his presence at the altar.... Christ, the only Son of God the Father ... lets him have his way therein. ...'

The intrinsic point of these, and other, examples, is the firm intention of the Church to present itself, and to act as, the Church of priesthood and the Church of the masses. The Church of priesthood, visualised as a strongly centralised institution, with its unifying force at Rome, in the person of the Pope, found its culmination in the declaration of papal infallibility, whereas the Marian propaganda and the dogma of the Immaculate Conception manifested itself as the Church of the masses.

It has been said of the Catholic Church that it is always permeated with the spirit of the masses, while Max Scheler called it a 'mass asylum'. But the Bonn Catholic theologian, Nikolaus Monzel, openly agreed with this description, saying 'it seems indubitable that the majority of Church members belong to the passive or receptive type, and that precisely because this type corresponds to the average person'. On the other hand, it was to this Church of the masses that the creative individual, who attracted the attention and disfavour of his spiritual superior and of his community, had to be sacrificed. It is therefore important to compare the ever more narrow-minded and ghetto-like Catholicism of the middle and late nineteenth century with the free and creative spirit which prevailed in its earlier decades.

German Catholicism owed its initial liberation to Napoleon. Under his influence the ecclesiastical polities of the Holy Roman Empire, the sanctuary for centuries for younger sons of the aristocracy, were dissolved. The measure also brought about a very positive religious factor in the shape of the Catholic Enlightenment, irrespective of the contempt in which it was held by the Romantic Movement and the Restoration.

With 1815, and lasting until 1960, there began the period of the concordats. It was precisely in his belief in the redemptive power of concordats, regardless of the sort of régime with which he was dealing, that Pope Pius XII showed himself to be a great son of this Catholic nineteenth century. 'The era of concordats laid the groundwork for innumerable disputes that cluttered the century.' It took time before the concordats could take full effect in universities, theological seminars, publications, and secular schooling in the various German states. But during that space of freedom in the first part of the century there arose two creative spirits who towered over practically any others produced by German Catholicism during the rest of the age: Johann Adam Möhler and Franz von Baader.

MÖHLER

The main work of Johann Adam Möhler (1796–1838) took shape at Tübingen. He arrived in 1826, nine years after the Roman Catholic theological faculty had been moved there by the Württemberg government, right into the heart of Protestant academic culture – an experiment that proved surprisingly successful. The earlier of his two major works, *The Unity of the Church, or The Principle of Catholicism as Shown by the Attitude of the Church Fathers in the First Three Centuries*, had been published in the preceding year. Its outlook was diametrically opposed to de Maistre's and Bonald's denunciations of the Greeks and their acclamation of the Roman Church as a static, pyramidal power structure in religious and political affairs. In 1832 his second great work appeared, *Symbolism: Doctrinal Differences between Catholics and Protestants as Evidenced by Their Symbolic Writings*. In this same year the anathema against the Greek, and free, spirit was pronounced in the form of the encyclical *Mirari Vos*. Seen in the light of the fatal development which was set in motion by this work and which lasted until approximately 1960, Möhler's achievements must be regarded as a warning and plea not to extinguish the basic spirit of the Church and the animating factor of love.

Möhler saw the community of believers as 'a great fraternal bond for mutual encouragement in life' while the 'ever fruitful source of the community of believers is within the pale of the Church'. The latter is a unity of opposites because it is a choir composed of the most varied voices and, as such, needs the free play of individualists within it. 'From this there arises the duty, for the Church, to allow the most generous treatment to the free play of individualities and not to impose unnecessary restraints.' This precept of toleration also holds good for the behaviour of one member towards another.

Möhler's interpretation of the dignity of man and of the Church as the community of saints, as well as the fraternal bond between all believers, did not come easily to him. Among other things he had to throw off an early training in Jansenism. He was a supporter of the episcopal system of thought, widely held in the late eighteenth and early nineteenth centuries, that was fully prepared to recognise the Bishop of Rome as *centrum unitatis* but not as the absolute monarch propounded by de Maistre and his Roman followers. Their train of thought, as they frankly admitted, was that Russia with its Church was a rotting corpse, the Greek spirit was the spirit of chaos and anarchy, and both of them could only be subjugated and tamed through a rigorously organised and tightly disciplined Roman centralism with an infallible pope at its head. The wooing of Russia by Rome throughout the nineteenth century and after failed because it was based on the mistaken concepts of de Maistre and his Roman friends and heirs. It was in vain that Franz von Baader, in the spirit of Möhler, issued his warning against the refusal to understand the totally different Greek Orthodox and Russian religious outlook which will always defend itself against any assumption of overlordship from outside and which ultimately remains invincible.

Möhler could not avoid seeing that during the past fifteen hundred years the Church had sustained severe intellectual loss simply because of its incapacity to contain within itself, as a productive play of opposites, what it deemed to be heresy. He was also aware (like Franz von Baader) of the lethargy affecting many of the Catholic clergy as a result of the notion that scientific approach to religion was a Protestant prerogative. This was Möhler's point of departure in his *Symbolism*, on which he continued during the last six years of his life, and which he issued in five editions.

To enter into discussion with the Protestants and all the other sectarians of the past fifteen hundred years was the first task he set himself. He knew that no 'skilful negotiation' would restore lost unity. God himself was at work in the division between the denominations.

A Higher Power has reserved to Itself determination of the time, place, and way that the contradictions shall be resolved and will not leave unwarrantable human importunity unpublished. So, even though there can be no doubt whatever but that the peaceful side by side existence of the denominations intimates a future existence within one another, a return to former unity, yet that unification must be consummated wholly in the field of the spirit, openly and honestly, freely and consciously, . . . and on the basis of the unaltered ancient principles as well as on higher impulse.

Catholics and Protestants alike were guilty. Both would need to make a common confession of wrong. 'Aware of their guilt, both must proclaim that "It is we who have erred, all of us, it is only the Church that cannot err. We have all sinned, on earth the Church alone is blameless." The feast of reconciliation will follow on this open avowal of common guilt.' Möhler was utterly convinced that real reconciliation demanded first the most frank and harsh demonstration of differences. The sharper these were, the greater the tension, the greater would be the urge towards a genuine solution through a reconciliation of the differences.

Möhler's *Symbolism* has been called a 'theodicy of the schisms'. God educates mankind and history is the means that He employs. By adopting this Greek concept, Möhler ranged himself against Augustine, Bellarmine, and all Roman Catholic jurists who viewed history more in the light of man's trial for his crime. At the bottom of every great human aberration, he argued, there must lie a cry from the human heart and a great truth. Otherwise it would be inexplicable how generation upon generation could be ensnared in such an aberration.

In the preface to the first edition of *Symbolism* Möhler referred to the custom prevailing in 'all German Lutheran and reformed universities for many years past' of holding lectures on the doctrinal differences between Catholics and Protestants. He proposed that it should also become a Catholic practice as it was essential for Catholics to know something of other denominations. 'And what is less in accordance with our own self-respect than not to have examined most thoroughly and meticulously the true bases and foundations of our higher life and to convince ourselves how far we stand on solid ground or whether we have posted ourselves on a deceptive surface which hides a yawning chasm.' Döllinger, Loisy, the so-called Modernists, and not a few cultured Catholics were to discover that, in their own eyes, such was certainly the case.

'It is self-evident that the instruction in doctrinal differences must be imparted kindly, carefully, and charitably, with upright love of truth and without exaggeration.' That is, it was self-evident to Möhler – the German theologian, who, thinking of his Protestant colleagues at Tübingen, drew on their common spiritual traditions. In his work he drew up truly grand and detailed accounts of the doctrines not merely of the Lutherans and Calvinists, but the Anabaptists, Quakers, Moravian brethren, Methodists, Socinians, and Arminians too, and was always at pains to demonstrate the continuity of certain of these doctrines as far back as the Middle Ages and early eras of Christianity.

Möhler's delineation of the 'doctrinal differences between Catholics and Protestants as revealed by their symbolic writings' was monumental. He set out material for centuries of frank and free discussion. In the same year as the first edition of his work the encyclical *Mirari Vos* was published which defined all the sects he had so carefully analysed as inventions of the Devil and their adherents as his disciples who sought nothing but the destruction of all earthly and heavenly order. This was a case of two worlds where different languages were spoken, just as it was with Pope Gregory XVI and Lamennais, with Pope Pius XII and the French worker-priests. In Germany, instead of taking advantage of the opportunity that Möhler presented, there was already a strong trend in Catholicism in the opposite direction. It was this that led Franz von Baader, the most fertile and far-reaching German Catholic thinker of the nineteenth century, to take up his fight against the Church's 'petrification' add to adopt a radically anti-papal stance.

BAADER

Franz von Baader (1765–1841) is one of the 'great unknowns' of the nineteenth century. He was admired by Hegel, whose opinions were diametrically opposed to his; contemporary Russians and Frenchmen held him in esteem; Kierkegaard and Scheler used him as a source of inspiration; Berdyaev as a source of support. His is the imperceptible spirit behind the ecumenical movement.

To police agents in Russia and Prussia he appeared suspicious, to others half demon, half angel. He began his struggle against Rome and papal primacy at the age of seventy-five, two years before his death, and right up to the last moment everything about him was in a state of flux. He left numerous writings, but no system of ideas, for, to him, dialectic was the essence of life. Without it there could be no truth and no knowledge. Every thought, like life itself, was a piece of dialectic, and his work was deliberately incomplete: he wanted to provide the inspiration to thought, not the thought as such.

He began his journal on 12 April 1786 with the intention of recording his life as an experiment with God, nature, poetry, learning, and his own person. 'Morality is nothing but a higher form of physics applied to the mind and spirit.' Sin stunts good sense. There is no such thing as abstract truth; there is only living truth, incarnate in action and history.

Baader visited England from 1792 to 1796. His contact with Godwin, the revolutionary English 'youth movement', and, at one remove, the French Revolution, fascinated him. He was to turn against all these things later, but he always remained a fanatic for freedom and adhered firmly to his resolution of 1787 that '*Nobody* may impede me in my researches in any field whatsoever'.

His train of thought around 1800 was very close to that of Teilhard de Chardin some hundred and twenty years later. The universe glorifies God and creation spontaneously rises in unending prayer to Him. Baader hated every sort of dualism and supernaturalism. Spirit and matter were indivisible and correlated concepts. There is no God without nature, no Creator without creation. The Creation must constantly and perpetually continue to be created.

'Man may neither divide nor mix what God has joined by distinguishing one from another, external from internal, events of the past from actual experience, nature from spirit.' True reality is at once material and spiritual. Man's duty is to spiritualise the universe and to represent God in nature. Man's task is to evolve all his talents to a higher degree.

This evolution, man's true progress, is costly and dangerous. Like everything in the world he must pass through the fire of temptation. Each living thing is rooted in darkness and death, and life is always subject to death and mortal danger. Light is a continual triumph over darkness. Man's mission is to be God's collaborator in the temporal order, succeeding here to God as a son succeeds to a father. Man is a god in miniature and the denial of this true dignity of man is the worst enemy of goodness. The principle of creation is that there is nothing in the spirit which has not been in matter.

The philosopher of matter, Baader, was, as such, a philosopher of love. Love is indivisible. Sexually conditioned fear of God and fear of nature were the same dangerous error of the age. The love of man for God and for the earth must correspond. Woman is the 'keeper of love'. Baader frequently reflected on the deeply human significance of the kiss. Animals do not kiss. The embrace and the kiss are the outstanding hallmarks of mankind.

Love, sexual power and beauty, the spirit of God and grace are all inseparable. Baader, the scientist, mining engineer, and industrialist, was all too familiar, if only from his visit to England, with the terrible ugliness which arose in the nineteenth century. In his eyes puritanism and hideousness, as well as the struggle against affection and pity, all derive from the same source. Beauty is grace and, with a divine strength of love, hides the rigour of matter. Beauty is a stratagem of divine love and compassion. Art is a divine favour and is literally 'wonderfully beautiful'. As against the sexless and sexually hostile Kitsch of 'religious' nineteenth-century art, Baader emphasised that neither religious art nor any poetry worthy of the name must lose sight of 'the exalted significance of sexual love'.

Man's entire dignity lies in his capacity to think, and true faith is rational. 'Blind faith is the source of all errors and all afflictions in the Church.' True faith is free and knows no fear. Sadly Baader remarked in 1825 that respect for religion had been overthrown. 'Doubt as to religion's redemptive power is more or less general. Catholicism had in many instances become fossilised and the Church petrified; in Protestantism decay was dominant.'

There is no such thing as return to the *status quo ante*. New illnesses cannot be treated with old prescriptions. The great political and spiritual heresies were necessary. Frightened and lazy theologians were responsible for states of spiritual misery just as political reactionaries were the cause of revolutions. Every revolution is simply an impeded evolution. Political reaction, and obstacles placed in the way of science and freedom of thought, go hand in hand. Trying to retrieve simple faith by blocking scientific research is a mistake analagous to advising a fallen woman to return to her initial innocence or attempting to counter licentiousness with castration. True faith is anticipation of the future.

But where could the future be perceived? Baader looked towards Russia. His thinking urged him to action. Whereas the nineteenth century often enough gazed with fear, indeed terror, in the direction of the Russian colossus, and the Curia wooed the Tsar with a mixture of fright and hope, Baader wanted to win over the Russian Church as the third power which would liberate Roman Catholicism and Protestantism from their self-imposed shackles. In a letter of 1841 to Uvarov, the Russian Minister of Education, he analysed what to him constituted the great problem: the contemporary division in Western Europe between faith and knowledge. 'After the Papacy had gained full control of old Catholicism, it was inevitable that under its dictatorship the free evolution of religion's temper and spirit would stagnate. This in turn caused a gradual reaction which finally came to fruition in the Reformation.' The loser was knowledge, which in the Roman Church foundered on a false conservatism and in the Protestant Church on a false liberalism.

Baader placed his hopes in the first place on Tsar Alexander 1 and the latter's friend Prince Alexander Golitsyn, whom on the occasion of a banquet the Tsar had nominated Procurator of the Holy Synod. An epicurean and Voltairean, the Prince looked (for the first time) into the Bible and was much moved. In 1817 all spiritual and educational matters were entrusted to him, whereupon he became 'in a certain sense patriarch, pope, superintendent, chief rabbi, and mufti all in one'. He was now dedicated to a gigantic ambition: he wanted to find room for the practice of all religious forces and movements in the vast spaces of the Russian Empire. This was the reason for his invitation issued to English Quakers and particularly German Nonconformists to settle there. He hoped to find in Baader a congenial collaborator and appointed his 'correspondent' to supply regular reports on the state of religion in Europe.

Baader threw himself enthusiastically into this task, believing it to be the realisation of his mission to educate Russia for its role as mediator between Roman Catholicism and Protestantism. He organised for Golitsyn the religious emigration movement from southern Germany. Replacements were urgently necessary for the Jesuits who, on account of their successful propaganda on behalf of Rome in the highest aristocratic circles, were regarded by the Tsar and his Minister as dangerous enemies of the Russian Church and as political agents. He evolved plans for a Christian Academy which was to give Russia a thorough grounding in religious and secular sciences and thus not only spare it the revolutions of western Europe, but enable it to catch up, even surpass European thoughts. Baader and Golitsyn were foiled, however, by the resistance of Russian Orthodoxy and the change in Alexander, deeply influenced by Metternich, from liberal to reactionary views. The whole Russian Orthodox hierarchy watched with indignation as the 'anti-Christian' Golitsyn proposed to put it on the same level as foreign sects, Protestants, Catholics, and even non-Christians. For the Russian Church there existed only *one* orthodoxy. Golitsyn therefore failed.

In his later years Baader fought against the Russophobia existing in certain West European circles and tried to gain sympathetic understanding for the Eastern Church's theology. Herein he showed real knowledge of, and veneration for, the Orthodox concept of the Trinity. He viewed Rome, as represented by the Curia, with its trend towards the deification of the pope, and the simultaneous reduction of Christ to a papal cipher, as an invincible enemy. The papacy, in his eyes, had betrayed the fraternal and basically corporative character of the early Church; it was the enemy of true Christian catholicism. His writings and letters in his final period may seem one-sided, unjust, exaggeratedly sharp. But, looking back today on roughly a century's Inquisitorial treatment by the Church of Europe's leading Catholic intellects, his great worry about his own time and the future seems at least intelligible.

FRENCH CATHOLICISM POLITICISED

There had been a political quality in French Catholicism ever since the Middle Ages, starting with the struggle of French kings with the papacy, but it was not until the triumph of Bossuet over Fénélon, and the destruction of Port-Royal by the troops of Louis xiv, that the contemplative, mystic, intellectually spiritual forces in French Catholicism were finally driven underground. And when the Napoleonic concordat effected the restoration of the Church, it was nothing but a barren, bigoted, inwardly frightened and outwardly haughty religious machine which was incapable of deriving positive from the Revolution or its consequences.

In the early nineteenth century many of the fifty thousand livings were vacant. The Bourbon régime tried, with the aid of police and army, to re-Catholicise the country. The Church would have liked to take over, or destroy, the 'atheistic' universities. It was proposed that freedom of the press should be suspended. Bonald defended capital punishment for profanation of the host on the grounds that although Christ had asked forgiveness for his executioners, God the Father had not given it.

But the masses seceded from religion, and intellectuals, with the aid of eighteenth-century classics, managed to screen themselves against the attempts to reinstitute a 'unity of faith'. During those early years Voltaire and Rousseau sold by the thousand.

Large-scale quasi-religious, quasi-political operations were mounted to try and win over the public. Processions were instigated and thirty new bishops were consecrated – but the appointments were filled by members of the old aristocracy, who proved harsh, overbearing and reactionary. Full of disdain, the régime used the Church to serve its aim of subjecting the nation. Louis xviii avowed himself a freethinker and was fond of saying to his entourage that he had early thrown off the 'superstitious imaginings' of his childhood. Prominent aristocrats were frankly atheistic. Lamartine described their scornful, sceptical, purely formal orthodoxy in his *History of the Restoration* and Chateaubriand said in 1816 that the state expected only one thing of the Church; that it should create royalists. The state was out to found a Gallican Church. The ordinances of 16 June 1828 brought Church institutions (schools, seminars, and so on) under strict state discipline. In 1800 Chateaubriand had been introduced to Bonald in the home of Pauline de Beaumont. During the first decade of the nineteenth century they held closely similar views and published them in the same periodicals together with the young Lamennais. Yet by 1830 these three men embodied three separate outlooks.

BONALD

Louis-Gabriel-Ambroise Vicomte de Bonald (1754–1840) is one of the most outstanding examples of Restoration Catholicism. He had received a thorough, classical education at the Oratorian school at Juilly. In 1785 he became a mayor, in 1790 President of provincial administration. During the Revolution he emigrated and enlisted in the Army of the Princes. While at Heidelberg he wrote his *Theory of Power*. In 1797 he returned secretly to Paris, where he lived in hiding, producing during this period some of his most important work. In 1803 he joined Chateaubriand on the staff of *Mercure de France*, and later, that of *Conservateur*. He devoted himself entirely to the Restoration, evading Napoleon's efforts to recruit him in his service. In 1821–2 he became Vice-President of the Parliament, 1823 Minister of State, member of the Chamber of Peers, and, at Royal behest, member of the French Academy. He was famous at this period for his speeches against the legislation to permit divorce. In 1827 Charles x appointed him chairman of the newly formed censorship board, which position he held until the Fifth Republic. After the July Revolution he withdrew to his estates and there, at the age of eighty-four, he died.

By nature he was a grave, dignified man, but with a certain inflexibility, particularly in his thought. Like Bossuet and de Maistre, he rejected the idea of the Greek spirit and Greece: 'A nation of philosophers would be a nation of inquirers, and a nation must on penalty of its decline know and not inquire.' He considered that a Christian society had no need of philosophy but rather a strong government, a disciplined army, a well-ordered administration, a pious clergy and an authoritative religion. Philosophy, together with atheism, could only cause revolution. Nor did he believe in tolerance, which he considered merely an aspect of indifference and extreme stupidity, or liberalism, which represented the transitional stage of totalitarian dictatorship.

Bonald once wrote: 'It must not be forgotten that man is forever engaged in upholding or destroying society.' Society, in his view, was 'the image of God', 'the eternal order of things applied in time to the moral and physical maintenance of mankind.' 'Society produces itself and produces man' but revolutionaries, according to Bonald, thought that 'Man produces himself and produces society'. These two aphorisms were opposed to one another 'like armies'. (This particular contrast shows how the Revolution and socialism were rooted in humanity whereas reaction based itself substantially on inhumanity.)

'How does the general will of society or the social will best find expression' on the issue of legitimate power? The legitimacy of the Bourbons was founded, for Bonald, in the 'legitimacy of things', the legitimate state of affairs, which was that of France under Louis xiv. The essence of politics was to save man from man. He was constantly exceeding his limits, dissolute in his desires and vices. The main function of the state was 'repression' because it alone could prevent 'oppression' as manifested in the tyranny of man over man. 'Society knows no rights, only duties.' 'All laws (are) against mankind.'

There are two sorts of society, political and natural. The former consists of the political professions composed of the monarchy, the priesthood, and the senatorial aristocracy. It safeguards natural society, consisting of children, women, and the nation. 'Political society is composed only of families and only the family, never the individual, is of importance to it.' Europe, ruled by a few hundred big families of good society, princes, bishops, generals, and industrial leaders closely affiliated, was the good Europe that Bonald had in mind and of which 'good France' formed the core.

The people, being the mass of artisans and peasants, was in a 'state of enduring childishness'. 'A man who lives by a wage has no political freedom.' (On the subject Spaemann has remarked, 'This sentence, which might have been written by Marx, is an unsparing criticism of civil liberties as mere formalism.') Society is a society of God and man 'for the purpose of their mutual production and maintenance'. In his strictly political theology Bonald identified the community of saints with 'civil society'. The humiliated Louis xvi became Christ. Bonald believed imperturbably in his formula for salvation; 'God will be given back to society, the King to France, and peace to the world.'

An English Catholic, belonging to the school of free and humane English Catholicism, has said that it would be a mistake to underestimate Bonald's direct influence in his own day. He did immeasurable harm. His moral and intellectual qualities brought him to the top of the Catholic party in France where he contributed to the victory of reaction which lasted for more than a century. He fathered a Church which more than once disturbed the tranquillity of Europe's chancelleries and was still in some respects a terror to honourably liberal-minded men of Acton's generation. He was the creator of that peculiar form of 'Roman Catholicism' which its enemies called 'clericalism'. The Romantic ideas were buried, but Bonald's classical ideology survived. When the sociologists adopted his ideas and adapted them to modern conditions, they acquired almost paramount sway over French Catholics, thanks to the *Action Française* and its atheist leader, Charles Maurras. Whoever recalls the condemnation of the *Action Française* in 1926, which enjoyed the support of the preponderant part of the hierarchy, knows the fierce reaction it produced. The ideology which clergy and laymen in the twentieth century had so widely made their own was still Bonald's.

LAMENNAIS AND 'L'AVENIR'

During the second decade of the nineteenth century a young French Catholic *élite* came together at La Chênaie, Brittany, the estate of Hugues Félicité Robert de Lamennais (1782–1854). Priests and laymen, future politicians like Montalembert, and preachers such as Lacordaire, all belonged to this 'Lamennais school'. Spiritual enthusiasm was the dominating feature of this group: church, state and society were to be renovated. It was an intellectual climate which was to be re-encountered later among the *Professorini*, the intellectual sector of resistance to fascism, existing in Milan and Florence in the last decade of that régime.

The first number of *L'Avenir* was published on 16 October 1830 ('until today the most outstanding Catholic organ of the press: Waldemur Gurian, 1929), and it had an important precursor in Baron d'Eckstein's *Revue Catholique* (1826–30). Eckstein, a convert of German-Danish-Jewish origin, had been fighting against the *idéophobie* – fear of intellectual problems – which then ruled the upper and middle classes, the dangerous patronage of church by state, and the link between political espionage, police and pseudo-devotion. He understood the motto of Restoration as meaning the reduction of popular education, the cultivation of ignorance on the part of a clergy who were terrified of revolution and loss of power. He saw Europe as a banking house and major industrial undertaking, with financiers and industrialists whose wish was to make a 'docile beast' of the peoples.

Lamennais was similarly concerned with the state of the Church and its connection with society. On 18 July 1830, he wrote to Comte de Senft: 'Insofar as it has indissolubly linked, the issue of religion with a power that oppresses it, the episcopy with all its might is preparing the ground for a general decline of faith.' In the same year he had already written to the Comtesse that he could not see how existing society was to continue. Most families were unable even to afford funeral costs. European society was destroying itself with wars and civil wars. The majority of bishops favoured violent subjugation of the people by the government.

The July Revolution of 1830 (for which the Archbishop of Paris had prophesied glorious victory for Charles x) was directed against both throne and altar. Churches were stormed, crosses torn down in the streets and squares. Bishops fled France to take refuge in other parts of Europe, and the power of the state was taken over by an upper middle class, which, under the aegis of the bourgeois monarch, Louis Philippe, occupied all the important positions. That was the hour at which *L'Avenir* was born.

L'Avenir proposed to the liberals a pact, 'the century's great *magna carta*', as Lamennais called it, which would contain three main points: freedom of conscience and religion, freedom of press, freedom of education. It championed universal franchise and fought against the exploitation of the working classes, women and children: 'The question of the poor is a question of life and death for society because it is a question of life and death for five-sixths of the human race' (Lamennais, 1831). *L'Avenir* implored the clergy to show itself to be the true friends of the people. It opposed excessive French nationalism and supported understanding among nations and the freedom of all. Its intercession for the Poles aroused the especial animosity of the Tsar and Metternich, both of whom intervened at Rome to persuade the new Pope, Gregory xvi, to put an end to this 'scandal'. *L'Avenir* had no more than three thousand subscribers, but a very wide distribution, with the younger clergy eagerly awaiting each fresh issue. Its powerful enemies (Gallicans, Carlists, Old Royalists of every kind) organised a campaign of denunciation and slander throughout the country. In several dioceses bishops forbade its perusal. On 15 November 1831 the paper was provisionally banned.

On 23 April 1832, thirteen French bishops signed a letter to the Pope with a request for the condemnation of *L'Avenir*. On 15 August the encyclical *Mirari Vos* was published. On 10 September, in obedience to the encyclical, *L'Avenir* closed down. Back in Brittany, Lamennais first fell victim to deep despondency, then rage. On Easter Sunday, 7 April 1833, he held his last mass, removed his vestments, and broke with the Church. In 1854, during the night of Shrove Tuesday when Paris was thronged with revellers giddy with pleasure, Lamennais died. Napoleon iii's police held back the crowds; disturbances and open demonstrations against the régime were feared during the course of the funeral. A hundred years later good Catholics perceived in the man whom Metternich had wanted burned at the stake as a heretic a forerunner of social-minded Catholicism and Christian democracy. In 1961 the Roman Catholic *Encyclopedia for Theology and Church Affairs* gave the following appreciation: 'Lamennais was a man of superlative spirit, an intrepid pioneer for the freedom of the Church, a disinterested advocate for those lacking social rights. His transcendent importance and the tragedy of his life are gaining ever stronger recognition.'

OZANAM AND THE 'ÈRE NOUVELLE'

There were thirty-four million inhabitants in France in 1842, of whom four million were beggars, four million 'needy persons' and four million 'wage-earners without any sort of saving'. The electors numbered 190,000. The July Monarchy had in no way solved the *question des prolétaires* (Lamartine's phrase) but, if anything, rendered it more acute. Sala has described the massacre of the workers at Lyons in 1834, in his *The Workmen of Lyons on 1834*, which he had hoped would serve as an appeal and warning to the ruling classes.

But, like the generation of aristocrats who surrounded the restored Bourbons, the ruling classes were sceptical. The wealthy liberal enemies of the Church had nevertheless discovered its usefulness as a political factor. In the period 1834–48, the subject of education, totally spoiled the atmosphere of public affairs. A political church accused state-run universities of 'training prostituted intellects which ... seek the glorification of prison, incest, adultery and rebellion' (Abbé Combalet). And such politicised clericalism gave rise to a fierce anti-clericalism which lasted until 1914 and was only temporarily solved by the assassination of Jaurès and the outbreak of the First World War. Ozanam compared this situation in the Church with that which it had faced in the eighth century, when, tied all too long to the decaying Byzantine imperial throne, it sought alliance with the barbarians, and thus freedom. The proletarian masses were the 'barbarians of the modern age' and it was in alliance with this proletarian force that Ozanam saw the salvation of the Church.

Antoine Frédéric Ozanam (1813–53) had a much livelier personality than is often allowed. His father, a Jewish convert and republican, was a doctor who courageously threw up a fine career in Paris to work among the poor at Lyons. His mother was no less heroic; having watched eleven of her own children die in infancy, she founded a charitable organisation, the motto of which was 'serve and help'. Ozanam himself, as a boy, saw nothing but the misery prevalent in Lyons at that time. He studied law, history and literature, and, at the age of thirty, was appointed professor at the Sorbonne. At nineteen he had already written a small book which contains the basis of his philosophical ideas, and a year later, together with seven fellow students, had founded the Society of St Vincent de Paul: 'We are too young to be able to intervene in the social struggle. Before we engage ourselves on behalf of the entire community, we can try to help a few individuals.' He and his companions, all of middle-class families, went among the proletariat to try and gather experience.

In the years between 1832 and 1848 small groups of Catholic social reformers had been hard at work, often in the face of considerable hostility. It was partly as a result of this that in February 1848, the people, although still respecting religion as a whole, rebelled against secular authority. Priests were invited to bless the trees of liberty, and the Bishop of Paris,

Affre, followed by the senior clergy, welcomed the new government. Right-wing diehards, however, were only too ready to see in this the spread of communism and denounced the weakness of the Pope Pius IX, 'the Louis XIV of the Papacy'.

Catholicism's greatest chance of the nineteenth century was thrown away by the political leaders of the Catholic majority, who took the side of the middle classes against the people. It was a time for antagonism even within the party. Those associated with *L'Avenir* turned against each other, only a few rallying round Lacordaire and Ozanam. The overwhelming majority, split between various royalist and middle-class camps, found their main spokesman in Montalembert. A man with little regard for democracy, he considered that the lesson of the church could be summed up in two words, *s'abstenir et respecter*: that is, the poor should respect other people's property, law and order. He preached a gospel of suffering on earth and recompense in heaven, which met with immense applause.

Ere Nouvelle was founded in March, 1848, by Ozanam, Lacordaire and Abbé Maret. In the first issue, of 15 April, Lacordaire declared that in France there existed 'Two victorious forces . . .: the nation and religion, the people and Jesus Christ. If they part company, we are lost. If they understand each other, we are saved.' The paper implored Catholics to show discernment in social questions and to appreciate the acute misery of the poor. It maintained that the clergy should relinquish their rich livings and devote themselves to the care of the masses, sentiments which received public approval from the archbishop of Paris. By June *Ere Nouvelle* had reached an edition of twenty thousand copies. Yet despite its popularity, the Catholic Right began a campaign against it, immediately after publication, which lasted until its final annihilation.

In 1848 the Catholics of Rouen had unanimously elected to the National Assembly a firm believer in good order, a confirmed atheist, Adolphe Thiers, who was determined to put an end to the disorders provoked by the working classes. The communist spectre was evoked; Catholics were convinced that war was a suitable fate for the proletariat. In 1848 came civil war. Cavaignac had the Parisian workers mown down, and the Archbishop of Paris was killed by a stray shot, whilst trying to mediate between the barricades. Success was considered the victory of *France honnête* over *La France anarchique et corrompue*. There was general rejoicing among the Catholic Right, while Lamennais wrote 'These are the saturnalia of reaction and the bloody grave of the Republic'.

The cannonades of June 1848 had destroyed not only the hopes of February and March, but Ozanam's hopes of an alliance between Church and proletariat. That became clear when on 22 September the Socialist *L'Emancipation* described the enemies of the people as 'capitalism and the priests'. In September and October, *Ere Nouvelle* published a series of essays by Ozanam on *The Origins of Socialism, The Causes of Poverty, On Public Aid*, and *To the Prosperous*. He appealed to his wealthy co-religionists and the priests to join him in his 'crusade of love' and to tackle the social question frankly and courageously. His enemies decided that the time had come to put an end to this 'Jacobin' periodical, and proceeded to do so.

The Marquis de La Rochejacquelin put himself forward as a generous patron who wanted to ensure the economic future of *Ere Nouvelle*. After giving his word of honour as a gentleman that not a single member of the editorial staff would be dismissed nor the spirit of the paper changed, it passed into his hands. He took charge on 31 March 1849. Next day he threw out every one of the editorial staff, wrote a leading article as public rebuttal of the spirit of the paper, and, on 9 April, ceased its publication altogether. Sued, the noble Marquis paid thirty per cent of the agreed purchase price. On 17 May Lacordaire declared that the manœuvres of Montalembert and his party had been even more perfidious than those formerly employed against *L'Avenir*.

It seemed, as though the sacrifices made by the men of *Ere Nouvelle* had been to no purpose. Shortly before the end of the Republic, on 8 April 1851, Ozanam wrote to a friend, 'We (Catholics) do not have enough faith. We always want to restore religion by political means. We dream of a Constantine who will, at one stroke and with a single effort, bring back the nations into their stall. . . . An abyss is opening up. . . . '

CATHOLICS IN SEARCH OF DICTATORS

The life of Henri Lacordaire (1802–61), rich in its disappointments and the persecution which dogged him, belongs to Church history. Speaking from the pulpit of Notre-Dame at Paris (from 1835, with certain breaks, until 1851, the end of the Republic), he pleaded with French Catholics, magnificently, movingly, and in vain, to regard themselves also as the champion of their enemies. His speech in 1847 on the Irish independence fighter Daniel O'Connell was a monumental delineation of the spirituality and political inspiration of the men who stood behind the *Ere Nouvelle*:

He who serves freedom must demand it equally and effectively for all. Not only for his own party, but for that of his opponents. Not only for his own religion, but for all religions. Not only for his own country, but for the whole world. Mankind is one and its rights are everywhere the same, even though the practice of them varies according to the current state of morality and spirit. Whoever excepts one single individual from his demand for justice, whoever acquiesces in the bondage of one single individual, black or white, . . . is no upright man and does not deserve to be a brother-in-arms in mankind's sacred cause. Public conscience will always reject a man who demands exclusive freedom or is even indifferent to the rights of others. . . . That was never so with O'Connell. Never in the course of fifty years did his language lose the insuperable charm of frankness. His voice trembled for the rights of others as for his own. Its

257

accusation of every subjugation, from whatever quarter it came and upon whomever it fell, was clearly to be heard. Thereby he attracted to his cause – the cause of Ireland – spirits who were divided from his by chasms of opinion. Hands were stretched out to him in fraternity from the remotest parts of the world. For in the heart of the upright man who speaks for all, and in doing so seems sometimes even to speak against himself, there is an invincible logical and moral superiority which almost infallibly invokes reciprocity of feeling. Catholics, understand it well: if it is freedom for yourselves that you demand, then you must demand it for all people in all climes. If it is only for yourselves that you want it, you will never obtain it. Concede it where you are masters, so that it may be given you where you are slaves!

But this great doctrine, plea, and warning fell both then and later on deaf ears, as Catholicism's political leaders after 1848, Montalembert and Comte de Falloux made plain. 'Society is turning back to religion. Who leads this return? The upper classes. And so it must be, if this return is to be effective and enduring' (Falloux). The nation must 'be defended against the greed of the lower classes'. 'Stern war must be waged against Socialism', which threatens to destroy society (Montalembert, 22 May 1850). It was a topic of many Catholic pamphlets at the time. The writings of Wallon, Louis Reybaud, and Romieu-Trimalcion (whom Napoleon III was to appoint director of the Academie des Beaux-Arts) around 1850 anticipated the hate-filled atmosphere of the Dreyfus period. *Era of Caesars*, by Romieu-Trimalcion, was truly prophetic and indicative of what was desired.

Romieu saw salvation solely in 'the Church and the Army'. 'I have made my choice between guns and parleys.' The Army must first subjugate the people; afterwards it can be sent to Church, for 'a people which has been robbed of its faith will never voluntarily reconcile itself to its work-burdened poverty'. Personally the arch-Catholic Romieu was a Voltairean who admired Julian the Apostate, an Emperor who had had to deal with Christians 'preaching fraternity and especially equality like sectarians' (in other words, 'left-wing' and 'red' Christians like Ozanam and his fellows). Such individuals are ruinous to good order. It was regrettable that Switzerland, exercising a deplorable attraction, lay so close to France. But at least Russia could be relied on. Russia was Europe's best force for order, the Tsar representing a splendid combination of political power and spiritual authority. 'Guns alone can settle the problems of our century and they must settle them, even though they may have to come from Russia!'

Romieu's writing reflected the hysterical fear of revolution and vengeance for the massacre of 1848. It was also a reply to Donoso Cortés' speech, 'On the Situation of Europe in General', made in the Spanish Cortes on 30 January 1850. 'Tsar Nicholas I, Frederick William IV, Louis Napoleon, Metternich, Schelling and Ranke were under its spell. Translations into French, Spanish and Italian followed speedily on one another.' In Paris fourteen thousand copies were distributed. Together with Cortés' speech of 4 January 1849 about dictatorship, this was the most impressive and influential documentation of the fear which held Catholics in its grip after 1848. Cortés' own *Angst* was compounded of old Spanish Manichaean elements and the depression arising from his feeling of guilt at his suppressed homosexual tendencies: he accused himself of loving his brother more than was natural.

Donoso Cortés' abysmal pessimism impelled him to his frontal attack on nineteenth-century Europe. The people, he maintained, had become impossible to govern and the standing armies were civilisation's sole prop against relapse into barbarism. (That he was anything but a militarist himself is proved by his phrase 'A soldier is a slave in uniform'.) 'Freedom is dead.' The decay of religion began with Constantine. The Lutheran revolution was nothing but a gigantic infamy. A religious revival, were it possible, would be the only road of escape. It is here that Cortés reveals the secret shared by all political reactionaries: he did *not* believe in a religious revival. That was why the masses could be kept in place only by a dictatorship of armed force which alone could help against the 'satanic presumption' of the nineteenth century, against socialism and communism, against 'the dagger' which he had seen employed at Rome in 1848 to facilitate seizure of power. In 1852 Cortés wrote for Cardinal Fornai a memorandum, *Principal Current Errors According to Their Origin and Causes*, which provided important groundwork for the papal *Syllabus* of 1864. So Army and Church stood side by side, civilisation's sole representatives. Spain was Europe's oasis.

On 2 December 1851 the highly-talented and debt-ridden gambler Louis Napoleon seized power. In many respects his government can be designated the first Fascist régime, a prototype of Fascist propaganda and operation. Over twenty-six thousand arrests ensured the success of his *coup*. Nearly ten thousand individuals were deported as political prisoners to Africa or Devil's Island; 2,804 were held in France – relatively small numbers, by twentieth-century standards but large enough to signal the death of freedom. Montalembert summoned Catholics to support the election of Napoleon III in an open letter to Veuillot, published in *Univers* on 14 December 1851. He appealed to them in the name of defence of the Church, their womenfolk, and their families. 'For society against Socialism, for Catholicism against revolution!'

Napoleon III's reward included Montalembert's admission to the Académie Française. His inaugural address described the revolutionary disease which had affected France since 1789, adding (an attack on Lacordaire and Ozanam). 'Nobody worth taking seriously will pay any more regard to those new systems which claimed to derive democracy from Catholicism and to be able to see a commentary on the Gospels in revolution.' 'Democracy' is 'the universal explosion of presumption'. Forward! 'For Catholicism and against democracy!' In his reply to the address, Guizot the Protestant praised Montalembert's *belle docilité chrétienne*.

Bishops extolled Napoleon III as 'the instrument of Providence' and

Pater Ventura, during his Lent sermon in the chapel of the Tuileries, likened the resurrection of the Empire to that of Christ. On 28 January 1854 Veuillot, in the spirit of Cortés, proudly declared that the safety of the state rested with two allied armies: that of four-hundred-thousand soldiers and that of forty thousand priests, supplemented by fifty thousand nuns. Indeed Veuillot preached hate so vehemently that some bishops were taken aback and Montalembert began to regret the alliance between Catholicism and absolutism. He genuinely wanted to do penance, exposed Veuillot's 'scandalous teaching', and in a speech at Malines on 21 August 1863 confessed his alarm at Catholicism's self-betrayal. If a fresh revolution were to occur, the thought of what atonement the clergy would have to make was frightening.

That was the situation in 1870. Defeat in the war that was meant to solve all social problems broke the dam of twenty years' hate of the Church. In Parisian clubs revolutionaries called for the burning at the stake of priests and the destruction of all churches. None the less fifty-five out of the capital's sixty-seven churches remained open during the Commune. Thiers, in collaboration with Bismarck, drowned the Commune in blood. The *Journal des Débats* proclaimed the extermination of the Communards more important than victory against Prussia: 'Our Army has avenged its misfortunes through an inestimably great triumph.' Success in civil war – that was the Army's sacred mission!

The successful bourgeoisie at this point made a deal with popular anti-clericalism as it had previously done with clericalism. Its old ally, the Church, now useless, was abandoned to popular venom. And yet still the social problem was not solved, for all that Gambetta might say, 'There is no social problem. . . . Social evil, that is clericalism.'

The effect on the Catholics was to create desperate fears, which found relief in a mania for miracles. Lourdes, in its historical perspective, may be seen as an attempt at healing the national neuroses and fears of the Catholics. They placed all their hopes in the recovery of a monarch, or, as substitute, a dictator. Cardinal de Bonnechose tried hard to persuade Marshal MacMahon to perform a *coup d'état*, though in vain. This same prelate considered that compulsory primary education would be a public catastrophe.

It was at this stage that Pope Leo XIII began his efforts to reconcile French Catholics with the century and the state, in face of a majority opposition from France's cardinals and bishops. The old beliefs that the Republic was 'evil and satanic' were rejuvenated: to be a Catholic was to be a counter-revolutionary. The Pope's imploring admonitions (the encyclicals *Nobilissima Gallorum*, 1884, and *Immortale Dei*, 1885), were rejected. Anti-republican Catholicism became associated with anti-Semitism, and Catholics, inspired by these movements, tried to persuade General Boulanger to undertake a *coup d'état*. Their rage against the Pope was turned against his spokesman, Cardinal Lavigerie, who demanded positive affirmation of the Republic by Catholic France. The Catholic and Royalist Press, *Soleil, Patrie, Gaullois, Français, Moniteur*, was in an uproar. The Cardinal was regarded as a traitor.

In December, 1893, Pope Leo XIII wrote a letter to Germain, Bishop of Coutances, the contents of which were intended for the entire French episcopy: 'Advise your priests not to immure themselves within the walls of their churches and presbyteries, but to go among the people and whole-heartedly to concern themselves with the workers, the poor and the children. . . . The chasm between the priests and the people must be closed.'

THE DREYFUS AFFAIR

This *cause célèbre* was both the result of the royalist, anti-semitic Catholic Right's antagonism to the Catholic Social movement, and a welcome release for that antagonism. Even in our own day it has retained its importance, not merely in relation to the internal condition of France, but for the impressive evidence it reveals, in Armin Möhler's words, 'that France was from the outset of the nineteenth century the real country of origin for those right-wing political trends which evolved from the old conservatism via revolutionary nationalism into Fascist totalitarianism. France was the country of the fully matured right-wing philosophies of de Maistre, Bonald, and Maurras. The outstanding intellectual fathers of (those) totalitarian systems – Gobineau, Drumont and Georges Sorel – were Frenchmen. That is not all. In political practice too France was the most important field of experiment for the Right. Bonapartism and Boulangism are the real forerunners of modern Fascism. In the Dreyfus crisis there was seen the first anti-Semitic mass movement which differed fundamentally form earlier pogroms.' The first thing that must be appreciated is that the Dreyfus Affair, 'by no means concluded, is today still operative, part of a movement whose end cannot be fortold'.

Perhaps the classic example of this desire for extermination, for annihilation on the part of the Catholic anti-Semitic Right, occurs in a speech given by Father Didon during a prize-giving at his educational academy:

> When I speak of the necessity of power for a nation, let me emphasise that I mean naked force does not waver . . . and whose finest embodiment is the army. Of it can be said what is claimed for artillery, that it is the ultimate argument of the body politic and of nations. . . . The enemy is intellectualism, pretending to hold force in contempt, and the civilian order of things, trying to subordinate the army to itself. When the art of persuasion fails and love is exhausted, then the sword must be drawn, terror spread, heads fly, effective action taken and punishment meted out.

And on the 19 July 1898 he demanded the extermination of all Jews and enemies of France.

To the Catholic Right, which represented the vast body of French Catholics, Captain Dreyfus was a matter of indifference. It wanted nothing to do with him, and it was in vain that Mathieu Dreyfus appealed to Cardinal Richard, Archbishop of Paris, for the Church declined to intervene on the matter of legal revision. The basis of this issue was the need to settle accounts, once and for all, with the satanic Republic; to protect the army, which was so necessary to the nation and the Church, from 'insult'; to prepare the way for the success of a *coup d'état* by a military man (openly demanded, for example, in *Croix*, 19 January 1899). And the method to be used in order to stir the enthusiasm of the masses was anti-Semitism, although the majority of Frenchmen had, at that time, never personally encountered a Jew. If it were, however, possible to create in the minds of the masses the notion of the Jew as the prototype of traitor, German, freemason, Antichrist, the final struggle for power could begin. On 5 February 1898 in *La Civiltà Cattolica* appears the sentence: 'The Jew was created by God to act as spy wherever treason is brewing.' The periodical had been created to espouse the cause of Curial Absolutism and centralism. It fought against Modernism and against the Jewish-German-republican-masonic conspiracy incarnate in Dreyfus. Two points are manifest. The Dreyfus Affair was an affair of European Catholicism. The infallible army was none other than the infallible political Church on which the religious and political hopes of 'good Frenchmen' were pinned.

Alfred Dreyfus was born on 9 October 1859 the youngest son of a rich Jewish family at Mulhouse. He was twelve when Alsace was annexed to Germany, and his father emigrated to France. He was commissioned in 1892, and, as he admits, had but one objective in his life, 'vengeance on the infamous robber who has seized our beloved Alsace'. To find himself convicted of high treason seemed incredible. Despite the general dislike for him which was felt even by his well-wishers, he nevertheless compelled the respect of Barrès, his mortal enemy, who wrotes of the trial. 'Judas marches too well. . . . As he approached us, cap deep down over his brow, pince-nez on his racial nose, countenance severe and defiant, he called out, no, what am I saying, ordered, in an intolerable tone, "Tell all France that I am innocent!" '

The Dreyfus Affair was started by the rabid anti-Semitism of Major Marie-Charles-Ferdinand Walsin Esterhazy, a man of aristocratic origins, the tool of Colonel Henry of the General Staff, a spy, counter-spy, document forger, liar and slanderer, who died in England in 1923. He was a man of unstable and unhappy temperament, who indulged in dreams of pillage, assault and mass murder. He is, in fact, a symbol of a peculiar dialectic in neurotic nineteenth- and twentieth-century nationalism. Just as neurotic Christian anti-Semitism contains an element of hatred for Christ, so this nationalism had an element of hatred of its own nation. His loathing, on the one hand of the General Staff, on the other of Jews, increased during the Dreyfus Affair. He told a British journalist in February, 1898: 'It is almost impossible that this drama should end without violence. A hundred thousand corpses will lie in the streets of Paris. . . . As far as I am concerned, I ask nothing better than to lead my regiment against the Parisian Jews. I would slaughter them like rabbits, without hate or anger, in the public interest.' This event appears all the more obviously as a prologue to the orgies of

National Socialism in that Esterhazy spoke and acted on behalf of the whole French Right and the majority of French Catholics.

During this period Esterhazy remained in constant touch with Edouard Drumont, who put the paper, *Libre Parole*, at his disposal at all decisive moments. It was this paper which first designated Dreyfus a 'traitor', and on the so-called suicide of Hubert-Joseph Henry, the principal forger of documents incriminating Dreyfus, demanded the erection of a monument to him as a national hero. Doubtless Henry really did believe that his perjuries and forgery were serving his country, and the list of subscribers to the monument fund included the names of most of the important members of the aristocracy, as well as those of thirty-two generals and several hundred priests. The sentiments which accompanied the subscriptions were, to a degree, crude.

The Catholics' pact with the Devil (Péguy) and the alliance of conservative forces with the vulgar herd – two truly remarkable phenomena – were cemented with the aid of anti-Semitism and a feverish nationalism. French Catholicism succumbed to the great temptation of believing that, by means of anti-semitism, it could bind to itself, politically and religiously, the alienated masses. The vast majority of Catholics shared the view of the *La Civiltà Cattolica* which on 5 February 1898 quoted in support of its arguments the (forged) *Protocols of the Elders of Zion*, painting a picture of poor Christian France in the clutches of a German-Jewish-Protestant-freemason conspiracy. 'The Protestants have made common cause with the Jews. . . . The money comes primarily from Germany. *Pecuniae obediunt omnia* is the principle of the Jews. In every country of Europe they have bought bribable individuals and papers.'

The liberal pontificate of Leo XIII was incapable of rendering null this trend of a whole century. Under his totally unbending successor, Pius x, extremist clericalism allied itself to extremist nationalism, whose leader, Charles Maurras, was an unambiguous atheist. In January 1914 seven of his books and also his newspaper *Action Française* were put on the Index, but publication of the decree did not occur because the Pope reserved this to himself. Maurras of his own accord reported an utterance of Pius x which explains this policy: *Damnabiris, non damnandus* was what the Pope said of him.

Maurras possessed influential adherents in Rome, cardinals and bishops, and in France he had powerful patrons among the senior episcopacy. The Dreyfus Affair paved the way for the Pétain régime which delivered the Jews of France into the hands of Hitler's executioners. The first nuncio to the first post-Vichy French government, Cardinal Roncalli, subsequently Pope John XXIII, had no easy task, for the French Head of State demanded the removal of the preponderant portion of the French episcopacy from its dioceses. This episcopacy had, in its loyalty to Vichy, remained true to the traditions of the Dreyfus era.

On the front page of *L'Aurore*, on 13 January 1898 *J'Accuse* was published, Emile Zola's open letter to the president of the Republic. A lonely individual, he entered the lists against the strongest forces in France. As the loser in proceedings he brought upon himself, he finally fled to England to avoid imprisonment. The faith of the 'atheists', 'socialists' and 'unbelievers', which evolved in the years of struggle for justice and truth after the Dreyfus case, seemed ridiculous to their opponents who relied, quite cynically, 'only on themselves, on their power, their cunning, the superiority of their weapons'. Equally ridiculous, in their minds, was Zola, when he wrote, so simply, 'Bury the truth in the ground and it will develop such explosive force that, on the day it frees itself, it will destroy all around it.'

The honour of having cleared the way for the struggle for truth must belong to an insignificant little Jew who made his way laboriously through mountains of lies and forgeries, and paid for their publication out of his own pocket – Bernard-Lazare. He broke down under the effort, and was escorted to the grave by only a few Jews, loyal to the man who had defended them, a small number of friends, and bourgeois and Péguy.

HOPE IN FRANCE: CHARLES PÉGUY

Péguy had seen in the atheist Bernard-Lazare a man filled with the spirit of God, who bore unmistakable traits of genuine sanctity. 'I still feel his short-sighted gaze resting on me. I still see his so intelligent, benevolent, imperturbably clear and radiant expression, from which there emanated inexhaustible understanding, proven goodness.' He possessed 'a heart that bled for all the world's ghettos, and perhaps still more for open ghettos like Paris, than for closed ones. . . . A heart that bled for Rumania, Turkey, Russia and Algeria, for America and Hungary, wheresoever the Jew was persecuted, which, in a broad sense, means everywhere; a heart that bled for the Orient, for the Occident, for Islam and Christendom.' 'His heart was consumed by a fire, the fire of his people; he himself a blazing spirit; the glowing coal was on the lip of the prophet.'

Yet this delineation of the Jewish atheist Bernard-Lazare can equally be applied, in entirety, to its author, Charles Péguy (1873–1914). He was the prophet who wanted to open for France and the Church, the door to the twentieth century and to fellow-feeling. Everything that has been really alert, healthy, and fertile in the spirit and soul of French Catholicism during the twentieth century owes its inspiration to sparks struck by Péguy.

It was the Dreyfus Affair that first made Péguy conscious of his mission, and maybe he understood the significance of the case better than anyone else: 'It needs to be said, and with due solemnity, that the Dreyfus Affair was something special. It was an extremely important crisis for three historic entities which are themselves of the greatest importance': the history of Israel, the history of France, and the history of Christendom.

André Gide's famous aphorism, 'Catholics do not care for the truth', relates to the fact that Catholics very often seem totally incapable of being receptive to all facets of the truth. They recognise, like the men of *Vérité*

Française, only their own truth. Péguy, on the other hand, was a genuine 'witness of truth', recognising that the concealment of one iota of the truth of the Dreyfus Affair was capable of casting 'an entire nation into the condition of mortal sin'. He knew that the incapacity of Catholicism to face the bitterness of truth was fatal to itself.

Péguy's father, a master joiner at Orléans, had died shortly after his birth and his mother and grandmother had had to work to keep the family. At the age of sixteen he became an atheist-socialist, determined to fight for mankind's freedom and well-being. Although an atheist, he was elected head of one of the centres of Ozanam's Society of St Vincent de Paul. He made it a condition that he would not join the working sessions until after the prayer with which each meeting opened. His primary intellectual guides were Kant, Karl Marx and Ernest Renan. At the École Normale Supérieure he studied philosophy under Bergson which influenced his whole outlook. His contacts with Bernard-Lazare and others of his race opened Péguy's eyes spiritually and physically to the sufferings of mankind. He discovered that Jesus was a Jew and His incarnation 'true and complete', as well as the fact that the Jew and Man Jesus stands in indivisible solidarity with all men. A Christian's duty is to be brother to all his fellow-men.

In the Dreyfus Affair he underwent the painful experience which the outstanding Catholic writer Julien Green in 1944 summarised in the statement: 'Fighting against Divine love is the Christian's main occupation.' Péguy put it another way: Because they love no human beings, they believe that they love God. This sort of Catholicism was formulated in France around 1960 as a 'community of qualm and hate'. Péguy, however, embodied the Sophoclean principle that man is on earth to join in loving, not hating, his fellow-men. He rejected every kind of dogmatism. He knew that exorbitant human sacrifices were demanded 'in the name of unity and authority'. That was how he came to be found in January 1900, *Les Cahiers de la Quinzaine* as the mouthpiece of a free socialism which was to pave the way for the civilisation of the future. A handful of individuals, most of them Dreyfusards, joined him. At the same time, in a slow and painful process, Péguy worked towards recovery of the Catholic faith which still existed deep within him.

He took up the challenge presented by the Christian doctrine of hell, with its everlasting punishments. The more strongly he felt himself to be Catholic, the more passionately was he confirmed in his originally socialist-inspired conviction that 'We are solidly on the side of the damned. We shall not tolerate the inhuman treatment of men. We shall not tolerate that men are torn away from the gates of a *polis*. That is the great purpose which inspires us. We shall not tolerate any exception, whether in Heaven or on earth. An eternity of living death is a piece of perverse, inverted imagination.' 'Hell may or may not have been invented to deter sinners, but its effect has been far more to abash the best of Christians.' 'What today is absolutely certain is that the demand for belief in everlasting punishment has been the weightiest reason among the majority of serious Catholics for apostasy.'

Belief in hell had deadened Christians, destroying their alertness to the solidarity that exists between all men and all living things. It was therefore scarcely surprising that they overlooked the actual hell that they had helped to create, the hell of hate and the 'hell of money', the hell where man could no longer remain human, 'this modern hell wherein everyone who does not take a hand in the game loses'. He fought his way through to a faith in hope which surpassed not only the belief of the middle classes in progress, but also the Catholic hostility to progress. He viewed the history of mankind as the history of God's hope in man. For man to hope was to keep pace with the Creation's perpetual renewal. He who hoped lived wholly in the present, the radiant present of God and the present of man. Péguy resumed, in his own way, the great praise of the present that had been sung by Meister Eckhart and his contemporary Thérèse de Lisieux and (outside the Christian ambit) also by Nietzsche.

After 1905 Péguy lived in constant anticipation of war and, facing that issue, he reflected on fresh aspects of 'the infinite reality of the eternally young God'. 'The civil war in the Church' and a 'treasonous clergy' had betrayed hope and love. France was 'poisoned' through and through, by greed for money and power as well as by its professional politicians. The Socialists too had betrayed the revolution of man, the beauty of which left room for man's creative forces to extend themselves. To work and to be creative was to prove that Catholicism was an open road into an unobstructed future.

THE CHURCH IN CONFLICT

Péguy was called to the colours on 1 August 1914. He laid down his pen in mid-sentence. His last words were devoted to a defence of Bergson against the Roman bureaucrats, against the theologians, and against the fabricators of a system which had made of the Church 'an abortion in time'. He was killed in action on 5 September 1914.

The scene shifted to German-occupied Belgium during the First World War. At Ghent a lawyer fell under suspicion of conspiracy against the Occupation Authorities. A house-search was ordered. The officer in charge, a reservist and a member of a Catholic order, found hundreds of letters, memoranda, and documents. Most of them were marked 'Confidential, to be burnt'. The officer, on the instruction of his superiors, prepared a list of the pseudonyms and code-words involved. He kept one copy for himself and after 1920 published a part of his material as *The Jonikx Papers*. (Jonikx had been the name of the lawyer.)

What had been found was no less than a secret archive of those Catholics who, as a sort of Catholic freemasonry, had their centre in the *Sodalitium Pianum* of Monsignor Umberto Benigni at Rome. Benigni enjoyed the especial favour of Pope Pius x and was a very well-received guest in the home of Cardinal Merry del Val. From Rome he conducted, with the assistance of his collaborators at Paris, Vienna, Brussels, Milan, Cologne, Berlin, and so on, his campaigns of denunciation and espionage, preparing the political and ecclesiastical operations against professors and priests, theologians and laymen who were to be 'unmasked' as dangerous heretics because they were 'Modernists'. A centre of a similar nature was to be found at Lyons in the 1950s.

The witch-hunts organised by Monsignor Benigni, lasting in their initial stage until 1914, were themselves the product of a process set in motion by Gregory XVI's encyclical *Mirari Vos* in 1832. Henceforward the representatives of an outlook moulded at least two and a half thousand years earlier, came into violent conflict with the representatives of an outlook shaped by the nineteenth century. Gregory XVI, Pius IX, and Pius X knew that they must defend to the last a sacred and inalienable doctrine of the Church; the Modernists and the very various reformers, philosophers, theologians, and historians, drawn into the process of condemnation, obeyed the demands of conscience formed by the scientific outlook of their day.

The old Roman tradition, upheld by the Church in its entirety, understood right and religion, religion and politics, the authority of God and the authority of His deputy as existing in intimate connection with one another. Every prayer, every step, every gesture, every word during the ritual of Divine Service had to be observed with meticulous exactitude. The ritual would lose its redemptive power, were it to be altered one iota. The liturgy of the Roman Church transmitted the religious and political tradition of late antiquity. The pope, as Christ's deputy, was possessed of the keys to the kingdom of Heaven and of the power to damn. His assistants in the world were the Christian princes. Their task was to annihilate rebels and to wage wars in the service of God and the pope. *Bellum Deo auctore* was first proclaimed by St Augustine, who, after a long mental struggle, convinced himself of the justification for faith by coercion. The first defence for the burning down of a synagogue comes from St Ambrose. War was first considered a suitable missionary weapon by Gregory the Great. The efforts of Gregory XVI to obtain agreements with Metternich and the Tsar were as much in line with the illustrious, thousand-year-old tradition as were the plans for, and actual conclusions of, concordats of the papal Secretary of State, Cardinal Pacelli, subsequently Pope Pius XII.

NINETEENTH-CENTURY PAPAL VERDICTS*

Mirari Vos opened with the declaration that the pope had on accession to office (Gregory XVI was elected in 1831) immediately been cast into such a

---

* The authority for the quotations in this section is a collection of documents, *Man and Community in Christian Sight*, published in German at Fribourg in 1945. (A French edition had already appeared a year earlier.) The first chapter, 'The Eternal Foundations of Society and Modern Man', began with the encyclical *Mirari Vos* of 1832 and was followed by the papal circular letters *Quanta Cura* and the *Syllabus* both of 1864. Roman Catholic students and academic bodies received copies 'as a present from His Holiness Pope Pius XII'.

storm-tossed sea that, if God had not intervened, he would surely, thanks to the malevolent conspiracy of the godless, have drowned. He had seen the waters of revolution reaching to the threshold of God's citadel and had observed the licentiousness of the insurgents, who had not been deterred from bringing the signs of battle once more into papal proximity. There had remained no choice other than finally to use the rod against the obduracy of such people who had learnt nothing from the prolonged, merciful leniency with which the Church had treated them. The downfall of public order was in sight and the overthrow of all legal power approaching, a situation to be ascribed to the conspiratorial societies which were a focus for every heresy and blasphemy there had ever been. Help and protection could be provided only by the Holy See.

Injustice, impudent science, and unbridled freedom were celebrating insolent victories. Indifference and a passion for innovation went hand in hand. Pernicious indifference was the source of the utterly deluded opinion that all should enjoy freedom of conscience, an error which prepared the way for that excessive and unlimited liberty of opinions the spread of which could do nothing but harm to Church and State. It was a fact known since ancient times, and confirmed by experience, that states which had been rich, mighty, and renowned could be pitifully brought down by one specific evil – unchecked freedom of opinion, freedom of speech, passion for innovation. Into the same category could be brought that freedom which could not be sufficiently condemned and abhorred, a freedom which many promoted with utmost criminal zeal – the freedom to trade in books. What sensible person would ever argue that poisons should be accessible to all because perhaps there existed an elixir of life? Even in the days of the Apostles books had been publicly burned, and the evils of error would never be annihilated until their sources had been consigned to the flames.

The entire last part of the encyclical was devoted to the defence of established rulers and the condemnation of those who try to rob them of their authority. The loyalty of the ancient Christians towards the heathen Roman emperors was emphasised in order to argue that this glorious example, resulting necessarily from the sacred prescriptions of Christian religion, proved the guilt of those who, with abhorrent impertinence and malevolence, gave themselves wholly over to jarring and tearing down all the rights of authority and to leading the peoples, under the pretence of freedom, into slavery. This aim was identical with the criminal fantasies and intrigues of the Waldensians, the followers of Wyclif, and other sons of Belial, scandalous scum of humanity, justly placed under the anathema of the Holy See. These rebels together with Luther were ready to grasp every nefarious means to attain more easily and swiftly their purpose of being, above all, free.

Eighty years after the American Declaration of Independence and forty years after the French Revolution, regardless of the Catholic Poles under the yoke of the Tsar and the Christian Greeks under the dominion of the Sultan, Gregory XVI looked to the 'Princes' as sole protectors of the sacred walls of sacred Rome. The papal altercation with the nineteenth century, conducted in the spirit of an outlook that had been shaped in the millennium *preceding* Christ, reached, however, a monumental climax in Pius IX's *Quanta Cura* and the *Syllabus*, both issued on 8 December 1864.

The Pope quoted approvingly that passage in the encyclical of his predecessor where the demand for freedom of conscience had been labelled 'madness'. Paragraph Four of the *Syllabus* condemned in one sentence the 'plagues' of socialism, communism, secret societies, Bible societies, and clerical-liberal societies. Bishops were instructed to take up the sword of the spirit against them. Previous paragraphs had dealt equally negatively with 'pantheism, naturalism, and total rationalism', 'moderated rationalism', the recognition of other religions as possible roads to salvation and the notion of Protestantism as a form of the true Christian faith. The succeeding paragraphs dealt with numerous 'errors concerning the Church and her rights', the relations between the state, society, and the Church, and Christian marriage. Two points may retain particular interest for the present day. One is the condemnation of the mistaken notion that an excess arbitrariness on the part of the popes had been responsible for the division into the Churches of East and West. The second is the condemnation of the right of resistance to authority. This could affect not only Poles, Greeks, Italians, and others during the nineteenth century, but also German Catholics who were against the Hitler régime which had met with concordat endorsement.

The last paragraph but one of the *Syllabus* rounded trenchantly on every doubt relating to the necessity of the papal state's existence, and particularly the theory that abolition of the Holy See's temporal power would contribute immensely to the liberty and happiness of the Church. The last paragraph dealt with certain fundamental errors of 'contemporary liberalism'. The document closed with condemnation of the idea that the pope could and should reconcile himself to and make friends with progress and liberal trends of thought.

On 20 June 1888, in his circular letter *Libertas praestantissimum,* Pope Leo XIII confirmed in essence the solemn pronouncements of his predecessors, although he modified certain points. He remarked that it scarcely needed mention that unrestricted freedom of speech and the Press could find no justification and that it could never be sanctioned that freedom of thought, of the Press, of teaching, and indiscriminate freedom of religion should be promoted, defended, or allowed as though they were rights conferred on man by nature.

Particularly important in this connection was Leo XIII's encyclical against freemasonry, 'the secret precursor of liberalism' in *Humanum Genus*, dated 20 April 1884. Five years later to the day Adolf Hitler was born. The latter's interpretation of liberalism, democracy, and authority can, like Mussolini's interpretation of the authority of his black-shirted Party Church, be treated as a perversion of Curial authoritarian outlook. The fundamental similarities cannot, however, be overlooked.

Humanum Genus began with a version of the world's state of affairs which St Augustine had adopted from Tyconius (the Donatist bishop) and nine-teenth-century reactionaries had applied so splendidly to their own age. Ever since the Fall, wrote the Pope, mankind had been split into two hostile parties, one being that of the true Church of Christ and the other that of Satan. The second of these had currently entered into alliance with the widespread and well-organised league of so-called freemasons, under whose guidance and with whose help an embittered battle was being fought against the righteous. Without even trying to hide their objectives, they were impudently encouraging each other in hatred of God and frankly seeking the Church's downfall. The freemasons were the 'arch-enemies' of the 'Christian people', a sect not merely illegal but downright dangerous to the state. They were out to destroy all order and discipline, all authority, all family bonds, all marital ties. Upheaval and destruction were, however, the plainly-avowed aim of most of the Socialist and Communist cliques, linked as they were to one another, and freemasons should not venture to assert that they had nothing to do with the socialist's projects. Not only did they thoroughly aid and abet them, but shared their main doctrines.

This last claim was a risky one, but intelligible as part of an ecclesiastical concept deriving from the conviction that freemasonry was basically and intrinsically vicious and shameful. What was called liberty, equality, and fraternity was, from this perspective, simply a tissue of lies and deceit meant to lead nations astray. According to this encyclical of 1884 there existed a conspiracy of infernal sects akin to that proclaimed in the late eighteenth and early nineteenth centuries by French *abbés*, German theologians, and Metternich. Under the spell of a theological interpretation of history a macabre, over-simplified picture was drawn which paid no attention what-ever to the highly differentiated historical truth. This league of arch-enemies of the human race included not only Mozart, Goethe, Schiller, and members of the artistic and intellectual *élite* of the eighteenth and nineteenth centuries but kings and emperors too, not to mention (around 1884) a majority of Anglican bishops and dignitaries and a fair proportion of the French bourgeoisie, which sent its daughters to convent schools and had long been ready to use religion as a valuable prop for its dominion.

These papal circulars and addresses of the nineteenth century demonstrated an impressive religious and political belief in Eternal Rome and the eternal validity of the untouchable teachings of its Church, as well as a terror of being enveloped by the 'innovations' of a century abounding with 'fiends'. The neurotic exaggeration of certain sentences and statements evinces an intellectual and spiritual climate equally far removed from the serenity and spiritual gaiety of an Aquinas, as from the humanity of those heathens who, as fathers to freemasonry, sustained so angry an attack in *Humanum Genus*. The conflict was unavoidable and insoluble.

Politically its edge was sharpened by the struggle concerning the dogmatic definition of the Pope's infallibility. The *Syllabus* served to prepare the ground and a party was founded, whose protagonists in Britain and France may be regarded as Manning, Ward and Veuillot, which referred hymns to God and the Holy Ghost directly to Pope Pius IX, was imbued with an outlook steeped in archaism and magic on the subject of the redemptive power of his office.

'Witnesses to tradition? There is but *one* witness, and I am he!' That was the declaration which he flung in the face of Cardinal Guidi, a Dominican, the Archbishop of Bologna, formerly a professor of theology at Vienna and Rome, who during a major speech at the Vatican Council had dared affirm that the bishops were witnesses to tradition. He was summoned to the Pope that same day. The Holy Father was deeply stirred: a Roman bishop and cardinal had placed himself on the same level. This pope saw in every attempt at modification of his hotly asserted infallibility a rebellion against God, Christ, the Church, and himself. At the Vatican Council of 1870 he created an atmosphere that became increasingly intolerable.

IGNAZ VON DÖLLINGER AND THE FIRST VATICAN COUNCIL

Ignaz von Döllinger (1799–1890), Germany's greatest Catholic ecclesiastical historian during the nineteenth century, was one of the rare individuals who stood firmly by their conscience and their scholastic outlook. The outstanding tribute to him in his own century was paid, shortly after his death, by Lord Acton, his pupil and friend. In the *English Historical Review* he recalled how Döllinger as a young man had been an ardent reader of Romantic poetry, philosophy, and literature. Franz von Baader influenced him deeply. In literature his taste had inclined to Schlegel, Coleridge, Leopardi, and Gioberti, among the moderns. Among the older philosophers, on the harmony of opposites and dialogue between opponents, he had mainly favoured Nicholas of Cusa, Ramon Lull, and Postel.

In his early years the intellectually hot-blooded Döllinger became, under the influence of de Maistre, the most respected academic representative of ultramontanism. 'The Pope as highest teacher and protector of the Faith' and 'as the manifest representative of the Church's unity' was to him above everyone and everything. As incumbent of the chair for Church law and history at Munich University, he remained in this sense, until 1860, the highly-esteemed protagonist of the papacy. But in 1865 he wrote to Montalembert, 'I am very disillusioned. – So much had happened in the Church other than I thought it would twenty or thirty years ago when I painted it to myself in rosy colours.' In 1882 he confessed: 'My whole life has been a process of stripping myself of misconceptions, misconceptions to which I cling tenaciously.'

In 1861 the publication of *The Church and the Churches, or the Papacy and Temporal Power*, a description of the wretched state of the papal domains from the sixteenth to the nineteenth centuries, marks the beginning of the second period of Döllinger's life, a period which was to lead to excommunication and loneliness. He describes how, in the present time, the papal state rested solely on the military support of Napoleon III, and had long been declining. Criticism of the papal state led him further to the criticism of papal exercise of authority under Pius IX.

In August 1864, shortly before the appearance of the *Syllabus*, the Pope announced his intention of summoning a council, the aim of which would be the restoration of the Holy See's spiritual and temporal powers throughout the Church and in the papal state. In 1869 another article appeared, in *La Civiltà Cattolica*, the mouthpiece of the Pope, expressing the hope that the declaration of the Pope's infallibility respecting matters of faith would be greeted unanimously.

The majority of Catholic bishops and theologians were against such a statement, however, and the March and April editions of the Augsburg *Allgemeine Zeitung* contained a series of articles, written mainly by Döllinger, which were later published in book form under the title, *The Pope and the Council*. This book, in the view of the British Benedictine Abbot Cuthbert Butler, amounted to a vehement frontal attack on the papacy as a political factor, on its role as it had been understood and accepted for hundreds of years, and on all the temporal powers of the Church. The book was translated into various languages, and had a marked effect in Britain, France and America. On 2 December 1869 it was accordingly announced that the Pope had confirmed that the book was to be included in the Index, and therefore, that it was forbidden to read it.

Döllinger had pointed out that supporters of papal absolutism paid no regard to the Bible, history or tradition, quoting the statement of the Jesuit Peronne, that these were not necessary for a statement of faith. He commented that it was on the strength of this statement that Pius IX had, in 1854, turned the Immaculate Conception into a dogma.

Considerations for Bishops attending the Council on the Question of Papal Infallibility was compiled in 1869: 'This new doctrine is branded on the brow with the stamp of illegitimacy; it can and must never be raised to the dignity of religious truth.' 'It can be said that all theologians possessing a comprehensive knowledge of history and erudition in the Bible and the writings of Church Fathers have repudiated the new doctrine of papal infallibility.' Certainly on the eve of the Vatican Council the overwhelming majority of German bishops and laymen took the same view and during the Council itself, in March, 1870, Bishop Ketteler denounced its pronouncement as a crime, falling on his knees before the Pope, in an effort to prevent him from making the declaration of infallibility.

In September 1869 Germany's twenty bishops assembled in a synod at Fulda. Fourteen of them, including the archbishops of Cologne and Munich, signed a letter to the Pope in which they begged him on account of the deep unrest among German Catholics to renounce his intention to define the doctrine as dogma. At the Council the Austrian Cardinals Schwarzenberg and Rauscher manifested themselves from the outset as the opposition's staunchest leaders. Schwarzenberg fought for an open-minded Church;

Rauscher composed the famous counter-petition signed by one hundred and thirty-six bishops. The cultured, open-minded Catholicism in the opposition camp included forty-four German and Austro-Hungarian bishops, one German-speaking bishop from Switzerland, thirty-three Frenchmen, twenty-four North Americans, four Englishmen and Irishmen, seven Italians, nineteen Orientals, four Portuguese and Argentinians. The episcopacy from countries where a tradition of archaism and magic prevailed, as well as from South America, Spain, southern Italy, and Poland (with one exception), was almost unanimously for the dogma.

Pius ix was furious at the opposition's tenacity. To speed matters the way he wanted, fresh procedural rules, allowing the chairman to curtail every speech and debates to be curtailed at any time at the request of a majority, were introduced on 22 February 1870. On 22 March there was an outbreak of storm indignation when Bishop Strossmayer declared it to be neither just nor gracious to attribute every progress in religious error, indeed all the errors of the age, to Protestantism.

'I believe that Protestantism contains not merely one or two but a multitude of people who love Jesus Christ.' A 'murmur' arose and Cardinal Capalti retorted, 'So I beg you to desist from that sort of talk which, as I must frankly say, offends the ears of many bishops.' Strossmayer, who had frequently already roused the ire of the majority by his open-mindedness and his culture, was finally shouted down. The official record states, 'Most of the fathers howled him down.' Deeply concerned about Russia and the Eastern Church (whereas Pius ix was sharply against the Eastern Churches and wanted to see the Latinisation of the Uniate Churches brought about as speedily as possible), Strossmayer told the Council openly that it was lacking in freedom and truthfulness. On 19 May the Patriarch of Antioch, the first Oriental to be allowed to speak, confirmed that the definition of papal infallibility would be a slap in the face for the Orthodox Church and destroy all hopes of reunion.

On 23 May Bishop Ketteler declared that Christ had first chosen the Apostles and only subsequently given authority to Peter. All theological text-books dealt first with the Church and then with the Primacy. Theology was a positive science in which it was not possible to determine matters beforehand or to draw conclusions from a single principle. Actual history was involved. How had Christ ordered the Church and authority in it? What did the Apostles say? Through the doctrine of primacy now proposed, the divine establishment of the Church would be totally altered. It remained a matter for proof that the pope alone, independently and divided from the Church, was infallible. In the same way as the effort to repeal, in the secular state, every form of freedom and to introduce absolute rule was the precise reason for the downfall of monarchies, so, within the Church exaggeration of papal claims to authority would, if not lead to the downfall of the Church, still do it very great harm. *Absolutismus corruptio popurolum*. In matters of faith the bishops were not merely witnesses to the truth, but judges of it. That would, however, no longer hold good if the pope, without bishops, was to be held infallible.

The liveliest minds among the opposition emphasised again and again these two elements – the Church's growing absolutism and the revolutionary character of the proposed infallibility dogma. It meant the creation of a totalitarian, authoritatively-led Church which contradicted the inmost nature of Catholicism. *La dernière Heure* was the title of the last manifesto issued by the opposition. It expressed the hope that a new Council would be held in freedom. 'This Council has revealed to us all the degree to which absolutism can corrupt the best of institutions and the best of instincts.' On 17 July the hard core of the opposition sent a letter to the Pope, signed by fifty-five bishops, telling him that they were going home and would not attend the decisive session. On 18 July the vote on pronouncement of the infallibility dogma took place. There were five hundred and thirty-three *placet* voices and two *non placet*. They belonged to Riccio of Cajazzo in the kingdom of Naples, and Fitzgerald of Little Rock, USA. The voting took place to the accompaniment of thunder and lightning. A pane almost immediately over the papal throne was smashed and came clattering down. The following day war was declared between France and Prussia; Napoleon III, patron of the Papal States, withdrew his troops. During the next few months opposition cardinals and bishops, after severe struggles with their conscience and faced with no alternative except to leave the Church, submitted to the dogma. On 20 September, after a siege of Rome lasting several hours, the papal army capitulated on the orders of the Pope. Italian troops moved into the Eternal City marking the end of the Papal States. Exactly one month later Pius IX issued a papal letter which postponed the Council until better times.

Superficial observers of Roman Catholic history have suggested that declaration of the dogma of infallibility did no harm and that the fears of the German, French, and British theologians, bishops, and laymen evinced themselves as unfounded, since the pope barely makes use of his solemnly acknowledged *ex cathedra* power and the increased respect enjoyed by the papacy is in some degree to be ascribed to it. This interpretation is historically mistaken. Between 1871 and 1914 the declaration of infallibility did Catholicism great harm. Neither Pius IX nor Pius X seemed capable of noticing the fact, but late nineteenth-century popes like Benedict XV and Pius XI, have felt the effects.

The real victor of 1870 was not the pope but that body of 'Integralists' who had long since firmly decided to constitute itself as the party of infallibles and needed the pope as a cloak for its intrigues and schemes. ('Integralism' was the term applied in Germany, Holland, France, and Italy to a group which claimed for itself staunch adherence to Catholic principles in the teeth of their enfeeblement by others in the days of Modernism.) Its fanatical propaganda on behalf of the infallibility declaration beforehand in Veuillot's *Univers*, Cardinal Manning's *Tabret*, and *La Civiltà Cattolica* – and its triumph afterwards attest the fact. By constant invocation of the pope they were able to make themselves super-popes and to overwhelm their opponents, secular and ecclesiastic, with the claim of protecting the honour of the Holy See. But by enveloping the pope in such a secluded clique, by protecting him from the attacks of reformers, academics and scientists, they also made him a prisoner of the masses, of their fears neuroses, their mania for miracles, and excessive Mariolatry. For the episcopacy the pronouncement of dogma, however, transformed the question of conscience and historical research into one of Church discipline.

The efforts made by prelates, nuncios and senior ecclesiastics to secure Döllinger's submission did not cease until shortly before his death. The approaches were polite and, on the whole, sympathetic in tone. The archbishop of Munich wrote to plead with him in 1871, but, as Döllinger reminded him, a liberal wind, started in 1848, had also blown through German Catholicism. He condemned the Jesuits as champions of papal absolutism, saying that the theory of papal infallibility had been introduced 'into the Church by a long series of deliberate fabrications, and forgeries and . . . then spread and asserted by force. . . . ' He maintained that the new doctrine:

> seeks to establish the kingdom of this world which was precisely what Christ rejected . . . I cannot accept it either as a Christian or as a theologian or as a historian or as a citizen. As such I know that the tenacious ambition to realise this theory of world dominion has cost Europe rivers of blood, caused disorder and brought down whole countries, disturbed the fine organic constitution of the Church in olden times, and produced, nurtured and maintained its worst abuses.

LORD ACTON

John Emmerich Edward Dalberg-Acton, first Baron Acton (1834–1902) was related to or connected with many of the leading European families and with the men of the Whig dynasty. He was moulded on the one hand by the freedom of outlook of the English gentleman and on the other by the freely-roaming, intellectual breadth of mind which he met in the Döllinger household in Munich. He was himself a gentleman, a Roman Catholic, a European and a humanist. His greatest themes were freedom, tolerance, and justice, the need for all to recognise the sanctity of human life and the need for the crimes of ecclesiastical authorities to be depicted in exactly the same way as those of other authorities: 'Murder is always murder, whether committed by populace or patricians, by councils or kings or popes.' It has been said of him that 'never has a Catholic author written more ruthlessly about the past of his Church'.

Acton noted that almost twenty years after 1789 reaction could celebrate its triumph throughout Europe. During the course of the next fifty years important spokesmen for this nineteenth-century religious and political reaction, Bonald, de Maistre, Veuillot, and the *La Civiltà Cattolica*, were to extol the eradication of Huguenots in the Massacre of St Bartholomew's

Eve as an exemplary deed, exemplary precisely for contemporary times. This praise and celebration of religious and political murder, sanctioning the extermination of whole groups and classes of population, led Acton to publish in October 1869, just prior to the Vatican Council, his reflections on the events of 1572.

In 1858 – ten years after the occurrences that he considered decisive for Europe's future – Acton had already pondered the Church's situation in *Political Thoughts on the Church*. Current views about the Church's political attitude were highly contradictory. O'Connell, Count Montalembert, and Father Ventury declared it to be liberal, constitutional, and almost democratic, whereas Bonald and Father Taparelli gloried in its absolutist character. Acton appreciated that Catholicism as a religion alone was incapable of saving Europe any more than it had been able to preserve Antiquity. Currently the term 'Catholic state' was synonomous with misrule and maladministration. France, Spain, and Naples were far worse governed than Protestant states like Britain, Holland, and Prussia.

Acton regarded nationalism, successor to Europe's political shipwreck, as the principal disease of the age. In his great essay on the subject (July 1862) he revealed what were to be the causes of Europe's crises and catastrophes right up to the Second World War. He traced back the origin of this horror, nationalism in its new form, to the action of the 'old absolutism' of the 'Christian states' of Old Europe in partitioning Poland. The theory of 'unity', 'unification', and 'reunification' makes of the nation a source of despotism and revolution.

> The coexistence of several nations under the name state is . . . the best security of its freedom. . . . The combination of different nations in one state is as necessary a condition of civilised life as the combination of men in society. Inferior races are raised by living in political union with races intellectually superior. Exhausted and decaying nations are revived by the contact of a younger vitality.

Glancing towards Austria, he remarked on the great problems and potentialities of this state, where the cultural level of the different member-nations varied much but no single one could dominate the rest, and he compared Austria with the British Empire.

Acton was the pupil and friend of Döllinger, whom he introduced to the British public in two important essays written in 1861 and 1890. He was also spokesman for a liberal Catholic humanism of the kind propagated by Erasmus. As such he could not fail to come into conflict with the representatives of narrow-minded Roman Catholic dogmatism, itself an ecclesiastical parallel to the new nationalism, which had come into fashion since 1832 and was to last until 1914. When he was twenty-five, Acton founded the *Home and Foreign Review*, a bi-monthly magazine aiming to act as a forum for educated opinion and an outlet for frank discussion within the somewhat stuffy and bigoted atmosphere of British Catholicism. Cardinal Wiseman (and the Vatican) took exception to the paper's objectivity. Acton's reply (1862), calm, factual, and precise, is, in the magnificence of its love of liberty, high-mindedness, and dignity, a model case of altercation with an intransigent prince of the Church.

The crux of Wiseman's complaint had been that *Home and Foreign Review* had been too little partisan in 'the Catholic cause' and its 'interests', paying too little heed to Catholic instincts, motives, and aspirations and giving too much space to the ventilation of non-Catholic views. 'The principles of religion, government, and science,' Acton answered, 'are in harmony, always and absolutely; but their interests are not. . . . A false religion fears the progress of all truth; a true religion seeks and recognises truth wherever it can be found.'

The Catholic revivalist movement had, he continued, split in two directions, during the nineteenth century – that of the intellectually broad-minded and that of the politically partisan. Men like Bonald, de Maistre, and Donoso Cortés tried to trample their opponents underfoot by every available means, concerned in seeking their weaknesses and their own advantage, but no longer truth for its own sake. Therein lay the parting of the ways. 'These men only look to interests. They were prepared to chase chimeras if they only seemed to serve their cause, were fearful of every fresh discovery and all progress if it appeared 'harmful'. Their rejoinders to criticism were lies, slanders, wild accusations.

> They have lied before God and man . . . and against themselves they have justified those grave accusations of falsehood, insincerity, indifference to civil rights, and contempt for civil authorities which are uttered with such profound injustice against the Church.

> The present difficulties of the Church – her internal dissensions and apparent weakness, the alienation of so much intellect, the strong prejudice which keeps many away from her altogether, and makes many who had approached her shrink back – all draw nourishment from this rank soil. – The world can never know and recognise her divine perfection while the pleas of her defenders are scarcely nearer to the truth than the crimes which her enemies impute to her.

Acton ceased publication of the *Home and Foreign Review* in 1864 after its condemnation by the Vatican. *Conflicts with Rome* was his epilogue, and whoever experienced the liquidation of Catholic periodicals between 1948 and 1958 will not remain unmoved by his words of farewell. Only a few of the themes can be outlined here. Acton recalled the many and fatal conflicts, between science and literature on the one side and ecclesiastical authority on the other, which had recently done so much dishonour to the Church. Publication of his periodical had been prefaced by enunciation of the principle that 'Its aim will be to combine devotion to the Church with discrimination and candour in the treatment of her opponents; to reconcile freedom of inquiry with implicit faith'. He was now sacrificing the existence of the *Review* in defence of its principles and in order to be able to combine obedience to the Church with the conviction of intellectual freedom. He ended with the words: 'It (the *Review*) was but a partial and temporary embodiment of an imperishable idea – the faint reflection of a light which still lives and burns in the hearts of the silent thinkers of the Church.'

RENAN

Ernest Renan (1823–92) had once, as a young man, been pointed out to Döllinger by Dupanloup as one of the great hopes of Catholicism. As time went on, however, he seemed, to 'good Catholics', to be the very embodiment of 'impious science', of the 'academic anti-Christ'. Certainly, the influence he exercised in the second half of the nineteenth century on non-Catholic French intelligentsia was exceptional. When the episcopacy intervened successfully to prevent him from actively fulfilling the duties attached to his appointment to the Chair for Semitic Languages at the Collège de France, he turned this obstacle to his own advantage by making a trip to the East, in 1864–5 (his second, for he had already visited Palestine) and pursuing his own studies. In 1878 he was elected a member of the Académie Française. Six years later he became, and remained until his death, Director of the Collège de France. His *Life of Jesus* was one of the most widely read and hotly-debated books of the century.

It is worth taking a look at the life of this little Celtic boy from Tréguier, whose grave lies in the Panthéon at Paris. In his *Recollections of My Youth* (1883) Renan wrote: 'I love the past, but I gravitate towards the future. The world is going in the direction of a sort of Americanisation'; by this he meant that there was no longer any mass of believers. Religion had become, irrevocably, a matter of individual taste, and France seemed likely to evolve along the lines of British and American democracy; and although this would inevitably include mediocrity and vulgarity, 'American vulgarity would not have brought Giordano Bruno to the stake, or persecuted Galileo'. Renan closes the work with the words: 'As far as I am concerned, I am never more firmly rooted in my liberal faith than when I think of the miracles of the ancient Faith, and I am never more ardent in work for the future than when I have for hours heard the Bells pealing in the city of Is.'

Is was the city sunk below the sea off the coast of Brittany, and Renan was recalling the world of his youth, almost unchanged since ancient times. Treguier, where he was born, had been founded as a monastery in the late fifth century by Saint Tudwal or Tual, and Brittany was a land of Celts, a race capable of miracles and madness, a race with a heritage of saints, and strange and marvellous tales, the land of Saint Renan (or Ronan). Saint Renan, an arbitrary, violent saint, had great powers over the elements and as a child Renan had seen his father cured of a mortal fever by a smith who, magician and technician combined, had caused a cure by threatening the saint.

Renan's mother was of Basque descent, so that he had a doubly archaic heritage, and as a child he conceived a fascination for unusual personalities – martyrs, heroes and Utopian figures, associates of the impossible. It is against this background that his *Life of Jesus* should be understood. He was destined for the Church at an early age and was educated first at the seminary of Saint-Nicolas du Chardonnet in Paris, and later at that of Issy, a subsidiary of Saint-Sulpice (the main seminary in the diocese of Paris). He maintains that although it was usual at the time to denounce the alleged immorality of the clergy, he himself had, during those thirteen years, met only good priests.

On 6 September 1845, just before his consecration as subdeacon, Renan sent a long letter to the rector of Saint-Sulpice, telling him that he could no longer remain a Catholic. In his *Recollections* he said that historical criticism was responsible for his loss of faith. He did not know which way to turn, for on the one side stood theology, a wholly thirteenth-century construction with the greatness and infinite spaciousness of a Gothic cathedral, and on the other German intellect, to cross whose threshold was like going into a temple. His conscience was severely troubled by those doubts, yet it was not the political, doctrinal or moral failure of the Church that worried him, but the contradictions between the Synoptic Gospels and that according to Saint John, the flaws in the Holy Writ.

In the corrupt and turbulent Paris of the day Renan felt immensely lonely, but gradually recovered through the medium of scholarship. Augustin Thierry stood as intellectual father to him; the free and pious intellect emanating from Germany, was a source of deep satisfaction to him and seemed almost like the rise of a fresh Christianity.

In 1890 Renan compared the nations of Europe to the statues of heroes which flank the grave of Emperor Maximilian in Innsbruck, rickety bodies crushed by armour. It seemed to him that in the nineteenth century, with all the great scientific achievements to its credit, 'human destiny has become more obscure than ever'. The state of morality had dropped with the loss of faith in a supernatural reality, and he could not see how it was to be reinstated, or what was to become of man.

These thoughts were published in *The Future of Science*, a book which was not published until forty-two years after it had been written. Some of the passages evince quite clearly the optimistic spirit of 1848, and the idea that mankind had started to take its fate into its own hands. He felt sure that the revolution of the future would be the triumph of morality, a progress which nothing could overcome; that decline was a word which made no sense if applied to humanity as a whole, all processes of decadence being confined to very limited periods and social circumstances. Material and industrial progress would not be attained at the expense of the spirit, for 'when the material world has become completely subject to man, then the spirit will begin its great rule'.

Renan saw the history of mankind as that of a gigantic process of production, with the labours of millions of individuals, nations, civilisations and epochs often concentrated in apparently minute quintessentials. Yet in these quintessentials millions of dead continued to live and to illustrate his point. Renan recalled a childhood experience that had moved him deeply. He had gone with his mother to an old, deserted Breton cemetry. What had become of the many nameless, unknown dead? And the answer that came was: When Brittany is no more, there will be France; when France is no more, there will be humanity; when humanity will be no more, there will be God; and humanity will have contributed to His creation. 'Not one single member of humanity is superfluous.' 'Belief in immortality signifies fundamentally nothing else than this insuperable trust of humanity in the future. No deed dies.'

The prosperity of science and humanity demanded an infinite prodigality of strength, work, and sacrifice. Generations of scientists eventually produced a genius. After a century the work even of a genius of the very highest quality could be compressed into two or three pages. The One World required enormous quantities of people of every degree. 'Nothing is too dear when it is a matter of rendering an atom of truth available.' Today's and tomorrow's task was organisation of intellectual labour. 'I do believe, without being an adherent of literary and scientific Communism, that it is a matter of urgency to fight against the dissipation of energies and to focus on the work to be done.' 'The purpose of society is the broad and complete realisation of all facets of human life.' The state, seeing that its duty did not stop at organisation of the forces of law and order, but extended to providing the conditions for man's improvement of himself, owed science the erection of laboratories, libraries, and so on. 'How odd it is that science, the most liberal activity in the world, finds really generous support only in Russia!' — Here and in the following passage it should be borne in mind that the author was writing in 1848.

For Renan the outstanding problem for the nineteenth century was popular education. He looked with a mixture of horror and fascination at the rising masses: 'We have to make men of these brutes.' 'I am utterly convinced that, unless steps are quickly taken to educate the people, we stand on the edge of an outbreak of frightful barbarity. For should the people triumph, in its present condition, that will be worse than the ancient Franks and Vandals.' Europe had three great tasks to fulfil: expansion of the scientific spirit, education of its own barbaric masses, and the gradual education of the 'wild races' of Africa, Asia and elsewhere. In this connection Renan examined the 'favourite widespread notion' that modern, like ancient, civilisation must always be due for an invasion of barbarians who, 'let it be clearly understood, are to be sought nowhere else than among ourselves'. He rejected this 'decline and fall' theory. He granted that the dangers were great in that fear-ridden century, an era of false neo-Catholicism, false and cowardly scepticism, malevolent materialism on the part of hedonistic upper classes and superstitious barbarism among the masses. Nevertheless there were, and would continue to be, saints, truly pious individuals who believed in truth. 'Nothing great is ever produced without visions.' Without Utopia there could be neither healthy present nor future.

In 1871, during France's collapse, Renan published his ideas on the intellectual and moral problems of reconstruction. 'It was the dream of my life to work for the intellectual, moral, and political alliance of Germany with France, an alliance which would result in the exclusion of Britain . . . in order to lead the world towards a liberal civilisation. . . . My vision, I admit it, is destroyed for ever. A chasm has opened up between France and Germany. Centuries will not suffice to close it.' Germany had been his tutor and he owed the best in his culture to it. Now Wallenstein's soldiery had arrived.

With his gaze fixed on Germany, Russia and America, Renan proposed a new form of education, political policy, and social structure for France. Five or six fresh universities were to be founded along the German pattern, an active colonial policy pursued, and the nation shaped into a hard-working, disciplined people. 'A nation that does not colonise is irrevocably delivered up to Socialism, the war between the rich and the poor. Conquest of the country of an inferior race by a superior race, which installs itself in order to rule there, is not inherently shocking.' The Europeans constituted a master race, a race of competent soldiers whose mission was to subjugate the world. Under the spell of his great fear of socialism, communism, and German militarism, Renan evolved ideas appropriate to Rosenberg's *Myth of the Twentieth Century*.

His prognosis for German (expressed in letters to David Friedrich Strauss of 6 September 1870 and 15 September 1871) was distinctly gloomy. Germany was setting out on a racial policy the objective of which – repatriation of all Germans the world over into One Reich – would have unforeseeable catastrophic consequences. This racial policy would lead to 'wars of extermination' and to 'zoological' wars in the struggle for total victory by a 'pure race'. The Slavs would be in raptures at the concepts and principles of this German policy. One day the Slavs would enlist in their train the masses of central Asia, descendants of the hordes of Genghis Khan and Tamurlane. One day the Slavs would throw on to the scales of history all the weight acquired by the Bohemians, the Moravians, the Croats, the Serbs, and all the Slav peoples currently still under Turkish sway clustering around the great Muscovite conglomeration.

Gratitude was not to be expected from the Russians. 'One of the secret reasons for Prussia's malevolence towards us is that it owes part of its culture to us. One of Russia's causes for grudge will consist one day in having been civilised by Germans.' He wondered what the Germans would do when one day the Slavs demanded the return of Prussia, Silesia, Pomerania, and Berlin, since these all bore Slav names. 'When, pressing forward across the Elbe and the Oder, they will do what you have done this side of the Moselle.' 'Nation' is no synonym for 'race'. Every nation is a mixture of various races, a fact which German racialism overlooked. He considered that a healthy and sound life was only possible in association with very different individuals. He himself was not rich, but could not exist in a society where there were no rich people. He was no Catholic, but glad that there were Catholics, nuns to nurse the sick, country persons, and Carmelites. In the same way Germans should be prepared to tolerate what was unlike them. Valhalla would never be the kingdom of God. They should occupy themselves with the really great problems, the social questions, so as to hit on a rational and, as far as possible, just organisation of humanity. France had tried, though with too naïve a means, to solve these matters in 1789 and 1848. Now it was the Germans' turn to create a humane society, to reform the Church or find a substitute for it.

During the whole course of his life Renan never withdrew in silence before a problem. To his death he worked tirelessly on his ideas of the future of Europe and mankind and the questions that these ideas presented. Three instances are characteristic of his concern. The first was a speech he delivered on 2 February 1888, at the Society for the Propagation of the French Language. He considered that Europe ought to free itself from its condition of hate, and maintained that 'Fanaticism is impossible in French', for French teaches laughter. 'Teach all nations to smile in French.' On 9 May 1889, at the Paris World Exhibition, Renan asked Jules Lemaitre what he thought the future would bring, for he felt that even if the World Exhibition might represent men's last opportunity to enjoy themselves and be happy, it would still not be right to give way to fear and despair. The third instance occurred when Renan, in his address on admission to the Académie Française, summed up his hopes and fears with regard to the nineteenth century and the future: 'the future will have much to say against this dear old nineteenth century, but failure to recognise its charm will be to do it an injustice'. On the question of what would survive, he maintained that the future belonged not only to the strong, but to the unassuming; that the question of immortality was a naïve and vain one. He suggested that perhaps, in a thousand years, only two books known to the nineteenth century would be republished, Homer and the Bible. Impossible to tell which ideas the twentieth century would pick out of the wastepaper basket into which the revolutionary nineteenth century had carelessly thrown them.

The powerful impression left by Renan on his century was not, however, due to reflections such as these, known to comparatively few, but to the work of his early manhood, his *Life of Jesus*, which had been read throughout Europe, Russia and the Balkans. He acknowledged at the outset his debt to David Friedrich Strauss, but the originality of his own interpretation owed not a little to his travels in the Holy Land. In the preface he says quite clearly: 'To write the history of a religion it is essential in the first place to have believed in it (without that it is impossible to understand why it should have exercised a fascination and have satisfied human sensibility) and in the second place no longer to believe in it absolutely, for absolute faith is incompatible with giving an objective historical account.'

The greatest event in history was the revolution whereby the noblest sectors of humanity went over to a belief in the Trinity and the Incarnation of the Son of God. No environment, except that of the French Revolution, had been so suited as that prevailing around Jesus, for putting into motion the titanic forces hidden in the lap of humanity. Jesus did not have visions, for God was in Him, and the miraculous was, to Him, normal. His new religion was founded on purity of heart and the brotherhood of man. The Church betrayed all that. Jesus had embodied the most revolutionary idea and movement of any age. His enemies belonged to the 'party of order' which is the same in every age, narrow-minded, nationalist, unable to see beyond the day's events and its party political interests.

For centuries the Christian Moloch demanded unheard-of human sacrifices. That was why it was important to keep in mind that Jesus had not been the founder of dogmas, but had brought a new spirit into the world. 'He created the Heaven of pure souls and the Kingdom of God in man.' No revolution would ever divide mankind from the great spiritual and moral criterion set by Jesus. In this sense even those were Christians who differed in almost all points from past Christian tradition.

Jesus had emanated from Judaism and had stepped out of it just as Luther had discarded the Middle Ages, Rousseau the eighteenth century, and Lamennais Catholicism. For three years Jesus had led a life that in contemporary society would have brought him twenty times before the police. Jesus was the individual Who had rendered possible for mankind its greatest stride towards God. He knew Himself as the 'Son of Man' and the 'Son of God', but in a way that all men could achieve. He had never either seen Himself as the Incarnation of God or given Himself out to be such. He was a man and had had to struggle with the same passions as all others. No Angel of God, except His own conscience, had consoled Him. No Satan, other than each carries in his own breast, had tempted Him. No man, except Buddha, had ever so subdued his egotism and his own interests as Jesus had done. Whatever the future might bring, Jesus would not be surpassed and His cult would be constantly rejuvenated. 'All the coming centuries will proclaim that none among the sons of men is greater than Jesus.'

LOISY

Renan once said: 'The excommunicated members of a Church are invariably its *élite*. They are ahead of their time. Today's heretic is tomorrow's conformist.' It is an aphorism which Friedrich Heiler, the author of a biography of Loisy, and who had a deep knowledge of the suspect and persecuted theologians of the time, applied, justifiably, to Loisy.

Alfred Loisy (1857–1940) was the child of a peasant in the Haut Marne area, and even at an early age, obviously unsuited to agricultural work, a shy awkward boy, plagued by inner doubts. He was introduced to higher criticism by the great scholar Leopold Duchesne, at the Institut Catholique in Paris, studied Hebraic and Assyrian, and, between 1882 and 1858, obtained permission to attend Renan's lectures at the Collège de France. He never knew Renan personally, but was firm in his mind as to why he was so keen to listen to him – he wanted one day to beat him with his own weapons.

On 6 July 1883 Loisy noted in his diary: 'At the present time the Church is an impediment to mankind's intellectual progress. . . . It is, however, as impossible to hold back mankind as it is to get a river to flow back to its source.' He therefore saw the salvation of the Church in its taking the lead in scientific progress, but two days later he noted that ever since Copernicus had made the first irreparable breach in the Church, theologians had been totally occupied looking for heaven and hell.

Nine years later, in 1892, he commented on the fear haunting everyone in the Church, and did his best to alleviate the situation caused by mediaeval scholasticism and Jesuit teaching, feeling that the spirit of dogmatism should be replaced with the spirit of religion, that it was necessary to stir man's soul and liberate reason in order to safeguard the conscience. Religion, he maintained, was eternal, whereas theology was no more than a temporally conditioned theory of religion. He felt that death was only an illusion because there is life in everything, and that the responsibility for the future lay with the priesthood.

On 24 October 1892 Loisy met Meignan, the seventy-five-year-old Archbishop of Tours, a favourite of Pope Leo XIII, and recorded the following conversation. Meignan maintained that 'criticism has never existed within the Church', criticism of Bible, of dogma, being matters of which Rome really comprehended nothing. He maintained that the Curial clergy, while wild and fanatical, were still completely ignorant. Yet to oppose them was dangerous. The Jesuits controlled everything written on Biblical matters, and constantly the petrification of the Church was bound to proceed. The gap between faith and science was consequently bound to widen. He suggested that all men engaged in research could do was continue to work silently in a dark room, only trying, very gently, to open a window a little.

This was also Loisy's aim, but the first blow fell almost before he had started. He was dismissed from his post as theological teacher on account of the inept defence of his essay, *The Biblical Question*. D'Hulst, who defended the essay, suffered from the consequences of this for the rest of his life, and remarked to Loisy, 'You threw yourself in front of a moving train'. Loisy wondered: 'Does the government of the Church consist of nothing but blind and brutal machines?'

Generous financial assistance from Friedrich von Hügel enabled him to found the periodical, *Revue d'histoire et de littérature religieuse*, one of the most important of academic Catholic papers, to which Loisy sometimes contributed under the pseudonym, Jacques Simon. At this period he longed for a Church which would be 'the home of all souls', and for a revised papacy: 'It is time for the Catholic Church to seek among men not merely subjects, but to have for its sole preoccupation how to make them more like Christ.'

On 2 March 1899 Duchesne wrote to Hügel that the Church looked for support only to the masses and the princes, neither of whom was interested in reconciling the intelligentsia with religion. Whether one pope went and another came, it made little difference. There was an atmosphere of oppression and fear in Rome. After the death of Leo XIII a reactionary was expected on the chair of St Peter. 1900 was a year of struggle against the 'devilries' of the Modernists, set alongside those of the freemasons and Lucifer himself. Loisy recalls how, as late as November of that year, he had not even been denounced as suspect, yet only shortly afterwards he was termed 'almost heretical', and then immediately, 'heretical'. In the same year he fell out with Cardinal Richard of Paris, who accused him of falling victim to the influence of German writers.

In 1902 Loisy published, in Paris, a book entitled, *The Gospel and the Church*. Its impact was explosive. 'This little book made me the most notorious man in France' (Loisy to Hügel). 'Precisely among the younger generation of theologians the effect of this tract was like wildfire.' Buonaiuti, probably the most outstanding historical brain among Italian Modernists, but no friend of Loisy, confessed that 'Were it not for *The Gospel and the Church* I would not be what I am, a Roman priest excommunicated by Rome.' In the issue of *L'Univers* for 1 January 1903 Abbé Gayraud began the campaign against the volume, closely followed by *La Civiltà Cattolica* and a flood of hostile writings. On 17 January Cardinal Richard led the way in prohibiting perusal of the book by Catholics within his diocese; eight bishops followed his example. The accusation against Loisy was framed as a denial by him of Christ's divinity and the authority of the Church.

Yet his objective had been a defence of the Church against Harnack's *What is Christianity?* And Harnack himself was genuinely moved by the book's intellectual and religious seriousness, recognising it as an affirmation of faith in the Church. That could not prevent Loisy breaking down inwardly under the spate of attacks. 'The Church's present régime is surely a school for lies and vileness,' he confided to his journal. 'Fortune is on the side of the feeble-minded, the cowardly, and the liars. . . . It is important that the future of Catholicism should not be surrendered to a swarm of idiots and liars dragging an all too politicised papacy and extremely ignorant episcopacy in its train.'

'The new Pope,' he noted, on the election of Pius x, 'will have nothing more urgent to do than to put my books on the Index. The Pope's personality will not be as outstanding as that of Leo XIII and the machine will have to be reckoned with. Machines, as it happens, are always machines, meaning brutal.' Pius x, though personally very benevolent, did indeed become a prisoner of the Vatican machine which was soon to gather speed in the direction of persecution. While he had still been Cardinal Archbishop of Venice, the Pope's attitude about *The Gospel and The Church* had been quite impartial. 'At last a theological book which is not boring' (quoted in a letter from Genocchi to Loisy, 15–16 October 1903). Friedrich von Hügel's daughter, Gertrude, gained during an audience the impression of a kindly man burdened by the cares of office, rather like an uprooted peasant. Loisy often seemed to himself precisely this, so that the pending conflict, in which he and Pius x were to be involved in a personal clash, became one of peasant against peasant.

A decree of the Holy Office, published on 30 December 1903, placed five of Loisy's books on the Index. Rome had declined to accept two recantations because Loisy had tried to limit his subjugation to the question of discipline, invoking his conscience and scholastic studies on his own behalf. On 28 February 1904 he sent a letter to the Pope.

> Most Holy Father! I know all the benignity of Your Holiness and it is to your heart that I address myself today. I want to live and die in communion with the Catholic Church. I do not want to contribute to the destruction of faith in my country. I do not have it in my power to destroy in myself the effect of my works. As much as it lies in me, I submit to the judgement pronounced against my writings by the Congregation of the Holy Office. To bear witness to my goodwill and as an act of appeasement, I am ready to relinquish my work as a teacher and likewise to break off the scholastic publications on which I am engaged.

Among the reasons for writing this letter Loisy had in mind the many priests facing a spiritual catastrophe and looking to see what their fate would be.

Pius x's reply, written in Italian in his own hand, was sent to Cardinal Richard, who read it to Loisy. 'I have received from the Rev. Abbé Loisy a letter . . . which appeals to my heart. But this letter is not written from the heart.' The Pope demanded total subjugation 'in that he puts into practice the admonition delivered by the saintly Remigius to Clovis: *Incende quod adorasti, adora quod incendisti.*' [Burn what you have adored; adore what you have burnt.] This was an extraordinarily revealing document, requiring of the nineteenth- and twentieth-century scholar a return to an archaic condition of awareness which would tie it down to magical primordiality. Here were two irreconcilably opposed forms and nuances of awareness. That of the Pope, demanding the wholesale preservation of an unchanging sacred doctrine and of the body in whose lap this redemptive teaching and knowledge was guarded. That of Loisy, in the shape of his knowledge and conscience as scholar, could understand revelation now only in the way it had been defined in *About a Little Book*, Loisy's apologia for *The Gospel and the Church* which, in the form of seven letters, was a literary work of art justly to be compared with Pascal: 'What is called revelation cannot be other than the awareness that man has acquired of his relationship to God.'

An additional factor in the wrangle between the Cardinal, with his Breton obstinacy, and his compatriot, was the clash arising from these kindred temperaments. Richard reprimanded Loisy with the words 'That is the arrogance of the academic' and got the reply 'There also exists an arrogance of ignorance, Your Eminence. Those who know me are aware that no man is less demented about what he knows and less wedded to his own system than I am.' The Cardinal hereupon once more cast in Loisy's teeth the reproach of having swallowed the poison of German writings and in this way ruining France. Despairingly Loisy exclaimed, when Richard again mentioned the Pope's reference to the Merovingian Clovis, ancestor to the hallowed kingdom of France, 'That is senseless!' For the ardent legitimist Cardinal and for the Pope there could scarcely be a more honourable comparison than with Clovis. For the historian Loisy the demand that he should reduce himself to the intellectual level of the Merovingian monarch seemed abhorrently unreasonable.

The interview ended with the Cardinal's brusque dismissal of Loisy. 'The Head of the Church to which I had given my life, had dedicated thirty years of work, had always loved and still love, beyond which I neither wanted nor desired anything, found nothing else to say than "This letter, which appeals to my heart, is not written from the heart!" Yet it came from my heart! . . . ' The wound was unhealable.

Later it became clear to me that these men (the Pope and the Cardinal) were decent and meant for the best. They wanted to save my soul and therefore to kill my intellect. But I saw the régime at that hour in its parade of benevolent fanaticism, its charitable cruelty, its murderous goodness. When Pius x in 1910 condemned *Sillon*, I said to my friends, 'The Church of Rome has no heart'. I had known it since my reception by Cardinal Richard on 12 March 1904.

Anatole France complained once, 'Democracy has no heart'. Viewed as a machine and the embodiment of a principle, no institution in the world has a heart.

In an acute state of spiritual distress, Loisy recalled his parents – simple, honest, devout folk – and the memory of them wrung from him a cry of pain at the thought that he would not be allowed to rest beside them, although he had denied neither them nor their faith. 'I am with you and you are with me. I sense that you help me and encourage me and do not blame me. The same eternity in which you are, awaits me too. I make my way towards it confidently.' The peasant son Loisy was invoking the primal confidence in the primal communion of man with the earth and the protection it afforded as a force to aid him along the road towards illumination and awareness.

Loisy, against his conscience and conviction, made submission and thus attained four years' respite from excommunication. Anguish at the assault on his integrity kindled rebelliousness. That same year Catholicism began to appear to him as a fetter on humanity's moral and spiritual progress. 'We are no longer Christians.' A major revulsion was taking hold of him. The kingdom of God should be erected in this world. It was not permissible to console the poor, nor humanity as a whole, simply with a beyond.

The avalanche against Loisy and the Modernists was on the move. In an audience with the Pope, on 4 January 1906, von Hügel's daughter bravely undertook Loisy's defence. If His Holiness had read the exchange of letters between Loisy and her father, she told Pius x, he would have been edified. She reproached the Pope with 'persecution', a word against which he protested and went on to say, in an inimitable hotch-potch of Italian and French, *'Loisy est un brave homme, solamente un poco tête montée su certe idée'*. The remark revealed an instinctive understanding on the part of the peasant temperament of Pius x for the peasant obstinacy of Loisy – a good fellow, but gone wild about certain notions.

On 11 February and 10 August 1906 two encyclicals were published, *Vehementer* and *Gravissimo*, condemning the legal separation between Church and state in France. Loisy wrote an article which compared Pius x with Gregory vii, Innocent ii, and Boniface viii, in so far as the present Pope felt called upon to act as the political leader of nations. Although it appeared anonymously, Integralists intervened at the Vatican to urge the ultimate condemnation of this 'heretic'. Catholic publicists had for the last three years attacked him as a Dreyfusard. Now, it was alleged, a number of pupils at certain theological seminaries had taken for their slogan 'Loisy, Dreyfus, and disarmament!'

On 1 November 1906 Loisy celebrated his last mass, twenty-seven years and four months after his first. In 1907 he received the news of his excommunication. On 4 July of that year Pius x signed the Holy Office decree *Lamentabili saine exitu*, a syllabus of sixty-five 'depraved and disgraceful' passages, the majority of which were taken from *The Gospel and The Church* and *About a Little Book*. Torn out of their context, they were twisted with a sure Inquisitorial sense into damning evidence. Exactly two months later followed *Pascendi Dominici gregis*, the condemnation by encyclical of the Modernists. Intellectuals of very various convictions, men like Maurice Blondel, Lucien Laberthonnière, George Tyrrell, and Edouard Le Roy, many of whom thought very differently from Loisy and even opposed him, were convicted in common. The charge was general: the doctrine of Modernism led to atheism and the destruction of all religion. These 'enemies of the Church' could (with some justice) declare that 'Modernism' was an invention of their mortal enemies at the Curia.

The Loisy Affair, the Church's internal Dreyfus Affair, which contributed no less to the contamination of Roman Catholicism, was still not ended. The Integralist papers proceeded to allege that the 'blackguard Jew' Salomon Reinach, a prominent leader of the Dreyfusards, was Loisy's principal adviser: 'Loisy and Reinach, how symbolic!' Loisy's reply, that he had spoken to Reinach on one occasion only in his life, on 20 August 1902, was ignored. On the Feast of Thomas of Aquinas, 7 March 1908, his solemn 'grand excommunication' took place at Rome. He was fifty-one and felt physically old and exhausted. Spiritually, however, he experienced a deep feeling of peace within himself. Tyrrell's phrase about 'salvation-bringing excommunication' was true also for him. Not since early childhood had he been pervaded by such a sense of gladness and liberty. On 31 January, at Bergson's suggestion, he was appointed professor at the Collège de France. The Catholic and nationalist Press went wild. Mgr Baudrillat, in *Le Gaulois*, asserted that a German was at the back of every Loisy book. 'He knows German' was thrown at him as highest disparagement. Nonetheless on 3 May 1909, with appropriate ceremonial, he took over Renan's chair and closed his inaugural address with the words, 'And our care shall be for nothing but the truth'.

Five years earlier, when his works had been placed on the Index, Loisy had applied himself energetically to the history of Christianity and all other religions. What he learned, first dismayed him, then awakened in him fresh hopes and a new faith. He absorbed himself in the study – and here his archaic peasant heritage stood him in good stead – of earliest magical sacrifices, human sacrifices, and the primal forms of the Christian mass. No one prior to Loisy recognised so fully the ramified importance of the transubstantiation involved in the ceremony of sacrifice. The beginnings of religion had been as lowly, confused, and paltry as those of humanity. Later national religions evolved, and after that, religions of a different sort which promised to secure the individual soul's eternal salvation. The history of recent centuries had displayed a great crisis in these redemptive systems and now they were threatened as once the national cults of Late Antiquity had been. 'One is inclined to say that the modern soul seeks something more intimate, deeper, and perhaps also more real' (lecture given on 17 December 1912).

He was at pains to lay bare the roots of Christianity. The penetration of his examination, the radicalism of the theories he propounded, and the breadth of his argument rendered the eighteen hundred pages of his commentary on *The Synoptic Gospels* (1907) a disturbing experience for theologians of all the Christian denominations who asked themselves how Jesus should really be interpreted. Loisy saw Jesus here not as the founder of a new religion, but as a herald of the great hope in the early coming of the kingdom of God which, by divine miracle, would descend upon this earth. His ethic was both subordinate to and indissolubly bound up with the eschatological idea of the kingdom of God.

'Jesus' dream was brittle and finite, as is our knowledge. It seems to us just as paradoxical as our favourite notions will appear to our great-grandchildren. Nevertheless it contains the most precious nuclei of human truth and the most fertile principles of human progress through its recognition of the fact that man's Golden Age lies not in the past but in the future, that a man's worth depends on the way of thinking which inspires his conduct, that the true religion is that which comes from the heart, that religion essentially consists of love, love of one's fellow-men and love of God in one's fellow-men, that the self-denial of each is necessary for the good of all . . . and finally that our fleeting existence is impelled across an ocean of life into which it is submerged, in order to endure for ever, precisely at the moment when it apparently ceases to be. If the last word about everything is not nothingness – and it cannot be nothingness – then the Gospel is only apparently a fantasy and Jesus embodied the wisdom of God in man, while His death was simply a transition to immortality.' Half a century later Ernst Bloch, in *The Principle of Hope*, conceived similar ideas.

The First World War provided Loisy with the strongest impetus towards evolution of a post-Christian philosophy which was to try and incorporate the Christian verities. This was the time when his faith in a personal God was shattered. He was dismayed by the declaration in 1914 by ninety-three German academics and many Catholic theologians on behalf of the holy German war. During the war only national gods were allowed room: the God of the Germans, the God of the French, the God of the Italians. The French clergy celebrated the Feast of the Immaculate Conception under the motto *Christo regnante Regnum Galliae, regnum Mariae*, on which Loisy commented that it was difficult to choose between the two Gods, French and German. In his eyes the war showed that no Providence guided mankind's destiny, but that it did everything in its power, whether erring thousandfold or tearing itself apart, to live, to grow, and to better itself.

In *War and Religion*, published at Paris in 1915, Loisy diagnosed an utter failure on the part of the Christian Churches in the face of the catastrophe. In the second edition, which appeared a few months later, he dealt with 'two philosophers of war', that of Adolf Deismann, who had asserted that war was the revelation of the 'German God' and the characteristic form of German religion, and that of the British Modernist Maud Petre who, in *Reflections of a Non-Combatant*, called for the subdual of war through a transformation of social, political, and international conditions. In answer to a deeply pessimistic letter from Duchesne in the summer of 1917, Loisy wrote that, below his outer cover of materialism, new religious aspirations were growing in modern man in the direction of a new brotherhood of peoples and a new sense of justice. The future would bring 'a truly human widening of religion'.

In *War and Religion* stands the following passage: 'The Catholic Church has, under the name of "Faith", set up so many doctrines of belief incomprehensible to our intellect, as to allow many to persuade themselves, in an excess of reaction, that the future of humanity can only lie with a complete repudiation of religion.' That was wrong, he continued. Christianity must be transmuted into a fresh, higher, truly universal religion. The problem was how.

On 21 January 1915 Loisy entered in his journal: 'I have a presentiment of a new God Who will be an ideal of humanity and Who will be better, yes, better and truer than Christ, than even the ideal Pauline Christ with his concept of personal sacrifice as the ransom for sin, which is nonsense and must be replaced by simple devotion *usque ad mortem* to the surmised ideal.' A later entry ran: 'I believe in one humanity, the mother and creator of all earthly and spiritual things, and in duty and right, her only son; *deum de deo, lumen de lumine*; and in the loving surrender *qui ex matre filioque procedit* and through which humanity forms one community, *unam sanctam catholicam et apostolicam ecclesiam*. And we await *resurrectionem mortuorum*, the realisation of their ideal, *et vitam saeculi*, and we work for the coming of centuries that shall be happier than ours.' Faced with the murder of millions, Loisy here (1 January 1917) transmuted the creed of Holy Mother Church into a creed of belief in the maternal power and courage of humanity.

Again in *The War and Religion* he writes: 'The secret of death and the secret of life are deeper than the symbols of the old Faith. What is necessary is to believe in life until death. . . . The fight between life and death is no less wonderful for him who believes in the destiny of mankind, convinced that in this struggle, where families and individuals succumb, life is none the less victorious and humanity triumphs over death. *Mors et vita duello conflixere mirando. Dux vitae mortus regnat vivus.*' In 1916, the most bloody year of war, Loisy translated the Easter faith of the Church into a post-Easter faith in humanity. Again Ernst Bloch's *Principle of Hope* comes to mind, the 'red Good Friday' of the 'red hero' who knows no personal resurrection.

In his latter years the kingdom of God seemed to Loisy the fruit of the labours, pains, and sacrifices of millions of individuals through many centuries. He evolved a mysticism of contemporaneity.

Through the prevailing preoccupation with a beyond for which the present life has merely the value of preparation, a preparation consisting in the procurement of a place in the world beyond, the Christian denominations fail to appreciate the essential object of religion, which is the perfection and spiritualisation of living humanity, not a constant recruitment of candidates for a blessed immortality. Christianity was conceived on the basis of the world's approaching end. Since it is certain that the world does not end . . . a reversal of perspectives is indispensable. . . . The essential purport of our existence lies in the present, where we collaborate with the external working of the spirit. The realm of the spirit is the true Kingdom of God on earth, a kingdom that the spirit raises with man and through man. . . . Contemporary life – we cannot repeat it often enough – is the main site of our existence, and our task is to ennoble and to perfect this life which is our active participation in eternity. For in the lap of this living world lies the principle of the whole of life, the source of spiritual life and the true foundation of morality, the community with the spirit of love through work, through struggle, through sacrifice, through joy in renunciation. Our role is finished when, through death, we pass once more into the eternal mystery.

Peace finally came to Alfred Loisy. At Paris, in 1927, the Congress on the History of Christianity was dedicated to the occasion of his seventieth birthday. Charles Guignebert, of the Sorbonne, held the inaugural address. 'Bred in the Gospel and formed by Catholicism,' said Loisy in his reply, 'I have at least retained thereby the belief in, and the feeling and affection for, humanity. I believe that all nations are sisters and all men brothers. In my view men of learning must stand in the front rank of those who labour to organise peace on earth, to secure human progress through the co-operation of all peoples, and to procure an end to the bloody rivalries which have always brought ruin in their train.'

In his letter of thanks to Carl Clemen, of Bonn, who had transmitted the greetings of the universities of Bonn, Breslau, Giessen, Halle, and Wittenberg, as well as those of Germany at large, Loisy expressed the hopes he had placed in the youthful strength of the German people. 'Europe and the world needs you. You can be the creators of that European peace which is so vital to all European peoples.'

In 1933 and again in 1938 – two fateful years for Europe in which its Catholicism was brought into the service of barbarity – the Holy Office decreed an overall condemnation of all Loisy's writings. The Church's inner impotence in the face of Fascism was closely connected to its silencing and elimination of those free intellects and critical minds who, with better treatment, would have been its best fighters. The eighty-three-year-old Loisy died on 1 June 1940 when German troops stood at the gates of Paris. On 29 June a harsh obituary appeared in *Osservatore Romano*.

MODERNISM

In order to understand to the full the nature of Modernism, on which were centred the struggles and persecutions of half a century, we must turn to the comments of Maud D.Petre. In her work on Loisy, finished shortly before her death in 1942, she rejects yet again the misconceptions to which the term gave rise. Modernism had been in no way sectarian. Almost the sole link between the very different personalities involved had been the hope that the Church would not scorn the truths of science and history and that the religious substance of its dogma would be able to survive all attacks of sceptical criticism. Yet tragedy had been unavoidable, at least in so far as every war demands a certain number of victims. And this controversy had been war, war between the guardians of faith and the guardians and pioneers of science.

This had been a Catholic point of view. In 1908 Karl Holl revealed his ideas on the event as a Protestant theologian: 'In the Catholic Church an internal conflict has broken out which, as regards clash of principles, surpasses all previous crises with the exception of the Reformation.' Yet, rather than finding it a cause of satisfaction, he continues: 'Must we too not be slightly to blame if excellent men like Tyrell and Loisy feel a repugnance for Protestantism? Is their censure of Protestantism, that it is shackled and obdurate, so wholly unjustified? To my mind we have recently been able to make our own observations on that point. With deep shame we have read articles in Church papers which might have been copies straight out of a papal encyclical.'

The Modernists were in fact not, as this important Protestant scholar makes clear, Protestant, despite the accusations of the Integralists. They wished to remain within the Catholic Church. Yet it destroyed them. Maybe Tyrrell summed up the feelings of many of these men when he said before he died (asking that the words should be put over his grave): 'I was a Catholic priest. I defended Catholic principles against Vatican heresies.'

TYRRELL

George Tyrrell (1868–1909) was an Irishman, originally of Low Church origin, who became a Catholic convert. His religious education took place partly as a novice in England, where he experienced the harshness of Catholic discipline which was so significant in forming and hardening his own individuality. The other great influences in his life were the sea and death. The death of his maternal grandmother made an imperishable impression on the boy, and as for the sea: 'the memory of it stood forth in his mind as a kind of symbol of that universality, that ocean of human thought and inspiration, fed by innumerable tributaries since the beginning of the world – that vast Catholicity.'

Tyrrell became acquainted with Friedrich von Hügel in 1897 as the result of some contributions he had made to the Jesuit periodical, *The Month*, and it was an encounter which was to determine the course of his life and ideas. Von Hügel was already forty-five at that time, the son of an Austrian ambassador, married to the daughter of a Scottish general. He was the founder of the London Society for The Study of Religion, a medium he used to spread a sense of a catholicity which would do justice both to the needs of science and the modern age, and to religious tradition. For those Catholic reformers, theologians, priests and scholars who were caught up in the Modernist movement, he played an important part as the liaison between them and Vatican circles.

It was Hügel who first introduced Tyrrell to Higher Criticism, developing in him a feeling for the greatness and spaciousness of mysticism, as well as for a broad-minded catholicity. It was he who defended Tyrrell against the attacks of Integralists, spent his life, in fact, in an unceasing effort to induce Catholics to abandon their mediaeval mentality and adopt an attitude of fairness, decency and moderation in their conduct towards opponents. Despite many disappointments, he hoped for 'reform and relaxation of our present system of denunciation and censorship', finding in Rome a spirit of persecution, a dominance of secular, political ambitions which were utterly alien to any spirit of scientific criticism. Yet despite the fact that he wrote to Tyrrell in 1902 that 'those that try and push matters on must be more or less prepared for martyrdom', they both adhered rigidly to their one principle: 'truth first, authority second'. And after Loisy had been condemned by the papacy, Tyrrell even compared this papal authority to that of Tsarist absolutism, both being basically terroristic, a taint which neither a good pope nor a good Tsar could escape. There came a time, however, when the ways of the two friends were to diverge, for Hügel, while still not abandoning his old friend, could no longer accept Tyrrell's radicalism.

The major turning point in Tyrrell's life came with his separation from the Roman Church, a separation caused mainly by his openly expressed belief in the congregation of all men and things in God. He quoted in support of his belief the mystic Mother Julian of Norwich, but it could just as well have been Origen or popular mother-wit. At the end of time, he argued, the Holy Trinity would make all things well.

The Church and its role in the future was the prime topic of all Modernists. Tyrrell's contribution, printed for private circulation under the pseudonym Hilaire Bourdon in 1903 and then published for public consumption in 1910, was in fact called *The Church and The Future*. He did not mince his words. 'Newman's theory of development has never been accepted by the "officials".' The orthodox 'explication' theory did not suffice; there had been, and continued to be, a wealth of developments which did not exist in the early days of Christianity. His tone became harsher. 'Metaphysics (and scholastic theology is chiefly metaphysics), by reason of its necessary obscurity, is the department where mediocrity and slovenliness of thought can most easily mask itself under the semblance of profundity and where the intellectual charlatan can lie longest undetected.' It was only necessary to take a handful of men from the uneducated classes, who were possessed by a superstitious desire to learn and to rise in the social scale on the score of this learning, train them in scholasticism and rhetoric, inflate them with the pride and the belief that they held in their hands a spiritual power over life and death, 'and we have all that is needed to constitute one of the worst intellectual tyrannies the world has ever known.' Precisely this corporation of theologians were the pope's advisers and through him attained omnipotence. (Tyrrell at this point was thinking of the true victors in the struggle over the infallibility dogma.) 'It is their corporate interest to defend the extremist views of papal infallibility and ecclesiastical inerrancy.'

'By "official" Catholicism we mean therefore the system of these scribes and rabbis of the New Law who keep the key which they cannot use themselves and will suffer no one else to use. . . . Christ and that theological terrorism, known as "the Holy Office of the Inquisition",' had nothing whatever in common with one another except perhaps the Sanhedrin, which sentenced Jesus to death as a heretic.

The Church and Christianity constantly required new impulses to enliven Catholicism. 'Dead, pedantic classicism, servile and literal imitation of the past, the superstition of blind custom worship, would lead to the triumph of organised mediocrity over individuals genius and would end in petrification and death.' In every society, including the Church, the issue was to establish a sound relationship between progressive and conservative forces. The Church must above all see its role as that of a school in sanctity and Christian love. Christian faith is the fruit of Christian life in just the same way as it had been exemplified first by Christ and then the Church.

Tyrrell drew a grandiose picture of the life of the Church and the state of Catholicism through the ages. The absolutism confirmed by the Vatican Council needed to be dismantled. 'The Pope as Tsar and absolute theocratic monarch by divine right must, under the logic of the Christian idea, give place to the Pope as the actual *Servus Servorum Dei*, and not only in name, as the greatest, the first-born among many brethren. . . . The growth of organic, as opposed to mechanical, conceptions of society will reconcile his leadership with the fundamentally democratic character of the Church and will relax an impossible centralisation in favour of a freer and more spiritual unity.' Opposed to all this was the 'class-interest of the theologians' fighting for *their* papal infallibility and *their* dominion over the sciences.

With the blind conservatism of their class, and indeed appealing to mediaeval authorities without the slightest allowance for changed conditions, the "officials" still hope, by the old-world coercive and oppressive methods, by the *imprimatur*, and the Index, and the Inquisition, to keep from the faithful that flood of growing information and knowledge which surges up and pours around those worm-eaten, leaky barriers which, even in their best days, had not been proof against such forces.

These men saw the Devil at work everywhere. To them the freemasons and the loss of the Church's secular state were the cause of all contemporary evil. They claimed all right for their side and put the blame for all wrong on the other. Their efforts to 'safeguard' Catholics from the wickedness of the world, by the seclusion of their seminaries, schools, and national churches, were naïve and totally inadequate.

Tyrrell expressed the hope that, from within and without, a new spirit would spread through the Church and transform its climate. 'Public mind, opinion, and sentiment' invariably made their mark and would not fail to leave it on the Church. 'The Church is greater than what she has made, greater than the episcopate or the pope. What they do officially, they do simply in her name, as her servants, under her judgment.' 'The mind of the Church is not to be identified with the intellect of a class in the Church, i.e., of the theological schools whose understanding is logically developed by dialect, criticism, and other purely mental processes.'

Under the harsh pressure of historical reality a coalescence of divided Christianity was in train. 'It is not to the theologians, or to the officials, that we are to look for such a reform, but to the stern logic of history with its ruthless criticism of all unreality and to the spread of knowledge that no class-conspiracy can keep back for long, save to its own more utter discomfiture.' Christ's spirit was at work in the souls of millions of Catholics, non-Catholics and non-Christians, and was seeking a path from heart to heart through all the denominational barriers erected by the theologians.

The cry of the spiritually starving multitudes, robbed of the bread of life, will at last drown the chatter of idle theologians and wake the great heart of the Church to the weightier realities of the Gospel.

The reunion of Christendom, as conceived and desired by a large class of its advocates, would be perhaps the greatest calamity that could befall religion in general and Christianity in particular. It would mean the formation of a gigantic sect in league against the rest of the world, excluding and condemning five-sevenths of its religious life.

Tyrrell pleaded the cause of a 'liberal Catholicism', for which 'the final authority is Christ as progressively revealed in the life of the Church from first to last; it is the *consensus fidelium*, the spirit of Christianity, as embodied in the present, past, and future multitudes of those who live the life' of Christ. The liberal Catholic, knowing himself to be thus at one with Christ in the Church, will not be disconcerted by Church officials who issue instructions which he cannot square with his conscience, just as an Englishman who sided with the Boers, and in the Chamberlain era, had his windows smashed as a 'traitor', did not cease to be an Englishman, for all that public opinion was against him. 'If it be objected that such a procedure may be honest under a democratic constitutional monarchy where party government is recognised, but that it cannot be recognised under an imperial absolutism like that of the Church, one may answer that the liberal Catholic is just one who repudiates this notion of the Church, and that, what would be dishonest in one who accepts it, is perfectly honest for him.' 'That the Church of Christ should be governed by the methods of Russian autocracy and terrorism is an abuse that must revolt the conscience of every Christian who is even moderately imbued with the spirit of Gospel liberty; it is an abuse that deserves no respect. . . .'

Cardinal Mercier, in his pastoral letter for Lent 1908, called 'the English priest' Tyrrell the leading brain in Modernism. His works, which contained pages of profound piety to be read only with sincere gratitude towards the author, breathed a spirit permeated by the fundamental error of the German Döllinger. It was a Protestant spirit, and no wonder, seeing that Tyrrell had formerly been a Protestant. Tyrrell's reply to this attack by the French Cardinal ran to two hundred pages.

'Your Eminence, will you never take heart of grace and boldly throw open the doors of your great mediaeval cathedral and let the light of a new day strike into its darkest corners and the fresh wind of Heaven blow through its mouldy cloisters?' Tyrrell took the attitude of an independent Irish monk of the early Middle Ages rounding on a Frankish bishop. 'Indeed, it is no impreachment of your sincerity to suspect that, in the depth of your sub-consciousness, you agree with me more than you dare admit to yourself.' Because in Tyrrell's eyes the Church of the Pope and of Cardinal Mercier was completely bound to the past, he called his reply *Mediaevalism* and contrasted their Church with the open, live, and free one of the future.

Through Scylla and Charybdis appeared in 1907. The German edition appeared at Jena two years later. In his preface to the translation of his famous work Tyrrell remarked that the German origin of Modernism was its main crime in the eyes of Rome and sufficed to damn it, since nothing good could come out of the land of Luther and Protestantism. Nowhere was Catholicism so well drilled and organised, nowhere did it render its political intentions so obvious as in Germany. Consequently any movement which sought to interrupt the mechanical uniformity of its firmly closed ranks was instantly and energetically trodden underfoot. This was the reason why Modernism had not been able so far to gain a hearing among the countrymen of Döllinger, Deutinger, Kraus and Schell. His present contribution sought to steer between the Scylla of a crippling dogmatism which allowed of no improvement and the Charybdis of an all-devouring scepticism and negation, between authority which annihilated personality and individualism which destroyed society.

Modernism meant faith in Catholicism, but also faith in the modern world. In both instances this faith was so deep as to be able with calm confidence to be critical to the ultimate degree. Erasmus was preferable to Luther, and this fact was not invalidated by the admission that warm-hearted and more humane Catholicism had always been confined to a weak and down-trodden minority which had attracted to itself the disapproval of the majority.

Tyrrell welcomed the many points of contact between Catholicism and other religions. To be Catholic was to feel at one with all the world's religions and to recognise that every one of them, however feebly, was illumined by that one invisible Light which was a match for their deepest darkness. St Paul, Origen, Clement of Alexandria, and Tertullian supported this view. Catholicism was a people's religion, full of compromises and beset by thickets and tangles. Nevertheless God, as in nature, worked slowly but surely through the uninhibited strife between opposites.

The duty of religion was to convey God to man and to fill the soul with the inexhaustible riches of divine truth, goodness, and love. The Church was historically a young institution and the leaven of the Gospel was far from having gained the day. Religions evolved and were not manufactured as finished articles. Therein lay their strength and their dignity. It was impossible that the Church should penetrate the world without being penetrated by it.

Tyrrell was aware of life's dialectic and gave a dialectical interpretation to history and religions of all sorts, including Christianity. Jesus and the Judaism of His time were the most perfect representations of the two essential and always mutually hostile elements in every living religion, the progressive and the static. The latter, seeking to defend itself, would be driven into reaction; the former, into open rebellion. Truth would be attained by the clash of these opposites. Ultimately, the decisive question was whether thought developed architectonically or biologically. The one led to the walled Church and its tectonic theological systems which caved in if a single stone was loosed. The other resulted in a Catholicity accessible to all of life's change and growth. Christianity was nothing if it was not an interpretation of life and history.

Currently one class of theologists was trying to lead the Church with the aid of the masses and the mass spirit. The voice of the masses was not the voice of the people, but, looked at as a class, these theologians bore some stamp of the masses and the mass spirit. Not, as Tyrrell emphasised, that he was against theology as such. His objection was to its being turned into an '-ism'. He regarded 'theologism' as the father and chief of all heresies, the sword which had cut Christianity to pieces, the force which today kept multitudes of deeply religious individuals away from the Church or drove them out of it, the undoer of revelation and of theology, and the enemy simultaneously of faith and reason. In philosophy he understood the outcome of philosophic reflection on the facts of religious experience, the normative focus of these facts being Apostolic revelation. 'Theologism' was the terror of a closed system to which the world was indebted for the declaration of papal infallibility.

In 1870 the absolutism of officials had triumphed at Rome and was destroying the deepest substance of Catholicism in favour of a military dictatorship. (The Jesuit Tyrrell had the Roman Jesuits in mind.) Absolutism was a practical and speculative simplification which always appealed to the masses and their leaders as Hitler's rise to power was to show. As for sacerdotalism, it was the bureaucracy of the Church just as bureaucracy was the sacerdotalism of the state. It found expression in the first place in the comparatively vulgar and obvious view of the sheep as the source of the comfort and dignity of their shepherd. In a more refined and corrupting form it lurked behind the notion that the entire ecclesiastical apparatus existed for its own sake and not simply and solely as a means to the spiritual furtherance of those who supported it. However unselfish the intent, it was impossible to escape egotism if service was rendered to the egotism of a corporation, class, or trade union.

The machine at Rome was working at full blast to establish absolutism inside the Church by way of decrees, encyclicals, and 'police orders'. That was no cause for despair because the Church's path was positively strewn with the bleached bones of long-forgotten decisions and ordinances which had, in their day, been reversed as standing for all time. It was to be hoped that a democratic spirit would come to prevail in the Church, that democratic feeling which had been so active in the Early Church and had then been submerged. The immediate future admittedly seemed gloomy because the alienation of laymen was still increasing on account of the Church's absolutism. What was necessary was to concede laymen once more their original active participation in the life of the Church. Modernism and its opponents both belonged to the same process of living growth.

Hügel, after Tyrrell's death, wrote to Loisy that he had been 'a man, in a word, who deserved a very different lot, and a man whose influence, in large measure, will not pass away'.

HÜGEL

'True catholicism is the recognition and assimilation into one's own life of all religious and extra-religious truths and values.' This was Hügel's most fundamental belief, the belief of a man who had never been to school, whose education had rested in the hands of such different men as an Anglican friend of the family, a Rhenish Lutheran pastor, a Roman Catholic historian, and an English Quaker, and which had been tested at the age of eighteen when, during a year spent in Vienna, he underwent a severe religious crisis.

Hügel was the son of a man who regarded Vienna as his true home, and of a Scottish mother. He was married to Lady May Herbert, the daughter of Lord Herbert of Lea, and in 1914, basically because of his profound dislike of Wilhelmine Germany, he assumed British citizenship. His life was spent as mediator between the Catholic Church of Rome and those Catholics who, for one reason or another, had fallen away from the Church. He studied 'the differences between officialdom on the one hand and the living forces of religion around us and within us on the other'.

Creative individuality clashed with the authority of the Church which, relying on the majority, the average, demanded passive obedience and precise fulfilment of its injunctions 'as mechanically and repetitively as possible'. 'Every truly noble life is noble largely through having courageously risked all risks necessary to its own expansion, growth and fruitfulness', but authority desired safety and thus produced 'stagnation and sterility'. Authority was always a threat to the noblest and most personal qualities. Nevertheless, it was essential to the maintenance of the link between the mass and the individual.

The Church's life was a process of 'rhythmic inspiration and expiration', rendering it 'both progressive and conservative'. 'Church officials are no more the whole Church, or a complete specimen of the average of the Church, than Scotland Yard or the War Office or the House of Lords, though admittedly necessary parts of the national life, are the whole, or average samples, of the life and the fruitfulness of the English nation' (1904).

On 11 December 1918, writing to his dearly loved Anglican niece (whom he never made the slightest effort to convert), Hügel remarked on the fact that in all other religions God Himself was still the source of historical preparations for His fullest manifestation of Himself, each individual religion remaining a true revelation of God.

As far as Hügel was concerned, the basic sin of Christians was not, as the tradition following Augustine maintained, carnal lust: 'the central sin . . . is Pride and Self-sufficiency, distinctly more so than Impurity or Sloth.' And in 1920, looking back on the First World War, the excesses of nationalism and the three decades of persecution by the Church of its dissenting members, Hügel formulated the following profession of belief: 'I am deeply grateful to God that I most truly owe, and that I am keenly aware that I owe, to all the great typical races and nations far too much ever to totally condemn any one of them. What . . . would my religion be without its Jewish figure? What would my Theology be without the Greeks? What would my Church Order be without the Italians? . . . I want them all and I rejoice in them all.'

Hügel was only too aware of the heritage of thousands of years which went into the makings of religion, and formed so deep a part of the life of all Christians, and this being so, he felt that the essential task of Christianity was to perceive and accept the 'deep central truth' below the surface of every way of thought possessed by humanity. And after this essential fact, the second task of Christianity was the glorification, enrichment and trans-mutation of all human relationships, whether between man and woman, parents and children, nations, races or classes.

Interdependence – the slogan of a more recent sociology – was, for Hügel, experience of the community of saints, of all men, of all sinners, at all times. It found expression in a letter to his niece in 1919, where he defined it as the deep tie subsisting between all human souls, and exemplified it by saying that it was not simply a matter of praying, but of suffering, for one another.

On his seventieth birthday, Hügel recalled the most important experience he had gained from life: to want to help another soul along the road meant for the life-bringing soul, in the highest reality, an especially thorough, double atrophy of self; the Church, especially in its Roman Catholic form, had done much harm and caused many complications and suppressions which would not have existed without it. But he found consolation in those great, though few, saints who had overcome the hate and mass of antipathies in the Church. In a later letter he added that every truly noble life was most noble in that it bravely assumed all the hazards necessary to its own growth and fruitfulness.

Hügel, as an Austrian and British Catholic gentleman, had the courage to march between the fronts, knowing that his own maturation was only to be achieved in community with those who dared, hoped and suffered. At Rome he pleaded for years for moderation and understanding on behalf of the much persecuted Modernists. His friends Tyrrell, Loisy, Loyson, Romolo Murri, and the young priests at Milan could rely on his support. When the waves of persecution broke over the heads of the Italian Modernists, he arranged a three-day meeting with them at Molveno in Austrian South Tirol. Among those present were Fogazzaro, Casati, Scotti, Fracassini, Buonaiuti, Casciola, Mari, and Piastrelli. They included the author of the anonymous pamphlet *Quello che vogliamo, Lettera aperta a Pio X*.

ITALIAN AND GERMAN REFORMISM

Tyrrell called Pope Pius x the 'inventor of Modernism', and not without justification. *Pascendi Dominici gregis*, the encyclical of 3 September 1907, condemned a movement as heretical to the point of deserving destruction; a movement which was, in fact, not inherently heretical, which adopted no unanimous attitude, which was, through its total lack of homogeneity, hardly a movement at all, but an evolutionary process among modern intellectuals whose ways of thought were not only diverse, but often even contradictory. As in every youth movement there were errors, misunderstandings and extravagances. The term covered a wide circle of men from Jansenist reformers, priests of an archaic turn of mind, men of a mediaeval monk-like severity, demanding total reorganisation of the Church, and 'liberals' inspired by French and German higher criticism. In Italy, at the turn of the century, Modernism represented an unwieldy mass of professors, poets, theologians, young parsons.

One of the many formative influences on Modernism in Italy may be found in the 'liberal Catholicism' of Vincenzo Gioberti. The fragments of his principal work include the sentence 'Contemporary Catholic Christianity needs to do what the Jewish prophets, six hundred years before our era did – reform religion and bring it into harmony with science and civilisation.' Gioberti (1801–52), priest, émigré at Paris and Brussels, minister (1849–9) under Charles Albert of Savoy, attacked the Index and supported evolution of dogmas. He likened dogma to the seed which had lain buried for thousands of years in Egyptian tombs, but now upon its excavation was sprouting.

The Golden Age for Italy's young and open-minded clergy, who placed their hopes in Leo XIII (1890–1900), found literary expression in the periodical *Studi Religiosi*, founded at Florence in January 1901 by Salvatore Minocchi. It had enormous success. One of its results was the blowing of a fresh intellectual breeze through theological seminars. In 1905 the *Rivista storico-critico delle science teologiche* was first published in Rome, bringing together theologians with historical training who immediately after the appearance of the encyclical *Pascendi* issued an anonymous pamphlet, *The Modernists' Programme*, which refuted the encyclical word for word. They noted with satisfaction that the authors had even got the date of Pope Gregory IX's missive to the Parisian theologians wrong, writing 1223 instead of 1228, a small example of their utter lack of historical insight.

Nova et Vetera, the periodical founded with the active help of Hügel, came out in 1908. Towards the end of the year it published a long letter from Giovanni Papaini. After acknowledgement of the worthy efforts of these members of Modernism, it nevertheless reproached them with the fact that there was nothing in all their exertions which was directly and exclusively aimed at seeking the triumph of love in the world. This was precisely the complaint of 'friendly' critics – the critical labour of the Modernists was destructive without being constructive. *Nova et Vetera* took Papaini's rebuke very seriously. Its reply sought to explain, clearly and frankly, the Modernists' point of view, that they were merely forerunners of the Church and Christianity as it would be in the future, and that to render the old soil ripe for fresh growth required the removal of much rubbish and the elimination of many impediments.

Those Modernists who met Friedrich von Hügel at Molveno were made to realise how completely they differed among themselves in outlook, spirituality, objectives and planning. Much patient encouragement and promotion would have been necessary for their intentions to become mature and lucid. For this, however, there was no time: after the 1907 encyclical they were forced underground.

The traits of the French and German Modernists (of which the latter included some highly individual personalities), were quite distinct from those of the Italians, although they suffered the same persecution. In France men as different as Loisy, Blondel, Le Roy, Turmel, Saint-Yves, Labethonnière, and others, became victims of the wave of condemnations between 1908 and 1913. At the same period many periodicals were forced to cease publication, including *Demain, Les Annales de philosophie religieuse*, and *Revue d'histoire et de littérature religieuse*.

Many of the parsons and priests in Germany silently tolerated this warping of their consciences and knowledge, but one or two resisted, among them Albert Ehrhard, an ecclesiastical historian whose answer to an inquiry by the *Internationale Wochenschrift für Wissenschaft, Kunst und Technik* in January 1908, was extremely courageous. He confirmed that the constant curial condemnations constituted a mortal menace to conscience and theology and called them a sin against the Holy Ghost. Questions concerning the Bible, the evolutions of dogma, the apostleship, and others, did exist, and there was no point in trying to disguise the fact. If curial decisions were carried through in Germany, it would merely signify the end of the university theological faculties as had been the case in France and Italy.

One of the earliest German victims was Hermann Schell (1850–1906). The guiding principle of his life may be found in a sentence from his book on Christ: 'To be a man means to be a fighter, a seeker after truth, not a possessor of truth and reveller in truth.' He continues 'the only convincing apologetic is proof and demonstration of the Spirit'. In his six volumes of dogma (1889–1893) he tried to achieve an apologetical dogma which would be simultaneously polemic and ironic. As far as he was concerned, if Catholic science lacked the courage to express an opinion on major scientific questions, then it was neither a science nor Catholic. In 1897 he published an appeal to German Roman Catholics not to betray their duty to a contemporary intellectual life and provided two mottoes: 'Catholicism as a principle of progress' and 'the intellect for God and God for the intellect'.

In the same appeal Schell demanded from the Church a long overdue acknowledgement of culpability. This short work passed through six editions in the first twelve months. The following year Schell brought out *New Age and Old Faith*. On 15 December 1898 both pieces and his two main works on dogma and apologetics were, without explanation, put on the Index. On 1 March 1899 he surrendered in disciplinary obedience to his bishop and on the following Sunday announced his submission from the pulpit of the university chapel. Although the next five years were full of lecture activities in various German cities, the spring of his strength was broken. As the editor of a selection of his works, Paul-Werner Scheele, said in 1957, 'What sort of a vindication of the Church was to be expected from him who saw himself misunderstood and proscribed by many of its members and yet put his whole strength into praising and defending it?'

Schell wanted laymen and priests to collaborate in the great crisis of the time. He felt that all effort was menaced by those who 'neither perceive any need to increase the horizon of their thought nor understand how anyone can cherish such a need'. The authors of the encyclical *Pascendi* can hardly be more pithily described. The authors of this and the syllabus *Lamentabili sine exitu*, published two months earlier as an inventory of errors were Cardinal Billot and Pater Matiussi on the one hand and Pater Joseph Lemius, a personal friend of the papal Secretary of State Cardinal Merry del Val on the other hand, men who formed the core of the clique which surrounded the Pope, a deeply pious man but utterly out of touch with the age and barely conversant with any foreign language. A principal part was undoubtedly played by Cardinal Billot, a right-wing extremist who, indignant at the action taken (twenty years too late) by the subsequent Pope Pius XI against the *Action Française*, divested himself of the purple in 1927. It was a public demonstration of the secret workings of Integralism. If a pope did not suit the party, it intrigued against him or was prepared, in the last resort, to take to open rebellion.

Under the spell of these politicians, who in 1910 were to drive him to condemnation of the Christian Democrats, Pius X began his campaign of annihilation against the Modernists. In a public consistory he accused them of 'teaching in deceptive forms abominable errors . . . about adaptation to contemporary times' and admitted himself 'fearful in the face of this attack which is not a heresy but the substance and poison of all heresies, the aim of which is to undermine the foundations of faith and to destroy Christianity.' The only qualities which, according to the encyclical *Pascendi*, he could see in them were reprehensible 'curiosity' and 'presumptuousness'. He wished to 'tear away the masks' of these 'enemies of the Church' who 'are worse than all other enemies' since they 'lurk in the breast and lap of the Church'.

A 'savage passion to damn' (Walter Nigg) predominated in this encyclical. The outlook and language were identical with the Integralists and politicians of the 'Party of Order' that was so prominent in the Dreyfus Affair and the papal prouncement met with frenzied acclamation on the French and Italian Right. To this was very shortly added the jubilation of the Italian Left for it realised that at this point all hope of reconciliation between the Church and the modern world, the dream of the Liberals, had been utterly destroyed. Others joined in the exaltation (as they would do in the 1950s, after condemnation of the worker priests) – men like Benedetto Croce and Giovanni Gentile who mocked at the Modernists' delusion that it was possible to unite science and the Church.

French and Italian Modernists were quick to reply to the encyclical. They convicted it of forgery, fanaticism and unreasonableness. They rejected the accusation that a specific philosophy lay at the back of all their work, retorting that, as historical criticism – and not philosophy – was the point of their departure, the time had come, in Pascal's words, 'to lay the documents open on the table'.

> We are tired of seeing the Church degraded to a bureaucracy which jealously safeguards its remaining competencies and avidly seeks to regain former ones, and to a class of indolent men, who, after dedicating themselves to the priesthood, which means leading the life of an apostle, have arrived on the highest rungs of the hierarchy while guiltily absent from the seat of those fat livings they enjoy, and to an inert mass which, for all its proud, superficial glitter, borne up by the so easily attained and stupid admiration of the populace, simply hems the progress of society.

In contradiction to a fetishistic interpretation of scholasticism, they declared, as an example, that 'St Thomas was the true modernist of his age, the man who, with marvellous endurance and grandiose genius, attempted to merge faith with the outlook of his age. We . . . are the true prosecutors of scholasticism, there where it renders valuable service – in the establishment of a sensitivity which enables the Christian religion to adjust to the fluctuating forms of philosophy and civilisation in general.' They regarded themselves as rightful sons of the Church and reminded the Pope of Augustine's words, 'Divine Providence has often allowed, in consequence of the unruly behaviour of all too carnally minded men, the expulsion too from the Christian community of irreproachable individuals.'

Pius x, a friend and patron of the *Action Française*, very soon extended the persecution to 'political Modernism'. Its exponents were the supporters of a Christian democracy, French priests desiring a reconciliation with the Republic, or those who even ventured to think of a 'Christian socialism'. With expressions of hatred which had stood the test so well in the Dreyfus Affair, democracy was denounced as a 'modernist' heresy. In Italy the priest Romolo Murri with his *democrazia christiana* and in France the *abbés démocrates*, then Paul Naudet with his periodical *Justice sociale*, Pierre Dabry with *Vie catholique*, and Marc Sangnier with *Sillon*, were all ecclesiastically condemned. In this annihilation campaign, political and theological reaction worked hand in hand and cannot be distinguished. The *Sillon* case was exemplary.

On 25 August 1910 Pius x, in collaboration with the *Action Française*, officially condemned *Sillon*, the periodical of the Christian Democratic movement conducted by the disinterested Marc Sangnier. The reasons given in the letter of the Pope (that is, his wire-pullers) to the French episcopacy were twofold. First, 'the presumption of having evaded the guidance of the Church's authority' on the excuse 'of working in a field' (social affairs) 'which did not appertain to that of the Church'. Secondly, 'a worse evil', that '*Sillon* has in view the re-establishment and regeneration of the working classes'. The Pope backed this reasoning by reference to Leo xiii's encyclical

Graves de communi of 18 January 1901. The passages in question affirmed that there must be maintained 'the diversity of classes which is surely the attribute of well constituted society' and condemned as in the highest degree 'perverse' the presumptuous aspiration 'to pursue the abolition and nullification of the classes'.

After this the Curial Integralists let loose a wave of persecution, denunciation, and spying of which one of its victims, Ernesto Buonaiuti, said in 1943 that even more than thirty years later the wounded souls of many priests testified to the work of destruction. 'If the true dramas of history are those that are performed without witnesses in the temple of human conscience, then there have been few dramas in the modern age more tragic than the dramas produced in the souls of innumerable priests through the applications and consequences of the encyclical *Pascendi*.'

On 1 September 1910 Pius x's decree *Sacrorum Antistitum* accused the Modernists of undermining theological seminars with their propaganda and of being a secret society whose objective was the destruction of the Church. The *Corrispondenza Romana* and *Action Française* at once raised the hue and cry of a Modernist conspiracy along Carbonari lines and warned against Modernist spies in every nook and cranny. This became too much even for *Etudes*, the French Jesuit periodical, which protested in November 1910 against collective denunciation.

In the same decree Pius x ordered that every member of the clergy must annually testify on oath and according to a two-page long formula that they rejected 'the heretical assumption of an evolution in the dogmas' and historical methods of criticism as well as declaring from the bottom of their hearts that they 'agreed with all the condemnations, pronouncements, and precepts contained in the encyclical *Pascendi* and the decree *Lamentabili*'. 'This anti-modernist oath, which remains in force today still [Walter Nigg, writing in 1937] created the most grievous conflicts of conscience for countless Catholic priests and professors who could render the oath only with secret and admitted reservations.' This annual brain-washing of the Church's theological and academic intelligentsia contributed to the paralysis of European Catholicism, making it incapable during the First and Second World Wars of speaking an authoritative word of its own or taking up effectively the struggle with Fascism and National Socialism.

These were the days when Monsignor Benigni built up his secret society against the Modernists. *Sodalitium Pianum*, named after Benigni's patron, Pius x, who sent him a letter of congratulation each year, had the task of nosing out Modernists everywhere, arranging for their denunciation in the Catholic Press, and instituting their condemnation by the Church. This pious organisation was not dissolved until 1921. Benigni had earlier been the teacher at Rome of Buonaiuti, who inspired only the sarcasm of this deeply pessimistic reactionary. 'Do you really believe, my good fellow,' he asked Buonaiuti, 'that people are capable of any good in the world? History is a constant and despairing effort to vomit and all humanity needs is the

Inquisition.' Theological, anthropological, and historical pessimism constitutes, both inside and outside the Church, the foundation for totalitarian and absolutist régimes.

In the years preceding 1914 and in the early years of the First World War the small groups of Modernists who refused to take the oath required by Pius x's decree were hunted down. In spring 1913 Cardinal Andrieu of Bordeaux (he gave his blessing to *Action Française*) dissolved the last semi-Modernist periodical in France, the *Bulletin de la Semaine*. He pointed out that its trend was advantageous to German policy and ruinous to France's intellectual standing in the world. 1916 saw the subjugation of a last small group of priests.

The consequences of the Modernist dispute have remained catastrophic for European Catholicism right up to the present day. Viewed politically, the condemnation of Marc Sangnier and his Christian Democracy had its logical consequence thirteen years later in Italy and twenty-three years later in Germany. On 9 June 1923 Cardinal Vannutelli, dean of the Sacred College, recommended Don Sturzo to resign and to dissolve the Catholic party. This placed the forces of Italian Catholicism at Mussolini's disposal. In 1933 the Curia extorted the self-dissolution of the Centre Party in Germany after it had fulfilled its last task by voting in the *Reichstag* for Hitler's seizure of power. Under the spell of the firm belief in princes held by Pope Gregory XVI and his successors during the nineteenth century, Pius XII sought, for the Church, the protection of the 'Christian princes' of his day. Peron, Franco, and Salazar received the Vatican State's highest decoration – the Order of Christ. And Hitler seemed the leader-elect for the crusade against Bolshevism. Pius XII, the last of the nineteenth-century popes, was the last papal victim of the Integralist bureaucracy dominant since 1870.

As Papal Nuncio, he had been a man of enlightened and sceptical intellect who enjoyed talking to Adolf von Harnack about, for instance, the numberless forgeries existing in hagiology. As Pope, he was a lonely man who felt himself surrounded in the Vatican by 'Romans' whom he feared and tried to keep at a distance. Dependent on his own judgement and diplomacy, he was defeated by Hitler and proved incapable of protecting Catholics, whether in Germany, Hungary, Poland or elsewhere, or the Jews, about whose extermination he received regular reports. This deeply *Angst*-ridden and helpless Pope, after a short period of post-war respite during which Princes of the Church and Integralist groups, compromised by their connections with Fascism, National Socialism, and right-wing French extremists, had to exercise a certain restraint, allowed new waves of persecution to break over worker-priests, modern Jesuits, Dominicans, Carmelites, ecclesiastical historians, and Bible critics.

For the old problems arose again immediately after 1945. The major questions which had preoccupied the reformers, the scholars, and the Modernists were resumed, though cautiously, by the men of the *Théologie nouvelle*. As early as 1946 M.-Michel Labourdette, O.P., in charge of the

Revue thomiste, fired the first shot against modern 'relativism' and Lubac and Danielou. At Rome, Reginald Garrigou-Lagrange (another Dominican) began, in *Angelicum,* the drive against the Jesuits Bouillard, Lubac, Fessard, Pierre Teilhard de Chardin, as well as against numerous typewritten and duplicated anonymous treatises which had been circulating among the French clergy since 1934. In 1951 Giuseppe Martini remarked of the situation: 'Today the courageous vanguard of French Jesuits is advancing ideas which are not far removed from those of Tyrrell.'

Labourdette in 1947 distinguished between two sorts of Modernism; the one condemned by Pius x, and a Modernism in a broader sense which should not, as a way of thought, be condemned out of hand as heretical. This conservative French theologian was no out and out reactionary. In order to escape the vicious circle of the past, he wanted to establish a set of rules which would govern any disputes among theologians, which should include readiness to be self-critical, renunciation of malicious imputations and denunciations, and abandonment of anonymous and clandestine literature. During the following decade a certain amount of notice was taken of his recommendations.

In 1861, according to a report in *Orbis Catholicus,* an inquiry instituted by the International Federation of Catholic Social Research Institutes (FERES) came to the conclusion that 'on the whole, conditions during the last decades of the nineteenth century left the impression that Catholicism had manœuvred itself out of the stream of history and into a ghetto, thereby renouncing penetration of the world with its spirit.' As for the consequences of the encyclical, *Pascendi,*

> the repercussions of this condemnation affected the whole of ecclesiastical and theological life. The supporters of the conservative school of thought were in part roused to an extremity of Integralism directly reminiscent at its lowest level of a witch-hunt on the pattern of the sixteenth century. . . . Numerous theologians who had only just come out of recently founded Catholic faculties and institutes or German universities, were not merely subject to suspicion but in some cases suffered downright persecution. . . . The Index, vetos on speaking and publishing, and intrigues of the worst sort served Integralism as a means towards its reactionary ends, which it identified without hesitation with the true faith. It pretended to be, or was blind to the aim of its opponents, that of discovering the elements of truth in the modern non-Catholic and non-Christian systems of values, and interpreted orthodoxy, which it thought it was defending, as meaning that the Church as a concrete social reality was neither susceptible to nor needed any serious modification.

This inquiry rendered its report two years after the death of the last nineteenth-century pope, Pius XII.

ROME AND RUSSIA

In 1905 Charles Péguy wrote one of his finest works, *Les Suppliants parallèles*. It served as introduction to his poem, *Le Porche du Mystère de la deuxième Vertu*, dedicated to the events of 22 January 1905, 'Bloody Sunday', at St Petersburg, the day when the power of tsarism broke, when the people of Russia lost their faith for ever in the tsar as protector of the nation.

Throughout the nineteenth century the papacy and the tsar had looked to each other for mutual support against revolution, Enlightenment, democracy. Rome, moreover, relying on the successful missionary work of the Jesuits among Russian aristocracy, hoped to prove legatee to the moribund Orthodox Church. And not without reason. In 1800 it seemed as if the tsar himself might turn Catholic in order to save both religion and governmental power.

Papal diplomacy, the Jesuits and the Curia's lay assistants, in the form of influential Russian converts, persuaded tsarism that the Roman Church was the sole refuge against revolution, and Tsar Alexander I, under the influence of Metternich, was inclined to agree. In 1845 Tsar Nicholas I visited Pope Gregory xvi at Rome. The subject of their discussions – common measures for the suppression of revolution, communism and socialism. In August 1847, inspired by their common fears, a concordat, though short-lived, was reached.

Many links carefully woven on the part of the papacy, were destroyed by the Crimean War, and the declaration of infallibility on the part of the Vatican Council naturally increased the never quite dormant mistrust of the Russian Orthodox hierarchy. In its eyes political relations between tsarism and Rome meant the beginning of the end, a Western, political and religious take-over of Russia. When contacts became ever closer under Leo xiii and his secretary of State, Cardinal Rampolla, the Procurator of the Holy Synod wrote a letter to Tsar Alexander iii, warning him that any written agreement with Rome would mean a threat to the freedom of the Russian nation. 'Every utterance provides Rome with a weapon and a title which it then interprets according to its own discretion.' In its rejection of the possibility of a nunciature at St Petersburg, the Orthodox Church was completely at one with the Liberals and Social Revolutionaries.

In 1888 Leo xiii fancied the danger of world war to be imminent and placed his hopes in Russia. The well-known Austrian historian, Theodor von Sickel, reports of an audience he had with the Pope at this time that 'he described the unfailing results of a reconciliation of Russia with the West: the Eastern Question would be at once resolved and Islam defeated, while Russia, with the advice and support of the Church, would dictate peace in Europe and restore social order.' At this point the Pope, rising up and looking like a seer, added to the historian kneeling at his feet, 'And, when that happens, you Protestants will simply follow the Russian example.'

No one incarnated more impressively than Leo xiii this imperial concept of the nineteenth-century papacy. He had taken Innocent III for his pattern and 'even today the tombs of Popes Innocent III and Leo XIII, flanking the high altar of the Lateran Church to right and left, commemorate that missionary notion and the belief of Leo XIII in world dominion'. Whether or not this spiritual and ecclesiastically political imperialism seems now an extravagant version of late nineteenth-century imperialism, it was in any case the complete reverse of the Holy Alliance, the friendly alliance between the three major Christian Churches, as envisaged early on by Alexander I as well as Franz von Baader and his Russian and Prussian friends.

Immense efforts were made on the part of the Curia to effect an approach to its objective by direct and indirect diplomatic negotiations at Rome, Vienna, Paris, and St Petersburg. Yet they made no progress. Every time it seemed as though the so keenly desired moment of union between the Churches, and a closer political tie, was in sight, the Russians dodged. From time to time the papacy temporarily lost its nerve. Pius IX, for instance, during the course of a large audience given on 30 April 1877, complained of a 'heretical Great Power' which embittered his life. Not only the Russians, but the Catholic Czechs, too, felt this to be an affront. In a talk with the papal historian Ludwig von Pastor, on 12 December 1913, Pius X told him that Russia was the Church's greatest enemy and that the other Slav peoples should equally not be trusted. The Curia, on the eve of the First World War and under leadership of this same Pope, advocated a swift overthrow of Serbia by Austria-Hungary and feared the worst for Europe from Russia.

These immense hopes and immense fright were inseparable. The last of the nineteenth-century popes, Pius XII, although perhaps subconsciously, did see in Adolf Hitler the man of Providence who would lead the crusade against Bolshevism. The Eucharistic Congress, held at Budapest in 1938, was the forum for a policy speech by Pius when still Cardinal Pacelli which must be regarded as approval of such a plan. At Berlin, representatives of the Curia in due course had talks about the Church's future work in occupied Poland and Russia which found confirmation in the orders issued by the *Wehrmacht* High Command.

The papacy sacrificed its favourite Eastern daughter, Poland, to its imperialist notions. The pleas of French Catholics fell on deaf ears. The popes were tireless in summoning the Poles and their episcopacy to subjugate themselves obediently to the Tsars, and in condemning Polish uprisings. There is some reason for believing that Monsignor Benigni, during the course of his duties in the papal State Secretariat in 1905-6, advised the Tsarist Government of matters, the transmission of which amounted to a betrayal of the Catholic Church in the Russian–Polish territories. A report by the Saxon envoy at Munich on 14 March 1912, suggests that this betrayal related to information about the Polish revolutionary movement. After the breakdown of Poland in 1939, Foreign Minister Beck declared, 'One of those principally responsible for the tragedy of my country is the Vatican.' The efforts of Polish Catholics and bishops to go their own way after 1945 becomes perhaps more intelligible if the abandonment of Poland by the papacy during the nineteenth century is borne in mind, a performance complementary to that mortal sin of the two European conservative Powers, Prussia and Austria, the partition of Poland.

One small episode may serve to illuminate the fundamental reason why all Roman efforts to attain a firm footing in Russia for any length of time failed. In 1891 Vincenzo Vannutelli, a Dominican and nephew of the two influential Cardinals Vincenzo and Serafino Vannutelli, paid a visit to Russia with the full support of the Foreign Ministry at St Petersburg. A year later he published a book on his impressions. Its sub-title was 'A Religious Study of Russia'. Owing to its author's frankly expressed belief in the union of the Russian Orthodox Church with the papacy, engineered by a concordat between the tsarist government and the Holy See, it had international, political implications. On the one hand, it was a straightforward revelation of how once again the Integralists as they had done during the whole nineteenth century, could successfully still blind the popes with the false hope that it needed just a few more exertions to achieve the great work of 'union' under the sovereignty and leadership of the Holy See. On the other hand it thoroughly alarmed Pobedonostsev, the Procurator of the Holy Synod.

In a letter to the British periodical *Review of Reviews* the Procurator stated that he had told Father Vannutelli that the Russian people would never agree to submit to the yoke of papal authority, that its beliefs were incompatible with the dominant position of Christ's representative on earth, that all other differences respecting dogmas and ritualistic precepts and customs were unimportant, but that this one difference would always constitute an insuperable impediment to a merger between the two Churches because it would involve the abandonment of the Russians' spiritual individuality. The Tsar's own belief was indivisible from that of the Russian people. As far as his wishes in doctrinal matters were concerned, the Tsar stood to the Church as a son to his mother. The point that the Tsar was not going to commit matricide was clearly insinuated. Pobedonostsev did, however, do something to save the Dominican's face a little. He explained that the misunderstanding about a union of the Churches, which was specifically based on a conversation with himself, was presumably due to the fact that Vannutelli was inadequately versed in French, the language in which the interview had been conducted.

How about Russian? The language of the Russian soul, the Russian spirit, and the Russian intellect? There can be no doubt but that Rome's wooing of Russia was foredoomed for one specific reason. While popes, curial politicians, and their missionaries increased their efforts towards a political and ecclesiastical approach from decade to decade, 'Rome' withdrew intellectually and spiritually even farther, even faster, ever more obviously from the 'Greeks', the spirituality and the intellect of the Greek Fathers of the Church, as well as from those 'damned Greeks' whom Bonald and de Maistre had already identified as the source of all Europe's revolutions and outbursts of anarchy. 'Rome' continued to become ever more 'Roman', Western, dualistic, Integralist, and political. The glorification of Roman genius and the sovereignty of Latin were indicative. But whoever is seriously concerned with Russia has to face Greek genius and the traits of the Eastern Church. Erich Przywara, one of the most intelligent German Jesuits, gave a true appreciation of continuity when he remarked 'how, for instance, the Eastern Communist poster portraits cannot deny their descent from Eastern icons'.

12

Russia in Europe

In the nineteenth century Russians gazed towards Western Europe with the look both of an elder brother and of a younger son.

In the character of elder brother, as the older Christian, keeper of the Greek spirit and of the early, indeed primal, Christian traditions, the Russian knew himself to be a thousand years ahead of all Western Christians and Europeans. In his view, indeed, it was they who were the recreants and revolutionaries, immature individuals, lacking in spirituality, and understanding as little of the dialectic of heavenly love as manifested in the Holy Trinity, of the universe's transfiguration and the redemptive power of Him Who rose from the dead, as they did of Russia, mother of humanity, and its sacred rivers and peoples.

It was, however, in the character of younger son that there was a growing awareness of the immensity of Western achievement to be found in technology and industry, German philosophy, British political economy, French political thinking. Russian theologians in the renowned ecclesiastical academics studied Hegel, Schelling, Fichte, and developments in the contemporary Western world as keenly as any of the anarchists, revolutionary socialists, and early Marxists. Lenin's thought was permeated by Russian, Eastern, and Western European intellectual traditions.

From this twofold outlook arose a conflict of feeling which ranged from hate to love, attraction to repulsion, and created a condition of mental tension. It is of particular interest today because this is precisely the situation in which Arabs, Africans, and Asians are currently situated. They want to build up fresh social structures on the ruins of indigenous cultures which European civilisation has destroyed. Their purpose is on the one hand to exploit European and American facilities in order to overcome the political and military supremacy of 'Western' civilisation, and on the other hand to strike root again in the soil of their own immemorial ways. Russo–Asian and Russo–African sympathies are based on this common experience of a tension which allies action with reaction, a policy of offensiveness with defensiveness.

HOLY RUSSIA

Prince Andrei Kurbski, the friend, general and subsequent opponent of Ivan the Terrible (1533–84), was probably the first to use the phrase 'Holy

Russia'. But from the seventeenth century onwards there existed two 'Holy Russias', locked in mortal enmity. The Old Believers rebelled against the political intervention in Church affairs by Peter the Great. In the nineteenth century a total of more than twenty million Old Believers, the *Raskolniki*, and other sectarians formed the first underground movement (*podpolye*), a basis for the political underground which evolved in the 1860s. The secular authorities reacted against this movement with savage thoroughness: exile and imprisonment for the least dangerous, and more violent methods of punishment, or death at the stake, for the others. After the outstanding Avvakum had suffered this fate in 1682, the Old Believers began to evolve a 'Utopia of the Past', while they saw the present as a time when devils dominated Church and State. During the eighteenth century one wing of the *Raskolniki* created in the north a well-planned, though illegal, organisation.

THE ROAD TO PRAVDA

'When Napoleon invaded Russia, the Russian people for the first time became aware of its power. That was the beginning of freedom of thought in Russia.'

In Russia, as in Europe, the nineteenth century began with great hopes. Under the rule of Alexander I the aristocracy looked forward to their country being opened up to the culture, the benefits and beauty which Europe had to offer. Universities were established at Dorpat, Kazan, Kharkov and St Petersburg. The influence of German Romanticism began to make itself felt, and in Russia political and literary Romanticism became closely linked. Yet after 1815 a change came over Alexander I. The conduct of state affairs was handed over to the War Minister, General Arakcheyev, with his entirely militaristic ideas of rule. Resistance began to gather. Small revolutionary groups formed, culminating in the Decembrist uprising of 1825. This failed, however, owing to lack of popular support – which indeed its instigators had not even tried to gain. Nicholas I used every means within his power to prevent the nation's attaining freedom of thought, his efforts stimulated by fear of revolution such as he saw in Europe in 1830 and 1848. With the help of Count Benckendorff, the 'Third Department' was created, a secret state police force which relied primarily on spies and denunciations.

Despair at contemporary conditions and indignation at the political and spiritual misery of contemporary society became the spring of youthful patriotism. By the 1840s, two elements could be discerned – the Westerners and the Slavophiles. Both movements were much persecuted, and it is ironic to note that the Slavophiles, later to be accepted as orthodox ideologists of Tsarism and its Church, were originally the ones suspected of communist leanings.

Pushkin's great posthumous poem on the statue of Peter the Great in St Petersburg, in which he compared the Tsar, as the revolutionary from above, with Robespierre, displays the mixture of emotions that characterised

313

early Russian patriotism. Later Alexander Herzen was to say that he would not be surprised if a Tsar were to assume the role of a Spartacus since the principles and system of a Peter the Great left the way open equally well for the Prussian spiked helmet or the Jacobin red cap.

Nicholas I chose the spiked helmet. A generation of young intellectuals opposed his Germans with their Germans – Kant, Schiller, Fichte, Schelling, Oken, and, more slowly, Hegel.

BELINSKY AND GOGOL

The question posed constantly by Russian students, emigrants to Berlin, Geneva, Paris, London was, how could the intolerable state of affairs in Russia be altered? But even more pressing was the problem of reform to be undertaken from within the country's confines, when censorship and police kept constant surveillance. There was an answer: the careful assessment of future developments, an analysis of past and present, of home and foreign literature, from which could be formulated a wealth of critical comment on prevailing political and social conditions.

It was V.G.Belinsky (1811–48) who first appreciated the character of literary criticism as political criticism. He was a man to whom there have been many different reactions. Dostoevsky felt an unrelenting hatred for him and continued the feud in *The Possessed*, in the figure of Ivan Karamazov and in the chapter headed 'The Grand Inquisitor' in *The Brothers Karamazov*. Turgenev, a patriot despite his affinity to the West, honoured him. Berdyaev saw in him 'the progenitor of Russian intelligentsia'. The town where he spent his youth was re-named 'Belinsky' in 1948, and their respect for him has been shown in many other ways, in the erection of monuments, in commemorative stamps, in books and critical editions of his works.

Socially Belinsky belonged to that small middle class of minor officials, merchants and officers of middle rank, from which grew the Russian intelligentsia. His grandfather was a priest, his father an embittered naval surgeon, and later a country doctor. Belinsky ran away from home at the age of twelve, and lived throughout his life on the breadline. In order to evade official confinement to the Moscow students' quarter, and to develop a career of his own, he wrote a drama, *Dimitri Kalinin*, which, with strong Schillerian elements, dealt with the problems of peasant serfdom. The censorship stepped in before the play could even be printed; the author was expelled from the university and placed under police surveillance.

Overworked and consumptive, mortally ill for the last five years of his life, on 15 July 1847 Belinsky wrote a letter to Gogol which Alexander Herzen called his 'testament', and which should be regarded as 'a milestone in the history of Russian radicalism'. After 1849 anyone reading this letter in company in Russia could suffer the death penalty. Yet Ivan Aksakov, travelling across Russia in 1856 said: 'there is not a grammar school teacher who does not know the letter to Gogol by heart'.

The reason for Belinsky's letters was the publication of Gogol's *Selected Passages from Correspondence with Friends*, which though not uncritical of contemporary conditions, drew, with the aid of the excisions of censorship, an ecstatic picture of Russia as a harmony between God and man, Tsar, Church and people. To Belinsky the final published version seemed an utter distortion and he accused Gogol of attempting, through it, to put the Russians under the tutelage of the Church.

'Your book,' he wrote, 'does not breathe genuine Christian love, but exhales a morbid fear of death, the Devil, and hell. It is not sermons that it (the Russian people) needs – it has heard enough of those – nor prayers – it has repeated them often enough. What is needed is that the feeling for human dignity, lost in filth and ordure for so many centuries, should awaken in the people, that standards of law and equity, conforming not to the teachings of the Church but common sense and justice, should be established and strictly observed. Currently the most important national questions for Russia are the abolition of serfdom, the abolition of corporal punishment, and the strictest possible implementation of at least such laws as do already exist.'

You are standing, Belinsky warned Gogol, on the edge of an abyss. You link quite inadmissibly Christ and that Russian Church which has always been a supporter of the knout and the handmaiden of despotism. Christianity in Russia rests upon the shoulders of the Old Believers, the *Raskolniki*, of whom there are, however, but a few and whose spirit is not that of the common folk. The Russian Church, on the other hand, has nothing to do with that Christ Who taught and teaches freedom, equality, and fraternity. The Church has in the past evinced itself as

a hierarchy, an adulator of power, an enemy and persecutor of brotherhood among men – and it remains so to the present time.

The purport of Christ's teaching was revealed by the previous century's philosophical movement. And that is why any Voltaire, who, with the help of mockery, has extinguished the flames of fanaticism and ignorance in Europe, is obviously more a son of Christ, more flesh of His flesh and more bone of His bone, than all your popes, bishops, metropolitans and patriarchs, east or west. Do you really not know that? There's not a schoolboy to whom it's news.

The popes were held in contempt by the Russian people. Gogol might proclaim the Russian people to be the most pious in the world, but that was a lie. It 'is by nature profoundly unbelieving' but filled with superstition. Terror and suppression have resulted in apathy. In Russian writers alone does the Russian people see its leaders, defenders against and saviours from autocracy, orthodoxy, and Russification of all who live under tsarist sway.

Shortly before his death Belinsky summarised the faith which he had attained painfully and searchingly by many devious paths: 'God was my first thought, mankind my second, man my third, last, and only one.' To this he added the conviction of his youth, when he had defied the wrath of both his own father and that Little Father, the Tsar: Man must have compassion for his fellow-men and men must stand together against that 'tyrant God' whose terrestrial image is the Third Department police, penetrating every circle of friends and imperilling, if not actually spoiling, every intimate human relationship.

Dying, Belinsky's thoughts concentrated on the beauty of Russia. He was too ill properly to appreciate Europe. At Dresden he merely noted that the Sistine Madonna looked like a cold-blooded daughter of the tsars. (In 1920 Pope Benedict xv pointed out that Mary and Jesus were of aristocratic stock.) At Paris he stayed with Herzen. Crossing the Place de la Concorde with Turgenev, shivering with fever, utterly exhausted, he saw nothing of the Paris around him, but spoke only of Gogol and Russia. The whole of the West was too much for this sick man whose sole longing was to meet death at home.

FOUR FRUITLESS ENCOUNTERS WITH THE WEST: PETSCHERIN

'I prefer Prometheus to Satan, though . . . even though I may be an atom, that leaves me master of my fate – I am looking for truth, not redemption, and I expect to find it in reason, not grace' – Turgenev, 1847.

This was to be the burden of generations of Russian intellectual manifestoes: truth, not as a science of salvation, but as a fact, founded on reason. Many of these young intellectuals sought such truth in the West, but there are four examples which reveal how shattering such an experience could be: Petscherin, a Russian who became a Roman Catholic; Bakunin, an anarchist; Herzen, an upper middle-class liberal; Dostoevsky, a neo-conservative.

V.S. Petscherin had been educated by a Hessian tutor, an ardent Bonapartist and admirer of Voltaire and Rousseau. As a young man he had received orders to go to Berlin in order to prepare himself for a professorship in philology at St Petersburg. The lectures of Eduard Gans, who traced a link between Hegel, Saint-Simon, and nascent socialism, made the same deep impression in him as they did on Karl Marx. His enthusiasm was equally aroused by Lammenais' *Words of a Believer*, wherein he saw 'the new faith that will renovate tumbledown Europe'. On his return to St Petersburg he found the official restrictions intolerable, fled to Switzerland, and drew up plans for the establishment of a free Russian colony in the United States. Although commissioned by a pastor of the Reformed Church to make a translation into French of D.F. Strauss's *Life of Jesus*, he was reduced to a state of utter penury. As a ragged beggar at Liège an awareness came to him, during the course of a divine service, of the 'wholly democratic character' of the Roman Catholic Church. He took for his model the monk Spiridon – a figure in a novel by George Sand – who lived by the light of reason and played an active social role. His loneliness induced him to join the Redemptorist Order.

A longer stay at Rome alienated him permanently from the Roman Church because he failed to find there the brotherhood and spirituality which he sought. With the permission of his superiors he left his Order in 1861 and sought comfort from the Cistercians. The last twenty years of his life were spent as the conscientious, and highly esteemed, chaplain to a hospital run by Dublin nuns. During this time he caught up with the entire materialistic culture on which radical youth in Russia was feeding. He was convinced that Russian and America signified the beginning of a new historical cycle. In 1885, the year of his death, the first Marxist cells were founded in Russia.

FOUR FRUITLESS ENCOUNTERS WITH THE WEST: BAKUNIN

The communists and anarchists had, for years, been divided by a mortal enmity, an enmity which caused Marx to attack Bakunin's *Summons to the Slavs*, in 1848, and which found its culmination in the elimination of the Catalonian anarchists by Stalinists during the Spanish Civil War in 1936.

Basically Bakunin represented a challenge, often overlooked by friends and enemies alike, a challenge to the state, to all Churches, parties and associations who impose their will on mankind, to give man, the individual, his freedom. Born in 1818, Michael Bakunin fought in every intellectual and political revolutionary front that Europe had to offer. He spent years wandering in Switzerland, France, Italy, Germany, and Austria. From 1848 to 1851, with two death sentences hanging over him, he was on the run from political authority. Finally he was handed over to the Russians and imprisoned in the fortress of St Peter and St Paul. In 1857 he was exiled for life to Siberia, but escaped in 1861 to Japan and made his way to the United States and Britain. He died at Berne in 1876.

Bakunin's background was aristocratic and cultured. His father had studied at Padua and seen the beginnings of the French Revolution in Paris; his mother was described from families of the old nobility. The estate to which his father withdrew early in life was a meeting-place for Russian intelligentsia and was reminiscent of Madame de Staël's Coppet. Romantic and revolutionary ideas mingled freely, with German idealist philosophy on the one hand and French intellectual notions on the other.

A love-hate relationship bound Bakunin to his father. For his four sisters he felt an almost incestuous love and grudged them any other man. His egocentric mother he held in contempt. At twenty-one he gave up a military career in order to study at Moscow University and then at Berlin, the mecca of Hegel's and Schelling's disciples. Before leaving Russia he had published a translation of one of Fichte's works and of Hegel's Nuremberg addresses, the first authentic Hegel text to be produced in Russian. At Berlin he visited Bettina von Brentano and was fond of quoting her in his letters, together with Fichte, Goethe, Schiller, George Sand, Leroux, Cabet, and others.

A letter to his sister, in late summer 1842, indicated his transition from a theologically-speculative frame of mind to a determination upon a radical and revolutionary course of action: 'It is in the nature of action to corroborate God within its own limits ... action is man's greatest glory and highest service in the face of God, demonstrating an act of self-confidence, a simple innocent heart, and man's eternal personality.'

Five years later he wrote from Paris, 'We shall not be happy until the whole world is in flames.' He proceeded to construct a mysticism of negation and struggle which Russian critics have analysed as a form of pseudo-Christian mysticism. He prophesied a new age and a new religion of life, man, and action. As 'the monk of revolution' (Herzen's description of him) and 'revolutionary ascetic', he demanded of revolutionaries total surrender to the revolution. He saw Prometheus as the model for the man of total revolution, which to him was something different from the revolution of totalitarians.

'There is in all this, as you will say, a considerable portion of mysticism. But who is not mystic? Is a drop of life possible without mysticism? Life is possible only where there is a *clear*, unlimited, ... undefined mystical horizon.' 'I seek God in men, in their love, in their freedom; and now I seek God in revolution.' 'I want, and there is nothing else that I earnestly desire, to preserve to the end and intact the sacred spirit of revolt.'

Revolt was to break out first in Europe, and then among the other awakening peoples. The accusation of Marx, Engels, and their followers that Bakunin was the representative of a Panslavism run riot was unfair. As Masaryk has indicated, Marx's loathing of things Russian bore distinct German traits. Bakunin drew the hatred of tsarist Russia on his own head by his defence of the Poles. He had no love for the Germans, deeming theirs a servile religion and even reproaching them with making a religion of servility. Above all he hated Germanic Russia and St Petersburg (the realm of Dubbelt and his German successors in the Third Department) as a 'Germany in disguise'. In Italy he sensed in Mazzini something of a forerunner of modern Fascism. He possessed an uncanny capacity for discerning totalitarian tendencies at a very early stage and basic qualities in persons and in intellectual and political movements. Perhaps because the properties of a monkish dictator, a Grand Inquisitor of total revolution, were inherent in his own nature.

An element of ancient iconoclasm was resurrected in Bakunin's struggle against all institutions and stimulated by his association in Paris with Proudhon. The state is the altar of political religion for sacrifice of the real society of men, he proclaimed; it is the Church's twin, the Moloch of mankind. In his famous Geneva speech of 1867, he prophesied mutual national, political, and cultural destruction in the process of a coming world war: 'States that are at all effective can only maintain themselves by misdeeds.'

Bakunin fought every sort of tyranny, not excluding that of a victorious proletariat. Workers will become bourgeois straight-away when they become statesmen, he said, and probably more bourgeois than the bourgeois themselves. 'We must first purify our own atmosphere and completely alter the environment in which we live, for it corrupts our instinct and our will and constricts our hearts and our minds.' In all peoples and in all ages revolution swiftly moves over into reaction unless it constantly rejuvenates itself from the springs of anarchy. – Bakunin's concept rested on an anarchistic interpretation of the Christian Gospel in the same way as in Bakunin's eyes mankind was Christ crucified and resurrected.

Marx, Engels, the communists, and by no means least, the German social democrats (whose road to self-annihilation, through reaction, he foresaw by nearly a century) had therefore reason to hate Bakunin. As a move to exterminate the social revolutionaries, who held him in high esteem and cited him against Lenin, the Bolsheviks in 1919 published from among the Third Department's documents Bakunin's penitent statement to the Tsar. This prison letter, in which Bakunin pleaded with the Tsar to put himself at the head of world revolution against the Germans, created immense excitement far beyond the borders of Russia. Although there was undoubtedly an element of calculation in what he wrote, it is also certain that his inmost motive was that of a Russian patriot who both feared the West and held it in contempt. The Tsar at any rate put a great many approving remarks in the margin and recommended the missive to his son as an instructive piece of composition.

FOUR FRUITLESS ENCOUNTERS WITH THE WEST: HERZEN

'It is now time both to reach and accept the conclusion that the bourgeoisie represent the ultimate form of Western civilisation. . . . On the one hand there are the middle class "haves" . . . . On the other the middle class "have-nots", who want to replace the former but lack the strength to do so.'

Bakunin could well have written these sentences, but in fact they express the convictions of Herzen who, after a long life as a rich *émigré* in Europe, learnt to despair of the West. In his eyes it was owned by soulless, satiated men, without any intellectual interest, whose sole purpose in life was success. Even the workers, once they achieved the heights of middle-class status, merely perpetuated its mediocrity. This had already been proved in both France and Germany.

Marx hated Herzen, whom he termed a 'cossack' and a free-roving Russian individualist. Yet Herzen was in fact half-German, the son of Ivan Yakovlev, a wealthy member of the Russian aristocracy, and of a totally illiterate German maidservant. He had a sheltered childhood, and, given the free run of his father's library, made an early acquaintance with Goethe,

Schiller and the French classics. His education lay in the hands of a French emigrant whom his father engaged as tutor.

For a time, around 1843, Herzen became interested in Slavophilism, though it was not long before he saw through the efforts of this movement to regenerate a Byzantine theology by means of notions from Hegel's and Schelling's philosophy. In the same year he married, secretly, his beautiful cousin, Natalie, fleeing with her to Europe where he proceeded to lead the life of the wealthy in the main capitals of the West. His love for his wife ended tragically when his protégé, the writer Georg Herwegh, became her lover, a scandal of great import to the intellectual world of the time, and which had the side-effect of turning Herzen's son into a very bourgeois professor at Berne.

In June 1848 Herzen witnessed the violent suppression of the workers' uprising in Paris, and this, with all other experiences of Europe in this year, finally destroyed his hopes of the West being the leader in any movement towards world freedom.

Henceforward he sought refuge more and more in a faith based upon the redemptive powers inherent in the Russian people. 'I belong to the Russian people with every fibre of my soul,' he wrote towards the end of his life. His was the inspiration behind the populist movement which led Russian aristocrats and intellectuals to seek to prepare the common people for the assumption of power and responsibility.

Following upon the early death of his still much-loved wife in 1852, Herzen retired from Switzerland and France to London. Here he founded a Russian-language publishing house and two periodicals, *Polar Star* and *The Bell*. The latter was smuggled into Russia and, much read in official circles, in its heyday it enjoyed considerable esteem. Exceptionally well-informed on all matters concerning corruption, the paper made Herzen for some years the most respected spokesman, even inside Russia, for an enlightened liberal and radical individualism.

Eventually, however, this individualist incurred the displeasure not merely of those who disagreed with him, but also of practically all his supporters, without this actually rebounding to his credit. To youthful revolutionaries at home he seemed too romantic, too 'soft', too academic, too 'conciliatory'. His initial welcome for the new government of Alexander II and its liberation of the serfs offended the many sworn enemies of any tsarist régime. Russians of every political shade were furious at his courageous interventions on behalf of the Poles after suppression of the Polish uprising in 1863, seeing him as a traitor to the Russian cause. Yet in his eyes the Russo-Polish understanding which he sought to achieve would have provided a firm basis for the future of a free and brotherly Europe. His home was the meeting-place for Italian, French, Polish, Hungarian, and German *émigrés*.

The sounding of *The Bell* ceased and in 1867 Herzen left London to continue wandering Europe until on 21 January 1870 he died. An effort to ring *The Bell* in French created but a feeble echo. Lonely and ageing rapidly, he was preoccupied with the future, foreseeing the onslaught of major wars which would sap the strength of states and Churches alike. In this sense he took a positive view of socialism and communism as the harbingers of a new world for to him they contained 'the *membra disjecta* of the great formula for the future'. As early as 1844 he had prophesied a new Christianity to follow on the old, a new Gospel which would create men prepared to lead a fraternal life.

His political objective for Russia was the achievement of a pluralistic, decentralised and agrarian 'Communism', moulded in the shape of independent associations and co-operatives, capable of bargaining with the state. To this degree Bakunin and Herzen came quite close to each other. Their differences lie in Herzen's warning against impatience, iconoclasm, too impetuous destructiveness. 'For minds to mature takes time,' he taught. In his eyes it was difficult enough to render even *one* new idea intelligible to even *one* person, let alone whole peoples. It was essential to proceed slowly, else great misfortunes could arise. Bandages should not be removed before wounds are healed.

Herzen compared the purity of the Apostles and the early Christians with the purity of the Huguenots and Jacobins.

> Fighters for freedom in the first stage of an armed conflict have always been saintly, like Cromwell's Ironsides, and therefore strong. I don't take seriously people who prefer destruction to the great resources of development and compromise. Sermons are what men need, untiring, incessant sermons. Sermons directed equally at workers and employers, farmers and the middle classes. We need apostles rather than front-line officers and demolition snipers. Apostles who will preach to the enemy as well as our own hosts. To preach to the enemy is to perform a great act of love. It is not the fault of those on the other side that they live beyond the mainstream of modern life. . . . I pity them like I do sick people, like not quite normal individuals who stand on the edge of an abyss with a load of treasures. That load is going to pull them down. You have to open their eyes, not tear them out, so that they too may save themselves, if they so desire.

In his last years Herzen appeared to young Russians as 'finished' and 'out-of-date' as he seems important and interesting to us today. With his critical but sympathetic outlook he understood the Slavophiles and the Westerners, the revolutionaries and the liberals, and also the reformers around Alexander II. In his own way he reconciled east and west in his own person.

FOUR FRUITLESS ENCOUNTERS WITH THE WEST: DOSTOEVSKY

In a famous controversy of the 1860s between Turgenev and Herzen, which then led to the breach between the two friends, Turgenev remarked, 'God forfend that we should fall into a blind veneration for everything Russian simply because it is Russian. God save us from narrow-minded and, to be honest, ungrateful attacks on the West and, above all, on Germany. . . . The surest sign of strength is to know one's own weaknesses and imperfections.

It was a warning that Fyodor Mikhailovich Dostoevsky (1821–81) should have taken to heart. Himself a serious pathological case, this man from the underground, in his capacity of 'plebeian imperialist' (Bohatec) and Russian messiah, hated the West from the depths of his tormented soul. In his great novels he not merely conducted an autopsy on the state of Russian society, but painted hate-laden pictures of the West which contributed fatefully to the deepening of neuroticism in Russia, just as their success in the West constituted a part of its sickness of mind in the decades preceding the First World War. Dostoevsky, who knew Herzen well and often took him as a model, could have applied to himself one of his remarks: 'We are not only the doctors, we are also the affliction.'

Russia's war propaganda and hate campaign against the West, beginning in the 1880s, is only intelligible in the strict context of the neuroticism which afflicted the top and middle strata of Russian society and the fears besetting the leading figures of the Tsarist régime. The atmosphere harmonised wholly with Dostoevsky's thought, which had indeed prepared the ground for it.

Yet of all Russia's great writers, with the exception of Pushkin and Turgenev, none owed more to the West than Dostoevsky. In early youth he was fired with enthusiasm for Molière, Corneille, Racine, Schiller, Dickens, George Sand, Balzac, Shakespeare. To this list were later added Victor Hugo, Alexandre Dumas, Sue, Soulie, and de Kock, his membership of the Petrashevsky Circle and Marx. All this rich endowment with Western European ideas was insufficient ever to inspire him with a genuine sympathy for the European outlook. Instead he hated and looked down on all Europeans and was irritated by all personal contact with Westerners, whether Germans, French, Poles, Italians, Jews. He underwent a major mental crisis in Siberia. As a result of this he parted finally from any attempt at compromise with European views and notions of a Europeanisation of Russia. Instead he became a strange venerator of tsarism and a Russian imperialist who enthused over the concept of an Asiatic Russia. Siberia was the cradle for his messianic imperialism and played for him a part similar to that of Algeria in the minds of many Frenchmen in the nineteenth and twentieth centuries.

Dostoevsky was constantly on the search for fresh victims to feed his pathological hate-complex, but the initial force of it fell on the Poles. There was a special reason for this. Apart from any cultural or political factors, he was well aware that his own traits as well as his name revealed his Polish origin. He used to enjoy saying that, should he discover a drop of Polish blood in his veins, he would immediately 'purge' himself and it was precisely as a prisoner of the Tsar in Siberia that he evolved his fancies about Russian dominion over Poles, Balts, and Lithuanians. All the same, he knew Polish very well and his daughter liked to think of a family connection with the well-known aristocratic Polish Dostoevsky family. This was in fact a mistake; the doctor who was the father of the great writer was himself the son of an Orthodox Russian priest.

In the final analysis, Dostoevsky's hatred of Poles was a self-hatred which he manifested in the most fascinating personalities of his great novels. Seldom has a man become so productive out of the chasms of his self-loathing and will to self-destruction. In this respect, as in others, he was close to Kierkegaard. Both men were possessed by a compulsive desire to 'do penance'. In his first masterpiece he sought in the character of Raskolnikov to 'lay bare' and to atone for his 'crime' in having belonged to the Petrashevsky Circle and having been intellectually a revolutionary.

In his first letter from Paris, dated summer 1862, he described the French capital as a hideous, revolting place and Frenchmen as false, money-grabbing, and standing on the lowest rung of human culture. Similar terms were applied to Germany and Switzerland. Berlin reminded him, to its disadvantage, of St Petersburg. His impression of London was altogether apocalyptic, a kingdom of Baal, a man-eating monster. His perspective was that of Blake, Bunyan, and Engels. He waxed indignant over the fat, prosperous, self-assured bishops of the Church of England, who did not bother about the common people, and forgot all about their opposite numbers in the tsarist Church. At Geneva, in 1868, he foresaw the victory of higher Russian morality the world over and proclaimed the right of Russia, as patron of justice, to rule over the whole Slav world. He demanded full-scale Russian rearmament, strategic railways and cannons, lots of cannons. Constantinople must be conquered.

Dostoevsky's theology of hate against the 'corrupt West' contained many of the slogans of German nationalist and later National Socialist propaganda, as well as a good part of the Stalinist anti-Western arsenal of abuse. The idea of civilisation is 'in western Europe identical with the notion of the need to reduce a portion of humanity to the level of animals so that the rest can live in easy circumstances'. The motivating interests of European civilisation are 'trade, shipping, markets, factories'. It is a disgusting civilisation because its maintenance is simply a mask for economic imperialism and the French one is stamped with intolerable pride, self-satisfaction, and conceit. Even Germany for the past nineteen centuries has represented nothing but a purely negative protest, a single sterile Protestant performance. Even a German drunkard was far more stupid and far more ridiculous than a Russian one.

In this mood Dostoevsky became an enthusiastic admirer of Bismarck, went into raptures about the Franco-German War, and insisted on a Russo-German alliance for the conquest of the world. It would need millions of dead to ensure Russo-German global dominion. The remark was made on the occasion of his famous memorial address for Pushkin, who thought very differently from him.

'I believe in Russia.' Mankind's revival could occur only at the instance of 'the Russian God' and certainly not at that of the Pope who by his distortion of Jesus Christ was responsible for the spread of atheism throughout Europe. Dostoevsky hated Roman Catholicism as only the monks of Athos and members of the Orthodox Church have been capable of hating the 'foul, corrupt West'. He reserved an especial hate for the Jesuits as the dangerous missionaries and pioneers of Catholicism and in them he sensed something of that intellectual and spiritual imperialism which inwardly devoured him.

In the last piece he ever wrote, Dostoevsky, having avowed in many different forms his faith as a convert (briefly, a Europeanised Russian must be a foe of the Russian people) and repeated it with neurotic compulsiveness, tore off the last of the veils with the cry, 'To Asia!' With Napoleon in mind, he asked, 'What have we gained by our service to Europe? Only Europe's loathing.' Russians must liberate themselves from the menial-like fear of the past two centuries of being termed 'Asiatics'. By turning to Asia, Russia will be given back its dignity and self-respect. 'In Europe we are no more than Tartars, but in Asia we shall be Europeans.' 'The Russian is not simply a European, but an Asiatic too. Perhaps indeed our expectations lie more in Asia than in Europe. Yes, indeed more than that. It may be that in our future, destiny will play the principal part.'

Some outstanding members of the Petrashevsky Circle met again in Siberia as exiles and performed notable feats there in their desire to turn it into a model of a land of liberty. In their eyes the path towards a revolutionary re-shaping of the whole of Russia lead through Siberia. These were the people to whom Dostoevsky owed so much. In his penury one of them had lent him money, in the libraries of others he had pursued his reading and became acquainted with David Friedrich Strauss, Cabet, Proudhon, and at the home of another he had been chosen to read to the assembled circle Belinsky's letter to Gogol. That, indeed, had been the main ground for his arrest. His revenge for that on these friends, patrons, and well-wishers of his years of early manhood (his seizure by the police took place in 1849) was terrible. Ever and again they recurred in his novels as 'nihilists', satanic conspirators, and incarnations of evil.

As is well known, he was sentenced to death and, in a disgraceful piece of comedy, reprieved just before execution. In place of capital punishment he was condemned to four years' forced labour in Siberia. The shock effects produced by the near-fulfilment of his execution, already vividly imagined, as well as the period of penal servitude (described in *The House of the Dead*) were both magnificent and dreadful. Dostoevsky undertook a brain-washing of himself, a meticulous and painful process of 'voluntary' re-education, a re-orientation of his consciousness. There exists only one comparably imposing and powerful phenomenon, that is the case of Augustine, who revised the outlook of his sixteen years as a Manichee and, having apparently succeeded, in his old age and in the struggle with Pelagius, reverted to the channels of thought of his youth. The abortive convert Augustine was the father of the Inquisition, the extermination of heretics, and the death of the theology of hope. Dostoevsky was the sole denouncer of the Russian revolutionary intelligentsia, his friends, the Petrashevsky Circle. So critical an observer as Peter Scheibert has written of its members that they were 'the last group who by character and origin were essentially aristocratic and in the main filled with the spirit of the noble ideal of humanity. This did not prevent them at the same time being the first technologists of revolution, pure men of action ... who were concerned with directly snatching power.'

Dostoevsky also recurrently described himself in the distorted figures of his friends of 1848–9 – and that constitutes the fascination of his infernal visions, his pictures of the Russian underground. That was his own journey into hell, *before* his arrest, had seemed to him a heavenly journey to an earthly Paradise, a liberated and Europeanised Russia.

THE PETRASHEVSKY CIRCLE

Butashevich-Petrashevsky was a member of a respected aristocratic family, and it was in the library of his house in St Petersburg, a library which contained the works of Fourier and the French social Utopians, of Proudhon, Marx, Feuerbach and Bruno Bauer, that a group of young intellectuals used to meet. This was the Petrashevsky Circle, the 1849 'conspiracy' about which Tsar Nicholas I had become so agitated.

Petrashevsky himself believed in the reform of administration in both Russia and the European states. The former was to be reconstructed along general lines with each nationality forming a component part, and all politics were, in future, to base their organisation on their universities, not on the armed forces. It was Petrashevsky and his friends who were the first men in Russia to heed the link between the Industrial Revolution and the political, as well as intellectual, changes in society which were inevitably to follow. It was a group which, meeting in 1848, had an outlook which today seems far more modern than that of any other group of revolutionaries before 1917.

Petrashevsky wanted to propagate his ideas through a periodical and a dictionary of foreign words and expressions. The first volume of the dictionary passed censorship safely, but the second was seized. In the periodical the essay on 'New Christianity' combined practical planning and scientific interests with a form of Messianism. A contribution on political opposition contained the sentence, 'It seems outlandish, even criminal, to some, but it really amounts to none other than discovery of the law of conflicting forces.' An article on rhetoric said that, although there is nothing authoritative or supernatural in the universe which is not in conformity with human nature, and mankind's power is founded on and maintained by the power of utterance, speech is impossible in a state where every talent is in opposition and the words of the wise are accounted lunacy because society is unused to rational thought.

The leading light of this Circle was Fourier. One of the participants in the Friday evening discussions, which took place from November 1848 onwards, proposed that the world should be divided into two halves and allocated to Fourierism and Communism respectively, so as to be able subsequently to compare the results obtained by the two systems. Not dissimilar plans have been put forward in our own day by American and Russian technocrats. Petrashevsky thought the first step should be to establish a large phalanstery, a sort of model Fourierist collective, and to win over the Tsar to this idea. There is no doubt that he would have been glad to place himself at the Tsar's disposal, because he realised that the gigantic tasks he envisaged, starting with liberation of the peasantry would require enormous powers and possibly a despot, a new Peter the Great of the type desired by Leibniz.

Dostoevsky malevolently called Petrashevsky, a chatterer and intriguer. Others of the Circle, under prison interrogation and during cross-examination, as well as in their memoirs, spoke unfavourably of him. Nevertheless, both in arrest and at his trial, he stood firmly by his own notions and even evolved them further. One of them which was taken particularly amiss was his 'revelation' of the Gospels as the products of ecclesiastics avid for power. He continued his criticism of the Russian Church imperturbably: spiritual academies should be abolished so as to allow the clergy, released from their ghetto, to relinquish their prejudices. For the academies there should be substituted theological faculties where representatives of all creeds, including the Old should be allowed to teach. Persecution of the latter should cease. If they were not won over by tolerance, they would form the core of every future uprising.

Discovery and arrest of the Circle was the work of Dubbelt, the Russo-German chief of the Third Department. There was never a real conspiracy. The positive achievements of the Circle members in Siberia draw attention to two points. The first is the loss to the tsarist government sustained by the condemnation of these practical and imaginative men who were so thoroughly suited to undertaking the difficult task of beginning to turn agrarian, archaic Russia, imbued with magic-lore, into an industrial state. The second point concerns Dostoevsky. By his terrifying pictures of Russian revolutionaries as 'atheists', 'anarchists', 'nihilists', and men possessed by the Devil, this dreadful reactionary fed and increased the fear in governing circles and the neurotic outlook of the leading social strata. Stavrogins and Ivan Karamaszovs were seen everywhere. What was not perceived was that, from beginning to end, Dostoevsky was engaged in a series of fearful public self-accusations, confessions, and mangling self-dissections.

CHERNYSHEVSKY

Nikolai Gavrilovich Chernyshevsky (1828–89) was the son of an Orthodox priest at Saratov. He received his initial education at a theological college and in 1848–9, as a student at St Petersburg, joined the Petrashevsky Circle.

His readings of Belinsky, Herzen, Feuerbach, and Helvetius made a deep impression on him and he also participated in the political and social discussions of the group centred around Nvedensky, 'the father of Nihilism'. In 1853, after two years as headmaster of a secondary school at Saratov, he became a teacher at the St Petersburg Military Academy. In 1856 he took over editorship of *The Contemporary*, the radical-democratic periodical, and remained in charge until 1862 when it was banned and he himself arrested. On the basis of forged evidence and the testimony of a spy, he was sentenced to fourteen years' penal servitude in Siberia. Transported in 1864, he spent eight years doing forced labour and was then interned for another eleven years. In 1889 he at last returned to Saratov and died there in October of the same year.

While awaiting trial, Chernyshevsky wrote, *What is to be Done?*, a novel which is masterly in its treatment of contemporary questions, the discussion of which would have been forbidden absolutely by the censorship, in allegoric and pictorial form. As he himself said: 'It is forbidden to speak of certain things directly. Let us therefore speak of irrelevant subjects, so long as they have some point of contact with the idea in hand.'

The novel was dedicated to Chernyshevsky's loyal wife, the mother of his two sons, in whom he tried to inculcate intellectual integrity through his letters from Siberia.

'In the early morning of 2 July 1856,' it begins, plunging the reader straight into the social situation. The heroine's name was Vera Pavlova. Her evolution into a free, independent woman, capable of thinking for herself, is one of the book's main themes and her personality is meant to serve as a model for young people who needed to be awakened out of a fatalistic resignation.

The most important theme was that of the 'new individuals'. Whereas a very large part of middle- and upper-class society led apathetic and corrupt lives, a new type of individual was (so the book claimed) coming into being, men of sound, strong character, honourable and able. Formerly decent individuals had been all too rare and thinly scattered, but the number was growing rapidly. 'Indeed, after a while, such instances will become customary and, slightly later still, there will be no others, because everybody will be decent. Things will be fine then.' Addressing Vera, the author said, 'I am telling the story of your life because you, as far as I know, are one of the first women whose life had been finely moulded.'

George Sand had delineated the French figuratively as a young woman awakening to a new life of her own. Turgenev, writing to Herzen, envisaged Russia as 'a young woman' who, 'has a somewhat greater power of attraction, I believe, than her older (European) sisters'. Vera is a nascent Russian with the beauty of dawning.

Vera marries the medical student, Lopuchov, against the will of her mother who wants to pair her off to greater material advantage. As a result she comes into contact with a circle of young people who do not share her mother's conviction that man will always remain a fool of knave, parasite, whorer, drinker, good-for-nothing or weakling. Lopuchov, his friend Kirsanov, and Vera spend their evenings discussing the chemical foundations of agriculture in accordance with Liebig's theory. Vera opens a needlework establishment on a monthly profit-sharing basis for her young female staff. Kirsanov learns French by reading the Geneva New Testament through eight times: 'By the ninth occasion he could already understand every word.' In Lopuchov's study hangs a photograph of the 'saintly greybeard', Robert Owen.

Kirsanov says to Lopuchov, 'What we both regard as a normal life will only become a fact when social ideas and customs alter. Society has got to be re-moulded, and it will be re-moulded through the evolution of life. Whoever has already been remoulded, helps one of his fellows. . . . The Golden Age will come, Dimitri, we know that, but it is a long way off yet. The Iron Age is passing, it has almost gone, but the Golden Age is still not here.'

Who will usher in the new age? That demands an entirely new sort of individual, a race of fighters which will stake all it has. The prototype is Rachmetov, the descendant of Tartars and ancient European aristocratic stock, members of which distinguished themselves in the eighteenth and early nineteenth centuries. His 'small' share of the family inheritance is some four hundred souls and eighteen thousand acres, whereas that of the whole clan is some seventy-five thousand souls. He is an 'unusual' man and a 'rigourist' (Chernyshevsky's paraphrase for 'revolutionary') who lives austerely and intends to carry on doing so until such time as all people have attained full enjoyment of life. He works with his hands, but is also a voracious reader (especially of important Western literature, such as Malthus, Adam Smith, Ricardo, John Stuart Mill) who adheres firmly to the rule, 'Every book that I read must be so packed with content that it saves me studying a hundred other books.' He runs his finger along Kirsanov's collection of volumes with the comment, 'Well-known. . . . Nothing original. . . . Nothing original. . . . Nothing original', applying the epithet to works of Macaulay, Guizot, Thiers, Ranke, Gervinus. He seizes, however, *Observations on the Prophecies of Daniel and the Apocalypse of St John.* 'There's something well worth close attention!' He falls in love on one occasion, but draws back when the woman offers herself to him. 'I must struggle the love inside me. Love for you would tie my hands. Indeed, they are bound already, but I shall free them again, although it will take time. I cannot permit myself to love.' This monk-like asceticism of the total revolutionary was to become exemplary.

The new generation is to evolve in a new sort of partnership between husband and wife. Hitherto women have been held down by force and similarly impeded in their intellectual and professional development. 'Officially,' says Vera, 'every career in public life is closed to us women, and in practice very many; nearly all fields of activity in ordinary life are too.' The author advises the young man who truly loves his wife to continue to regard her as his affianced who has the right to break the bond if she is dissatisfied with him. 'Unfortunately there are still ten antediluvian individuals for every new one. Naturally, though, in an antediluvian world you have an antediluvian species.' The new man will grow with love. 'He who has not experienced how love arouses all man's powers does not know true love. . . . Only he who helps the wife he loves to attain independence really loves. . . . Only he whose thoughts become clearer and his arms stronger through love really loves.'

In Vera's dreams there are visions, invoked by verses of Goethe and Schiller, of man's great and splendid future. There are visions of woman's rise through the centuries from slavery and low estate to liberated beauty. And there is a vision of womanhood who says, 'My realm is small as yet and I must still protect my supporters against the hostility of those who do not know me. Therefore I do not as yet wholly manifest my will. Only when my dominion extends the whole world over and every creature is fine of limb and pure in heart, then shall I reveal myself as I am in complete loveliness.' This is a refurbishment of the ancient Johannine apocalypse of Holy Wisdom and a fresh communication of man's freedom.

Cherneshevsky described paradisial future landscapes which are reminiscent of Jean Paul and Fourier. 'New Russia' is situated in the south of the Empire, a gigantic territory in which figs, sugar-cane, wheat, rice, and date-trees grow where there was desert before. (The Soviet Union is trying to transform these visions into earthy reality.) There are houses of aluminium and large, tent-shaped roofs over gigantic building complexes. There are fewer cities than there used to be because people live more in the country. Individuals are happy in their work and their evenings are spent at the theatre, in museums, libraries, or lecture-halls or in domestic intimacy. 'No, real pleasure is unknown as yet because there is no such life as would be necessary to enjoy it and the people requisite to it do not as yet exist.' Many generations must pass before this reality can be fulfilled, but a picture of more immediately pleasurable reality is offered by the marriage of Katerina Vassilyevna, one of the young and new generation, to Beaumont, the rich American.

Would one call this a happy ending? Siberia and twenty years of imprisonment lay ahead for the author of this propagative novel, written in a cell of the Fortress of St Peter and St Paul in 1862–3.

What is to be Done? signified in the first place an invitation to Russian youth and intelligentsia to venture on the experiment of a new life – as reformers, as revolutionaries, as anarchists, as populists. It was in 1862 that there began a cleavage among the progressive intelligentsia between a revolutionary and a moderate democratic group (which led to Conservatism). Until 1905 the struggle between these two groups constituted an important element in the domestic history of Russia. Both of them failed. The revolutionaries disappeared in the wave of arrests, the terrorists were executed or sent to

Siberia, the populists were either not understood or rejected by the peasantry whom they wanted to educate (a débâcle described by Turgenev in *Virgin Soil*). The reformist moderate groups never got a real opportunity, thanks to the victories constantly achieved by reactionaries under the two Tsars, Alexander III and Nicholas II (1881–1917). The rise of the Marxists and then the triumph of Lenin over various Marxist directions and anti-Marxist revolutionaries and reformers, the success of the single doctrine, the single strategy, the single party, and the single man, was due by no means least to the catastrophes which befell the many and variegated individuals who ventured, each on his own account, to put into practice the experiment of a new life.

THE FACE OF REACTION

During the years 1881 to 1904 Konstantin Petrovich Pobedonostsev (1827–1907), 'reaction's sole important ideologist', had exercised almost complete power over Alexander III and Nicholas II. His predecessor as Procurator of the Holy Synod, Count Protasov, had already brilliantly demonstrated how the Church could be controlled by all means available to the state, while itself in turn, with every means at its disposal, exerting dominion over the people. Spirituality made him, as with many others who hold the reins of Church politics, very uneasy, and he tended to suspect all theological academies of Protestant leanings. In his view the sole function of the Church was to serve the interests of the state, and therefore priests needed to be trained only to meet the requirements of the ordinary people, as well as being able to give agricultural instruction, act as regimental surgeons, or fulfil other useful but lowly purposes of secular authority.

During the important years of his control the Procurator was supported by Afanasij Drozdov, a man extremely well-versed in theology, but a mere obscurantist owing to a total lack of faith. A sound Hebrew scholar, he was familiar with all the relevant literature from the Church Fathers to Strauss and Bruno Bauer. He was, however, also the first Russian to pay for the privilege of knowledge with loss of faith. He lived in complete retirement, never reading a mass or preaching a sermon, and although he wrote a great deal, he burned everything he wrote. It is not difficult to find many parallels to Drozdov among Roman Catholics of the last century and this. They hold leading positions in the Church and theology, and are distinguished by their scepticism and irony, by their humaneness in private, and severity in official dealings.

Drozdov, his own hope gone, sought to protect Christianity from total dissolution by Draconian means: for example, the Scriptures, because it was possible for them to prove an inspiration for revolution, ought, according to him, to be withdrawn from the laity and be replaced by the Lord's Prayer. (Similar measures have, indeed, often been employed by the Catholic Church). He was 'intellectually . . . quite close to the future revolutionaries'.

The difference was that, unlike them, he had no confidence in the future, and tried with all his might, even at the price of treason to the Holy Ghost, to hold up progress. He and Pobedonostsev had in common their vision of the Church as the state's last 'resource for the maintenance of order, with chaos following on its heels'.

Pobedonostsev, by profession a lawyer and scholar, was an intellectual of a sceptical turn of mind, and, in some ways, far more 'modern' as an individual even than Lenin. But, as is quite common for this type of personality in the West, this leader of 'blackest reaction', as he was only too often called by young revolutionaries, was, in fact, a renegade of modern thought. He did not merely consider modern science harmful; spirituality and theology could be equally so in his opinion. In *Moscow Conversations*, published in 1896, he explains that the Russian people were to be safeguarded against Western European rationalism and belief in human good nature. The 'law of natural persistence' was to be upheld, meaning that outdated institutions, the Church (founded on ritual), and historical legends (instead of historical research) must be maintained. This required the strictest censorship; secondary schools should be open only to children of the well-to-do; the administrative autonomy in the universities should be dissolved, and higher educational courses for women (who had no direct access to university studies) suspended.

The effect of those views can be seen in the dismissal of famous scientists and scholars (the chemist Mendeleyev, the biologist Metchnikov, the sociologist Kovalevsky), the summons to the historian Kluchevsky to retract his 'liberal sentiments', and the veto on the works of John Stuart Mill, Herbert Spencer, and Karl Marx (although the censorship had passed the first volume of *Das Kapital* in 1872).

KATKOV AND RUSSOPHILISM

The new Russophilism which sprang to life in the 1880s found an outstanding journalistic representative in the headstrong personality of Katkov who, as 'dictator of Moscow', had dared lay down the law to the Tsar, and to oppose the Minister for Foreign Affairs. Forty years earlier, acting as correspondent for progressive liberal publications at Berlin, he had associated with the circle of Russian students and with the intelligentsia who surrounded Bettina. Once back in Russia he used nationalism as a means to an end, in which his business relations with protectionist Russian industrialists played no small part. A cynic and a profound believer in *Realpolitik*, he considered Bismarck 'if he were younger and found a partner', would not be 'disinclined to sacrifice the Hapsburg Empire'.

With this ambitious, self-confident man and his collaborators as the mouthpiece for politics, business and ideology, the press was turned into an instrument of militant Russophilism. It was in vain that Austrian and German diplomats tried to point out to the Tsar that a nationalism so artificially instilled could set the whole world and Russia on fire. Their very fear of revolution was one of the most real causes of its possible occurrence. 'It is the years of whipped-up fanaticism ... that have brought matters to the point where a policy of Communism is being pursued with national slogans,' the Austrian military attaché wrote home in November 1887.

Nevertheless Katkov (like Pobedonostsev, a frightened man beneath the layer of intellectualism) was sincerely convinced that only a stringent form of nationalism could preserve the country from revolution and the dissolution of established society. Since Russia was unfamiliar with chauvinism on the lines known in Poland, Bohemia, and France, it must be organised. In fact, it was a gigantic process of 'self-destruction', undertaken in the form of Russification of the Empire's non-Russian peoples. The Church was used, among other instruments, as the government's henchman, with the result that faith in God and faith in the Tsar were both destroyed.

On the evening of Bloody Sunday, 9 January 1905, Father Gapon, a Russian Orthodox priest and the leader of the crowd of St Petersburg workmen who had tried to approach the Tsar with a petition, issued a proclamation: 'The bullets of the imperial soldiery which killed bearers of tsarist pictures' (in the procession) 'shot through those pictures and killed our belief in the Tsar.' In his subsequent letters to the Tsar, Gapon prophesied the horrors of the coming revolution. The massacre demolished the tsarist charisma and the old religious tradition which had upheld the Tsar as the protector of the people.

In 1908 the priest Grigory Petrov wrote to the Metropolitan Antonius,

There is no such thing as a Christian emperor, a Christian government, and a Christian society. The upper classes dominate the lower. A small group dominates the rest of the population.... The lower classes have been excluded from everything, power, science, art, and even religion. They have made religion their servant.

... Christianity was made the state religion, but the state did not hereupon cease being heathen.... The Gospels were diverted from their spacious mission of establishing the Kingdom of God in society and the state into the narrow path of personal virtue and individual redemption ...

For the Church none of the existing political systems is perfect, final, and untouchable. Such a polity is a thing of the future. It is the polity of the coming Kingdom of God ...

According to the monkish view, but which the Church's ruling dignitaries also propagate, anything done against the state is thereby done against the Church, against Christ, and against God too. That reduces the Church's great task, the redemption of mankind, to the puny role of bodyguard to the temporal autocratic order.

This was the Church which in 1901 excommunicated Tolstoy who had perceived in its bellicosity and obedience to the state a radical negation of Christian faith.

The sons of Orthodox clergy who had no prospect of being accepted into theological academies and making a Church career lent a ready ear to revolutionaries. The Church, for its part, blessed the tsarist flags and pictures under whose protection and leadership millions of Russian peasants went to war in 1914. It blessed the war into which a frightened, overweening Tsar slithered under the guidance of his wife.

NICHOLAS II

In October 1905 Nicholas II promised Russia a constitution. Any politician who dared to even mention the word during the next eleven years, however, did so at his own peril. The main wish of his government in 1905 was that socialist elements in the country should be grouped together in a major uprising which would make possible the ultimate destruction of the movement. It hoped, in other words, to be able to act on the reactionary precedents of Paris in 1849 and 1870–1. Various facts reveal the truth of this hope: Admiral Dubassov, Governor General of Moscow, assured a French journalist after the suppression of the local uprising, that authorities had deliberately closed their eyes to military preparation, and on 15 December 1905, the Tsar wrote to his mother: 'although the Moscow events are very distressing, and cause me much pain, it does seem to me that they are turning out for the best.'

In 1914, he hoped that the war too would 'turn out for the best', just as he had hoped to be able to restore autocracy by means of a *coup d'état*. Super-Russians of German origin joined hands with Old Russian absolutists, gaining ever more influence with the Tsar. 'Not for nothing did the satirist, Saltikov, call the ministers and governors from the ranks of the Baltic Barons, "Germans with Russian souls". . . . '

The Tsar was completely under the influence of the Tsarina. But why did the people, whose soul, according to the words of Paleologue, the French Ambassador, the Tsarina had so completely assimilated, display such undisguised hatred for her? The answer is simple. To vindicate her new position, this German appropriated to herself with a calculating thoroughness all the traditions and ideas of the Russian Middle Ages, the sorriest and harshest of all, at a time when the people were making immense efforts to free themselves from its own mediaeval barbarity. This Hessian princess was possessed by the demon of autocracy. Risen from petty principality to heights of Byzantine despotism, she was loath to step down from them at any price. In the Orthodox faith she found the mysticism and the magic appropriate to her new position. The more plainly detestable the old régime was shown to be, the more firmly she believed in her vocation. With her strong character and her capacity for arid, unfeeling extravagance, the Tsarina complemented the irresolute Tsar by dominating him.

That was the view of Leon Trotsky, one of the Revolution's most important participants and historians, in his *History of the Russian Revolution*.

The last Tsarina prescribed for the last Tsar, a twofold treatment for his pathological nature. The first was by way of deriving strength from her own heavily charged neurotic nature and the second through clinging to the advice of 'our friend', Rasputin.

On 13 March 1916 she wrote to him, discouraging him from any move, 'But don't give the ministers any power, towards a constitution, which is what they are all bent on now. Things will become calmer and improve, but they need to feel your strong hand. For years I have been told the same thing – "Russia loves to feel the whip". That is its nature!' As late as 6 December of the same year another note ran, 'Bang your fist down on the table for once, remain firm, be the master. Listen to what your resolute wife and Our Friend have to say. Trust us.' The sexual element in this political advice is manifest: the Russian people are to be thrashed back into righteousness as muzhiks had always thrashed Russian women. 'I suffer for you as for a delicate, tender-hearted child that needs guidance, but listens to evil counsellors while the Man sent by God tells him what should be done.'

It was in the fateful year 1905 that the Tsarina procured for her feeble husband-cum-child the 'man of God, Grigory' (as the Tsar noted in his diary on 1 November). Rasputin, the peasant with the scars on his skull dating from horse-stealing, was responsible for reviving an atmosphere of magic and archaism at the tsarist court. His task, in the Tsarina's eyes, was to transmit a share of his virility to the Tsar and to heal the sick heir to the throne. She met the demand for a reasonable Council of Ministers by dispatching to the Tsar at General Headquarters an apple (the traditional aphrodisiac) that Rasputin had given her and an impassioned plea to 'Remember that even Monsieur Philippe [a French charlatan and hypnotist] said there must be no constitution, for that would be your own and Russia's downfall. ... Be Peter the Great, Ivan the Terrible – Crush everything underfoot.'

The Metropolitan of St Petersburg and Archbishop Varnava, who could barely read or write, owed their offices to Rasputin, and the Senior Procurator of the Holy Synod maintained himself in office through his assistance. The leadership of the Orthodox Church appeared to have passed, via the Tsar, into the hands of a peasant whom Paleologue, a descendant of Byzantium's last ruling house, embraced as an *illumine*. A century after Madame de Krudener and her circle of *Illuminati* had inspired Alexander I with the concept of the 'Holy Alliance', the demonic primal power of the Russian peasantry took possession, of the decadent court in the person of Rasputin.

After the murder of Rasputin, who had been against the war and pro-German, the Empire lasted only some ten weeks. The Revolution began on 23 February 1917, with demonstrations by women textile workers (who included many conscripts' wives), the most exploited members of the proletariat in St Petersburg. So the revolution erupted from below and at female initiative. Vera, the heroine of Chernyshevsky's *What Is to be Done?*, had (it will be recalled) set out to arouse the political consciousness of her female employees.

The Bolsheviks had little, practically nothing, to do with the Russian Revolution at its outset. They waited, hesitantly.

LENIN

In December 1901 in *Brdzola* (The Struggle), the first journal in the Caucasus which managed to evade censorship, an essay was published on 'The Russian Social Democratic Party and Its Immediate Tasks'. The second part began with the following passage:

> Not only the working class had been groaning under the yoke of Tsardom. Other social classes too are strangled in the grip of autocracy. Groaning is the hunger-swollen Russian peasantry. . . . Groaning are the small town-dwellers, petty employees . . . petty officials, in a word, that multitude of small men whose existence is just as insecure as that of the working class and who have reason enough to be discontented with their social position. Groaning, too, is the lower and even middle bourgeoisie that cannot put up with the Tsarist knout and bludgeon, especially the educated section of the bourgeoisie. . . . Groaning are the oppressed nationalities and religions in Russia, among them the Poles and the Finns driven from their native lands and injured in their most sacred feelings. Autocracy has brutally trampled over their rights and their freedoms that were granted to them by history. Groaning are the unceasingly persecuted and humiliated Jews, deprived even of those miserable rights that other Russian subjects enjoy – the right to live where they choose, the right to go to school, *et cetera*. Groaning are the Georgians, the Armenians and other nations who can neither have their own schools nor be employed by the state and are compelled to submit to the shameful and oppressive policies of Russification. . . . Groaning are the many millions of members of Russian religious sects who want to worship according to the dictates of their own conscience rather than to those of the Orthodox priests.

The author of this denunciation was just twenty-two years old, had attended the theological seminary at Tiflis, had composed patriotic Georgian verses and secretly read Victor Hugo, Darwin, and Thackeray as well as Gogol, Chekhov, and Saltykov-Shchedrin, and was called Joseph Dzhugashvili, later to become famous under the name of Joseph Stalin.

He went on to manifest an invincible mistrust of the bourgeoisie: 'Though discontented, they are still quite well-off and therefore gladly cede to the working class and to the ordinary people at large the right to expose their backs to Cossack whips, to fight on barricades, and so on.' The industrial working class therefore ought to assume the leadership. If autocracy was overthrown by the people led by proletarian socialists, the result would be 'a broad *democratic constitution*, giving equal rights to the worker, the oppressed peasant and the capitalist'.

About nine months earlier a Munich social democrat, Hans Kaiser, of Schleissheimer Strasse 106, took on two new tenants: Comrade Meyer and his wife. Comrade Meyer was an unobtrusive lodger, worked a good deal in his room, and liked the local beer. After visits to Berlin, Leipzig, and Nuremberg, he had settled in Munich at the beginning of September 1900. Here, apart from his contacts with German social democrats and Polish revolutionaries, he set about publication of a periodical, *Iskra* (The Spark). Comrade Meyer was in fact Vladimir Ilyich Ulyanov (1870–1924), the son of an ennobled school inspector and a lawyer by profession, who became a revolutionary after the execution of his brother in 1887, spent the years 1896–9 in exile in Siberia, and thereafter was generally known as Lenin. In 1903 he assumed leadership of the majority group in the Russian Social Democratic Party, the Bolsheviks. In 1912 he began publication of *Pravda* (The Truth), in 1917 he returned to Russia in a sealed train under the aegis of the German High Command, and in 1922 he founded the Union of Soviet Socialist Republics. The first Collected Edition of his works was issued, in twenty volumes, in 1923–6.

Sixty years after Lenin's stay at Munich an extremely spry old gentleman, fond of his wine, was often to be met at the monthly meeting between conservative professors and journalists in one of the city's good restaurants. He was Fedor Stepun, former member of the Kerensky Government who, together with other non-communist members of the intelligentsia, had been expelled from Russia in 1922. His memoirs had just been re-issued and their pages contain a vivid picture of Lenin in the early days of his seizure of power:

> The monumental scale on which Lenin ... proceeded to lay down the basis for Communist society can only be compared with the report of the Creation as told in the First Book of Moses.
>
> Day after day his dreadful 'Let there be' thundered through Russia, confused and plunged into gloom by the Revolution.
>
> The soldiers – they were to be diplomats and, at their own responsibility and risk, arrange armistices with the enemy.
>
> And the workers – they were to control industry, look into the manufacturers' books and decide for themselves production goals as well as prices of the products.
>
> And the poor – they were to become masters of the soil and take into their safekeeping the estates of the rich.
>
> The peoples of Russia were to become the lords of their fate, their right of self-determination extending even to the right of secession from the federal state.

And the schoolchildren – they were to become the governors of their schools, masters and parents bowing to their collective will, for the children, not the greybeards, were the guarantors of the happiness of the coming world.

And the artists – they were to become the prophets of the future. Praise be to the Futurists who smash the old artistic forms just as the Revolution is smashing the old ways of life.

And God shall be denied and His Church destroyed so that Communism may rule the globe.

That was the way one decree after another was promulgated. Yet Communism failed to arrive.

Towards the end of the nineteenth century, in the weariness following on the failure of the Populists and the catastrophe of their terrorist wing, a number of outstanding Russian thinkers turned Marxist: Bulgakov, Berdyaev, Frank, Tuhan-Baranovsky, and others. Pre-eminent among them was Plekhanov, the first great Marxist theoretician in Russia and an uninhibited thinker. He parted company with the Bolsheviks in 1903 and later with the Mensheviks too. Another important figure, often attacked by Lenin, was Alexander Malinovsky (1873–1927), who worked under the pseudonym of Bogdanov. Believing the essential issue to be the 'creative transformation of being' rather than 'evolution', he replaced 'dialectic' with 'organic process'.

Lenin's first polemic was directed against the Populists. *Who are These 'Friends of the People'?* contains the sentence 'Knowledge of historical necessity in no way reduces the role of the individual in history.' Nine years later, in 1903, he went through a severe internal crisis which was connected with that of the Social Democratic Party as such. Plekhanov, Vera Zasulich, and Paul Axelrod wanted to develop it along federal democratic lines whereas Lenin insisted on a strongly disciplined centralism. This had already been stated in *What Is to be Done?* In 1904 he brought out *One Step Forward, Two Steps Back*, launching his relentless fight against former friends and allies. For the first time he displayed that destructive will-power which led Trotsky in *Our Political Tasks*, published at Geneva in the same year and dedicated to 'My dear teacher Paul B. Axelrod', to liken him to Robespierre.

At this decisive moment he fortified himself with the study of radically individualistic revolutionaries who were distinguished by their thorough-going hostility to Marxism and party machinery, but whom he nevertheless regarded as kindred spirits. They included Zaichnevsky, who had proclaimed: 'We shall proceed more consistently than the great Terrorists of 1792. We shall not be deterred if the downfall of the present régime demands three times the quantity of blood spilt by the Jacobins. In unshakeable belief in ourselves, in our strength, in the sympathy of the people for our cause, in belief in the glorious future of Russia, to whom will fall the mission of being the first country to put socialism into practice, we shall proclaim the watchword "Seize the hatchet!" '

It is worth recalling that the hatchet had been the major weapon employed in all the many peasant disturbances and risings of which there were one hundred and forty-five in the years 1826–34, two hundred and sixteen in 1835–44, three hundred and forty-eight in 1845–54, and four hundred and seventy-five in 1855–61 (the last date being that of the emancipation of the serfs). After Alexander II's reforms there were no less than twelve hundred such uprisings. Whereas the population in towns only increased from six to twelve million between 1861 and 1892, that of the countryside rose from fifty-five to eighty-two million. More than half of the peasants lived at starvation level and, since political emancipation had not been accompanied by land reform, had no choice but either to join the city proletariat or to emigrate beyond the Urals.

The Populists and other revolutionaries, right up to 1917, thought of the workers as 'peasants in the towns' who would one day want to return to the land. Lenin feared these peasant masses because he knew what an explosive force they represented. He wanted to see them tamed and kept in order by a band of professional revolutionaries who would be harsher yet more disciplined than these chaotic masses. 'Russia has been used to the rule of one hundred and fifty thousand aristocratic estate owners. Why,' he demanded, 'should not two hundred and forty thousand Bolsheviks take over the same task?'

The question was put at the time of the October Revolution, but Lenin had in effect been asking it for the past fifteen years. Provide an organisation of revolutionaries and Russia can be turned upside down, was the opening claim of *What is to be Done?*, as well as his first shot in the struggle for control of the Party. Under prevailing conditions, he maintained, democratic conditions inside the Party rendered it impossible to lead the movement against tsarism. To fit himself for this fight, as its leader, he threw himself wholeheartedly into a battle of wits with the ideas of other Marxists, bourgeois philosophers, and Hegel. The singular and awesome part is that, in all these years up to 1914, he looked on language as a lethal weapon. An expression of opinion was to him a very serious matter. Whoever erred therein had lost his right to life and a place in history. His contempt and scorn are worthy of Marx.

Lenin's intense preoccupation with Hegel enabled him eventually to work out a dialectic that was not only truly original but to which he was to owe his greatest achievement. What saved Bolshevism and rendered foundation of the USSR and world communism possible was not the October Revolution (which could have been crushed), but his attitude to the Brest-Litovsk negotiations. The exactions of the Central Powers were outrageous, amounting to a political destruction of the Russian state which would have included divestment of its most important industries. Members of the Bolshevik Party, no less than others, rejected these demands in a storm of indignation. Nevertheless, after the fiercest of altercations, Lenin got his way and made peace, a peace which allowed troops of the Central Powers to occupy wide tracts of Russian territory and to enforce the secession of the Ukraine and Baltic provinces. To him all this was simply part and parcel of the beginning of the gigantic new conflicts involving the Russian revolution, the world revolution (due to begin, as he thought, in Germany), and the uprising of the masses, first in Europe, then Asia. He knew that the preceding hostilities, fought largely along nineteenth-century lines (poisonous gas, tanks, and aircraft played no primary role), had simply been the signal for the twentieth-century's really big contests.

He had a thorough appreciation of the value of constructive imagination. 'Even in the most straightforward generalisation, in the most elementary general notion (such as "table"), a minute piece of imagination is involved. (Vice versa it is nonsense to deny the part that imagination plays even in the strictest discipline. See Pissarev on useful dreams as a spur to work . . .)' In *What Is to be Done?* he had already cited this same author: 'The discrepancy between dream and reality is innocuous provided that the dreamer firmly believes in his dream, closely observes life, compares his observations with his dreams, and conscientiously works towards the materialisation of his dream picture.' To this quotation he added a comment of his own: 'Unfortunately our movement is all too poor in dreams of this sort.'

Lenin's original concepts of the Soviet state and the 'dictatorship of the proletariat' were dreams on the part of a political imagination which could justly claim to have its origin among the great French Enthusiasts of 1792 and later. Lenin, a genuine revolutionary, was a dreamer who belonged to that category. He took the Paris Commune of 1871 as his pattern for the Soviet state. To him the dictatorship of the proletariat meant 'the organisation of the avant-garde of the oppressed into the ruling class for the purpose of holding down the oppressors'. When the people, freed from capitalist exploitation and its effect on the soul, shall have become accustomed to 'adhering to the elementary rules of living together, known since ancient times and preached in all precepts for thousands of years, keeping them without force, without sanction, without subordination, and without that special apparatus of coercion calling itself the state', then it will really be possible for the state to wither away. He admitted that he had no idea how quickly that could happen.

'As long as there is a state, there is no freedom. When there is freedom, there will be no state.' Lenin's aphorism was a heritage plucked from the fire of Bakunin and other anarchists and nihilists. This same Lenin became the architect of a coercive state reminiscent of those Egyptian and Mesopotamian Empires which relied on massive armies of slave workers for their achievements.

It was Leon Trotsky, his great partner and comrade-in-arms, who brilliantly put into effect Lenin's policy at Brest–Litovsk. It was Trotsky who built up for Lenin's evolving state the Red Army which, during the years of the Civil War and War Communism until 1924, demonstrated itself as *the* instrument on which this state rested. It was Trotsky who, in August 1904 after leaving *Iskra* in April, published *Our Political Tasks*, the 'most strident bill of impeachment that any Socialist had ever drawn up against Lenin'.

Lenin, Trotsky alleged, wanted to erect an 'orthodox theocracy'. 'Lenin's methods lead to this: the party organisation at first substitutes itself for the party as a whole; then the Central Committee substitutes itself for the party as a whole; then the Central Committee substitutes itself for the organisation; and finally a single "dictator" substitutes himself for the Central Committee. . . . ' Lenin had proudly acknowledged himself to be a Jacobin, but Trotsky insisted on a sharp distinction being drawn between Jacobin and social democrat. Although he did not deny similarities between them, the social democrat had no use for the guillotine. 'A Jacobin tribunal would have tried, under the charge of moderation, the whole international Labour movement, and Marx's leonine head would have been the first to roll under the guillotine. . . . ' Robespierre used to say, 'I know only two parties, the good and the evil citizens', and this aphorism 'is engraved on the heart of Maximilian Lenin', whose 'malicious and morally repulsive suspiciousness is a flat caricature of the tragic Jacobin intolerance. . . . ' Lenin's follower wanted a 'dictatorship over the proletariat by way of an absolutely uniform party'. In view of the leaflets advocating this, 'one felt a shiver running down one's spine'. With real vision Trotsky foresaw the dangers and tasks awaiting the future revolutionary government in Russia:

> The tasks of the new régime will be so complex that they cannot be solved other than by a competition between various methods of economic and political construction, by long 'disputes', by a systematic struggle not only between the socialist and the capitalist worlds, but also between many trends inside socialism, trends which will inevitably emerge as soon as the proletarian dictatorship poses tens and hundreds of new . . . problems. No strong, 'domineering' organisation . . . will be able to suppress these trends and controversies. . . . A proletariat capable of exercising its dictatorship over society will not tolerate any dictatorship over itself. . . . The working class . . . will undoubtedly have in its ranks quite a few political invalids . . . and much ballast of obsolescent ideas, which it will have to jettison. . . . But this intricate task cannot be solved by placing above the proletariat a few well-picked people . . . or one person invested with the power to liquidate and degrade.

Twenty years later Trotsky was to plead for free competition of ideas and trends in almost the same words before the tribunals of Bolshevism. Those were the courts of Stalin who became the murderers of men, having already become the greatest of all murderers of the imagination, artistic, social and human, and even, first and foremost, of imaginative political perception. Stalin, so orthodox, persecuted the political prophets (starting with 'Marx's leonine head') with a destructive passion reminiscent of that applied by some of the Old Testament kings against their prophets. It shocked even the mortally sick Lenin, whose warning against the new dictator failed to reach either the Party or the people as a whole.

THE GREAT EXODUS

'Vladimir Lenin has awakened Russia from sleep and will not let it become engulfed again' (Gorky). He found to hand a Russian youth prepared for the most radical experiments in art, science, education, and society alike. In practically every field of the arts it had been playing a truly pioneer role. In architecture there were men like Vladimirov, Tatlin, Shuesev, Viesnin, Sobolev, and, above all, Ginsburg, Gobolov, and Ladovsky. In sculpture, Alexander Archipenko, Naum Pevsner (pseudonym, Gabo and Antoine Pevsner, Puni (Gallicized as Jean Pougny), and Ossip Zadkine. In painting, Kandinsky, Kawlensky, Chagall. In music, Stravinsky. In writing, there were both groups and individual talents. There was the Moscow Arts Theatre. The exponents of philosophy were men of extreme intelligence. On the eve of the First World War there was no advanced intellectual form that did not have its following, and on the eve of the Revolution alert minds caught, in the excited, fear-ridden, hopefully expectant air of St Petersburg and Moscow, the sound of preparation for a drama of unique grandeur: the greatest political and social experiment in history. A gigantic realm, whose people lived in mediaeval or even more primitive conditions, was to be transformed into an industrial and technological super-state of the twentieth century, an experiment which, as they hoped, was to be accompanied by the most daring flights of imagination in the fields of artistic, architectural, literary, and educational endeavour. The juncture between the two magnificent sets of experiment did not take place. Repeatedly begun, it ended time with the destruction of everything offered by the creative intelligentsia. Those artists and writers who had not already gone, of their own free will, to Paris, Munich, or London were either expelled or liquidated, in both the physical and psychological sense.

By 1922 the most respected authors had left the country; Ivan Bunin, Nikolai Berdyaev, Leonid Andreyev, Vyacheslav Ivanov, Dimitri Merezhkovsky, Zinaida Hippius, Boris Saizev, Alexei Remizov, Konstantin Balmont, Michail Artsybashev, Ivan Shmelyov, Mark Aldonov, Vladislav Khodasevich, and Alexander Kuprin, Marina Zvetyeva, Ilya Ehrenburg, Alexei Tolstoi as well as Dimitri Mirsky, all of whom later returned. One of the last to go was Maxim Gorky, who, together with Lenin, despite an advanced condition of consumption, fought with everything in his power to save Russia's cultural values. Practically all the writers who did remain behind soon ceased voicing their opinions: Andrei Bely, Valeri Brusov, Nikolai Gumilyev, Anna Akhmatova, Ossip Mandelshtam, Fyodor Sologub, Mikhail Kuzmin, Maximilian Voloshin.

Simultaneously, though, new literary groups and mini-groups sprang out of the ground like mushrooms, from Petrograd to the Far East, propagating in manifestoes printed on wrapping paper the most ridiculous ideas, wanting to throw all hitherto existing culture into the 'dustbin of history'. Members of every kind of avant-garde and even so-called proletarian authors saw that they got themselves talked about. There were many charlatans and nine-day wonders among them, but also many talented individuals. There was the Agitprop writer Demyan Bedny, Bogdanov's proletarian culture, the cosmists Kirrilov and Gerassimov, the futurists Mayakovsky and Khlevnikov, the imaginists around Yesenin, the constructivists Selvinsky and Vera Inber, the peasant writers Vassilyev, Kluyev, Lyychkov and Orechin, the 'Serapion Brothers' Fedin (after E.T.A. Hoffmann), Vsevolod Ivanov, Soschenko, Tikhonov and Kaverin, the formalists Shklovsky, Tinyanov, and others.

Even in those early, chaotic years three writers absorbed the greatness and the tragedy of the Revolution to the full: Blok, Yesenin, and Mayakovsky.

In Western Europe the expulsion of the silencing of artists, writers, and political or religious thinkers during the nineteenth century was less noticeable because it was spread over a longer period and submerged in a broad flow of events and a certain progress. The suicide of a young poet like Chatterton or Kleist might attract a certain amount of local attention (as in Berlin, in the case of Kleist), but it generally passed unnoticed, like Nerval's suicide during the Paris World Exhibition of 1855.

In Russia, however, insofar as it had not already left the country during the tsarist period, an alert, variegated, creative intelligentsia was annihilated within a few decades. There was really only one common denominator between the main groups and the highly individualistic personalities concerned – they were harbingers of the future. But it was in the name of the future that they were annihilated by the masters of the future. This annihilation began with Lenin, spread during the days of the Civil War, and under Stalin became a matter of bureaucracy and systematic application.

External destructive forces began to be complemented by similar internal trends. It is this which renders the Russian tragedy even more complex and terrible. The self-immolation of the Old Believers had, before the Revolution, already been paralleled by the attitudes of certain conscience-stricken sections of the intelligentsia.

The frenzy of the Bolshevik revolution against intellectual values fused the loathing of the Moscow masses for the alien St Petersburg culture with the echo of the intelligentsia's ascetic rejection of its own culture. Russian artists, writers, and other members of the intelligentsia spontaneously discredited their own art and their own achievements on account of 'the people's misery'. Tolstoy raged fiercely against his own work and what seemed to him the corruption of wordly culture. The traits of a Syrian–Byzantine asceticism become visible. Culture is to be sacrificed to the people because it smacks of the anti-social.

'The repudiation of freedom of intellect and freedom of research, insofar as they did not serve what was regarded as salvation, therefore constituted a part of Russian intellectual tradition. Bolshevism simply radicalised it on an enormous scale. What had originally been a spontaneous and deliberately austere renunciation of the free, abstract, and personally satisfying pursuit of intellectual matters, until such time as the salvation of men in general should be attained, became the point of departure for clapping the fetters of Marxism on Russia's bid for salvation' (Emanuel Sarkysianz).

There was of course an abyss between the peasant masses, stuck fast in the Stone Age, the lower middle classes, and the intelligentsia. Russian literature was far ahead of the evolution of the nation's intellectual life. 'When the popular masses spontaneously rose against tsarist dominion, the world of letters did not have the people behind it. Of what use to it were its inestimable treasures? They were inestimable treasures that foundered' (Adolf Stender-Petersen). Stalin could rely on 'healthy popular sensibility' in his campaign against the 'unpatriotic' and anti-party body of intellectuals and artists. Nevertheless, older and more potent than Stalin, murderer of the Revolution and murderer of the harbingers of the future, the Russian Revolution itself grew out of ideas and trends which are brought into focus by the will to destruction as well as the will to self-destruction of a section of the intelligentsia. They are genuinely Russian and genuinely religious trends in which a will to destruction and re-creation merge. In Bakunin, Kropotkin, and Lenin the age-old desire to the Creation and to install man as lord and shepherd of the universe take a political turn.

COSMOCRACY*

I use the word Cosmocracy to express the idea of the Russian people as the bringers of salvation and colonisers of cosmic space. The ideal demanded a type of individual very different from the selfish *petit bourgeois*, clinging to his earth-bound (Western) civilisation, on whom Herzen, Dostoevsky, Lenin, and other great Russian thinkers poured their scorn. To create the image of *homo cosmonauta* and provide for his physical and spiritual needs was an aim shared by Russian inventors and religious philosophers during the nineteenth century. It was a line of thought that, although its course (like most of history's vital trends) remained obscure, has led straight to contemporary Russian exploration of outer space. One of those who was preoccupied with plans for such cosmic flights was Kibalchich, the engineer-assassin whose bomb killed Tsar Alexander II.

Nikolai Fedorov (1828–1903), whose essays, during his lifetime, remained provincial publications, is, nevertheless one of Russia's most gifted thinkers. Initially he exercised a strong influence on Dostoevsky, Tolstoy, and Solovyev, 'but elements of his chiliastic visions of the apotheosis of all

* (This word is the author's invention and represents, as the opening sentence indicates, a fusion of two notions, one spiritual and one physical.)

matter can be traced in the most extreme of ultra-Bolshevist, pseudo-materialistic developments of Russian Messianism, in poetry, and in the machine-worship of the early Bolshevik period.'

Fedorov, politically a perfervid monarchist, was the son of a Prince Gagarin and a peasant woman (or perhaps a Circassian captive) and lived a life of the utmost simplicity. He censored philosophers for attaching more importance to thought than action. In that way they were contributing to the death of philosophy. The Scriptures provide a programme for our terrestrial activity: 'the concept (of the Gospels) is neither subjective nor objective, but prospective'. Man's task was 'not merely to visit all the worlds of the universe, but to populate them'. *That* is the purpose of mankind's creation.

To Fedorov it was a deeply wounding notion that the living should be separated from the dead and that all the world should behave as though this were a fact that must be accepted. He wanted to see the forces of nature mobilised in order that the dead might be awakened, because progress constructed on corpses is amoral. Ascending into the cosmos, man must take with him his ancestry as 'pious Aeneas' did when he carried his ailing father on his back out of burning Troy.

Man's task is to achieve the great fraternity of the living and the dead. 'What is important is not living for oneself (egotism), nor living for others (altruism), but to live with all, for all.' 'History as a whole has until now consisted of the destruction of nature and men's mutual extermination. Modern civilisation, lacking in fraternity, amounts to murder and suicide. Only fear, force, and utilitarian considerations hold it together. Everything serves warlike purposes, every invention, highway, and means of communication.' 'Science is under the yoke of manufacturers and merchants. . . . Formerly science was the handmaiden of theology. Nowadays it is the handmaiden of commerce.'

In this connection Fedorov attacked the industrialist and capitalist West in terms that were more radical and vehement (if this is possible) than any uttered by Stalinist communism. Western science and technology, in his view, did not serve a solid and essential 'subdual of savage natural forces', but their exploitation. He would have liked personally to implore the Tsar, as potential master of immense natural forces, to take the taming of them in hand himself, so that mankind could as a result be freed from hunger, sickness, and death. The Tsar, not the Pope, should prove, as the 'sovereign of souls', to be mankind's liberator.

Fedorov was by no means hostile to the West. In 1891 he observed attentively American attempts to create rain through artillery barrages. There was at the time a famine in Russia, caused by drought and the combination of circumstances caused him to propose that, in future, armies should be employed as mankind's forces of peace for the control and utilisation of natural forces. It is Man's hostile attitude to nature that has caused its forces to become infernal. His real task is to keep it in check responsibly and piously while assuring its protection.

The apotheosis of the universe was to be advanced by man's active intervention. Geography should be a sacred science, seeing that the whole earth is a single Holy Land. 'Man's regulative process' (a favourite expression) shall help to extend his realm 'to all the stellar systems until the universe has been finally spiritualised'. 'The gravity, which ties us to the earth, must be overcome.' The task of science is to manipulate and dispose of 'all the world's atoms and molecules' so as, among other things, to accumulate and to revivify the corpses of our ancestors. Solar energy must be used. A static, eternal Heaven, with a concomitant hell, was a notion to be rejected.

As long ago as 1932 N.A.Setnitsky, formerly professor at Harben, drew attention (in *On the Ultimate Ideal*) to the strong influence exerted by Fedorov's ideas on certain specific Soviet plans and undertakings: the connection between knowledge of natural forces and their application to social problems, the fight against famine, the opening up of the Russian waterways, and so on. Almost twenty years later N.O.Lossky remarked that it was conceivable that, at a time when man's extraordinary progress in science and technology was rendering ever more daring projects possible, Fedorov's philosophy might carry increasing weight.

Red Kremlin was the title of a poem in which V.Kirillov identified world revolution as the ultimate resurrection. In 1842 Bakunin had proclaimed, 'Mankind is God in matter. . . . Man's destiny is to bring Heaven to earth.' In 1908 Lunacharsky (the first Soviet Minister of Education) linked the inculcation of socialism with the coming of a new man and a new world. Pious Russians knew the meaning of 'red' long before 1917. The colour was a synonym for beauty and redemptive strength. Red was the colour of blood, of the Resurrection, of cosmic and terrestial Easter.

A leading contemporary Orthodox theologian, G.P.Fedotov, sees the main element in the Russian concept of salvation in the ideal of Mother Earth's redemption. The theme had already occurred in the earliest eschatological work of the Kiev period, wherein it was said that the transfiguration of nature would exceed the bliss of the saints on the new earth. 'Mother Earth is the Mother of God and the hope of mankind' (Dostoevsky). 'Our world is *the* world which by a miracle becomes the divine one' (Karsavin, the Orthodox theologian). 'The Redemption was formulated collectively, not individually, in the Orthodox Church, not merely as redemption within the community (as, for instance, in Catholicism), but as community in the Redemption itself.' From the idea of the unity of all living things and collective redemption there flows a current which transforms the 'Red' Revolution into the realisation of the redemption of all living beings, a process rendered easier by the absence from Orthodox piety of the Western European concept of *persona*. Redemption comprised every man and living creature. 'The beasts of the field were my brothers,' wrote Alexander Dobrolyubov, describing the Mother of God calling the calves into Paradise – and that in 1918! Was Lenin, who on his deathbed spoke of St Francis, aware of this proximity of primal Franciscan eschatology to Russian piety?

One of the first decrees of the Soviet authorities, No. 2 of 10 November 1917, proclaimed: 'The October Revolution began under the universal watchword of release. The peasants are freed . . . from the landowners. . . . The soldiers are freed from the generals. . . . Everything that lives and is viable is freed from its odious fetters.' Those were Red Easter tidings in Red October 1917.

RED EASTER

Chiliastic notions pervaded Russia from the days of Alexander I. In the second decade of the twentieth century the adherents of one such movement regarded Lenin as the Messiah. For another, in the Leningrad area, the Soviet star, became by association with the star of Bethlehem, the object of a cult.

Sergei Yesenin, a poet of peasant origin who in 1925 shot himself in the Hotel Angleterre at Leningrad and wrote a last poem in his own blood, addressed the Revolution in the following terms: 'I have seen a new manifestation of Christ in which death does not triumph over truth. . . . A threatening peal of church bells over Holy Russia. . . . It is the ramparts of the Kremlin that weep. Rise now, o Earth, upon stars' lances. I will pluck out the beard of God Himself. I will tug at His white hairs and say, "God, I remould you" . . . '

Yesenin's forefathers were Old Believers and it was with the force of their long-damned ardour that he now praised the new redeemers: 'Praised be God and goodwill unto men. One has appeared with a new faith, without Cross and without torment. . . . A new redeemer rides upon a mare into the world. Our faith is in vigour, our faith is faith in ourselves.' Yesenin defended Christ against the defamations of the Bolshevik Demyan Bednyi.

The Left social revolutionary Invanov-Rasumnik compared the Revolution, in *Russia and Ionia* (1920), to the birth of Jesus at Bethlehem. A sect calling itself 'New Testament' endowed Lenin, as bearer of the 'Third Testament', with the redemptive power revered by the Fraticelli followers of Joachim of Flora. In early Bolshevik poetry, a radical Messianism was linked with a vision of man redeeming the world by his art or technique, (*Techne*, Greek for art = craftsmanship, is related to both *tiktein* and *teknon*. witness and child.) The new Trinity assumed in Gastev's *Machine Paradise* the appearance of 'Three suns, three laws of nature: the ancient forces of nature, man's self-imposed labour, shining reason, and the Godhead's luminous sense. Triumph, resound victoriously, O reborn nature. Praise the iron Messiah, hero of the new day. Boundless freedom lies in his brown hands, mankind's dawn in his iron sinews.'

The Messiah of Iron was also the description chosen by V. Kirillov: 'Here he is, the earth's redeemer, the lord of titanic powers, amidst the hum of wires, the scintillation of machines, the glitter of electric suns. It was thought that he would come in a robe of stars, with the aureole of divine mysteries, but he came in the soot of factories and slums. Now he strides over abysses of oceans, insuperable, irresistible. . . . He brings the world a new sun.'

'We shall not thrust upward to those wretched heights called Heaven,' proclaimed Gastev in *We Dared*. 'Heaven is the creation of the passive, the idle, and the fearful. Let us thrust down! Let us dig shafts with fire, metal, gas, and steam, the biggest tunnels in the world. . . . May we merge with the earth, it is in us and we are in it. Born of the earth, we shall return to it. . . . The earth, wrought of iron, will become the furnace of the universe. And when . . . the earth can no longer endure and bursts its shell of steel, it will bring forth fresh creatures whose name will be man no longer. The new-born will then no longer heed the small and lowly heaven, which will have been lost in the explosion of their birth, but will at once move the earth into a new circle of the firmament, jumble the map of suns and planets, build new storeys atop the skies . . . and harmonies of unknown provenance will ever again resound across the unimaginably and indiscernibly far horizons.'

Yessenin, a poet whose thought was quite different from Gastev's, also foresaw the establishment of links between planets and Milky Ways 'when men will have grasped the marriage between earth and heaven'. Here, and in other writings, primal traditions about the universe and ancient memories of the sacred marriage between heaven and earth were mobilised on behalf of the new Easter, the grandiose Red Easter which was to be witness to the birth of *homo cosmonauta*, man's resurrection and ascension. Jean Paul, had also dared to dream of this a century before. Now it was to be realised by the 'Messiah of Iron'.

Nevertheless a long Good Friday was to precede this Red Easter, a way of the Cross for the Russian people, through civil war, in the struggle to preserve the victory of the Revolution. The proletariat, said Lunacharsky in 1918, climbs Calvary as the new Messiah and, crucified, will be resurrected; the uprising of the working class will kill God but create a new religion which 'to the highest degree' will comprise earlier religions.

Even in Marxist poetry of the Lenin era it is the pathos of the proletariat's martyrdom, not the Utopia of happiness, that forms the main subject. The official Soviet anthology for 1924 included Kirillov's poem *To the Proletariat*: 'In you alone is the vindication for centuries of torment. All those who have fallen in the cause of light are merged with you and await your answer and vengeance. The dreams of the crucified, the damned of centuries, awake in you . . . bring faster the sacred tidings of liberty. . . .'

Alexander Blok, the greatest Left social revolutionary poet and, with Mayakovsky, the greatest laureate of the Revolution's hopes, noted once that in order to understand Christ it was necessary to become like a poor and downtrodden path: trampled, you must plunge into a dark ravine, leaving all, forgetting all, to perish there like withered grass. During the

Civil War, in order to encourage the new 'Red Army', the Bolsheviks had two million copies of Blok's *The Twelve* printed.

The poem's protagonists are twelve Red Army men. They march through snowy tempests and the night, the Red Flag in front, fear and the enemy hard behind:

> 'Freedom, freedom, freedom let there be
> And no Cross, no Cross besides!'

The Twelve become an epitome for the Apostles:

> 'Striding, striding, striding . . .
> Famine scurries after.
> Ahead the flag, bloody, streaming,
> And, invisible in snow,
> Securely does He go,
> Gently, storm-free goes ahead,
> Snowy lustre rippling all about,
> Rose-white haloed, Christ is in the lead.'

Nikolai Gumileov, another poet, criticised the introduction of Christ from an artistic point of view. Blok replied, 'I don't like the end of *The Twelve* either. I wish it was different. When I had finished, I was myself surprised. Why Christ? But the more I looked, the clearer I saw Him. And at the same time I said to myself, "A pity, but Christ!" ' In his diary he noted, 'There is no doubt about Christ being out in front. The issue is not "whether they are worthy of Him", but, far worse, that He is once more with them and, for the present, none other. . . . '

THE VICTORY OF RED REACTION: STALIN

Red reaction won: the red *petit bourgeois* and the red bureaucracy with the help of the *apparat*, the party machine, and of 'administrative' terror. Sentences to labour camps and 'liquidation' were an affair of the 'administration'.

An outsize *petit bourgeois* built up this realm of red reaction – Stalin. A genius of mediocrity, he was also a genius at hiding his own plans. Indeed, often enough he was not aware of them himself, for he was not merely lacking in imagination, but actually hated and tried to destroy it whenever he found it. And that meant killing men. He made his way forward, carefully looking to right and left, through the ideological discussions and political struggles of the years 1900–24, always watching, always listening, not always understanding the intellectual issues but knowing how to turn them to his own advantage. By 1920 he had made the transition from relative tolerance to a belief in terror. The opposition between the 'Westerner' Lenin and the 'Easterner' Stalin became ever clearer, but did not prevent him, after Lenin's death, from instituting the Lenin cult so as to prepare the way for his own. His language, his style, his prolix rhetoric betrayed his Orthodox training.

'The oath to Lenin, which he read at the second congress of the Soviets, remains to this day the fullest and the most organic revelation of his own mind. In it, the style of the "Communist Manifesto" is strangely blended with that of the Orthodox Prayer Book; and Marxist terminology is wedded to the old Slavonic vocabulary. Its revolutionary invocations sound like a litany composed for a church choir.' Each paragraph of this litany began 'In leaving us, Comrade Lenin ordained . . . '

Lenin had been able to envisage a socialist society only within an international framework. Stalin, since international revolution failed to mature, drew the harsh conclusion that there must be 'socialism in one country'. In other words, communism is a closed society, enclosed within the precincts of the Party Church 'which is always right' and fights against its numerous internal and external enemies with every means at its disposal: schooling and propaganda, co-ordination in every sphere of life, enormous uniform organisations directing the farm, the factory, the army, the police, and cultural affairs.

Stalin and colleagues re-barbarised Russia, eliminated progressive thought or drove it underground. This ex-seminarist had a primitive, religious, vital confidence in himself. He was traditionalist and revolutionary alike, seeing himself as a new Moses who had the strength and austerity to lead his people through the wastes of hunger, poverty, and threat of war, into the promised land.

In 1931 he threw aside the cloak with which he had earlier covered his appeal to Russian nationalism. Speaking to business executives in February, he said: 'To slacken the pace would mean to lag behind; and those who lag-behind are beaten. We do not want to be beaten. . . . We are fifty or a hundred years behind the advanced countries. We must make good this lag in ten years. Either we do it or they crush us.'

Therein lay Stalin's greatness. He knew that 'they' were preparing to crush Russia. Just ten years later Hitler, with Western capital and the blessing of the Church dignitaries (who saw in him the leader of the 'crusade against Bolshevism'), invaded the Soviet Union. But then Stalin had managed, regardless of crises, catastrophes, and breakdowns, to mobilise, to industrialise a thoroughly 'underdeveloped' country whose preponderant majority of peoples had until that time barely more than an archaic outlook on life. Thousands upon thousands of human sacrifices were laid on the 'altar of the Fatherland war' in preparation for its occurrence.

Stalin was not only stirred, thrown into gloom, and stimulated into fresh outbursts of energy by his awareness of these sacrifices but also by the fear of still not having sufficient time at his disposal, of being betrayed and sold to the enemy. The material for the accusations against principal generals of the Red Army which led to their trial and the major purges of 1937–8, may very well have derived from Nazi SS sources. The ageing Stalin bears a resemblance to certain tsars, such as Alexander II, who fled before their fears like mortally wounded creatures.

The features of not one but several great tsars seemed to be revived in the Georgian Bolshevik who now ruled from their Kremlin. At one time he showed a trait of family likeness to the Iron Tsar, Nicholas I. At another he looked more like Peter the Great's direct descendant: was he not building industrial Russia in a way similar to that in which Peter the Great built his St Petersburg, on the swamps and on the bones of the builders? Again, in the years of the Second World War, he would assume the postures and imitate the gestures of Alexander I. Now, in the period of the great purges, he more and more resembled Ivan the Terrible, raging against the *boyars*.

Hitler's attack on Moscow began in October 1941. From the top of the Lenin Mausoleum Stalin inspected the 7 November parade of troops and volunteer division, who marched straight from the Red Square to the front at the outskirts of the city. He reminded the soldiers of the Civil War, when 'three quarters of our country was in the hands of foreign interventionists. . . . The enemy is not so strong as some frightened little intellectuals picture him. The devil is not so terrible as he is painted. . . . Germany cannot sustain such a struggle for long. Another few months, another half year, and Hitler's Germany must burst under the pressure of her crimes.' He invoked the spirit of the saints and warriors of Imperial Russia. 'Let the manly images of our great ancestors – Alexander Nevsky, Dimitry Donskoy, Kusma Minin, Dimitry Pozharsky, Alexander Suvorov, and Mikhail Kutuzov – inspire you in this war!'

He proclaimed the hostilities of a holy war for Holy Russia; the Church came to his support. He did not leave the Kremlin, but immured himself for four years in this holy citadel of Old Russia. Hitler ordered that 'the Kremlin was to be blown up to signalise the overthrow of Bolshevism', but the old man inside it proved to be the stronger. In April 1944 he made his first approach for an understanding with Pope Pius XII, an approach that he repeated five times between 1945 and 1948 (Stated in a letter to the author of 6 December 1962 by Father Robert Leiber, s.j., who was for many years secretary to Pope Pius XII.) His proclamation of the war as the 'Fatherland war' was in analogy to the epic of 1812, just as his aspirations, methods, gestures and caprices resembled those of Alexander I. The Georgian appears to have seen himself as a reincarnation of Alexander I, who, among other things, had wanted to acquire Poland and the Balkan Peninsula. 'The tension between Russia and her western allies was as acute in 1945 as it had been in 1815. The secretiveness of the diplomacy of both rulers, their tactics in taking their allies by surprise, and their alternation of conciliatory and strong-arm attitudes, caused the same confusion and embarrassment among their allies.'

Stalin had his eyes on other coming conflicts long before the victory of

1945 and, to be ready for them, he transformed the Soviet Empire into an armed fortress. The task of the economically, militarily, and politically associated satellite states was to constitute the approaches to this stronghold. Its keep was entrusted to the Party, whose responsibility was defence of the true doctrine against divergents to the right and to the left. Stalin wrote its catechism, *On Dialectical and Historical Materialism*, himself. He continually tried to safeguard the Party against the 'leftist deviation' of the Utopians, who exaggerated the part played by ideas, and the 'rightest deviation' of the 'economists', who underestimated it. The sole sane doctrine of political theology was, for him, 'dialectic' and 'science', in the sense that he understood these terms.

'Dialectical materialism,' he laid down in his catechism, 'is the outlook of the Marxist-Leninist Party.' During the semantic dispute in 1950, he wrote in *Pravda* that 'Marxism is the science of nature and society's laws of development, the science of the revolution of the oppressed and exploited masses, the science of the victory of socialism in all countries, the science of the erection of the Communist society'.

'Dialectic' is the instrument of this 'science'. 'Dialectic as against metaphysics, regards nature not as a condition of rest and immobility, as standstill and immutability, but as a condition of continual movement and change, continual renewal and evolution in which something is always being created and growing, something dies and becomes out-of-date.' But that was a dangerous thesis, and Stalin knew it. Dialectic could, in the wrong hands, prove the Party's and orthodoxy's total undoing. Hence it was essential to control dialectic. That was why he made such efforts to prevail with his All-Russian monolithic interpretation against 'red heretics' like Tito and his Yugoslav theoreticians and practitioners.

With Marx the dialectical method had been an instrument for analysis of the contradictions appertaining to the epoch of industrial capitalism. With Stalin it became 'an instrument for justification of the Party's position of leadership and Soviet conditions. Whereas Marx was concerned with revealing invisible contradictions, Stalin was out to disguise visible ones.' Dialectic was transformed into dogma, a weapon to stifle life and movement. The result was catastrophic. In the name of dialectic a neo-Byzantine rigidity was acclaimed and practised. During the last years of Stalin's life his Church was in danger of sheer fossilisation. No movement, no experiment at any price. Inflexible, within and without, the Stalinist leaders of the Red Church saw life devolving on the heretics beyond its walls, in Yugoslavia, in Hungary, in Poland, and, not least, in China.

In the space of less than a century (of we reckon Marxism to have begun in 1847) and in Russia in less than seventy years (1880), the Marxist movement, in a curious correspondence to the 'acceleration' of man's history in the nineteenth and twentieth century, progressed as a redemptive doctrine over a distance which equalled that covered by Christianity in nearly two thousand years. It was a road littered with the sacrifice, between 1903 and

1953, of theologians as great as any since the days of Origen. The constancy of 'Red heretics' during this short time, facing expulsion or extermination, in groups or individually, compares with Christian martyrdom as regards firmness of faith in the redemptive destiny of their Church.

THE RED ORIGEN: TROTSKY

Leon Trotsky, the Red Origen, in all the years of his exile and his struggle against the Stalinist Church, never lost faith in communism. Trotsky, creator of the Red Army, was an intellectual who exemplified for many intellectuals, in Western Europe and across the Atlantic, a belief in the revolution and in a future socialist society such as Stalin never had. Stalin, like all dictators, absolutists, and authoritarian characters, was a pessimist without trust in mankind. Trotsky relied on mankind with a spiritual optimism such as was demonstrated by the Greeks, Pelagius, and the men of the Enlightenment.

Leon Trotsky (1879–1940), inventor of that frightful heresy, Trotskyism, suspicion of mere mental adherence to which was enough to hang a man in the eyes of the Stalinist Church, came from a prosperous Jewish family. In his early teens his enthusiasm was kindled by John Stuart Mill, Bentham, and of course Chernyshevsky. Arrested for the first time for clandestine activity in the early weeks of 1898, he was taken for examination to a prison in Odessa and, during his eighteen months there, read the Bible simultaneously in English, French, German and Italian for linguistic exercise. Exiled to Siberia, he wrote essays on Zola, Hauptmann, Ibsen, d'Annunzio, Ruskin, Maupassant, Gogol, Herzen, Belinsky, Gorky, and others. His first publication, a critical obituary of Nietzsche, appeared in December 1900. A more direct epitome of his own outlook was to be found in the invocation to the twentieth century written a few months later, *On Optimism and Pessimism, on the Twentieth Century, and on Many Other Things*. The optimist, replying to the mockery of the philistine, says:

> *Dum spiro spero!* .... If I were one of the celestial bodies, I would look with complete detachment upon this miserable ball of dirt and dust. ... I would shine upon the good and the evil alike. ... But I am a *man*. World history which to you, dispassionate consumer of science, to you, book-keeper of eternity, seems only a negligible moment in the balance of time, is to me everything! As long as I breathe, I shall fight for the future, that radiant future in which man, strong and beautiful, will become master of the drifting stream of his history and will direct it towards the boundless horizon of beauty, joy, and happiness! ...

The nineteenth century has in many ways satisfied, and has, in even more ways, deceived the hopes of the optimist. ... It has compelled him to transfer most of his hopes to the twentieth century. Whenever the optimist was confronted by an atrocious fact, he exclaimed, 'What, and this can happen on the threshold of the twentieth century!' When he drew wonderful pictures of the harmonious future, he placed them in the twentieth century.

And now that century has come! What has it brought with it at the outset?

In France the poisonous foam of racial hatred; in Austria – nationalist strife . . . ; in South Africa – the agony of a tiny people which is being murdered by a colossus; on the 'free' island itself – triumphant hymns to the victorious greed of jingoist robbers; dramatic 'complications' in the East; rebellions of starving masses in Italy, Bulgaria, Rumania. . . . Hatred and murder, famine and blood . . .

It seems as if the new century this gigantic newcomer, were bent at the very moment of its appearance to drive the optimist into absolute pessimism and civic nirvana.

– Death to Utopia! Death to faith! Death to love! Death to hope! thunders the twentieth century in salvoes of fire and in the rumbling of guns.

– Surrender, you pathetic dreamer. Here I am, your long-awaited twentieth century, your 'future'.

– No, replies the unhumbled optimist: You – you are only the *present*.

In Trotsky* there existed an unquenchable faith in the future which survived both his disappointment in Lenin in 1903–4, and the failure of French and German socialists in 1914. The pamphlet *The War and the International* (1914) against German social democracy, had, in its American edition, a direct influence on President Wilson. Two years later his scorn for chauvinist French war socialism found expression in his 'Open Letter' addressed to Jules Guesde, the pioneer of French Marxism who had become Minister of War:

> The socialism of Babeuf, Saint-Simon, Fourier, Blanqui, the Commune, Jaurès, and Jules Guesde – yes, of Jules Guesde, too – has finally found its Albert Thomas to deliberate with the Tsar on the surest way of seizing Constantinople. . . . Step down, Jules Guesde, from your military automobile, get out of the cage where the capitalist state has shut you up, and look around a little . . . .

Trotsky, who acknowledged his debt to German social democracy and, in his Vienna years, was a member of the Austrian Social Democratic Party, spoke of German socialisms's capitulation in 1914 as 'one of my most tragic experiences'. His belief in a good future was similar to that of Victor Hugo. And, as with Hugo in 1848 and 1870–71, it was to be tragically tested. Such a man was no match for Stalin. He watched with horror how, under the slogan of fighting against 'Trotskyism' the release of the *petit bourgeois* in the Bolshevik was consummated.

* His real name was Lev (or Leon) Bronstein. He adopted that of Trotsky (which had belonged to one of his former jailors in Odessa) only to facilitate his escape from Siberia in 1902.

'I have been repeatedly asked, and sometimes I am asked even now, "How could you lose your power?" ' Commissar of War from 1918 to 1925, 'master' of the Red Army, Trotsky was branded a heretic (officially, on account of his doctrine of permanent revolution) by Stalin after Lenin's death in 1924, expelled from the Party and banished to Mongolia in 1927. He was finally expelled from the Soviet Union in 1929. He ascribed his elimination primarily to the rise of a 'new type' of people whom Djilas was subsequently to apostrophise as 'the new class' – party bureaucrats who constituted a closed and strongly conformist society of their own and who condemned him for his 'individualism, aristocratism, and so on'.

'During a bottle of wine together or on the way home from the ballet, one self-satisfied bureaucrat said to another "He never has anything in his mind except the permanent revolution".' That was Trotsky's own description of the ascent of a bureaucracy of Red 'officials' (Friedrich von Hügel's term for their fellows in the Curia) solely concerned with maintaining and improving their own position, killers of hope, Utopia, the good future, – and men.

In his exile at Alma Ata, on the Chinese border, Trotsky received a letter from his friend Rakogsky, sympathising with him on the death of his daughter. 'You have long borne the heavy cross of the revolutionary Marxist. . . . ' In the years between 1918 and 1958 an enormous potential of hope, 'Red hope', was dashed to pieces, the hopes of socialist and communist artists, intellectuals, revolutionaries, and writers whose ideas were ground to bits by the Stalinist Party Church while physically they were harried to death and murdered. Herein Europe's nineteenth century reverberated once more with one of its grimmest echoes. The massacres of hope in 1793, 1815, 1832, 1848 and 1870 found their parallel in the slaughter of good hope on the part of the Stalinist Church in its struggle against those heretics whom it deemed its own, meet for annihilation. The vilest of these heretics was Trotsky. After long pursuit the assassins finally attained their aim. In 1940, in Mexico, he was brutally murdered.

Early Bolshevism contained, as did sixteenth- and eighteenth-century chiliastic movements, an element of religious and political faith in the coming of a Great Peace. The future, peace, and global revolution belonged together. The Bolsheviks came to power because they promised peace, but they could not achieve peace because they had to go on fighting. One of the most outstanding of Trotsky's speeches demonstrated this frightful dilemma. Its occasion was an address, on the day before the inauguration of the actual peace talks at Brest-Litovsk, to a joint session of the government, the Central Executive of the Soviets, the Soviet and town council of Petrograd, and leaders of trade unions:

Truly this war has demonstrated man's power and resilience, which enables him to endure unheard-of sufferings. But it has also shown how much barbarity is still preserved in contemporary man. . . . The King of nature, he has descended to the trench-cave, and there, peeping out

354

through narrow holes, as from a prison cell, he lurks for his fellow man, his future prey. . . . So low has mankind fallen. . . . One is oppressed by a feeling of shame for man, his flesh, his spirit, his blood, when one thinks that people who have gone through so many phases of civilisation – Christianity, absolutism, and parliamentary democracy – people who have imbibed the ideas of socialism kill each other like miserable slaves under the scourge of the ruling classes. Should the war have this outcome only that people return to their mangers, to pick the miserable crumbs thrown from the tables of the propertied classes, should this war finish with the triumph of imperialism, then mankind would prove itself unworthy of its own sufferings and of its own prodigious mental effort, which it has sustained over thousands of years. But this will not happen – it cannot happen.

Having risen in the land of Europe's former gendarme, the Russian people declares that it desires to speak to its brothers under arms . . . not in the language of guns, but in that of international solidarity of the toilers. . . .

He appealed to 'our brothers in Germany', to the German and Austrian peoples, then hesitated, veering between hope and doubt.

If the voice of the German working class . . . does not exercise a powerful and decisive influence. . . . Peace will be impossible. . . . (But) if it should turn out that we had been mistaken, if this dead silence were to reign in Europe much longer, if this silence were to give the Kaiser the chance to attack us . . . we would fight to the last drop of our blood. . . . The weary and the old ones would step aside . . . and we would create a powerful army of soldiers and Red Guards, strong with revolutionary enthusiasm. . . . We have not overthrown the Tsar and the bourgeoisie in order to kneel down before the German Kaiser.

Under the most difficult circumstances Leon Trotsky, after 1918, built up the Red Army. The war went on, in Russia, in the world, and evolved into global civil war.

Index

Sell, Friedrich C., 153–4
Selvinsky, 342
Senft, Comte de, 253
Setnitsky, N. A., 345
Shakespeare, William, 108, 111, 113, 157, 322
Shaw, George Bernard, 2, 52, 186, 201, 233
Shelley, Percy Bysshe, 13–17, 19–21, 67, 91, 101, 186, 200
Shklovsky, 342
Shmelyov, Ivan, 341
Shuesev, 341
Sickel, Theodore von, 308
Siguenza, Count, 102
Slowacki, 80
Smiles, Samuel, 216
Smith, Adam, 328
Sobolev, 341
Sologub, Fyodor, 341
Solovyev, Sergei, 341
Sorel, Georges, 261
Sorokin, Pitirim A., 235
Soulie, 322
Soumet, Alexandre, 99
Southey, Robert, 18, 98
Souvestre, Emile, 230
Spaemann, Robert, 252
Spaventa, Bertrando, 226
Spencer, Herbert, 331
Spengler, Oswald, 170
Stael, Ann Louise, 75, 102, 111, 317
Stalin, Joseph (Dzhugashvili), 55, 127, 335, 340–3, 348–54
Stapledon, William Olaf, 229
Steffens, 113
Stein, Charlotte von, 63
Stein, 144
Stendhal, 52, 90
Stender-Petersen, Adolf, 343
Stenzel, Gustav, 147
Stephen, Sir James, 222
Stepun, Fedor, 336
Stifter, Adalbert, 192
Stirner, Max (Schmidt, J. K.), 41, 114, 130, 135–6, 138–9
Stocker, Adolf, 240, 336
Stockton, T. R., 2, 227
Stolberg, Friedrich Leopold, 36, 61

Strauss, David Friedrich, 114, 128, 130–4, 176, 193, 281–2, 316, 324, 330
Stravinsky, Igor, 341
Streseman, Gustav, 154
Strossmayer, Joseph, 273
Stumm-Halberg, Karl Ferdinand, Baron, 170, 172
Sturzo, Don, 306
Sue, Eugene, 322
Superviela, Juan de Arnaza y, 76
Suttener, Artur Gundaccar von, Baron, 234
Suttner, Bertha von, 231, 233–5
Suvorov, Alexander, 350
Swedenborg, Emanuel, 16–17
Swetschin, Mme, 8
Sweven, Godfrey, 228
Swinburne, Algernon Charles, 223

Taine, Hippolyte, 96, 226
Talleyrand, 4, 25
Tapelli, 276
Tatlin, 341
Tennyson, Alfred Lord, 79, 221
Teilhard de Chardin—see Chardin, Teilhard de
Tertullian, 297
Tessara, Gabriel Garcia y, 76
Thackeray, William Makepeace, 335
Théot, Cathérine, 5
Thérèse of Lisieux, 266
Thierry, Augustin, 83, 279
Thiers, Adolphe, 256, 260, 328
Thomson, James, 14
Tieck, Ludwig, 55–6, 140
Tiersch, Friedrich, 147
Tikhonov, 342
Tille, Alexander, 170–3
Tinyanov, 342
Tirpitz, Alfred von, 159, 225
Tisza, Count, 226
Tito, Marshal Josip, 351
Tocqueville, Alexis de, 6, 207, 210
Tolstoy, Alexei, 341
Tolstoy, Dimitri, 226
Tolstoy, Leo, 95, 106, 192, 236, 332, 342–3
Towianski, Andreas, 79–80
Traub, Gottfried, 239